FRAGMENTS

of

NUMENIUS

of Apamea

TRANSLATION and COMMENTARY

BY

ROBERT PETTY

The Prometheus Trust

The Prometheus Trust
28 Petticoat Lane
Dilton Marsh, Westbury
Wiltshire, BA13 4DG, UK

A registered charity, number 299648

Fragments of Numenius of Apamea

2012

Robert Petty

ISBN 978 1 898910 52 7

Robert Petty asserts the moral right to be
identified as the author of this book.

British Library Catalogue-in-Publication Data
A catalogue record for this book is
available from the British Library.

Printed and bound in the UK by Biddles, part of the
MPG Books Group, Bodmin and King's Lynn

FRAGMENTS of NUMENIUS of Apamea

R Petty

Platonic Texts and Translations

Volume VII

Contents

Foreword i

Introduction ix

The Text and Translation 1

Commentary 103

Bibliography 225

Index I - Subject 233

Index II - Vocabulary and proper names 237

Foreword

Gregory Shaw

Damascius, the last *diadochus* of the Platonic Academy, maintained that Platonists in the 6th century C.E. followed two distinct paths: the way of the philosopher and the way of the theurgist. He writes:

> There are those who prefer philosophy, like Porphyry and Plotinus and many other philosophers, and those who prefer theurgy, like Iamblichus, Syrianus, Proclus and the rest of the hieratics. But Plato, realizing that strong arguments can be advanced from both sides, united them in a single truth by calling the philosopher a *Bacchus*. For, if the man who has freed himself from generation were to stand in the middle, he would draw both ways to himself. And it is clear that Plato calls the philosopher a *Bacchus* in his desire to exalt him ....[1]

Prior to the division into hieratics and philosophers stands the Platonic *Bacchus*, the one who combines both. In the 6th century these two streams of Platonism may also be distinguished by their texts: the *Chaldean Oracles* for theurgists; Plotinus' *Enneads* for philosophers. A remarkable but virtually ignored fact is that there was a single source for these divergent streams, one font for both the *Oracles* and the *Enneads*. There was, indeed, a philosophic *Bacchus* to whom both theurgists and philosophers were indebted. He was known as Numenius of Apamea, a mysterious and fundamentally important religious thinker of the

---

[1] Damascius, *In Phaed.* I. 172, modifying the translation of Polymnia Athanassiadi, *Damascius: The Philosophical History*, text with translation and notes (Athens: Apamea Cultural Association, 1999) 57. Also see *The Greek Commentaries on Plato's Phaedo*, Vol. II, Damascius, text and translation by L. G. Westerink (Westbury, The Prometheus Trust, 2009).

2nd century C.E. Recognized even in antiquity as a primary source for Plotinus' *Enneads*, persuasive evidence suggests that he also influenced the composition of *Ta Logia*, the divine recitations known since the 11th century as the *Chaldean Oracles*.

Numenius was a seminal and eclectic philosopher living in Apamea, at the crossroads of the East and West. While he identified himself as a Pythagorean Platonist, Numenius is notorious for having "invoked the nations of renown, citing the initiations, dogmas, and fundamental rituals that the Brahmans, the Jews, and the Egyptians celebrated in agreement with Plato" as expressions of one and the same wisdom.[2] In light of this ecumenical breadth it is perhaps not inappropriate to designate Robert Petty's translation and commentary on the fragments of Numenius as a *terma*, a word used by Tibetan Buddhists to describe a buried spiritual treasure discovered at the appropriate time. Petty's work is clearly a *terma* for Platonic scholars; it is a critical and clearly written contribution to our understanding of later Platonism. His translation of the fragments of Numenius lucidly reflects the Greek original, and his examination of both primary and secondary sources is a carefully written and much-needed resource. For all who study late antique philosophy this translation and commentary of Numenius' fragments is truly a treasure whose time has come.

Written as a Ph.D. thesis in 1993 under the direction of Birger A. Pearson (who also directed Ruth Majercik's text, translation and commentary on the *Chaldean Oracles*) Robert Petty's work on Numenius languished for nearly 20 years on the second floor of UC Santa Barbara's Davidson Library. As a fellow Ph.D. student with Robert in the 1980's, I knew the quality of this work, and had often encouraged him to publish it since a scholarly English translation of Numenius's fragments was sadly lacking.

---

[2] *Fragments of Numenius of Apamea*, translation and commentary by Robert Petty (Westbury: The Prometheus Trust, 2012) fragment 1a.

Fortunately, in 2010, Petty took the initiative to scan his thesis and send it to me as an electronic file; he generously suggested that I share it with anyone who might find it of use. I immediately made the file available to the *International Society for Neoplatonic Studies (ISNS)* online forum. Within weeks, Tim Addey, editor with *The Prometheus Trust*, contacted Robert about having his work published. The present publication is the result of this fortunate confluence of events.

Numenius is now recognized as one of the most critical thinkers in the history of Platonism. One might reasonably argue that it is Numenius and not Plotinus who initiated the Neoplatonic turn in the Platonic school yet, in many respects, Numenius still remains a mystery to us. What distinguishes the Neoplatonists is their blending of philosophical reflection with personal experience, deepened through reading and commenting on Platonic and Pythagorean texts. While Plotinus has been credited with initiating this phase of Platonism, Numenius lies behind him; a point not missed by late antique philosophers. As Petty points out in his *Introduction*, Plotinus was accused of plagiarizing Numenius, and his writings were studied in Plotinus' school. While the genius of Plotinus remains unmatched for sheer brilliance and subtlety of insight, his lines of speculation and the questions he addressed had already been engaged by the Apamean, Numenius.

Numenius recognized that the purpose of Platonic philosophy was to bring about an *experience* of depth and wisdom. And for this experience a certain method was needed, a practice of contemplative reflection that united the soul with the divine. The aim of the Platonic dialogues was, therefore, divinization and Numenius studied the Socratic *elenchus* not for its logic but for the psychological transformation it effects. He thus initiated the practice of interpreting figures in the dialogues as representing aspects of consciousness in different phases or psychological states, a method of reading the dialogues that is clearly evident in the later Neoplatonic commentaries; for Numenius, Plato's dialogues were not simply logical exercises or cosmological maps but spiritual exercises, guides for divinization.

Numenius also recognized the exercise of contemplative reflection in the practices of other sacred traditions. Because he was convinced of the hieratic purpose of Platonism, Numenius severely criticized former leaders of the Platonic school, the skeptical Academics, for having forgotten the essence of their tradition, lost in their empty logical analyses. Numenius prioritized the syntax of Neopythagorean metaphysics that provided a symbolic choreography for engaging reality. Numenius entered these speculations and distinguished levels of divinity: the god beyond the cosmos and the god who creates and pervades the cosmos, sometimes looking to its divine source and sometimes falling into the material cosmos. Numenius also recognized that the god beyond the cosmos remains hidden within it, but these Numenian speculations are far better left explored in Petty's fine commentary.

It is also significant, as noted above, that Numenius probably influenced the composition of the *Chaldean Oracles*, the revelations of the gods venerated by Platonists from Iamblichus to Damascius. That some of these revelations bear remarkable similarity to extant fragments of Numenius, that he lived in Apamea where the oracles were received, and that he was a contemporary of the *Juliani*—the entranced channelers of the *Oracles*—has rightly led scholars to suspect a cross-fertilization of ideas and practices between Numenius and the Chaldean prophets. Numenius, then, was likely a key figure in the framing of the "Bible" of later Platonism, the *Chaldean Oracles*, and he may have been responsible as well for transferring Hermetic notions of the soul's subtle body into the Platonic tradition where it played an essential role after Plotinus.

Plotinus agreed with Numenius on the purpose of Platonic philosophy. Philosophy was mystagogy, and this was made even more explicit by post-Plotinian Neoplatonists such as Proclus who refers to Plato as a hierophant of philosophic *mystagogia*. In these later Platonists we see the Numenian Plato, a teacher of divine wisdom liberated from the distortions of the Academics. It is this Numenian view of Plato that was embraced by virtually all subsequent Platonists of late antiquity as well as by Renaissance Platonists. Yet, unlike Plotinus or Iamblichus, Numenius was not honored by his Platonic heirs. He is singled out for criticism and even condemnation by Platonists from Iamblichus to Proclus, and later, Macrobius. Perhaps this was due to Numenius' celebration of figures such as Moses and Jesus; although not abrasive to Platonists in the mid-2nd century C.E., by the 4th century and later, when Platonists suffered at the hands of Christians, the affirmation of the traditions of their oppressors would not have been appreciated. On the other hand, the criticism he received may have been due more to his dualist cosmology or possibly his dualist understanding of the soul. We simply do not know why he was dishonored by later philosophers, but it is one of the great ironies of Platonism that the initiator of the last and most creative phase of the tradition was not recognized for his seminal contributions. His fragments, in fact, were largely preserved not by Platonists but by Christians such as Eusebius and Origen.

There has long been a need for a reliable English translation of the fragments of Numenius. Robert Petty's translation and commentary not only brings these fragments to life, he also sheds a great deal of light on other spiritual and philosophic influences in 2nd century C.E. including the Gnostics, the Hermetists, the Chaldeans, as well as the Neopythagoreans. His lucid and economic prose provides a voice we can trust. Petty carefully outlines what these fragments say and how they might best be understood. This is no mere catalogue of sources or of secondary scholarship. Petty has honed his critique and enters vexed questions of influence and sources with his own well-reasoned and persuasive opinion. For those who need an English translation of Numenius' fragments as well as an authoritative explanation about how these fragments were understood in their historical context, we now have an excellent scholarly source. This is, indeed, an intellectual treasure for all students of ancient thought.

Stonehill College,
Easton, MA

For Lisa

ACKNOWLEDGMENTS

This book began as a doctoral dissertation suggested and supervised by Professor Birger A. Pearson at the Department of Religious Studies, University of California, Santa Barbara. It was completed over a period spanning ten years, interrupted by several lengthy residences in Greece. I wish to thank Professor Pearson for his unfailing patience and steadfast loyalty during that time. He has provided a model of profound and meticulous scholarship that his students can only hope to approximate. I would also like to thank the great Homeric scholar Professor Apostolos Athanassakis, Department of Classics, UCSB, not only for years of sage counsel, but also for introducing me to some magical corners of Crete and Northern Greece that I would have otherwise missed. Professor Gregory Shaw, Department of Religious Studies at Stonehill College, provided the graceful Foreword, has been a creative and stimulating friend since we were graduate students at UCSB, and began the process that led to the publication of this text. All of which merits my profound gratitude.

Two of my Greek teachers deserve mention here. Professor David Sansone, Department of the Classics at the University of Illinois, Champaign-Urbana did much of the heavy lifting when I was attending his classes there. Dr. Robert Renehan, Professor Emeritus at the Department of Classics, UCSB, initiated me into the finer nuances of the language.

Special thanks must go to Tim Addey and Dr. Crystal Addey. Tim graciously offered to publish this work, shepherded it through the press and also performed the onerous task of preparing the indices. And in the midst of a very busy schedule Crystal found time to assist in the typing and proofreading of the Greek text. I thank her for her help and encouragement.

Finally, my deepest gratitude goes to Lisa Taylor, a true Muse, whose grace, patience and affection makes all things possible.

INTRODUCTION

A Life and Works

The references to Numenius in Porphyry's Vita Plotini have assured him a unique position in the history of Middle Platonism. From that work we learn several interesting facts. The first is that the works of Numenius were among those read during the meetings of Plotinus' school.[3] This in itself is not all that remarkable, for the list of such writers which Porphyry provides is lengthy enough. It is the next notice in the Vita that has provided Numenius with more notoriety than his fragmentary literary remains alone could have done. At the beginning of Chapter 17 we read the following:

> When the people from Greece began to say that Plotinus was appropriating the ideas of Numenius, and Trypho the Stoic and Platonist told Amelius, the latter wrote a book to which we gave the title *On the Difference between the Doctrines of Plotinus and Numenius*.[4]

This Amelius is an interesting figure in himself. Earlier in the treatise when he is introduced Porphyry tells us that he had copied out nearly all the works of Numenius and knew most of them by heart. Amelius would, then, be the obvious choice to defend Plotinus from the charges of the 'Greeks', who may have been members of the Athenian Academy. In the letter he wrote to Porphyry accompanying this work, he makes it clear that the accusation against Plotinus was not a single occurrence. At 17, 16 he states that he would never have condescended to acknowledge those 'most praiseworthy' individuals (πανευφήμων ἀνδρῶν) who

---

[3] *Vita Plotini*, 14
[4] *Vita Plotini*, 17 (Armstrong trans.).

have continually attempted to derive the Master's doctrines from Numenius (τὰ Τοῦ ἑταίρου ἡμῶν δόγματα εἰς τὸν Ἀπαμέα Νουμήνιον ἀναγόντων), but he agrees with Porphyry that it provides an opportunity to cast Plotinus' teaching into a more accessible form. At the beginning of Chapter 18 Porphyry concludes the subject by stating: "I thought this letter worth inserting, to demonstrate not only that people in his own time thought that he was making a show on the basis of plagiarism from Numenius, but also that they considered him a driveller and despised him because they did not understand what he meant..."

These remarks alone have naturally made the examination of Numenius' thought an important aspect of any serious study of Plotinus, but certain other elements found within his writing make him what John Dillon has described as the "most fascinating figure in second-century philosophy."[5] It is all the more to be lamented that we possess only a handful of verbatim fragments, which, as in the case of Atticus, are preserved in the *Praeparatio Evangelica* of Eusebius. These are supplemented by scattered references made by the Neoplatonists, most notably Iamblichus and Proclus.

This slim collection of evidence provides no information about Numenius' life except for the fact that he was born in Apamea, an important center of trade in the Orontes valley of northern Syria. Puech[6] has vividly portrayed the intense swirl of religious and philosophical currents that swept through the area. In addition to the more orthodox Hellenic philosophical elements, it was made up of wandering Christian missionaries, Hellenized Jews, Jewish-Christians, and Gnostics of both Jewish and Christian coloration.

---

[5] John Dillon, *The Middle Platonists* p. 361. Cf. R. T. Wallis, *Neoplatonism*, p. 33: "Numenius is now commonly recognised as the most important and influential thinker of the second century A. D".

[6] "Numénius d'Apamée et les théologies orientales au second siècle," pp. 750-751.

As Puech points out and will be seen later, Numenius was not immune to these influences. But as Dillon[7] suggests, it is not necessary to assume that Numenius remained in Syria all his life. Indeed, although we have no firm evidence of activity elsewhere, the presence of so much that is typically Alexandrian in his thought, and the influence he exerted over Plotinus (who received his philosophical training in Alexandria), make it tempting to think that at least a part of his career was spent in that city.[8]

Numenius' chronology has been well settled by scholarly consensus. Clement of Alexandria (*Strom.* I 22) is the first writer who mentions him. Beutler[9] lists several indications that might place him in the first half of the second century, but the consensus places his floruit somewhere around 150 C. E. This would make him a contemporary of Marcus Aurelius, Taurus and Albinus.

His major philosophical work appears to have been the treatise *Concerning the Good* (Περὶ τἀγαθοῦ) which consisted of at least six books. The first several books are devoted to a preliminary metaphysical analysis of the first principle, τὸ ὄν or τἀγαθόν, while the later books present a theological discussion of various aspects of a First God (πρῶτος θεός) and a Second God (δεύτερος θεός) which in turn is split and gives rise to a Third God (τρίτος θεός). The work is cast in the form of a dialogue between a teacher (perhaps Numenius himself) and an interlocutor who is addressed as ὦ ξένε in fr. 14. From the fragments that we have it looks as if this second speaker played the limited role of answering simple questions and asking for information (see fr. 3, 4a and 5). Dillon makes the cogent observation that the treatise "gives the impression much more of an Hermetic dialogue than of a Platonic one." He goes on to say that Numenius' Stranger is no

---

[7] *op. cit* p. 361.
[8] Cf. Giuseppe Martano, *Numenio d' Apamea*, pp. 10-12; Christoph Elsas, *Neuplatonische und gnostische Weltablehnung in der Schule Plotins*, p. 54 and n. 220
[9] "Numenios." Pauly-Wissowa, Suppl. VII, col. 665.

less active than Theaetetus in the *Sophist*, but concludes: "...the tone of the main speaker's pronouncements is much more hieratic than that of any Platonic main speaker...The main speaker in *On the Good* reminds one of nothing so much as of Hermes instructing Tat"[10]. This is especially significant in light of the numerous other points of contact between Numenius and the *Corpus Hermeticum* that will be found throughout the commentary.

Other works that we know of are *On the Secret Doctrines of Plato* (Περὶ τῶν παρὰ Πλάτωνι ἀπορρήτων = fr. 23), of which our only fragment presents a facile allegorization of the character Euthyphro, from the Platonic dialogue of the same name. Numenius says in this fragment that Plato used Euthyphro as a symbol for the collective religious beliefs of the Athenians, and thus escaped the charge of impiety which proved the undoing of Socrates. He repeats this theme in fr. 24, 1. 50 where he states that Plato, "once having concealed himself between clarity and obscurity, wrote in safety (ἀσφαλῶς μὲν ἐγράψατο)." Origen provides us with titles of four other works. At Contra Cels. IV, 51 (fr. lc) he lists some of the writings in which Numenius allegorized Jewish scripture: *Hoopoe* (Ἔποψ), *On Number* (Περὶ ἀριθμῶν), and *On Place* (Περὶ τόπου). Dillon believes there may be a pun on ἐποπτεία in the title ἔποψ[11] and that the treatise *On Number* was probably a typical essay in Pythagorean numerology.[12] We may get a glimpse of what *On Place* might have been like by looking at the beginning of Tractate II of the *Corpus Hermeticum*, which consists of a brief examination of τόπος inspired by Plato's *Laws* 839b. Origen (*Contra Cels.* V, 57 = fr. 29)

---

[10] Cf. Hans Lewy, *Chaldaean Oracles and Theurgy* p. 314, n. 7: "His principle work, Περὶ τἀγαθοῦ, was a dialogue which may have resembled those of Plutarch."

[11] *op. cit.*, p. 365. Cf. Aeschylus fr. 304: ἐπόπτην ἔποπα τῶν αὑτοῦ κακῶν. The bird is also mentioned at *Phaedo* 85c in the beautiful passage concerning the song of the swan as it nears death.

[12] *op. cit.*

also informs us of a work of at least two books entitled *On the Indestructability of the Soul* (Περὶ ἀφθαρσίας ψυχῆς) in which Numenius apparently used marvel tales to support his arguments.

Ironically, the most lengthy extracts preserved by Eusebius tell us the least about Numenius' own philosophy. Fragments 24-28 are taken from a work entitled *On the Divergence of the Academics from Plato* (Περὶ τῆς τῶν Ἀκαδημαϊκῶν πρὸς Πλάτωνα διαστάσεως) which constitutes a polemic against the Sceptical Academy from Arcesilaus to Philo of Larisa. The Stoics also receive rough treatment at the hands of Numenius here, and Antiochus is criticized for adopting their teachings. Numenius displays several facets of his personality in this tract that do not appear elsewhere: the brutal polemicist, the gossip and the comedian; and it offers an important, if not totally dependable source for our knowledge of the Middle Academy.

B Theology

Numenius professed a doctrine of three gods, a fact that has attracted attention ever since late antiquity,[13] and has prompted some hasty scholarly conclusions.[14] Yet when viewed carefully, his teaching can be seen to be little more than a natural outgrowth of prevailing traditions. As Dillon has pointed out,[15] Moderatus, another so-called Neopythagorean[16] who taught in the first century, also set forth a triadic theology which was most likely an interpretation of the first three hypotheses of the *Parmenides* of Plato.[17] Numenius too shows traces of that dialogue's influence,

---

[13] See fr. 21.
[14] See notes to fr. 17.
[15] *op. cit.* p. 367.
[16] See notes to fr. 1b.
[17] See Dodds, "The *Parmenides* of Plato and the Origen of the Neoplatonic One," pp.137-138.

but he was also guided to some extent by the famous yet curious passage from the Second Epistle of Plato(?) (312e): "It is in relationship to the king of all and on his account that everything exists, and that fact is the cause of all that is beautiful. In relation to a second, the second class of things exists, and in relation to a third, the third class."[18] Numenius alludes to this text in fr. 24, 1. 41 where he makes the incredible statement that "Socrates posited three gods" (τρεῖς θεοὺς τιθεμένου Σωκράτους), explaining further that Plato received this doctrine from Socrates who in turn took it over from Pythagoras. This confusing turn of events was straightened out by Merlan[19] who first asked, "what is Numenius really talking about? (Wovon spricht Numenius eigentlich?)." He dismisses the 'usual' interpretation which merely sees Numenius ascribing his own doctrine to earlier thinkers,[20] and shows how the Platonic Letter might be construed in a way that would lead one to believe that the doctrine of 312e was actually that of Socrates.

This question appears to be rather superficial once one actually begins to examine Numenius' theology, for in essence he posits only two gods. The Third God appears only when the Second God, the Demiurge, comes into contact with matter and is 'split' by it.[21] The Third God thus constitutes that part of the Demiurge

---

[18] Trans. L. A. Post. For the influence of the Letter on Numenius see Merlan, "Drei Anmerkungen zu Numenius," pp. 138-139; Dillon, *op. cit.*
[19] *op. cit.*
[20] Martano, (*Numenio d'Apamea*, p. 72, n. 3) provides a classic example of this interpretation: "Numenio ha la solita mania, una specie di malattia di moda comune ai filosofi suoi contemporanei (e che Plotino ereditò), di voler attribuire ai sommi maestri dell'antichità le proprie e del tutto nuove idee allo scopo di consolidarne le basi col ricorso alia indiscutibile autorità di quelli. E a Numenio era quanto mai facile attribuire a Socrate--il cui pensiero non era noto direttamente--la sua dottrina trinitaria."
[21] See fr. 11, 12-13 and note.

involved with the material realm, while the other part performs the activity which is most fitting to it, *i. e.* the contemplation of the First God, the ground of Being. Dillon stresses the fact that the division between a First God and a demiurgic Second God is a common Neopythagorean trait, but also points out that even the Platonists who do not distinguish between two gods, such as Philo, Plutarch or Atticus, still assign demiurgic activities to the Logos of God.[22] The tendency in this period to emphasize the absolute transcendence of God required that creation, and its attendant involvement with matter, be assigned to a subordinate entity of some kind.

It is probably safe to assume that Numenius' most important theological statements are those preserved by Eusebius and which form part of Book IV or V of *Concerning the Good*. Numenius prefaces this discussion of the First and Second Gods with a section (Books I-II) devoted to more purely ontological concerns. There, while setting forth a rather scholastic[23] delineation of Being (τὸ ὄν), the Incorporeal (τὸ ἀσώματον) and the Good (τἀγαθόν), all of which are interchangeable, he introduces the descriptive terms that will be later applied to his Gods. The Incorporeal, in contrast to matter is 'fixed' (ἕστηκε), and is without beginning (fr. 4a). Being exists outside of time in an eternal present, it is thus eternal (ἀίδιον), secure (βέβαιον), and unchanging (ἀεὶ κατὰ ταὐτὸν καὶ ταὐτόν); it neither increases or diminishes, and does not move spatially (fr. 5). It is utterly simple (ἁπλοῦν), and cannot be compelled to abandon its self-identity (fr. 6). The Good can only be comprehended by a form of mystical cognition that transcends every type of empirical knowledge (fr. 2).

---

[22] *op. cit.*
[23] Cf. Festugière, *Révélation*, IV, p. 139: "En ce qui concerne Numénius, on a pu voir que toute l'argumentation du π. τἀγαθοῦ est typiquement scolaire et suppose la connaissance de Platon."

When we come to view the First God, it is clear that he is merely Being, or the Good, clothed in theological garb.[24] He is simple (ἁπλοῦς), and indivisible (fr. 11); he is Father and King, completely devoid of activity (ἀργός; fr. 12). In fr. 15 we read first that he is 'fixed' (ἑστῶς), but then with conscious paradox Numenius says that this 'stasis' of the First God is his natural 'movement', by which salvation is spread throughout the cosmos. This dispersal of divine energy is described using the common image of a single flame igniting many torches without being diminished (fr. 14). In fr. 16 the First God is described as Mind (νοῦς, but see notes *ad. loc.*), and the cause (αἴτιον) of Form and Essence. He is expressly equated with the Good, being labeled "the Good itself (αὐτοαγαθόν)." None of this is really exceptional when viewed against the backdrop of prevailing Middle Platonic/Neopythagorean traditions. But once we begin to examine the Demiurge of Numenius, certain elements emerge that are atypical and which have attracted a good deal of scholarly attention.

The majority of the extant remarks concerning this deity take the form of direct comparisons with the First God, most of which are unfavorable and constitute what Dillon calls "a mild downgrading of this entity."[25] While the First God is simple, the Second is 'double' (διττός, fr. 16) since it has been split by its contact with matter (fr. 11). The First God is fixed, motionless, unchangeable in his self-contemplation, the Second is in motion (κινούμενος, fr. 15), and prone to desire (λαμβάνει...τὸ δ' ὁρμητικὸν ἀπὸ τῆς ἐφέσεως, fr. 18). The First God is the 'only Good' (fr. 16), and the Second, his imitator (μιμητής,) is Good only through participation in that higher deity (fr. 19 and 20). Numenius also employs several more positive images to portray his Demiurge. In fr. 13 he is described in terms of a farm laborer

---

[24] Cf. Festugière, *op. cit.*, p. 126: "Or, ce qui commande la théologie du π. τἀγαθοῦ, c'est l'assimilation du Premier Dieu à l'ἀγαθόν"; p. 127 "Le Premier Dieu est donc le Bien en soi."

[25] *op. cit.* p. 369.

who receives the seeds of souls from the First God and then transplants and disperses them throughout creation. Fr. 18 presents the metaphor of the ship's pilot: just as a pilot guides his ship navigating by the stars above, so the Demiurge guides the material realm, gazing upwards towards the First God and navigating by the Forms.

So on one hand, the Second God performs all the functions of a typical Platonic Demiurge by imposing structure upon the chaos of matter, and attending to his completed creation. On the other, we see that his creative activity was prompted by a desire for matter (ἐπορεξάμενος τῆς ὕλης, fr. 11), a motive that is more befitting an Hermetic deity than a Platonic one. This topic will be further discussed below in the section concerning Numenius' relation to the 'Platonic Underground'

C Cosmology

One of the images from the *Timaeus* which exercised a profound influence on the later tradition is that of the 'Receptacle' or 'Nurse' of Becoming found at *Tim.* 49a-c; 52e-53b,[26] There the primordial elements are described as a chaotic, fluid swirl of constant intermixture and separation. This of course is merely a graphic representation of the Platonic axiom (inherited from Heraclitus) that the material realm is in a continual state of change, and that corporeal objects 'are always coming to be and passing away but never really are' (see notes to fr. 8, 1. 5). In the verbatim fragments Numenius expends some effort establishing the instability of matter, describing it as a violent river (ποταμὸς γὰρ ἡ ὕλη ῥοώδης καὶ ὀξύρροπος, fr. 3) and emphasizing its tendency to dissolve and disperse itself (fr. 4a). Fr. 18 presents the poetic image of the Demiurge imposing a structure (ἁρμονία) on matter lest it "escape or wander away."

---

[26] Cf. Festugière, *Révélation* II, p. 118: "On perçoit ici l'origine de cette doctrine de la matière mauvaise qui tiendra une si grande place dans la mystique hellénistique".

xviii *Fragments of Numenius*

Thus far Numenius merely appears to be putting his own stamp on the scholastic formulations concerning matter (see notes to fr. 4a 1. 1, and 1. 5). Fortunately, however, we have a witness for his more developed cosmology in the fourth century Christian writer Calcidius (fr. 52), who shows Numenius adopting a minority position within the tradition. In his commentary on the *Timaeus* Calcidius catalogues the interpretations of various schools, and in the section on the Pythagoreans expressly uses Numenius as his source (see note to fr. 52, 1. 1). Here we learn that Numenius employed the common Academic term 'unlimited dyad' (duitatis indeterminata = ἀόριστος δυάς; see note to fr. 4a, 11. 2-3), to designate matter, and held that this entity was co-eternal with God (fr. 52, 1. 9: inornatum illud minime generatum aequaevum deo). Only after the Demiurge has organized matter can it be said to have a beginning in time. This stance places him with Plutarch and Atticus against the mainstream tradition, beginning with Speusippus,[27] which interpreted the creation described in the Timaeus as a timeless and eternal process. As with Plutarch and Atticus, Numenius' uncompromising dualism forced him to see the structuring of matter as a discrete event within a temporal framework.

The dualism is expressed in no uncertain terms. In 11. 9-14 of this fragment Numenius mounts a polemic against a monistic branch of Pythagoreanism which sought to derive the infinite dyad from the monad itself (see note *ad loc.*). He then attacks the Stoics for labeling matter a neutral entity when it should be viewed as 'utterly harmful' (1. 23: plane noxiam). Just as God is the cause of all good, matter is the source of all evil (1. 24: Deum quippe esse...initium et causam bonorum, silvam malorum). The final step is taken when he praises Plato for teaching that there were two world souls, one good, the other evil (1. 41: unam bencficentissimam, malignam alteram, scilicet silvam). The Latin

---

[27] Dillon, p. 7.

here indicates that Numenius identified the evil soul with matter itself, a position that would seem to separate him from Plutarch and Atticus. For this and Plato's 'doctrine' of two world souls, see notes *ad. loc.*

D The Soul

Numenius' cosmic dualism had its counterpart in his doctrine of the human soul. Porphyry (fr. 44) informs us that Numenius was among those who departed from the Platonic tradition which viewed the soul as composed of parts, and posited instead two separate souls, the 'rational' and 'irrational (τὸ λογικὸν καὶ ἄλογον). The difference between this position and the mainstream tradition might be merely semantic since it was common for Platonists, in a rather loose way, to refer to the separate parts of the soul as individual entities. However, another aspect of Numenius' doctrine, *i.e.* his teaching concerning the descent of the soul, points us away from this interpretation, and indicates that he was indeed adopting a non-traditional stance.

Both Porphyry (fr. 31) and Proclus (fr. 35) preserve a teaching of Numenius which describes the soul's descent to earth and return through two 'gates' in the heavens. The gate of descent is located at Cancer, the return is made through the gate of Capricorn. This probably originates in a Numenian commentary on the Myth of Er (*Rep.* 614b-621d), since Proclus adds that Numenius transferred the entire subterranean realm described there to the heavens (see note to fr. 35, ll.) Macrobius (fr. 34) furthers our knowledge by describing the soul's descent to earth through the planetary spheres where it obtains the various characteristics it will exhibit during the course of its embodiment. Some scholars have traced the source of this *descensus* through Porphyry back to Numenius, but this derivation has been questioned (see notes to fr. 34). While the issue of Macrobious' ultimate source remains vexed, it is safe to assume that Numenius held a doctrine of the same kind,[28] and

---

[28] Cf. Dillon, *op. cit.* p. 376; R. T. Wallis, *Neoplatonism*, p. 35

it is probable that his doctrine of a discreet second soul is related to it. Since this constellation of ideas had its widest diffusion in Hermetic and Gnostic circles, it will receive more detailed treatment in the section below.

E Numenius and the Platonic Underworld

Dillon[29] has admirably coined the term 'Platonic Underworld' to characterize important religious movements which flourished in Numenius' era, that are saturated with the terminology and concepts of Middle Platonism, *i.e.* Gnosticism, Hermeticism, and the *Chaldean Oracles*. While introducing the term, he emphasizes the relevance that these movements have for the study of Numenius. Indeed, it is this aspect of Numenius' philosophy that is in many ways the most interesting, and which has attracted the most scholarly attention.

Numenius' Demiurge is the element of his philosophy that most clearly displays gnostic influence. According to this scenario (fr. 11) the creation of the material cosmos comes about through a kind of divine 'fall'. It occurs when the Second God abandons his contemplation of the First God, glances towards matter and feels desire for it. In his desire to 'attend to matter' or to 'care for it' (ταύτης ἐπιμελούμενος), he becomes forgetful of himself (ἀπερίοπτος ἑαυτοῦ γίγνεται). And as stated above, He comes into contact with the material realm and is 'split' by its dyadic nature. This desire of the Demiurge is reiterated in fr. 18. It would appear that the inferior position of the Second God in relation to the First, which was mentioned above, stems from this 'fallen' nature. Numenius adds to the Gnostic flavor here by proclaiming (fr. 17) that the Demiurge is the only god that most men were aware of, since they are totally ignorant of the First God's existence.

---

[29] *Op. cit.*, pp. 384ff.

The distinction between an ineffable (see note to fr. 2, 1. 11), utterly transcendent high god, and an inferior Demiurge has prompted several scholars to see Valentinian influence within Numenius' theology. Zeller[30] was wisely tentative in this matter, but for Norden[31] the Valentinian derivation was obvious and indisputable. The blunt rashness of this assertion was attacked by a number of scholars (see notes to fr. 17), among whom was Lewy[32] who provided a two pronged rebuttal. He accused Norden on the one hand of failing to take into account the developments within Platonism that led to the distinction between a First and Second God (see notes to fr. 11), while drawing attention to his failure to recognize Valentinus' "receptivity to the Platonism of his time." But it was Bousset[33] who set this issue in the clearest light. First, with respect to Valentinianism, he suggests that the figure of the Demiurge is a foreign body within Christian Gnosticism. He points out that in the Valentinian speculation the figures of Sophia and the Demiurge are always bound up with the Hebdomad and the Ogdoad, and thus the meaning of the Platonic original is overlaid and lost. But more to the point is his introduction of the Anthropos myth in the *Poimandres* as an analogue to the drama of Numenius' Demiurge. In that famous narrative (ch. 13-15) the Primal Man is lured into involvement with material nature by the narcissistic desire for his own image which he sees reflected in her waters. As Bousett points out, this is much closer to what we have in Numenius than anything in Valentinianism. But he goes too far in saying that Numenius derived his Demiurge from the

---

[30] *Philosophie der Griechen*, III² p. 237, n. 4; p. 242, n. 3.
[31] *Agnostos Theos*, pp. 72-73, 109. He was followed by Puech, *op. cit.* p. 775. Dodds, *Proclus*, p. 308 says that Numenius "shows a knowledge of Valentinianism." Cf. Kramer, *Der Ursprung der Geistmetapkysik*, p. 79
[32] *op. cit.*, p. 319, n. 25.
[33] *GGA*, pp. 714-716.

Hermetic tradition.[34] As was shown above in the section on Theology, Numenius inherited the Demiurge from the Middle Platonic tradition. It is only the unique and dramatic flourishes with which he embellishes his Second God that are derived from Hermeticism. In this connection attention should be called to fr. 18, where the Demiurge is described binding the material realm together in a 'structure' (ἁρμονία). This exact term also appears in the Anthropos myth. Just before his fall into matter, the Primal Man bends through the 'structure' established by the Demiurgic Mind (δημιουργὸς νοῦς,) in order to get a glimpse of the lower nature (ch. 14). While Numenius could have been using Tim. 36e as his source for this term, the manner in which he uses it is closer to the Poimandres, and Dillon[35] is correct in suspecting that he used it "with a consciousness of its Hermetic significance."

Numenius' teachings concerning the soul also show likely Hermetic influence. He held the common belief that on its way to incarnation the soul descended through the planetary spheres, acquiring a different 'psychic' layer as it passed through each. Upon death, the soul remounted to the heavens discarding these 'accretions' in the sphere in which it had received them. Chapters 24-26 of the *Poimandres* have been cited repeatedly by scholars as a classic exemplar of this widespread doctrine. Numenius' two-soul theory is also best explained in this context. Iamblichus[36] preserves an Hermetic teaching stating that man has two souls, one from the First God, the other from the 'revolution of the heavens'. There are Gnostic parallels also. Clement[37] informs us that Basilides and his son Isidorus held a doctrine of a second 'accreted' soul, and Bardesanes' teaching of 'a soul from the seven' is clearly within this tradition. For a full discussion of this matter see the introductory note to fr. 34.

---

[34] He is criticized for this by Beutler, col. 670 (bottom)-671.
[35] *op. cit.*, p. 370
[36] *De Mysteriis*, 8, 6.
[37] *Stromateis* 2, 20, 113

Puech[38] struggled to attribute Numenius' cosmic dualism to Gnostic influence, but this was quickly and correctly brushed aside by Dodds[39] who points to precursors in the Pythagorean tradition. Besides, as mentioned above, Numenius' dualism is closely related to that of Plutarch and Atticus, both of whom are viewed as well within the Middle-Platonic tradition.

As a final note to the issue of Numenius' gnosticizing tendency, it should be kept in mind that it had clear limits. Although his Demiurge shows Gnostic traits, he is still viewed as 'good' (ἀγαθός), even though it is through his participation in the First God that he is so (fr. 19 and 20). And the end result of his impassioned contact with matter is an ordered Cosmos which is still described in Platonic terms as being "the beautiful Cosmos which has been embellished by participation in the Beautiful" (fr. 16: ὁ καλὸς κόσμος, κεκαλλωπισμένος μετουσίᾳ τοῦ καλοῦ). Although Elsas[40] has sought to establish Numenius as the source and inspiration for the Gnostics within Plotinus' school, it should be remembered that Plotinus had his works read and discussed there because in his view he was a good Platonist.

The final branch of the 'Platonic Underworld', the *Chaldean Oracles*, displays numerous similarities with the teachings of Numenius which have been noted and commented on by Festugière[41] and Krämer[42] The clearest parallels are found in the theological statements of the two systems. Numenius' First God, inactive and transcendent, is mirrored in the First Mind of the Oracles who is said to have 'ravished himself' away from all contact with lower levels of reality (fr. 3: ὁ πατὴρ ἥρπασσεν ἑαυτόν). As with Numenius, the 'Fathers'' transcendence is preserved by entrusting creation to a Second Mind:

---

[38] *op. cit.*, pp. 767ff.
[39] "Numenius and Ammonius," p. 7.
[40] *Neuplatonische und gnostiche Weltablehnung in der Schule Plotins*, passim.
[41] Révélation, III, pp. 53-58.
[42] *Der Ursprung der Geistmetaphysik*, pp. 66-68.

> For the First Transcendent Fire does not enclose
> its own Power in matter by means of works, but
> by Mind. For Mind derived from Mind is the
> Craftsman of the fiery cosmos, (fr. 5, Majercik trans.)

> For the Father perfected all things and handed them
> over to the Second Mind, which you - the entire human race
> call the First Mind, (fr. 7)

Like Numenius' 'double' Second God, the Second Nous of the Oracles, in its function as World Soul, is 'dyadic':

> ...beside this one sits a dyad-
> For it has a double function: it both possesses the
> Intelligibles in its mind and brings sense-perception
> to the worlds, (fr. 8)

As fr. 7 quoted above indicates, the First Mind is unknown to the masses, who mistake the Demiurge for the ultimate deity. Numenius parallel to this in fr. 17 is so striking that it has raised the question of dependence of one system upon the other. For the scholarly debate on this vexed question, see the notes to fr. 17.

F Numenius and Plotinus

The fact that Plotinus was accused by his own contemporaries of plagiarizing Numenius has naturally led to a search for Numenian echoes within the Enneads. Thedinga,[43] who claimed to have found entire passages from Numenius inserted into the Enneads by Porphyry, represents the most extreme example of this attempt. His approach has been criticized by Brehier[44] and

---

[43] "Plotin oder Numenios?", *Hermes* 52 (1917), pp. 592-612 (1. Teil); *Hermes* 54 (1919), pp. 249-278 (2. Teil), *Hermes* 57 (1922), pp. 189-218 (3. Teil).

[44] See his Notice to *Ennead* I. 8

Martano.⁴⁵ Martano himself occasionally spreads his net a little too wide. For example he points to Plotinus' use of the term 'King' in connection with the One as an echo of Numenius (fr. 12).⁴⁶ However, not only does this use of the term originate with Plato, but it was so widespread in the Middle Platonic tradition, beginning with Xenocrates, that it is meaningless to derive it from Numenius (see note to fr. 12, l 11). Dodds has summed up the entire enterprise by saying that "the harvest has been small",⁴⁷ and has gathered together the most critically secure group of parallels between the two philosophers.

The passage that made the most profound impression on Plotinus is the poetic description of the vision of the Good found in fr. 2. Numenius' use of the phrase "alone with the alone" (1. 9: μόνῳ μόνον) is echoed at I. 6. 7: ἕως ἄν τις...αὐτῷ μόνῳ αὐτὸ μόνον ἴδῃ; VI. 7. 34: ἵνα δέξηται μόνη μόνον; and VI. 9. 11: φυγὴ μόνου πρὸς μόνον. While Dodds cautions us that the phrase was a common one,⁴⁸ it was not widespread in this context and the other expressions borrowed from this fragment serve to indicate that this one was taken along with the rest. This is clearly illustrated by the following parallel. After the words μόνῳ μόνον Numenius continues his description: "there, where there is neither human being nor any other living being, nor corporeal object large or small (ἔνθα μήτε τις ἄνθρωπος μήτε τι ζῷον ἕτερον, μηδὲ σῶμα μέγα μηδὲ σμικρόν)." At VI. 7. 34, the same chapter where he had used the phrase μόνη μόνον, Plotinus has the following: οὔτε σώματος ἔτι αἰσθάνεται...οὔτε ἑαυτὴν ἄλλο τι λέγει, οὐκ ἄνθρωπον, οὐ ζῷον, οὐκ ὄν, οὐ πᾶν. Dodds tentatively suggests that this could be an "unconscious echo"⁴⁹ but he is perhaps being overly cautious. In 1. 12 Numenius

---

⁴⁵ *op. cit.* p. 101.
⁴⁶ *op. cit.* p. 105.
⁴⁷ "Numenius and Ammonius", p. 16.
⁴⁸ *op. cit.* p. 17.
⁴⁹ *ibid.*

employs the old poetic word ἀγλαΐα (splendor) to describe the Good, and we find several instances of its use in Plotinus: I. 6. 9 (describing virtue) ἕως ἂν ἐκλάμψειε σοι τῆς ἀρετῆς ἡ θεοειδὴς ἀγλαΐα; III. 8. 11 (describing Νοῦς) ἐν πάσῃ ἀγλαΐᾳ κειμένου; V. 8. 12 (of the contents of the Intelligible realm) τὴν αὐτῶν ἀγλαΐαν ἀσμενίσας; I. 7. 21 (of Νοῦς and its ζωή): εἶναι δ' αὐτὰ μεστὰ μὲν ἀγλαΐας The passage which appears to be most directly inspired by Numenius occurs at VI. 9. 4: εἰ δὲ μὴ ἦλθε τις ἐπὶ τὸ θέαμα, μηδὲ σύνεσιν ἔσχεν ἡ ψυχὴ τῆς ἐκεῖ ἀγλαΐας. Another clear borrowing is seen in the phrase used at 1. 14: ἐποχούμενον ἐπὶ τῇ οὐσίᾳ (seated above Essence). Dodds points to the echo at I 1. 8, ἐποχούμενον τῇ νοητῇ φύσει, adding that this metaphorical use is not attested before Numenius.[50] A final influence from this fragment is seen in Numenius' rare use of βολή in 1. 8 with the meaning of 'a glance'. Plotinus employs the same meaning in his early treatise on Beauty (I. 6. 2): Ἔστι (sc. τὸ καλόν) μὲν γάρ τι καὶ βολῇ τῇ πρώτῃ αἰσθητὸν γινόμενον.

The final verbal parallel that Dodds mentions is Numenius' image of the sea of matter as 'rough water' (κλύδων) found in fr. 33. In V. 1. 2 Plotinus refers to the 'turmoil of the body' (ὁ τοῦ σώματος κλύδων). To this list might be added several suggestions by Martano. The first is in reference to fr. 54 where Macrobius states that Numenius interpreted the name Apollo as meaning 'the one and alone' (unum et solum). The same derivation appears in the Enneads at V. 5. 6: τάχα δὲ τὸ "ἕν" ὄνομα τοῦτο ἄρσιν ἔχει πρὸς τὰ πολλά. ὅθεν καὶ Ἀπόλλωνα οἱ Πυθαγορικοὶ συμβολικῶς πρὸς ἀλλήλους ἐσήμαινον ἀποφάσει τῶν πολλῶν. The interpretation, attributed by Plotinus to the Pythagoreans, also appears in Plutarch (see notes to fr. 54). It is possible that Plotinus obtained this from a Pythagorean source, but it is more likely that this conforms to the claim of Martano that when Plotinus refers to 'the Pythagoreans', he is usually

---

[50] op. cit., p. 18.

drawing on Numenius.[51] Another parallel adduced by Martano which deserves attention is that between fr. 5 and Plotinus' essay (III. 7) 'On Time and Eternity'. Fr. 5 provides an analysis in miniature of the nature of linear time and its relation to eternity (αἰών) where true Being resides. Plotinus' essay, as its name implies, is a more detailed treatment of the subject, which goes well beyond the elementary remarks of Numenius. The examination of time and eternity was a commonplace within the tradition (see notes to fr. 5), but it is probably safe to assume that Plotinus derived some inspiration from Numenius on this matter.

Aside from mere verbal parallels, the most significant doctrinal similarities have been noted by Dodds.[52] He observes that both systems have three divine Principles. In both, the First Principle, Numenius' First God and Plotinus' One, are identified with the Good, and both display the qualities of absolute simplicity and utter transcendence. In both, the Second Principle exercises 'intellection' (νόησις,) and the Third employs 'discursive reason' (διάνοια; see notes to fr. 22). As Dodds puts it: "To the eyes of the uncritical, this alone would appear enough to substantiate a charge of plagiarism."[53]

Numenius' assertion that the soul shared an "indistinguishable identity" (ἕνωσιν...καὶ ταυτότητα ἀδιάκριτον) with its divine Grounds (ἀρχαί, fr. 42) was adopted by Plotinus as a "very important article of faith."[54]. This can be seen in a number of passages; cf. IV. 8. 8: οὐ πᾶσα οὐδ᾽ ἡ ἡμετέρα ψυχὴ ἔδυ, ἀλλ᾽ ἔστι τι αὐτῆς ἐν τῷ νοητῷ ἀεί; II. 9. 2: ὁτὲ δὲ τὸ χεῖρον αὐτῆς καθελκυσθέν συνεφελκύσασθαι τὸ μέσον· τὸ γὰρ πᾶν αὐτῆς οὐκ ἦν θέμις καθελκύσαι; VI. 4. 14: οὐδὲ γὰρ οὐδὲ νῦν ἀποτετμήμεθα; VI. 9 9: οὐ γὰρ ἀποτετμήμεθα οὐδὲ χωρίς ἐσμεν. Similarly, Numenius' belief that each soul encompasses

---

[51] *op. cit.*, p. 100.
[52] *op. cit.*, pp. 18-24.
[53] *op. cit.*, p. 19.
[54] *op. cit.*, p. 22.

"the Intellible World, the gods and daemones, the Good, and all the prior types of Being" (fr. 41: ἐν τῇ μεριστῇ ψυχῇ τὸν νοητὸν κόσμον καὶ θεοὺς καὶ δαίμονας καὶ τἀγαθὸν καὶ πάντα τὰ πρεσβύτερα) is reflected in Plotinus' famous remark that "each of us is a noetic world" (ἐσμὲν ἕκαστος κόσμος νοητός, III. 4. 3)[55].

Dodds concludes his analysis with the important statement that "two of the main structural laws or postulates of Neoplatonism are explicitly formulated by Numenius."[56] The first is the 'principle of participation' which states that 'all things are in all things' (fr. 41: ἐν πᾶσιν ὡσαύτως πάντα εἶναι). This appears in Plotinian statements such as ἐξέχει δ' ἐν ἑκάστῳ ἄλλο, ἐμφαίνει δὲ καὶ πάντα (V. 8. 4). The second is the principle of 'undiminished giving' which is articulated by Numenius in fr. 14. According to this doctrine, the divine source remains unchanged as it emanates its power to the lower levels of being (τὰ δὲ θεῖά ἐστιν οἷα μεταδοθέντα, ἐνθένδε ἐκεῖθι γεγενομένα, ἐνθένδε οὐκ ἀπελήλυθε). Dodds emphasizes that "this is cardinal for Plotinus" and points to IV. 9. 5 and III. 9, 2 where Plotinus, like Numenius, uses the example of communicated knowledge to illustrate the principle.

A final relationship between the doctrines of Numenius and Plotinus, which is briefly hinted at by Dodds[57] and stated explicity by Wallis,[58] is Plotinus' transferal of Numenius' language concerning the Demiurge's relations with matter to the individual soul itself. As described above, in fr. 11 Numenius portrays his Second God as abandoning contemplative unity by 'looking at matter' (διὰ τὸ τὴν ὕλην βλέπειν), an image Plotinus uses in connection with the soul at I. 8 4: ἔχει (sc. ἡ ψυχή) ἤδη ὕλην, βλέπουσα εἰς ὃ μὴ βλέπει. Numenius' Demiurge then "becomes forgetful of himself" (fr. 11: ἀπερίοπτος ἑαυτοῦ γίγνεται) due to

---

[55] *ibid*.
[56] *op. cit.*, p. 23.
[57] *op. cit.*, p. 21.
[58] *The Neoplatonists*, p. 35.

his involvement with matter. Plotinus combines this language with the figure of the ship's pilot (also employed by Numenius; see above and notes to fr. 18) at IV. 3. 17. Likening individual souls to pilots in stormy seas, he says that due to their concentration on the care of their ships, they "become unaware that they are forgetting themselves" (ἀμελήσαντες αὑτῶν ἔλαθον). Wallis cogently explains this transferal of doctrine by saying "the implication that matter can affect a divine being for the worse and rob it of Intellectual contemplation was too offensively Gnostic for Plotinus."[59] Dodds[60] takes great care to point out that Plotinus use of Numenian concepts to portray the soul appears in his early treatises, but that after a final break with Gnosticism this type of language disappears. Dodds labels this an "emancipation from Numenian influence".

G Text, Translation, and Commentary

The text followed here is that established by Des Places in his Budé edition. He follows Thedinga's example by combining actual verbatim fragments with the testimonia of later writers in a single numerical order. While this is somewhat misleading, it greatly facilitates ease of reference. The translation includes all fragments, but the commentary deals only with those fragments which are directly related to Numenius' own philosophy. Therefore the lengthy extracts from *On the Divergence of the Academics from Plato*, while often entertaining and which constitute an essential source for the Sceptical Academy, are omitted from the commentary.

---

[59] *ibid.*
[60] *Pagan and Christian in an Age of Anxiety*, pp. 25-26.

Numenius

Fragments

Text and translation

Περὶ τἀγαθοῦ

I

Fr. 1 a (9 a L.)

(Eus., *Pr. ev.*, IX, 7, 1 ; p. 411 b-c V.;

I, p. 493, 22-494, 7 Mras)

b Καὶ αὐτοῦ δὲ τοῦ πυθαγορικοῦ φιλοσόφου, τοῦ Νουμηνίου λέγω, ἀπὸ τοῦ πρώτου Περὶ τἀγαθοῦ τάδε παραθήσομαι·

c Εἰς δὲ τοῦτο δεήσει εἰπόντα καὶ σημηνάμενον ταῖς μαρτυρίαις ταῖς Πλάτωνος ἀναχωρήσασθαι καὶ συνδήσασθαι
5 τοῖς λόγοις τοῦ Πυθαγόρου, ἐπικαλέσασθαι δὲ τὰ ἔθνη τὰ εὐδοκιμοῦντα, προσφερόμενον αὐτῶν τὰς τελετὰς καὶ τὰ δόγματα τάς τε ἱδρύσεις συντελουμένας Πλάτωνι ὁμολογουμένως, ὁπόσας Βραχμᾶνες καὶ Ἰουδαῖοι καὶ Μάγοι καὶ Αἰγύπτιοι διέθεντο.

Fr. 1 b (9 b L.)

(Origenes, *Contra Celsum*, I, 15; I, p. 67, 21-27 Koetschau;

I, p. 114, 33-116, 8 Borret)

Πόσῳ δὲ βελτίων Κέλσου καὶ διὰ πολλῶν δείξας εἶναι ἐλλογιμώτατος καὶ πλείονα βασανίσας δόγματα καὶ ἀπὸ πλειόνων συναγαγὼν ἃ ἐφαντάσθη εἶναι ἀληθῆ ὁ Πυθαγόρειος Νουμήνιος, ὅστις ἐν τῷ πρώτῳ Περὶ τἀγαθοῦ, λέγων περὶ τῶν
5 ἐθνῶν ὅσα περὶ τοῦ θεοῦ ὡς ἀσωμάτου διείληφεν, ἐγκατέταξεν αὐτοῖς καὶ τοὺς Ἰουδαίους, οὐκ ὀκνήσας ἐν τῇ συγγραφῇ αὐτοῦ χρήσασθαι καὶ λόγοις προφητικοῖς καὶ τροπολογῆσαι αὐτούς.

Concerning the Good

1a (9a L.)

And from the Pythagorean philosopher himself, I mean Numenius, I will set forth these remarks taken from the first book of Concerning the Good:

And with regard to this it will be necessary, after discussing and drawing conclusions from the testimonies of Plato, to go back further and bind them together with the statements of Pythagoras; and to invoke the nations of renown, citing the initiations, dogmas, and fundamental rituals which they celebrated in agreement with Plato—all those which the Brahmans, Jews, Magi, and Egyptians have established.

1b (9b L.)

But how much superior to Celsus is the Pythagorean Numenius, who has demonstrated in many instances that he is most eloquent, and who has closely examined more doctrines and has collected from more sources the ones which appeared to be true. In the first book of Concerning the Good, while speaking about the nations which perceive God to be incorporeal, he placed among them the Jews also, not hesitating to employ the words of the prophets in his writing and to allegorize them.

Fr. 1 c (32 L.; cf. Test. 17)
(Id., *ibid.*, IV, 51; I, p. 324, 18-23 Koetschau;
II, p. 316, 14-20 Borret)

Ἐγὼ δ' οἶδα καὶ Νουμήνιον τὸν Πυθαγόρειον ... πολλαχοῦ τῶν συγγραμμάτων αὐτοῦ ἐκτιθέμενον τὰ Μωϋσέως καὶ τῶν προφητῶν καὶ οὐκ ἀπιθάνως αὐτὰ τροπολογοῦντα, ὥσπερ ἐν τῷ καλουμένῳ Ἔποπι καὶ ἐν τοῖς Περὶ ἀριθμῶν καὶ ἐν τοῖς
5 Περὶ τόπου. Ἐν δὲ τῷ τρίτῳ Περὶ τἀγαθοῦ...

Fr. 2 (11 L.)
(Eus., *Pr. ev.*, XI, 21, 7-22, 2; p. 543 b-d V.;
II, p. 48, 17-49, 13 Mras)

b Πάλιν δὲ καὶ ὁ Νουμήνιος ἐν τοῖς Περὶ τἀγαθοῦ τὴν τοῦ Πλάτωνος διάνοιαν ἑρμηνεύων, τοῦτον διέξεισι τὸν τρόπον·

Τὰ μὲν οὖν σώματα λαβεῖν ἡμῖν ἔξεστι σημαινομένοις ἔκ τε ὁμοίων ἀπό τε τῶν ἐν τοῖς παρακειμένοις γνωρισμάτων
c 5 ἐνόντων· τἀγαθὸν δὲ οὐδενὸς ἐκ παρακειμένου οὐδ' αὖ ἀπὸ ὁμοίου αἰσθητοῦ ἐστι λαβεῖν μηχανή τις οὐδεμία, ἀλλὰ δεήσει, οἷον εἴ τις ἐπὶ σκοπῇ καθήμενος ναῦν ἁλιάδα βραχεῖάν τινα τούτων τῶν ἐπακτρίδων τῶν μόνων μίαν, μόνην, ἔρημον, μετακυμίοις ἐχομένην ὀξὺ δεδορκὼς μιᾷ βολῇ κατεῖδε
10 τὴν ναῦν, οὕτως δεῖ τινα ἀπελθόντα πόρρω ἀπὸ τῶν αἰσθητῶν ὁμιλῆσαι τῷ ἀγαθῷ μόνῳ μόνον, ἔνθα μήτε τις ἄνθρωπος
d μήτε τι ζῷον ἕτερον μηδὲ σῶμα μέγα μηδὲ σμικρόν, ἀλλά τις ἄφατος καὶ ἀδιήγητος ἀτεχνῶς ἐρημία θεσπέσιος, ἔνθα τοῦ ἀγαθοῦ ἤθη διατριβαί τε καὶ ἀγλαΐαι, αὐτὸ δὲ ἐν εἰρήνῃ, ἐν
15 εὐμενείᾳ, τὸ ἤρεμον, τὸ ἡγεμονικὸν ἵλεω ἐποχούμενον ἐπὶ τῇ οὐσίᾳ. Εἰ δέ τις πρὸς τοῖς αἰσθητοῖς λιπαρῶν τὸ ἀγαθὸν ἐφιπτάμενον φαντάζεται κἄπειτα τρυφῶν οἴοιτο τῷ ἀγαθῷ ἐντετυχηκέναι, τοῦ παντὸς ἁμαρτάνει. Τῷ γὰρ ὄντι οὐ ῥαδίας, θείας δὲ πρὸς αὐτὸ δεῖ μεθόδου· καὶ ἔστι κράτιστον
20 τῶν αἰσθητῶν ἀμελήσαντι, νεανιευσαμένῳ πρὸς τὰ μαθήματα, τοὺς ἀριθμοὺς θεασαμένῳ, οὕτως ἐκμελετῆσαι μάθημα, τί ἐστι τὸ ὄν.

Ταῦτα μὲν ἐν τῷ πρώτῳ.

1c (32 L.)

And I know also Numenius the Pythagorean who in many places in his writings sets forth the words of Moses and the prophets, and not unconvincingly allegorizes them, as in the so-called Epops, and in concerning Number, and in the book Concerning Place. And in the third book of Concerning the Good…

2 (11 L.)

And again Numenius, interpreting the thought of Plato in Concerning the Good, proceeds in this fashion:

We can grasp the concept of corporeal entities by drawing analogies from similar objects and from characteristics inherent in things at hand. But there is no means whatsoever to conceive of the Good from anything at hand, nor in turn, from an analogous sense object. But it will have to be as if someone situated on a high vantage point were to spot, with one keen glance, a small fishing boat—one of these single, light craft—alone, solitary, cradled between the waves. In this way must one, after going far from sense objects, have converse with the Good, alone with the Alone. There, where there is neither any person nor any other living thing, no corporeal object large or small, but rather a divine solitude, absolutely indescribable and ineffable; there the abodes, haunts and splendors of the Good are found; and the Good itself, the gentle sovereign one, graciously seated above Essence.

But if someone, by adhering to sense objects imagines that he is flying toward the Good, and once satiated believes he has encountered the Good, he completely misses the point. For in reality there in need of a divine, rather than a casual approach towards it. And it is best, by ignoring perceptible objects, and by applying fresh enthusiasm towards mathematics and contemplating number, thus to master a lesson: what Being is.

These things are in the first book.

Fr. 3 (12 L.)

(Eus., *Pr. ev.*, XV, 17, 1-2 ; p. 819 a-b V.;

II, p. 381, 10-17 Mras)

a Ἀλλὰ τί δή ἐστι τὸ ὄν; ἆρα ταυτὶ τὰ στοιχεῖα τὰ τέσσαρα, ἡ γῆ καὶ τὸ πῦρ καὶ αἱ ἄλλαι δύο μεταξὺ φύσεις;
b ἆρα οὖν δὴ τὰ ὄντα ταῦτά ἐστιν, ἤτοι συλλήβδην ἢ καθ' ἕν γέ τι αὐτῶν;

5 - Καὶ πῶς, ἅ γέ ἐστι καὶ γενητὰ καὶ παλινάγρετα, εἴ γ' ἔστιν ὁρᾶν αὐτὰ ἐξ ἀλλήλων γιγνόμενα καὶ ἐπαλλασσόμενα καὶ μήτε στοιχεῖα ὑπάρχοντα μήτε συλλαβάς;

- Σῶμα μὲν ταυτὶ οὕτως οὐκ ἂν εἴη τὸ ὄν. Ἀλλ' ἆρα ταυτὶ μὲν οὔ, ἡ δὲ ὕλη δύναται εἶναι ὄν;

10 - Ἀλλὰ καὶ αὐτὴν παντὸς μᾶλλον ἀδύνατον, ἀρρωστίᾳ τοῦ μένειν· ποταμὸς γὰρ ἡ ὕλη ῥοώδης καὶ ὀξύρροπος, βάθος καὶ πλάτος καὶ μῆκος ἀόριστος καὶ ἀνήνυτος.

3 (12 L.)

But what is Being then? Is it the four elements: earth, fire, and the other two intermediate natures? Do these constitute reality, either taken together or individually?

~ Indeed, how could they, these things which originate and will be taken back again? Especially if one can see them emerging from one another and interchanging, remaining neither as individual elements nor as a composite.

~ As corporeal, then, they could not be Being. But since these are not, could matter be Being?

~ But this is the least possible of all, due to its inability to remain steady. For matter is a river with strong, erratic currents, and it is unending and without limit in depth, width and length.

Fr. 4a (13 L.)
(Eus., *Pr. ev.*, XV, 17, 3-8; p. 819 c- 820 a V.;
II, p. 381, 18-382, 19 Mras)

819c Καὶ μετὰ βραχέα ἐπιλέγει·

Ὥστε καλῶς ὁ λόγος εἴρηκε φάς, εἰ ἔστιν ἄπειρος ἡ ὕλη, ἀόριστον εἶναι αὐτήν· εἰ δὲ ἀόριστος, ἄλογος· εἰ δὲ ἄλογος, ἄγνωστος. Ἄγνωστον δέ γε οὖσαν αὐτὴν ἀναγκαῖον 5 εἶναι ἄτακτον, ὡς τεταγμένα γνωσθῆναι πάνυ δήπουθεν ἂν εἴη ῥᾴδια· τὸ δὲ ἄτακτον οὐχ ἕστηκεν, ὅ τι δὲ μὴ ἕστηκεν, οὐκ ἂν εἴη ὄν. Τοῦτο δὲ ἦν ὅπερ ἡμῖν αὐτοῖς ὡμολογησάμεθα ἐν τοῖς ἔμπροσθεν, ταυτὶ πάντα συνενεχθῆναι τῷ ὄντι ἀθέμιστον εἶναι.

10 - Δοξάτω μάλιστα μὲν πᾶσιν· εἰ δὲ μή, ἀλλ' ἐμοί.

- Οὔκουν φημὶ τὴν ὕλην οὔτε αὐτὴν οὔτε τὰ σώματα εἶναι ὄν.

d - Τί οὖν δή; ἦ ἔχομεν παρὰ ταῦτα ἄλλο τι ἐν τῇ φύσει τῇ τῶν ὅλων;

15 - Ναί· τοῦτο οὐδὲν εἰπεῖν ποικίλον, εἰ τόδε πρῶτον μὲν ἐν ἡμῖν αὐτοῖς ἅμα πειραθείημεν διαλεγόμενοι· ἐπειδὴ τὰ σώματά ἐστι φύσει τεθνηκότα καὶ νεκρὰ καὶ πεφορημένα καὶ οὐδ' ἐν ταὐτῷ μένοντα, ἆρ' οὐχὶ τοῦ καθέξοντος αὐτοῖς ἔδει;

- Παντὸς μᾶλλον.

20 - Εἰ μὴ τύχοι δὲ τούτου, ἆρα μείνειεν ἄν;

- Παντὸς ἧττον.

- Τί οὖν ἐστι τὸ κατασχῆσον; Εἰ μὲν δὴ καὶ τοῦτο εἴη 820a σῶμα, Διὸς Σωτῆρος δοκεῖ ἄν μοι δεηθῆναι αὐτὸ παραλυόμενον καὶ σκιδνάμενον· εἰ μέντοι χρὴ αὐτὸ 25 ἀπηλλάχθαι τῆς τῶν σωμάτων πάθης, ἵνα κἀκείνοις κεκυκημένοις τὴν φθορὰν ἀμύνειν δύνηται καὶ κατέχῃ, ἐμοὶ μὲν οὐ δοκεῖ ἄλλο τι εἶναι ἢ μόνον γε τὸ ἀσώματον· αὕτη γὰρ δὴ φύσεων πασῶν μόνη ἕστηκε καὶ ἔστιν ἀραρυῖα καὶ οὐδὲν σωματική. Οὔτε γοῦν γίγνεται οὔτε αὔξεται οὔτε 30 κίνησιν κινεῖται ἄλλην οὐδεμίαν, καὶ διὰ ταῦτα καλῶς δίκαιον ἐφάνη πρεσβεῦσαι τὸ ἀσώματον.

4a (13 L.)

And a little further he adds:

So the argument has been well put, saying that if matter is infinite it is without limit, and if unlimited it is incomprehensible. And if incomprehensible, unknowable. And, I suppose, being unknowable it must necessarily be without order, since ordered things would quite easily be known. But the unordered is not stable, and what is unstable could not be Being. This is what we agreed upon among ourselves in the previous discussions: that to apply all of these qualities to Being is an act of impiety.
~ Let it definitely be so resolved by all. And if not, at least by me.
~ I say then that neither matter itself nor corporeal entities constitute Being.
~ What, then? Do we have anything else besides these in the nature of the All?
~ Yes. This is nothing complicated to speak of, if we first examine the following point, discussing it together among ourselves: Since corporeal objects are by nature dead things and corpses carried about and not remaining in the same state, do they not require a principle of cohesion?
~ Absolutely.
~ And if they were not to obtain this, would they persist?
~ Absolutely not!
~ Then what is the binding force? If, in fact, this also were a corporeal object it would appear to me to be in need of Zeus Soter, since a body is constantly dissolving and dissipating. If, however, the cohesive principle must be exempt from the passivity of corporeal objects, so that it can ward off destruction from these churning entities and control them, it doesn't seem to me to be anything other than the Incorporeal alone. For this alone of all natures is fixed and stable and in no way corporeal. Furthermore it never emerges into being, nor does it increase, nor does it move in any other motion whatsoever. And because of this it appeared quite fitting that the Incorporeal take precedence.

Fr. 4b (Test. 29 L.)
(Nemesius, Περὶ φύσεως ἀνθρώπου, 2, 8-14;
p. 69-72 C. F. Matthaei, Halle, 1802 ;
P. G., 40, c. 537 b- 541 a)

Κοινῇ μὲν οὖν πρὸς πάντας τοὺς λέγοντας σῶμα τὴν ψυχὴν 70m ἀρκέσει τὰ παρὰ Ἀμμωνίου τοῦ διδασκάλου Πλωτίνου καὶ Νουμηνίου τοῦ Πυθαγορικοῦ εἰρημένα· ἐστὶν δὲ ταῦτα·

Τὰ σώματα τῇ οἰκείᾳ φύσει τρεπτὰ ὄντα καὶ σκεδαστὰ καὶ
5 διόλου εἰς ἄπειρον τμητά, μηδενὸς ἐν αὐτοῖς ἀμεταβλήτου ὑπολειπομένου, δεῖται τοῦ συνέχοντος καὶ συνάγοντος καὶ ὥσπερ συσφίγγοντος καὶ συγκρατοῦντος αὐτά, ὅπερ ψυχὴν λέγομεν. Εἰ τοίνυν σῶμά ἐστιν ἡ ψυχὴ οἱονδήποτε, εἰ καὶ λεπτομερέστατον, τί πάλιν ἐστὶν τὸ συνέχον ἐκείνην; ἐδείχθη
10 γὰρ πᾶν σῶμα δεῖσθαι τοῦ συνέχοντος, καὶ οὕτως εἰς ἄπειρον, ἕως ἂν καταντήσωμεν εἰς ἀσώματον. Εἰ δὲ λέγοιεν, καθάπερ οἱ Στωικοί, τονικήν τινα εἶναι κίνησιν περὶ τὰ 71m σώματα, εἰς τὸ εἴσω ἅμα καὶ εἰς τὸ ἔξω κινουμένην, καὶ τὴν μὲν εἰς τὸ ἔξω μεγεθῶν καὶ ποιοτήτων ἀποτελεστικὴν εἶναι,
15 τὴν δ' εἰς τὸ εἴσω ἑνώσεως καὶ οὐσίας, ἐρωτητέον αὐτούς, ἐπειδὴ πᾶσα κίνησις ἀπό τινός ἐστιν δυνάμεως, τίς ἡ δύναμις αὕτη καὶ ἐν τίνι οὐσίωται. Εἰ μὲν οὖν καὶ ἡ δύναμις αὕτη ὕλη τίς ἐστιν, τοῖς αὐτοῖς πάλιν χρήσομαι λόγοις· εἰ δὲ οὐχ ὕλη ἀλλ' ἔνυλον (ἕτερον δ' ἐστὶ τὸ ἔνυλον
20 παρὰ τὴν ὕλην· τὸ γὰρ μετέχον ὕλης ἔνυλον λέγεται), τί ποτ' ἄρ' ἐστὶν τὸ μετέχον τῆς ὕλης; πότερον ὕλη καὶ αὐτὸ ἢ ἄυλον; εἰ μὲν οὖν ὕλη, πῶς ἔνυλον καὶ οὐχ ὕλη; εἰ δὲ οὐχ ὕλη, ἄυλον ἄρα· εἰ δὲ ἄυλον, οὐ σῶμα· πᾶν γὰρ σῶμα ἔνυλον.

4b (Test. 29 L.)

Therefore, in rebuttal to those who assert that the soul is a body, the statements made in common by Ammonius, the teacher of Plotinus, and Numenius the Pythagorean will suffice. They are as follows:

Since corporeal objects by their own nature are liable to alteration and disintegration, and are completely divisible into infinity with no aspect in them remaining unchanged, they are in need of something holding them together, and uniting them, and as it were compressing and controlling them. This is what we call soul. If, therefore, the soul is a body of any kind, even the most subtle, what, in turn is holding it together? For it was shown that every body requires something to bind it together, and it is thus on into infinity until we arrive at the Incorporeal. But if some were to say, as do the Stoics, that there is a movement around bodies which produces a tension, moving into the interior as well as towards the exterior, and that the movement towards the exterior produces dimension and quality while that towards the interior produces unity and essence, it will be necessary to ask them: since every movement originates from a force, what is the force and what is its essence? Now if the force itself is some kind of matter, we will once again employ the same arguments. And if it is not matter but material (and material differs from matter, for that which participates in matter is said to be material), what, then, is that which participates in matter? Is it matter itself or is it immaterial? Now if it is matter, how can it be material and not matter? And if it is not matter, it must be immaterial. And if its immaterial, it is not body because every body is material.

Εἰ δὲ λέγοιεν ὅτι τὰ σώματα τριχῇ διαστατά ἐστιν, καὶ ἡ
ψυχὴ δὲ δι' ὅλου διήκουσα τοῦ σώματος τριχῇ διαστατή ἐστιν
καὶ διὰ τοῦτο πάντως καὶ σῶμα, ἐροῦμεν ὅτι πᾶν μὲν σῶμα
τριχῇ διαστατόν, οὐ πᾶν δὲ τὸ τριχῇ διαστατὸν σῶμα. Καὶ
γὰρ τὸ ποσὸν καὶ τὸ ποιόν, ἀσώματα ὄντα καθ' ἑαυτά, κατὰ
συμβεβηκὸς ἐν ὄγκῳ ποσοῦται. Οὕτως οὖν καὶ τῇ ψυχῇ καθ'
ἑαυτὴν μὲν πρόσεστι τὸ ἀδιάστατον, κατὰ συμβεβηκὸς δὲ τῷ
ἐν ᾧ ἐστι τριχῇ διαστάτῳ ὄντι συνθεωρεῖται καὶ αὐτὴ τριχῇ
διαστατή. Ἔτι πᾶν σῶμα ἤτοι ἔξωθεν κινεῖται ἢ ἔνδοθεν·
ἀλλ' εἰ μὲν ἔξωθεν, ἄψυχον ἔσται, εἰ δ' ἔνδοθεν, ἔμψυχον.
Εἰ δὲ σῶμα ἡ ψυχή, εἰ μὲν ἔξωθεν κινοῖτο, ἄψυχός ἐστιν· εἰ
δ' ἔνδοθεν, ἔμψυχος· ἄτοπον δὲ καὶ τὸ ἔμψυχον καὶ τὸ
ἄψυχον λέγειν τὴν ψυχήν· οὐκ ἄρα σῶμα ἡ ψυχή. Ἔτι ἡ
ψυχή, εἰ μὲν τρέφεται, ὑπὸ ἀσωμάτου τρέφεται· τὰ γὰρ
μαθήματα τρέφει αὐτήν· οὐδὲν δὲ σῶμα ὑπὸ ἀσωμάτου
τρέφεται· οὐκ ἄρα σῶμα ἡ ψυχή (Ξενοκράτης οὕτω συνῆγεν)·
εἰ δὲ μὴ τρέφεται, πᾶν δὲ σῶμα ζῴου τρέφεται, οὐ σῶμα ἡ
ψυχή.

But if they say that corporeal objects are extended in three dimensions, and that the soul, since it permeates all of the body is also extended in three dimensions, and is therefore necessarily also a body, we will respond that while every body is extended in three dimensions, not every thing that has extension in three dimensions is a body. For example, quantity and quality, which are incorporeal in themselves, are according to circumstance delimited in a solid. Thus it is that the soul too, in and of itself, is inherently without dimension; but according to circumstance, when viewed in conjunction with its host object which is three dimensional, the soul itself seems to have three dimensions.

Further, every body is either moved externally or internally. But if it is moved externally it will be without soul, and if internally, ensouled. And if the soul is body: if it is moved externally it is without soul, and if internally it is ensouled. But it is absurd to say that both the ensouled and the soulless are soul. Therefore the soul is not a body.

Further, if the soul is nourished, it is nourished by the Incorporeal. Therefore the soul is not a body. (Xenocrates argued this way.) And if it is not nourished, while every body of a living being is nourished, the soul is not a body.

II

Fr. 5 (14 L.)

(Eus., *Pr. ev.*, XI, 9, 8-10, 5; p. 525 b – 526a V.;
II, p. 25, 21-27, 2 Mras)

Πλείους μὲν οὖν εἰς τὴν τούτων ἐμβεβλήκασι θεωρίαν· ἐμοὶ δ᾽ ἐξαρκεῖ τὰ νῦν ἀνδρὸς ἐπιφανοῦς Νουμηνίου τοῦ Πυθαγορείου παραθέσθαι λέξεις, ἃς ἐν τῷ Περὶ τἀγαθοῦ δευτέρῳ συγγράμματι ὧδέ πῃ διέξεισιν·

5 Φέρε οὖν, ὅση δύναμις ἐγγύτατα πρὸς τὸ ὂν ἀναγώμεθα καὶ λέγωμεν· τὸ ὂν οὔτε ποτὲ ἦν οὔτε ποτὲ μὴ γένηται, ἀλλ᾽ ἔστιν ἀεὶ ἐν χρόνῳ ὡρισμένῳ, τῷ ἐνεστῶτι μόνῳ. Τοῦτον μὲν οὖν τὸν ἐνεστῶτα εἴ τις ἐθέλει ἀνακαλεῖν αἰῶνα, κἀγὼ συμβούλομαι· τὸν δὲ παρελθόντα χρόνον οἴεσθαι χρὴ ἡμᾶς
10 διαπεφευγότα ἤδη διαπεφευγέναι ἀποδεδρακέναι τε εἰς τὸ εἶναι μηκέτι· ὅ τε αὖ μέλλων ἐστὶ μὲν οὐδέπω, ἐπαγγέλλεται δὲ οἷός τε ἔσεσθαι ἥξειν εἰς τὸ εἶναι. Οὔκουν εἰκός ἐστιν ἑνί γε τρόπῳ νομίζειν τὸ ὂν ἤτοι μὴ εἶναι ἢ μηκέτι ἢ μηδέπω, ὡς τούτου γε οὕτως λεγομένου ἓν γίγνεταί τι ἐν τῷ
15 λόγῳ μέγα ἀδύνατον, εἶναί τε ὁμοῦ ταὐτὸν καὶ μὴ εἶναι.
- Εἰ δ᾽ οὕτως ἔχει, σχολῇ γ᾽ ἂν ἄλλο τι εἶναι δύναιτο, τοῦ ὄντος αὐτοῦ μὴ ὄντος κατὰ αὐτὸ τὸ ὄν.
- Τὸ ἄρα ὂν ἀΐδιόν τε βέβαιόν τέ ἐστιν ἀεὶ κατὰ ταὐτὸν καὶ ταὐτόν. Οὐδὲ γέγονε μέν, ἐφθάρη δέ, οὐδ᾽ ἐμεγεθύνατο
20 μέν, ἐμειώθη δέ, οὐδὲ μὴν ἐγένετό πω πλεῖον ἢ ἔλασσον. Καὶ μὲν δὴ τά τε ἄλλα καὶ οὐδὲ τοπικῶς κινηθήσεται· οὐδὲ γὰρ θέμις αὐτῷ κινηθῆναι, οὐδὲ μὲν ὀπίσω οὐδὲ πρόσω, οὔτε ἄνω ποτὲ οὔτε κάτω, οὐδ᾽ εἰς δεξιὰ οὐδ᾽ εἰς ἀριστερὰ μεταθεύσεταί ποτε τὸ ὄν οὔτε περὶ τὸ μέσον ποτὲ ἑαυτοῦ
25 κινηθήσεται, ἀλλὰ μᾶλλον καὶ ἑστήξεται καὶ ἀραρός τε καὶ ἑστηκὸς ἔσται κατὰ ταὐτὰ ἔχον ἀεὶ καὶ ὡσαύτως.

5 (14 L.)

While many have embarked upon the study of these matters, it is sufficient for me at this time to set forth the words of the distinguished Pythagorean Numenius, which he lays down in the second book of his writing *Concerning the Good* as follows:

Come then, as close as our strength permits, let us proceed towards Being and discuss: Being never was nor will it ever come to be, but it exists always in a definite time—the present only. Now if someone wishes to call this present eternity, I too agree. And with respect to past time, we must believe that having escaped, it has already fled and run off into 'no longer existing'. The future, in turn, does not exist yet, but promises that it will be able to come into existence. Thus it is not reasonable to think that somehow Being either does not exist, or exists no longer, or does not yet exist, because if stated in this way one great impossibility arises in the argument: namely, that the same thing both exists and does not exist at the same time.
~ But if that were the case, scarcely anything else would be able to exist, since Being itself would not exist with respect to Being itself.
~ Therefore Being is eternal and stable, always absolutely the same. It has not come to be and perished, nor has it increased and decreased; indeed, it never became more or less. And in addition to these aspects it will not move spatially. For it is not proper for it to move, either backward or forwards, either up or down; Being will not range about to the right or left, nor will it ever move itself about its center. But rather it will establish itself, and will be stable and fixed, remaining the same always and identically.

Fr. 6 (15 L.)
(Eus., *Pr. ev.*, XI, 10, 6-8; p.526 a-c V.;
II, p.27, 3-14 Mras)

a   Καὶ ἑξῆς μεθ' ἕτερα ἐπιλέγει·

Τοσαῦτα μὲν οὖν μοι πρὸ ὁδοῦ. Αὐτὸς δ' οὐκέτι σχηματισθήσομαι οὐδ' ἀγνοεῖν φήσω τὸ ὄνομα τοῦ ἀσωμάτου· καὶ γὰρ κινδυνεύει νῦν ἤδη ἥδιον εἶναι εἰπεῖν μᾶλλον ἢ μὴ
5 εἰπεῖν. Καὶ δῆτα λέγω τὸ ὄνομα αὐτῷ εἶναι τοῦτο τὸ πάλαι
b ζητούμενον. Ἀλλὰ μὴ γελασάτω τις, ἐὰν φῶ τοῦ ἀσωμάτου εἶναι ὄνομα οὐσίαν καὶ ὄν. Ἡ δὲ αἰτία τοῦ 'ὄντος' ὀνόματός ἐστι τὸ μὴ γεγονέναι μηδὲ φθαρήσεσθαι μηδ' ἄλλην μήτε κίνησιν μηδεμίαν ἐνδέχεσθαι μήτε μεταβολὴν κρείττω ἢ
10 φαύλην, εἶναι δὲ ἁπλοῦν καὶ ἀναλλοίωτον καὶ ἐν ἰδέᾳ τῇ αὐτῇ καὶ μήτε ἐθελούσιον ἐξίστασθαι τῆς ταυτότητος μήθ' ὑφ' ἑτέρου προσαναγκάζεσθαι. Ἔφη δὲ καὶ ὁ Πλάτων ἐν
c Κρατύλῳ τὰ ὀνόματα ὁμοιώσει τῶν πραγμάτων εἶναι αὐτὰ ἐπίθετα. Ἔστω οὖν καὶ δεδόχθω εἶναι τὸ ὂν ἀσώματον.

Fr. 7 (16 L.)
(Eus., *Pr. ev.*, XI, 10, 9-11; p.526 c-d V.;
II, p.27, 15-25 Mras)

c   Εἶθ' ὑποκαταβὰς ἐπιλέγει·

Τὸ ὂν εἶπον ἀσώματον, τοῦτο δὲ εἶναι τὸ νοητόν. Τὰ μὲν οὖν λεχθέντα, ὅσα μνημονεύειν ἔστι μοι, τοιαῦτα γοῦν ἦν. Τὸν δ' ἐπιζητοῦντα λόγον ἐθέλω παραμυθήσασθαι τοσόνδε
5 ὑπειπών, ὅτι ταῦτα τοῖς δόγμασι τοῖς Πλάτωνος εἰ μὴ συμβαίνει, ἀλλ' ἑτέρου γε χρῆν οἴεσθαί τινος ἀνδρὸς μεγάλου, μέγα δυναμένου, οἵου Πυθαγόρου. Λέγει γοῦν
d Πλάτων (φέρ' ἀναμνησθῶ πῶς λέγει)· Τί τὸ ὂν ἀεί, γένεσιν δὲ οὐκ ἔχον; καὶ τί τὸ γιγνόμενον μέν, ὂν δὲ οὐδέποτε; τὸ
10 μὲν δὴ νοήσει μετὰ λόγου περιληπτόν, τὸ δ' αὖ δόξῃ μετὰ αἰσθήσεως ἀλόγου δοξαστόν, γιγνόμενον καὶ ἀπολλύμενον, ὄντως δὲ οὐδέποτε ὄν'. Ἤρετο γὰρ δὴ τί ἐστι τὸ ὄν, φὰς αὐτὸ ἀγένητον ἀναμφιλέκτως. Γένεσιν γὰρ οὐκ ἔφη εἶναι τῷ ὄντι· ἐτρέπετο γὰρ ἄν· τρεπόμενον δὲ οὐκ ἦν ἀΐδιον.

6 (15 L.)

And next, following other remarks he adds:

This much, then, has furthered my argument. As for myself, I will no longer make a pretense nor will I say that I do not know the name of the Incorporeal. For indeed it is likely that by now it is more pleasing to speak than not. And in fact I say that its name is this very thing which has been investigated all along. But let no one laugh if I say that the name of the Incorporeal is Essence and Being. And the reason for the name 'Being' is the fact that it has not originated nor will it be destroyed, it does not accept any movement whatsoever or any change great or small. It is simple and unchangeable and exists in the same form, neither wishing to emerge from its identity nor is it compelled to do so by another. Plato too said in the Cratylus that names themselves are applied through similarity to their objects. Therefore let it be resolved that Being is incorporeal.

7 (16 L.)

Then, further down he adds:

I stated that being is incorporeal, and that this in turn is the noetic. The matters discussed, as far as I can recall, were of such kind. But I want to support the argument in question by suggesting only this: if the statements do not coincide with the teachings of Plato, it must be supposed that they are consistent with those of some other great and powerful man, such as Pythagoras. Now Plato says (well, let me recall how he says it): "What is that which exists always, having no beginning? And what is that which comes to be but never exists? The one can be grasped with intellect along with reason, but the other is surmised by opinion and irrational sense perception, since it is always coming to be and perishing but never really existing." He asked 'what is Being?' asserting indisputably that it is without origin. For he denied that Being has a beginning, because if it did it would change, and in undergoing change it would not be eternal.

Fr. 8 (17 L.)

(Eus., *Pr. ev.*, XI, 10, 12-14; p.526 d-527a V.;
II, p.28, 1-11 Mras)

526d Εἶτα ὑποβάς φησιν·

Εἰ μὲν δὴ τὸ ὂν πάντως πάντη ἀΐδιόν τέ ἐστι ἄτρεπτον καὶ οὐδαμῶς οὐδαμῇ ἐξιστάμενον ἐξ ἑαυτοῦ, μένει δὲ κατὰ τὰ αὐτὰ καὶ ὡσαύτως ἕστηκε, τοῦτο δήπου ἂν εἴη τὸ τῇ
5 'νοήσει μετὰ λόγου περιληπτόν'. Εἰ δὲ τὸ σῶμα ῥεῖ καὶ
527a φέρεται ὑπὸ τῆς εὐθὺ μεταβολῆς, ἀποδιδράσκει καὶ οὐκ ἔστιν. Ὅθεν οὐ πολλὴ μανία μὴ οὐ τοῦτο εἶναι ἀόριστον, δόξῃ δὲ μόνῃ δοξαστὸν καί, ὥς φησι Πλάτων, 'γιγνόμενον καὶ ἀπολλύμενον, ὄντως δὲ οὐδέποτε ὄν';

10 (Pergit Eusebius): Ταῦτα μὲν οὖν ὁ Νουμήνιος, ὁμοῦ τὰ Πλάτωνος καὶ πολὺ πρότερον τὰ Μωσέως ἐπὶ τὸ σαφὲς διερμηνεύων. Εἰκότως δῆτα εἰς αὐτὸν ἐκεῖνο τὸ λόγιον περιφέρεται δι' οὗ φάναι μνημονεύεται·

'Τί γάρ ἐστι Πλάτων ἢ Μωσῆς ἀττικίζων';

III

Fr. 9 (18 L.)

(Eus., *Pr. ev.*, IX, 8, 1-2; p.411d – 412a V.;
I, p.494, 9-18 Mras)

411d Καὶ ἐν τῇ τρίτῃ δὲ βίβλῳ Μωσέως ὁ αὐτὸς τάδε λέγων μνημονεύει·

Τὰ δ' ἑξῆς Ἰαννῆς καὶ Ἰαμβρῆς Αἰγύπτιοι ἱερογραμματεῖς, ἄνδρες οὐδενὸς ἥττους μαγεῦσαι κριθέντες εἶναι, ἐπὶ Ἰουδαίων ἐξελαυνομένων ἐξ Αἰγύπτου. Μουσαίῳ γοῦν τῷ Ἰουδαίων
5 ἐξηγησαμένῳ, ἀνδρὶ γενομένῳ θεῷ εὔξασθαι δυνατωτάτῳ, οἱ παραστῆναι ἀξιωθέντες ὑπὸ τοῦ πλήθους τοῦ τῶν Αἰγυπτίων οὗτοι ἦσαν, τῶν τε συμφορῶν, ἃς ὁ Μουσαῖος ἐπῆγε τῇ Αἰγύπτῳ, τὰς νεανικωτάτας αὐτῶν ἐπιλύεσθαι ὤφθησαν δυνατοί.

412a Διὰ δὴ τούτων ὁ Νουμήνιος καὶ τοῖς ὑπὸ Μωσέως ἐπιτελεσθεῖσι παραδόξοις θαύμασι καὶ αὐτῷ δὲ ὡς θεοφιλεῖ γενομένῳ μαρτυρεῖ.

8 (17 L.)

Then, further down he says:

If, then, Being is completely, in every way eternal and unchanging, and absolutely, in no way departing from itself, but remains consistently and identically fixed, this would be "that which is grasped by intellect and reason". And if the body flows and is swept along by rapid change, it runs away and does not exist. Accordingly is it not great madness to deny that this is indeterminate, and surmisable by opinion alone, and as Plato says, "coming to be and perishing but never really existing"?

Numenius says these things while interpreting at once both the teachings of Plato and the more ancient statements of Moses. Quite appropriately therefore that saying is ascribed to him in which he is reputed to ask:

For what is Plato but Moses speaking Greek?

III

9 (18 L.)

And also in the third book the same (Numenius), while discussing these matters, makes mention of Moses:

Next come Jannes and Jambres, Egyptian priestly scribes, men judged to be inferior to no one in magic at the time when the Jews were being driven out of Egypt. At any rate these were the ones deemed worthy by the majority of the Egyptians to stand before Musaeus, the leader of the Jews, a man was most powerful in prayer to God. And of the catastrophes which Musaeus brought upon Egypt, they were seen to be capable of destroying the most powerful.

By these remarks, then, Numenius testifies both to the incredible marvels effected by Moses and to his being dear to God.

Fr. 10 a (19 L.)

(Orig., *Contra Celsum*, IV, 51; I, p. 324, 23-27 Koetschau;
II, p.316, 20-24 Borret)

Ἐν δὲ τῷ τρίτῳ Περὶ τἀγαθοῦ ἐκτίθεται καὶ περὶ τοῦ Ἰησοῦ ἱστορίαν τινά, τὸ ὄνομα αὐτοῦ οὐ λέγων, καὶ τροπολογεῖ αὐτήν· πότερον δ' ἐπιτετευγμένως ἢ ἀποτετευγμένως, ἄλλου καιροῦ ἐστιν εἰπεῖν. Ἐκτίθεται καὶ
5 τὴν περὶ Μωϋσέως καὶ Ἰαννοῦ καὶ Ἰαμβροῦ ἱστορίαν.

Fr. 10 b

See Fr. 52.

10 (19 L.)

And in the third book of *Concerning the Good* he sets out a story about Jesus also, without mentioning his name, and allegorizes it. Whether successfully or unsuccessfully it remains for another time to say. He also sets out the story about Moses and Jannes and Jambres.

IV vel V

Fr. 11 (20 L.)
(Eus., *Pr. ev.*, XI, 17, 11-18, 5; p. 536d-537b V.;
II, p. 40, 9-41, 5 Mras)

536d   Ὁ δὲ Νουμήνιος τὰ Πλάτωνος πρεσβεύων ἐν τοῖς Περὶ τἀγαθοῦ τάδε καὶ αὐτὸς περὶ τοῦ δευτέρου αἰτίου λέγων διερμηνεύει·

   Τὸν μέλλοντα δὲ συνήσειν θεοῦ πέρι πρώτου καὶ
5 δευτέρου χρὴ πρότερον διελέσθαι ἕκαστα ἐν τάξει καὶ ἐν
537a εὐθημοσύνῃ τινί· κἄπειτα, ἐπὰν δοκῇ ἤδη εὖ ἔχειν, τότε καὶ δεῖ ἐπιχειρεῖν εἰπεῖν κοσμίως, ἄλλως δὲ μή, ἢ τῷ πρωϊαίτερον πρὶν τὰ πρῶτα γενέσθαι ἁπτομένῳ σποδὸς ὁ θησαυρὸς γίγνεσθαι λέγεται. Μὴ δὴ πάθωμεν ἡμεῖς
10 ταὐτόν· θεὸν δὲ προσκαλεσάμενοι ἑαυτοῦ γνώμονα γενόμενον τῷ λόγῳ δεῖξαι θησαυρὸν φροντίδων, ἀρχώμεθα οὕτως· εὐκτέον μὲν ἤδη, διελέσθαι δὲ δεῖ. Ὁ θεὸς ὁ μὲν πρῶτος ἐν ἑαυτοῦ ὤν ἐστιν ἁπλοῦς, διὰ τὸ ἑαυτῷ συγγιγνόμενος διόλου μή ποτε εἶναι διαίρετος· ὁ θεὸς
15 μέντοι ὁ δεύτερος καὶ τρίτος ἐστὶν εἷς· συμφερόμενος δὲ
b τῇ ὕλῃ δυάδι οὔσῃ ἑνοῖ μὲν αὐτήν, σχίζεται δὲ ὑπ' αὐτῆς, ἐπιθυμητικὸν ἦθος ἐχούσης καὶ ῥεούσης. Τῷ οὖν μὴ εἶναι πρὸς τῷ νοητῷ (ἦν γὰρ ἂν πρὸς ἑαυτῷ) διὰ τὸ τὴν ὕλην βλέπειν, ταύτης ἐπιμελούμενος ἀπερίοπτος ἑαυτοῦ
20 γίγνεται. Καὶ ἅπτεται τοῦ αἰσθητοῦ καὶ περιέπει ἀνάγει τε ἔτι εἰς τὸ ἴδιον ἦθος ἐπορεξάμενος τῆς ὕλης.

IV vela V

11 (20 L.)

Numenius, while representing the thought of Plato in *Concerning the Good*, also elaborates on the second cause himself and interprets it in this way:

One who intends to have some understanding of the First God and Second must first distinguish each thing in sequence and with a degree of orderliness; and next, if at this point it appears to hold together well, then one should also endeavor to speak sensibly, otherwise not. Or else, as the saying goes, the treasure turns to ash for him who grasps rashly before the preliminaries are established. May we not experience the same thing. But having called upon God, so that by becoming his own interpreter he might show us with a word a treasure of meditations, let us begin in this way (it is necessary first to pray and then make distinctions): The First God, who exists in himself, is simple, because being completely self-contained he is never divisible. However the Second and Third Gods are one. And coming into contact with matter (which is a dyad) he unifies it, but is divided by it since it possesses a passionate character and is constantly flowing. Now by not being close to the noetic (for he would be close to himself), because he glances at matter and becomes concerned for it, he becomes unmindful of himself. And he touches the perceptible, treats it with care and brings it further up to his own character through his yearning for matter.

Fr. 12 (21 L.)
(Eus, *Pr. ev.*, XI, 18, 6-10; p. 537b-d V.;
II, p.41, 6-22 Mras)

537b Καὶ μεθ' ἕτερά φησι·

Καὶ γὰρ οὔτε δημιοργεῖν ἐστι χρεών τὸν πρῶτον καὶ τοῦ δημιουργοῦντος δὲ θεοῦ χρὴ εἶναι νομίζεσθαι πατέρα τὸν πρῶτον θεόν. Εἰ μὲν οὖν περὶ τοῦ δημιουργικοῦ ζητοῖμεν,
5 φάσκοντες δεῖν τὸν πρότερον ὑπάρξαντα οὕτως ἂν ποιεῖν
c ἔχειν διαφερόντως, ἐοικυῖα ἡ πρόσοδος αὕτη γεγονυῖα ἂν εἴη τοῦ λόγου· εἰ δὲ περὶ τοῦ δημιουργοῦ μὴ ἔστιν ὁ λόγος, ζητοῦμεν δὲ περὶ τοῦ πρώτου, ἀφοσιοῦμαί τε τὰ λεχθέντα καὶ ἔστω μὲν ἐκεῖνα ἄρρητα, μέτειμι δὲ ἑλεῖν τὸν λόγον,
10 ἑτέρωθεν θηράσας. Πρὸ μέντοι τοῦ λόγου τῆς ἁλώσεως διομολογησώμεθα ἡμῖν αὐτοῖς ὁμολογίαν οὐκ ἀμφιβητήσιμον ἀκοῦσαι, τὸν μὲν πρῶτον θεὸν ἀργὸν εἶναι ἔργων συμπάντων καὶ βασιλέα, τὸν δημιοργικὸν δὲ θεὸν ἡγεμονεῖν δι' οὐρανοῦ ἰόντα. Διὰ δὲ τούτου καὶ ὁ στόλος ἡμῖν ἐστι, κάτω τοῦ νοῦ
15 πεμπομένου ἐν διεξόδῳ πᾶσι τοῖς κοινωνῆσαι συντεταγμένοις.
d Βλέποντος μὲν οὖν καὶ ἐπεστραμμένου πρὸς ἡμῶν ἕκαστον τοῦ θεοῦ συμβαίνει ζῆν τε καὶ βιώσκεσθαι τότε τὰ σώματα κηδεύοντα τοῦ θεοῦ τοῖς ἀκροβολισμοῖς· μεταστρέφοντος δὲ εἰς τὴν ἑαυτοῦ περιωπὴν τοῦ θεοῦ ταῦτα μὲν ἀποσβέννυσθαι,
20 τὸν δὲ νοῦν ζῆν βίου ἐπαυρόμενον εὐδαίμονος.

Fr. 13 (22 L.)
(Eus., *Pr. ev.*, XI, 18, 13-14, p. 538b-c V.;
II, p.42, 15-21 Mras)

538b Ὁ Νουμήνιος ἐπάκουσον οἷα περὶ τοῦ δευτέρου αἰτίου θεολογεῖ·

Ὥσπερ δὲ πάλιν λόγος ἐστὶ γεωργῷ πρὸς τὸν φυτεύοντα,
c ἀνὰ τὸν αὐτὸν λόγον μάλιστά ἐστιν ὁ πρῶτος θεὸς πρὸς τὸν δημιουργόν. Ὁ μέν γε ὢν σπέρμα πάσης ψυχῆς σπείρει εἰς
5 τὰ μεταλαγχάνοντα αὐτοῦ χρήματα σύμπαντα· ὁ νομοθέτης δὲ φυτεύει καὶ διανέμει καὶ μεταφυτεύει εἰς ἡμᾶς ἑκάστους τὰ ἐκεῖθεν προκαταβεβλημένα.

12 (21 L.)

And after other remarks he says:

For in fact it is not necessary that the First God create; rather he should be considered the father of the Demiurgic God. Now if we were to investigate the demiurgic aspect, asserting that necessarily what is antecedent would be exceedingly capable of creating, this would be a suitable approach for the argument to take. But if the discussion does not concern the Demiurge and we are investigating the First God, I reject what has been said; let those things be unspoken and I will seek to seize the argument by tracking it from another direction. However before the argument is captured, let us form an indisputable agreement among ourselves: namely, that the First God is devoid of any activity whatsoever and is King, while the Demiurgic God rules as he moves through the heavens. And it is through this one that we too have our journey, when Intellect is sent below along a path to all those who have been allotted a share in it. Therefore, when God looks and turns himself towards each of us, it happens that bodies live and are sustained by the rays of God. But when God turns back towards his own vantage point they are extinguished, while Intellect continues to live, enjoying a life of bliss.

13 (22 L.)

Listen to the type of theology that Numenius propounds concerning the Second Cause:

Again, just as there is a relation between the one who tills and the one who plants, so it is exactly the same relation that exists between the First God and the Demiurge. The 'One Who Is' sows the seed of every soul into all things that have a share in him, while the lawgiver plants and separates and transplants into each of us the seeds which have been previously cast down from above.

Fr. 14 (23 L.)

(Eus., *Pr. ev.*, XI, 18, 15-19, p. 538c-539a V.;
II, p. 42, 22-43, 13 Mras)

538c Καὶ ἑξῆς δὲ πάλιν περὶ τοῦ πῶς ἀπὸ τοῦ πρώτου αἰτίου τὸ δεύτερον ὑπέστη τοιάδε φησίν·

Ὁπόσα δὲ δοθέντα μέτεισι πρὸς τὸν λαμβάνοντα, c ἀπελθόντα ἐκ τοῦ δεδωκότος (ἔστι <δὲ> θεραπεία, χρήματα, 5 νόμισμα κοῖλον, ἐπίσημον), ταυτὶ μὲν οὖν ἐστι θνητὰ καὶ ἀνθρώπινα, τὰ δὲ θεῖά ἐστιν οἷα μεταδοθέντα ἐνθένδ' ἐκεῖθι γεγενημένα ἔνθεν τε οὐκ ἀπελήλυθε κἀκεῖθι γενόμενα τὸν μὲν ὤνησε τὸν δ' οὐκ ἔβλαψε καὶ προσώνησε τῇ περὶ ὧν ἠπίστατο ἀναμνήσει. Ἔστι δὲ τοῦτο τὸ καλὸν χρῆμα 10 ἐπιστήμη ἡ καλή, ἧς ὤνατο μὲν ὁ λαβών, οὐκ ἀπολείπεται δ' αὐτῆς ὁ δεδωκώς. Οἷον ἂν ἴδοις ἐξαφθέντα ἀφ' ἑτέρου λύχνου λύχνον φῶς ἔχοντα, ὃ μὴ τὸν πρότερον ἀφείλατο ἀλλ' ἢ τῆς ἐν αὐτῷ ὕλης πρὸς τὸ ἐκείνου πῦρ ἐξαφθείσης. Τοιοῦτον τὸ χρῆμά ἐστι τὸ τῆς ἐπιστήμης, ἣ δοθεῖσα καὶ 15 ληφθεῖσα παραμένει μὲν τῷ δεδωκότι, σύνεστι δὲ τῷ λαβόντι 539a ἡ αὐτή. Τούτου δὲ τὸ αἴτιον, ὦ ξένε, οὐδέν ἐστιν ἀνθρώπινον, ἀλλ' ὅτι ἕξις τε καὶ οὐσία ἡ ἔχουσα τὴν ἐπιστήμην ἡ αὐτή ἐστι παρά τε τῷ δεδωκότι θεῷ καὶ παρὰ τῷ εἰληφότι ἐμοὶ καὶ σοί. Διὸ καὶ ὁ Πλάτων τὴν σοφίαν 20 ὑπὸ Προμηθέως ἐλθεῖν εἰς ἀνθρώπους μετὰ φανοτάτου τινὸς πυρὸς ἔφη.

Fr. 15 (24 L.)

(Eus., *Pr. ev.*, XI, 18, 20-21, p. 539a-b V.;
II, p. 43, 15-21 Mras)

539a Καὶ πάλιν ὑποβὰς ἑξῆς φησιν·

Εἰσὶ δ' οὗτοι βίοι ὁ μὲν πρώτου, ὁ δὲ δευτέρου θεοῦ. Δηλονότι ὁ μὲν πρῶτος θεὸς ἔσται ἑστώς, ὁ δὲ δεύτερος b ἔμπαλίν ἐστι κινούμενος· ὁ μὲν οὖν πρῶτος περὶ τὰ νοητά, ὁ 5 δὲ δεύτερος περὶ τὰ νοητὰ καὶ αἰσθητά. Μὴ θαυμάσῃς δ' εἰ τοῦτ' ἔφην· πολὺ γὰρ ἔτι θαυμαστότερον ἀκούσῃ. Ἀντὶ γὰρ τῆς προσούσης τῷ δευτέρῳ κινήσεως τὴν προσοῦσαν τῷ πρώτῳ στάσιν φημὶ εἶναι κίνησιν σύμφυτον, ἀφ' ἧς ἥ τε τάξις τοῦ κόσμου καὶ ἡ μονὴ ἡ ἀίδιος καὶ ἡ σωτηρία 10 ἀναχεῖται εἰς τὰ ὅλα.

14 (23 L.)

And next, once again addressing the manner in which the Second issued from the First Cause, he makes the following remarks:

All things which once given proceed to the receiver by departing from the one who has given them (be it service, goods, plated metals, or inscribed coins), these things, then, are mortal and human. But divine gifts are such that once having been shared, coming from there they have not departed from there; and being here they benefit the one receiving without diminishing the giver, who is additionally benefited through the recollection of things he once knew. And this is the beautiful possession: beautiful knowledge, which benefits the one receiving while the one who has bestowed it is not deprived of it.

It is as if you were to see a lamp with a flame lit from another, which it has not taken away from the first, but has merely ignited its own material at the fire of that one. Just such a possession is knowledge, which once given and received remains with the giver, while the same knowledge is joined to the receiver. And the cause of this, O Stranger, is in no way human, rather it is because the condition and essence which adheres to knowledge is the same with God who gives it as it is with you and me who receive. That is why Plato too said that wisdom came to mankind through the agency of Prometheus along with and exceedingly bright fire.

15 (24 L.)

And again, further down he next says:

These are the lives of the First and Second Gods. That is, the First God will be motionless, the Second in contrast is moving. The first is involved with the intelligibles, the Second with intelligibles and perceptibles. Don't be amazed if I have spoken thus, for you will hear much that is still more remarkable. For corresponding to the characteristic movement of the Second I assert that the characteristic stability of the First is an innate movement, from which the order of the world, its eternal permanence, and its salvation are poured out into the all.

V

Fr. 16 (25 L.)
(Eus., *Pr. ev.*, XI, 22, 3-5, p. 544a-b V.;
II, p. 49, 13-50, 8 Mras)

a Ἐν δὲ τῷ πέμπτῳ ταῦτά φησιν·

Εἰ δ' ἔστι μὲν νοητὸν ἡ οὐσία καὶ ἡ ἰδέα, ταύτης δ' ὡμολογήθη πρεσβύτερον καὶ αἴτιον εἶναι ὁ νοῦς, αὐτὸς οὗτος μόνος εὕρηται ὢν τὸ ἀγαθόν. Καὶ γὰρ εἰ ὁ μὲν δημιουργὸς
5 θεός ἐστι γενέσεως, ἀρκεῖ τὸ ἀγαθὸν οὐσίας εἶναι ἀρχή. Ἀνάλογον δὲ τούτῳ μὲν ὁ δημιουργὸς θεός, ὢν αὐτοῦ μιμητής, τῇ δὲ οὐσίᾳ ἡ γένεσις, <ἣ> εἰκὼν αὐτῆς ἐστι καὶ μίμημα. Εἴπερ δὲ ὁ δημιουργὸς ὁ τῆς γενέσεώς ἐστιν
b ἀγαθός, ἦ που ἔσται καὶ ὁ τῆς οὐσίας δημιουργὸς
10 αὐτοάγαθον, σύμφυτον τῇ οὐσίᾳ. Ὁ γὰρ δεύτερος διττὸς ὢν αὐτοποιεῖ τήν τε ἰδέαν ἑαυτοῦ καὶ τὸν κόσμον, δημιουργὸς ὤν, ἔπειτα θεωρητικὸς ὅλως. Συλλελογισμένων δ' ἡμῶν ὀνόματα τεσσάρων πραγμάτων τέσσαρα ἔστω ταῦτα· ὁ μὲν πρῶτος θεὸς αὐτοάγαθον· ὁ δὲ τούτου μιμητὴς δημιουργὸς
15 ἀγαθός· ἡ δ' οὐσία μία μὲν ἡ τοῦ πρώτου, ἑτέρα δ' ἡ τοῦ δευτέρου· ἧς μίμημα ὁ καλὸς κόσμος, κεκαλλωπισμένος μετουσίᾳ τοῦ καλοῦ.

VI

Fr. 17 (26 L.)
(Eus., *Pr. ev.*, XI, 18, 22-23, p. 539 b-c V.;
II, p. 43, 22-44, 3 Mras)

b Ἔτι τούτοις καὶ ἐν τῷ ἕκτῳ προστίθησι ταῦτα·
Ἐπειδὴ ᾔδει ὁ Πλάτων παρὰ τοῖς ἀνθρώποις τὸν μὲν
c δημιουργὸν γιγνωσκόμενον μόνον, τὸν μέντοι πρῶτον νοῦν, ὅστις καλεῖται αὐτοόν, παντάπασιν ἀγνοούμενον παρ' αὐτοῖς,
5 διὰ τοῦτο οὕτως εἶπεν ὥσπερ ἄν τις οὕτω λέγοι·῏Ω ἄνθρωποι, ὃν τοπάζετε ὑμεῖς νοῦν οὐκ ἔστι πρῶτος, ἀλλ' ἕτερος πρὸ τούτου νοῦς πρεσβύτερος καὶ θειότερος'.

16 (25 L.)

In the fifth book he says this:

If Essence and Idea comprise the noetic, and Intellect has been acknowledged as superior to these and their cause, only Intellect itself has been found to be the Good. For if the Demiurge is the god of becoming, it suffices that the Good be the principle of Essence. Further, the Demiurgic God corresponds to the Good, being its imitator, just as becoming corresponds to Essence, since it is its image and copy. And if the Demiurge is the 'good' of becoming, surely the 'demiurge' of Essence will be absolute Good, inherent in Essence. For the Second, being double, independently creates his own Idea as well as the cosmos since he is Demiurge; afterwards he is wholly contemplative.

In drawing our conclusions let these four terms indicate four things: 1) the First God who is absolute Good, 2) the imitator of this one, the good Demiurge, 3) Essence, of one kind for the First, of another for the Second, 4) the copy of this, the beautiful cosmos, which has been embellished through participation in the Beautiful.

VI

17 (26 L.)

And in the sixth book he makes these further additions:

Plato knew that among mankind only the Demiurge is known, while the First Intellect who is called absolute Being is completely unknown among them. For this reason he spoke thus, as if one were to say: "O men, the one which you surmise to be Intellect is not the First, rather there is another Intellect before this one which is more august and more divine."

Fr. 18 (27 L.)

(Eus., *Pr. ev.*, XI, 18, 24, p. 539 c-d V.;
II, p. 44, 4-13 Mras)

c   Καὶ μεθ' ἕτερα ἐπιλέγει·

Κυβερνήτης μέν που ἐν μέσῳ πελάγει φορούμενος ὑπὲρ πηδαλίων ὑψίζυγος τοῖς οἴαξι διϊθύνει τὴν ναῦν ἐφεζόμενος, ὄμματα δ' αὐτοῦ καὶ νοῦς εὐθὺ τοῦ αἰθέρος συντέταται πρὸς
d 5 τὰ μετάρσια καὶ ἡ ὁδὸς αὐτῷ ἄνω δι' οὐρανοῦ ἄπεισι, πλέοντι κάτω κατὰ τὴν θάλατταν· οὕτω καὶ ὁ δημιουργὸς τὴν ὕλην, τοῦ μήτε διακροῦσαι μήτε ἀποπλαγχθῆναι αὐτήν, ἁρμονίᾳ συνδησάμενος αὐτὸς μὲν ὑπὲρ ταύτης ἵδρυται, οἷον ὑπὲρ νεὼς ἐπὶ θαλάττης [τῆς ὕλης]· τὴν ἁρμονίαν δ' ἰθύνει,
10 ταῖς ἰδέαις οἰακίζων, βλέπει τε ἀντὶ τοῦ οὐρανοῦ εἰς τὸν ἄνω θεὸν προσαγόμενον αὐτοῦ τὰ ὄμματα λαμβάνει τε τὸ μὲν κριτικὸν ἀπὸ τῆς θεωρίας, τὸ δ' ὁρμητικὸν ἀπὸ τῆς ἐφέσεως.

Fr. 19 (28 L.)

(Eus., *Pr. ev.*, XI, 22, 6-8, p. 544 c-d V.;
II, p. 50, 9-18 Mras)

b   Καὶ ἐν τῷ ἕκτῳ δὲ ἐπιλέγει·

c   Μετέχει δὲ αὐτοῦ τὰ μετίσχοντα ἐν ἄλλῳ μὲν οὐδενί, ἐν δὲ μόνῳ τῷ φρονεῖν· ταύτῃ ἄρα καὶ τῆς ἀγαθοῦ συμβάσεως ὀνίναιτ' ἄν, ἄλλως δ' οὔ. Καὶ μὲν δὴ τὸ φρονεῖν, τοῦτο δὴ
5 συντετύχηκε μόνῳ τῷ πρώτῳ. Ὑφ' οὗ οὖν τὰ ἄλλα ἀποχραίνεται καὶ ἀγαθοῦται, ἐὰν τοῦτο ἐκείνῳ μόνον μόνῳ προσῇ, ἀβελτέρας ἂν εἴη ψυχῆς ἔτι ἀμφιλογεῖν. Εἰ γὰρ ἀγαθός ἐστιν ὁ δεύτερος οὐ παρ' ἑαυτοῦ, παρὰ δὲ τοῦ πρώτου, πῶς οἷόν τε ὑφ' οὗ μετουσίας ἐστὶν οὗτος ἀγαθός, μὴ
10 ἀγαθὸν <εἶναι>, ἄλλως τε κἂν τύχῃ αὐτοῦ ὡς ἀγαθοῦ
d μεταλαχὼν ὁ δεύτερος; οὕτω τοι ὁ Πλάτων ἐκ συλλογισμοῦ τῷ ὀξὺ βλέποντι ἀπέδωκε τὸ ἀγαθὸν ὅτι ἐστὶν ἕν.

18 (27 L.)

And after other remarks he adds:

A helmsman, I imagine, carried along on the high seas, seated high above the rudder, steers the ship with the tiller but his eyes and mind have been directed straight to the ether towards the regions above, and his course proceeds above through the heavens while he sails below along the sea. In this way also the Demiurge, once having bound matter together in a harmony so that it might neither escape nor wander away, sits above it as if above a ship on the sea. He directs the harmony, steering with the Ideas, and instead of the heavens he looks toward the God above who attracts his eyes; and he obtains discernment from contemplation, but impulsiveness from desire.

19 (28 L.)

And in the sixth book he adds:

Things that participate in the Good participate in no other respect but through intellection only. In this way, then, they would benefit from the union with the Good, otherwise not. And indeed, as regards intellection, this function has fallen to the First alone. Therefore, if this function alone adheres only to that being by whom other things are tinged and made good, it would be foolish to remain in doubt. For if the Second is good not through himself but by means of the First, how can he, through participation with whom this one is good, not be good, especially if the Second participates in him as the Good? Thus Plato delivers the reasoned conclusion to the keen of sight: the Good is one.

Fr. 20 (29 L.)
(Eus, *Pr. ev.*, XI, 22, 9-10, p. 544 d V.;
II, p. 51, 2-9 Mras)

Καὶ πάλιν ἑξῆς φησι·

Ταῦτα δ' οὕτως ἔχοντα ἔθηκεν ὁ Πλάτων ἄλλη καὶ ἄλλη χωρίσας· ἰδίᾳ μὲν γὰρ τὸν κυκλικὸν ἐπὶ τοῦ δημιουργοῦ ἐγράψατο ἐν Τιμαίῳ εἰπών· "'Ἀγαθὸς ἦν"· ἐν δὲ τῇ Πολιτείᾳ
5 τὸ ἀγαθὸν εἶπεν "ἀγαθοῦ ἰδέαν", ὡς δὴ τοῦ δημιουργοῦ ἰδέαν οὖσαν τὸ ἀγαθόν, ὅστις πέφανται ἡμῖν ἀγαθὸς μετουσίᾳ τοῦ πρώτου τε καὶ μόνου. Ὥσπερ γὰρ ἄνθρωποι μὲν λέγονται τυπωθέντες ὑπὸ τῆς ἀνθρώπου ἰδέας, βόες δ' ὑπὸ τῆς βοός, ἵπποι δ' ὑπὸ τῆς ἵππου ἰδέας, οὕτως καὶ εἰκότως ὁ
10 δημιουργὸς εἴπερ ἐστὶ μετουσίᾳ τοῦ πρώτου ἀγαθοῦ ἀγαθός, <ἀγαθοῦ> ἰδέα ἂν εἴη ὁ πρῶτος νοῦς, ὢν αὐτοάγαθον.

Fr. 21 (Test. 24 L., fr. 36 Thedinga)
(Proclus, *In Timaeum*, I, 303, 27-304, 7 Diehl)

Νουμήνιος μὲν γὰρ τρεῖς ἀνυμνήσας θεοὺς πατέρα μὲν καλεῖ τὸν πρῶτον, ποιητὴν δὲ τὸν δεύτερον, ποίημα δὲ τὸν τρίτον· ὁ γὰρ κόσμος κατ' αὐτὸν ὁ τρίτος ἐστὶ θεός· ὥστε ὁ κατ' αὐτὸν δημιουργὸς διττός, ὅ τε πρῶτος θεὸς καὶ ὁ
5 δεύτερος, τὸ δὲ δημιουργούμενον ὁ τρίτος. Ἄμεινον γὰρ οὕτω λέγειν ἢ ὡς ἐκεῖνος λέγει προστραγῳδῶν, πάππον, ἔγγονον, ἀπόγονον. Ὁ δὴ ταῦτα λέγων πρῶτον μὲν οὐκ ὀρθῶς τἀγαθὸν συναριθμεῖ τοῖσδε τοῖς αἰτίοις· οὐ γὰρ πέφυκεν ἐκεῖνο συζεύγνυσθαί τισιν οὐδὲ δευτέραν ἔχειν ἄλλου τάξιν.

20 (29 L.)

And again, he says next:

Plato set these matters out, making distinctions here and there. For example, in the *Timaeus* he wrote about the Demiurge in the common way saying: "He was good." But in the *Republic* he stated that the Good is the Idea of the Good, implying that the Good is the Idea of the Demiurge, who has appeared to us to be good through the First and only. For just as men are said to be modeled after the Idea of a man, cattle after that of a cow, and horses after the Idea of a horse, so it follows that if the Demiurge is good by participation in the First Good, the First Intellect, being absolute Good, would be the Idea <of good>.

21 (Test. 24 L.)

Numenius proclaims three gods: he calls the First 'Father', the Second 'Maker', and the Third 'Product'. For the cosmos, according to him, is the Third God; so that according to him the Demiurge is double—the First God and the Second—and the creation is the Third. It is better to speak in this way, rather than the way he puts it, overly dramatizing: 'grandfather', 'son', 'grandson'. Indeed, in the first place the one who says this is numbering the Good together with these causes incorrectly. For by its nature that cannot be linked with anything nor take second rank to another.

Fr. 22 (Test. 25 L., fr. 39 Thedinga)

(Id., ib., III, 103, 28-32 Diehl)

Νουμήνιος δὲ τὸν μὲν πρῶτον κατὰ τὸ 'ὅ ἐστι ζῷον' τάττει καί φησιν ἐν προσχρήσει τοῦ δευτέρου νοεῖν, τὸν δὲ δεύτερον κατὰ τὸν νοῦν καὶ τοῦτον αὖ ἐν προσχρήσει τοῦ τρίτου δημιουργεῖν, τὸν δὲ τρίτον κατὰ τὸν διανοούμενον.

Περὶ τῶν παρὰ Πλάτωνι ἀπορρήτων

Fr. 23 (30 L.)

(Eus., Pr. ev., XIII, 4, 4-5, 2, p. 650 c-651 a V.;
II, p. 177, 25-178, 12 Mras)
(post citationem Euthyphronis, 5 e 6-6 c 7)

650c Ταῦτα ὁ Πλάτων ἐν τῷ Εὐθύφρονι. Διασαφεῖ δὲ τὴν διάνοιαν ὁ Νουμήνιος ἐν τῷ Περὶ τῶν παρὰ Πλάτωνι ἀπορρήτων ὧδέ πῃ λέγων·

d Εἰ μὲν γράφειν ὑποτεινάμενος ὁ Πλάτων περὶ τῆς
5 θεολογίας τῆς τῶν Ἀθηναίων εἶτα ἐδυσχέραινεν αὐτῇ καὶ κατηγόρει ἐχούσῃ στάσεις μὲν πρὸς ἀλλήλους, τέκνων δὲ τῶν μὲν μίξεις τῶν δ' ἐδωδάς, τῶν δ' ἀντὶ τούτων πατράσι τιμωρίας ἀδελφῶν τε ἀδελφοῖς ὑμνούσῃ καὶ ἄλλα τοιαῦτα· εἴπερ ὁ Πλάτων ταυτὶ λαβὼν εἰς τὸ φανερὸν κατηγόρει,
10 παρασχεῖν ἂν δοκεῖ μοι τοῖς Ἀθηναίοις αἰτίαν πάλιν κακοῖς
654a γενέσθαι ἀποκτείνασι καὶ αὐτὸν ὥσπερ τὸν Σωκράτην. Ἐπεὶ δὲ ζῆν οὐκ ἂν προείλετο μᾶλλον ἢ ἀληθεύειν, ἑώρα δὲ ζῆν τε καὶ ἀληθεύειν ἀσφαλῶς δυνησόμενος, ἔθηκεν ἐν μὲν τῷ σχήματι τῶν Ἀθηναίων τὸν Εὐθύφρονα, ὄντα ἄνδρα ἀλαζόνα
15 καὶ κοάλεμον καὶ εἴ τις ἄλλος θεολογεῖ κακῶς, αὐτὸν δὲ τὸν Σωκράτην ἐπ' αὐτοῦ τε καὶ ἐν τῷ ἰδίῳ σχηματισμῷ ἐν ᾧπερ εἰωθότως ἤλεγχεν ἑκάστῳ προσομιλῶν.

22 (Test. 25 L.)

Numenius assigns to the First a rank corresponding to the 'Living Being' and says that it contemplates by using the Second; the Second corresponds to Intellect and this principle in turn creates by using the Third, which corresponds to discursive intellect.

Concerning The Esoterica Of Plato

23 (30 L.)

Plato makes these remarks in the Euthyphro. And Numenius clarifies the intent in *Concerning the Esoterica of Plato*, saying something like this:

If Plato, after proposing to write about the theology of the Athenians then became annoyed with it and accused it of portraying the gods as having discords with one another, and as having incestuous relations with their children on the one hand, and eating them on the other; and accused it of reciting the revenges upon fathers for these deeds, and those of brothers upon brothers, and other such misdeeds; if then, seizing upon these things Plato were to make open accusations, it seems to me that he would present the Athenians with an occasion to become evil once again, by killing him also just as they had killed Socrates. And since he would not choose to live rather than speak the truth, but saw that he could not both live and speak the truth safely, he set Euthyphro in the role of the Athenians, being a boastful and dim-witted fellow, as poor a theologian as anyone, and put Socrates himself before him in the characteristic manner in which he was accustomed to confute each person with whom he conversed.

Περὶ τῆς τῶν Ἀκαδημαϊκῶν πρὸς Πλάτωνα διαστάσεως
I

Fr. 24 (1 L.)

(Eus., *Pr. ev.*, XIV, 4, 16-59, p. 727 a-729 b V.;

II, p. 268, 11-271, 6 Mras)

727a Τοιαύτη μέν τις ἡ αὐτοῦ Πλάτωνος ὑπῆρξε διαδοχή. Ὁποῖοι δὲ γεγόνασιν οἵδε τὸν τρόπον, λαβὼν ἀνάγνωθι τὰς ὧδε ἐχούσας Νουμηνίου τοῦ Πυθαγορείου φωνάς, ἃς τέθειται ἐν τῷ πρώτῳ ὧν ἐπέγραψε Περὶ τῆς τῶν Ἀκαδημαϊκῶν πρὸς
5 Πλάτωνα διαστάσεως·

b Ἐπὶ μὲν τοίνυν Σπεύσιππον τὸν Πλάτωνος μὲν ἀδελφιδοῦν, Ξενοκράτη δὲ τὸν διάδοχον τὸν Σπευσίππου, Πολέμωνα δὲ τὸν ἐκδεξάμενον τὴν σχολὴν παρὰ Ξενοκράτους ἀεὶ τὸ ἦθος διετείνετο τῶν δογμάτων σχεδὸν δὴ ταὐτόν, ἕνεκά γε τῆς
10 μήπω ἐποχῆς ταυτησὶ τῆς πολυθρυλήτου τε καὶ εἰ δή τινων τοιούτων ἄλλων. Ἐπεὶ εἴς γε τἆλλα πολλαχῇ παραλύοντες,
c τὰ δὲ στρεβλοῦντες, οὐκ ἐνέμειναν τῇ πρώτῃ διαδοχῇ· ἀρξάμενοι δ' ἀπ' ἐκείνου καὶ θᾶττον καὶ βράδιον διίσταντο προαιρέσει ἢ ἀγνοίᾳ, τὰ δὲ δή τινι αἰτίᾳ ἄλλῃ οὐκ
15 ἀφιλοτίμῳ ἴσως. Καὶ οὐ μὲν βούλομαί τι φλαῦρον εἰπεῖν διὰ Ξενοκράτη, μᾶλλον μὴν ὑπὲρ Πλάτωνος ἐθέλω. Καὶ γάρ με δάκνει ὅτι μὴ πᾶν ἔπαθόν τε καὶ ἔδρων σῴζοντες τῷ Πλάτωνι κατὰ πάντα πάντῃ πᾶσαν ὁμοδοξίαν. Καίτοι ἄξιος ἦν αὐτοῖς ὁ Πλάτων, οὐκ ἀμείνων μὲν Πυθαγόρου τοῦ
20 μεγάλου, οὐ μέντοι ἴσως οὐδὲ φλαυρότερος ἐκείνου, ᾧ
d συνακολουθοῦντες σεφθέντες τε οἱ γνώριμοι ἐγένοντο πολυτιμητίζεσθαι αἰτιώτατοι τὸν Πυθαγόραν.

Concerning The Divergence Of The Academics From Plato

I

24 (1 L.)

The succession of Plato was something such as this. Regarding the character of these men, read the following remarks of Numenius the Pythagorean which he has set down in the first book of *Concerning the Divergence of the Academics From Plato*:

Now during the time of Speusippus, the nephew of Plato, Xenocrates, the successor of Speusippus, and Polemon, who received the school from Xenocrates, the character of the teachings always remained nearly the same, due to the fact that this famous 'suspension' had not yet appeared, nor indeed had any other doctrines of that kind. But for the rest, by doing away with some doctrines and distorting others they failed to remain within the primary tradition. And once they had started from that point they continued to deviate, either quite rapidly or more slowly, by choice or through ignorance; perhaps indeed through another motive not lacking in ambition. However I do not wish to say anything derogatory concerning Xenocrates, rather I wish to speak on behalf of Plato.

For in fact it stings me that they did not both suffer and do everything in order to preserve for Plato, in all respects, in every way, complete uniformity of doctrine. And to be sure, Plato was worthy of them; not superior to the great Pythagoras, nor yet perhaps inferior to that man whose students, by closely following and revering him became the chief reason that Pythagoras is highly esteemed.

Τοῦτο δ' οἱ Ἐπικούρειοι οὐκ ὤφελον μέν, μαθόντες δ' οὖν ἐν οὐδενὶ ὤφθησαν Ἐπικούρῳ ἐναντία θέμενοι οὐδαμῶς, ὁμολογήσαντες δ' εἶναι σοφῷ συνδεδογμένοι καὶ αὐτοὶ διὰ τοῦτο ἀπέλαυσαν τῆς προσρήσεως εἰκότως· ὑπῆρξέ τε ἐκ τοῦ ἐπὶ πλεῖστον τοῖς μετέπειτα Ἐπικουρείοις μηδ' αὐτοῖς εἰπεῖν πω ἐναντίον οὔτε ἀλλήλοις οὔτε Ἐπικούρῳ μηδὲν εἰς μηδὲν ὅτου καὶ μνησθῆναι ἄξιον· ἀλλ' ἔστιν αὐτοῖς παρανόμημα, μᾶλλον δ' ἀσέβημα, καὶ κατέγνωσται τὸ καινοτομηθέν. Διὸ τοῦτο οὐδεὶς οὐδὲ τολμᾷ, κατὰ πολλὴν δ' εἰρήνην αὐτοῖς ἠρεμεῖ τὰ δόγματα ὑπὸ τῆς ἐν ἀλλήλοις ἀεί ποτε συμφωνίας. Ἔοικέ τε ἡ Ἐπικούρου διατριβὴ πολιτείᾳ τινὶ ἀληθεῖ, ἀστασιαστοτάτῃ, κοινὸν ἕνα νοῦν, μίαν γνώμην ἐχούσῃ· ἀφ' ἧς ἦσαν καὶ εἰσὶ καί, ὡς ἔοικεν, ἔσονται φιλακόλουθοι.

Τὰ δὲ τῶν Στοϊκῶν ἐστασίασται, ἀρξάμενα ἀπὸ τῶν ἀρχόντων καὶ μηδέπω τελευτῶντα καὶ νῦν. Ἐλέγχουσι δ' ἀγαπώντως ὑπὸ δυσμενοῦς ἐλέγχου, οἱ μέν τινες αὐτῶν ἐμμεμενηκότες ἔτι, οἱ δ' ἤδη μεταθέμενοι. Εἴξασιν οὖν οἱ πρῶτοι ὀλιγαρχικωτέροις, οἳ δὴ διαστάντες ὑπῆρξαν εἰς τοὺς μετέπειτα πολλῆς μὲν τοῖς προτέροις, πολλῆς δὲ τῆς ἀλλήλοις ἐπιτιμήσεως αἴτιοι, εἰσί τε ἑτέρων ἕτεροι στωϊκώτεροι καὶ μᾶλλον ὅσοι πλεῖον περὶ τὸ τεχνικὸν ὤφθησαν μικρολόγοι· αὐτοὶ γὰρ οὗτοι τοὺς ἑτέρους ὑπερβαλλόμενοι τῇ τε πολυπραγμοσύνῃ τοῖς τε σκαρ<ι>φηθμοῖς ἐπετίμων θᾶττον. Πολὺ μέντοι τούτων πρότερον ταὐτὰ ἔπαθον οἱ ἀπὸ Σωκράτους ἀφελκύσαντες διαφόρους τοὺς λόγους, ἰδίᾳ μὲν Ἀρίστιππος, ἰδίᾳ δὲ Ἀντισθένης καὶ ἀλλαχοῦ ἰδίᾳ οἱ Μεγαρικοί τε καὶ Ἐρετρικοὶ ἢ εἴ τινες ἄλλοι μετὰ τούτων. Αἴτιον δέ, ὅτι τρεῖς θεοὺς τιθεμένου Σωκράτους καὶ φιλοσοφοῦντος αὐτοῖς ἐν τοῖς προσήκουσιν ἑκάστῳ ῥυθμοῖς, οἱ διακούοντες τοῦτο μὲν ἠγνόουν, ᾤοντο δὲ λέγειν πάντα αὐτὸν εἰκῇ καὶ ἀπὸ τῆς νικώσης ἀεὶ προστυχῶς ἄλλοτε ἄλλης τύχης ὅπως πνέοι.

In this the Epicureans were not implicated; once having received instruction in no regard were they observed setting forth doctrines opposed in any way to Epicurus, but they agreed to be of like mind with a wise man, and because of this they too appropriately enjoyed that designation. And it was also the case in the highest degree with the later Epicureans themselves to say nothing at all contrary either to each other or to Epicurus concerning anything worthy of mention. But for them it is a transgression, or rather an impiety, and innovation has been condemned. Therefore no one even dares this, and their doctrines remain in much peace due to the constant harmony among themselves. The school of Epicurus resembles a true state quite free from faction, possessing one mind in common and one opinion. For this reason they were, and are, and as it seems, will be amenable to following.

The doctrines of the Stoics have been riven by faction, having started from the founders and not yet ending even now. And they gladly refute with a hostile reproof; some of them have remained ever constant, while others have already changed their position. Now the founders resemble an oligarchy, who surely by being at variance were the cause of much criticism among later Stoics, both toward their predecessors and toward one another. Some are more stoic than others, especially those who appeared more captious in technical matters. For these very men, since they surpassed the others were more prone to criticize in a meddlesome and quibbling manner.

However much earlier than these men, those who drew different concepts from Socrates experienced the same thing: Aristippus went off in his own direction, Antisthenes in another, and elsewhere in yet another the Megarians and Eretrians and others with them. The reason is that while Socrates was setting forth three gods and philosophizing about them in the rhythms appropriate to each, his auditors were unaware of this and believed that he was saying everything at random and always opportunistically from the dictates of chance—sometimes one thing, sometimes another, whichever way the wind blew.

55 Ὁ δὲ Πλάτων πυθαφορίσας (ᾔδει δὲ τὸν Σωκράτην μηδαμόθεν ἢ ἐκεῖθεν δὴ τὰ αὐτὰ ταῦτα εἰπεῖν καὶ γνόντα
d εἰρηκέναι), ὧδε οὖν καὶ αὐτὸς συνεδήσατο τὰ πράγματα, οὔτ' εἰωθότως οὔτε δὴ εἰς τὸ φανερόν· διαγαγὼν δ' ἕκαστα ὅπῃ ἐνόμιζεν, ἐπικρυψάμενος ἐν μέσῳ τοῦ δῆλα εἶναι καὶ μὴ
60 δῆλα, ἀσφαλῶς μὲν ἐγράψατο, αὐτὸς δ' αἰτίαν παρέσχε τῆς μετ' αὐτὸν στάσεώς τε ἅμα καὶ διολκῆς τῆς τῶν δογμάτων, οὐ φθόνῳ μὲν οὐδέ γε δυσνοίᾳ· ἀλλ' οὐ βούλομαι ἐπ' ἀνδράσι πρεσβυτέροις εἰπεῖν ῥήματα οὐκ ἐναίσιμα. Τοῦτο δὲ χρὴ μαθόντας ἡμᾶς ἐπανενεγκεῖν ἐκεῖσε μᾶλλον τὴν γνώμην,
65 καὶ ὥσπερ ἐξ ἀρχῆς προυθέμεθα χωρίζειν αὐτὸν
729a Ἀριστοτέλους καὶ Ζήνωνος, οὕτω καὶ νῦν τῆς Ἀκαδημίας, ἐὰν ὁ θεὸς ἀντιλάβηται, χωρίζοντες ἐάσομεν αὐτὸν ἐφ' ἑαυτοῦ νῦν εἶναι Πυθαγόρειον· ὡς νῦν μανικώτερον ἢ Πενθεῖ τινι προσῆκε διελκόμενος πάσχει μὲν κατὰ μέλη, ὅλος δ' ἐξ
70 ὅλου ἑαυτοῦ μετατίθεταί τε καὶ ἀντιμετατίθεται οὐδαμῶς. Ὅπως οὖν ἀνὴρ μεσεύων Πυθαγόρου καὶ Σωκράτους, τοῦ μὲν τὸ σεμνὸν ὑπαγαγὼν μέχρι τοῦ φιλανθρώπου, τοῦ δὲ τὸ κομψὸν τοῦτο καὶ παιγνιῆμον ἀναγαγὼν ἀπὸ τῆς εἰρωνείας
b εἰς ἀξίωμα καὶ ὄγκον καὶ αὐτὸ τοῦτο κεράσας Σωκράτει
75 Πυθαγόραν, τοῦ μὲν δημοτικώτερος, τοῦ δὲ σεμνότερος ὤφθη.

Plato was a Pythagorean (he knew that Socrates dispensed these same teachings from no other source than that, and that he had spoken in full awareness of this); in this way therefore he too bound things together, yet neither in a customary nor an obvious manner. And after arranging each detail in the way he considered most suitable, and concealing himself between clarity and obscurity, he wrote in security. Yet he himself provided the cause for the division which followed him, as well as the diversity of doctrines—not through jealousy, nor ill will to be sure; but I do not wish to make unbecoming remarks about venerable men.

And once we have learned this, we must call back our attention more to the point. And just as we proposed at the outset to separate him from Aristotle and Zeno, so now we separate him from the Academy, if God assists, and after making the separation we will leave him by himself now to be a Pythagorean. But now, since he has been torn apart more savagely than befits any Pentheus, he suffers in his limbs, but taken as a complete entity he is in no way subject to change and counter-change. Therefore, as a man assuming an intermediate position between Pythagoras and Socrates, he eased the gravity of the one down to the level of benevolence, and led the familiar cleverness and playfulness of the other away from irony up to the level of dignity and majesty. And in this respect, blending Pythagoras with Socrates, he appeared more human than the one and more serious than the other.

Fr. 25 (2 L.)

(Eus., *Pr. ev.*, XIV, 5, 10-6, 14, p. 729 b-733 d V.;

II, p. 271, 7-277, 9 Mras)

729b Ἀλλ᾽ οὐ γάρ τοι ταῦτα διαιτήσων ἦλθον, μὴ περὶ τούτων οὔσης νῦν μοι τῆς ζητήσεως, ἃ δὲ προὐδέδοκτο· καὶ εἶμι ἐκεῖσε ᾗ δὴ φροῦδος ἀναδραμεῖν δοκῶ μοι, μὴ καί που ἀποκρουσθῶμεν τῆς ὁδοῦ τῆς φερούσης. Πολέμωνος δ᾽
5 ἐγένοντο γνώριμοι Ἀρκεσίλαος καὶ Ζήνων· πάλιν γὰρ αὐτῶν μνηθήσομαι ἐπὶ τέλει. Ζήνωνα μὲν οὖν μέμνημαι εἰπὼν
c Ξενοκράτει, εἶτα δὲ Πολέμωνι φοιτῆσαι, αὖθις δὲ παρὰ Κράτητι κυνίσαι· νυνὶ δὲ αὐτῷ λελογίσθω ὅτι καὶ Στίλπωνός τε μετέσχε καὶ τῶν λόγων τῶν ἡρακλειτείων. Ἐπεὶ γὰρ
10 συμφοιτῶντες παρὰ Πολέμωνι ἐφιλοτιμήθησαν ἀλλήλοις, συμπαρέλαβον εἰς τὴν πρὸς ἀλλήλους μάχην ὁ μὲν Ἡράκλειτον καὶ Στίλπωνα ἅμα καὶ Κράτητα, ὧν ὑπὸ μὲν Στίλπωνος ἐγένετο μαχητής, ὑπὸ δ᾽ Ἡρακλείτου αὐστηρός, κυνικὸς δ᾽ ὑπὸ Κράτητος· ὁ δ᾽ Ἀρκησίλαος Θεόφραστον
15 ἴσχει καὶ Κράντορα τὸν Πλατωνικὸν καὶ Διόδωρον, εἶτα
d Πύρρωνα, ὧν ὑπὸ μὲν Κράντορος πιθανουργικός, ὑπὸ Διοδώρου δὲ σοφιστής, ὑπὸ δὲ Πύρρωνος ἐγένετο παντοδαπὸς καὶ ἴτης καὶ οὐδέν. Ὅ<θεν> καὶ ἐλέγετο περὶ αὐτοῦ ᾀδόμενόν τι ἔπος παραγωγὸν καὶ ὑβριστικόν·

20   Πρόσθε Πλάτων, ὄπιθεν [δὲ] Πύρρων, μέσσος Διόδωρος.

Τίμων δὲ καὶ ὑπὸ Μενεδήμου τὸ ἐριστικόν φησι λαβόντα ἐξαρτυθῆναι, εἴπερ γε δή φησι περὶ αὐτοῦ·

Τῇ μὲν ἔχων Μενεδήμου ὑπὸ στέρνοισι μόλυβδον θεύσεται ἢ Πύρρωνα τὸ πᾶν κρέας ἢ Διόδωρον.

25 (2 L.)

But I really have not come to discuss these matters, since my investigation is not presently concerned with them, but rather the subjects which were determined beforehand. And I will proceed to that point where it appears profitable to backtrack, lest we somehow be driven from the path which is leading us.

Arcesilaus and Zeno were students of Polemon; I will again make mention of them at the end. However I do recall saying that Zeno frequented Xenocrates and then Polemon, and then in turn lived the Cynic life with Crates. But now let it be reckoned to his account that he also had his share of Stilpon and the discussions of the Heracliteans. For when as fellow students with Polemon they became rivals of one another, they brought along allies into their mutual conflict. The one brought Heraclitus and Stilpon along with Crates; he became a warrior at the hands of Stilpon, by Heraclitus he was made austere, and by Crates a Cynic. The other, Arcesilaus, retained Theophrastus and Crantor the Platonist, and Diodorus, then Pyrrhon. By Crantor he was rendered adept at persuasion, by Diodorus he was made a Sophist, and at the hands of Pyrrhon he became flighty, reckless, and nothing. That is why a mocking and abusive verse was chanted concerning him:

Plato in front, Pyrrhon behind, Diodorus in the middle.

Timon reports that it was also after obtaining eristic from Menedemus that he was completely fitted out, since in fact he says this about him:

There with the lead of Menedemus in his heart
He will run to Pyrrhon, who is all meat, or to Diodorus.

Ταῖς οὖν Διοδώρου, διαλεκτικοῦ ὄντος, λεπτολογίαις τοὺς λογισμοὺς τοὺς Πύρρωνος καὶ τὸ σκεπτικὸν καταπλέξας διεκόσμησε λόγου δεινότητι τῇ Πλάτωνος φληναφόν τινα κατεστωμυλμένον καὶ ἔλεγε καὶ ἀντέλεγε καὶ μετεκυλινδεῖτο κἀκεῖθεν κἀντεῦθεν, ὁποτέρωθεν τύχοι, παλινάγρετος καὶ δύσκριτος καὶ παλίμβολός τε ἅμα καὶ παρακεκινδυνευμένος· οὐδέν τι εἰδώς, ὡς αὐτὸς ἔφη γενναῖος ὤν· εἶτα πως ἐξέβαινεν ὅμοιος τοῖς εἰδόσιν, ὑπὸ σκιαγραφίας τῶν λόγων παντοδαπὸς πεφαντασμένος. Τοῦ τε ὁμηρικοῦ Τυδείδου ὁποτέροις μετείη ἀγνοουμένου (οὔτ' εἰ Τρωσὶν ὁμιλέοι οὔτ' εἰ καὶ Ἀχαιοῖς) οὐδὲν ἧττον Ἀρκεσίλαος ἠγνοεῖτο. Τὸ γὰρ ἕνα τε λόγον καὶ ταὐτόν ποτ' εἰπεῖν οὐκ ἐνῆν ἐν αὐτῷ, οὐδέ γε ἠξίου ἀνδρὸς εἶναί [πω] τὸ τοιοῦτο δεξιοῦ οὐδαμῶς. Ὠνομάζετο οὖν

δεινὸς σοφιστής, τῶν ἀγυμνάστων σφαγεύς.

Ὥσπερ γὰρ αἱ Ἔμπουσαι ἐν τοῖς φάσμασι τοῖς τῶν λόγων ὑπὸ παρασκευῆς τε καὶ ὑπὸ μελέτης ἐφάρματτεν, ἐγοήτευεν, οὐδὲν εἶχεν εἰδέναι οὔτ' αὐτὸς οὔτε τοὺς ἄλλους ἐᾶν· ἐδειμάτου δὲ καὶ κατεθορύβει καὶ σοφισμάτων γε καὶ λόγων κλοπῆς φερόμενος τὰ πρῶτα κατέχαιρε τῷ ὀνείδει καὶ ἡβρύνετο θαυμαστῶς ὅτι μήτε τί αἰσχρὸν ἢ καλὸν μήτε ἀγαθὸν μήτε αὖ κακόν ἐστι τί ᾔδει, ἀλλ' ὁπότερον εἰς τὰς ψυχὰς πέσοι τοῦτο εἰπὼν αὖθις μεταβαλὼν ἀνέτρεπεν ἂν πλεοναχῶς ἢ δι' ὅσων κατεσκευάκει. Ἦν οὖν ὕδραν τέμνων ἑαυτὸν καὶ τεμνόμενος ὑφ' ἑαυτοῦ, ἀμφότερα ἀλλήλων δυσκρίτως καὶ τοῦ δέοντος ἀσκέπτως, πλὴν τοῖς ἀκούουσιν ἤρκεσεν, ὁμοῦ τῇ ἀκροάσει εὐπρόσωπον ὄντα θεωμένοις· ἦν οὖν ἀκουόμενος καὶ βλεπόμενος ἥδιστος, ἐπεί γε προσειθίσθησαν ἀποδέχεσθαι αὐτοῦ τοὺς λόγους ἰόντας ἀπὸ καλοῦ προσώπου τε καὶ στόματος οὐκ ἄνευ τῆς ἐν τοῖς ὄμμασι φιλοφροσύνης. Δεῖ δὲ ταῦτα ἀκοῦσαι μὴ ἁπλῶς, ἀλλ' ἔσχεν ὧδε ἐξ ἀρχῆς· συμβαλὼν γὰρ ἐν παισὶ Θεοφράστῳ, ἀνδρὶ πράῳ καὶ οὐκ ἀφυεῖ τὰ ἐρωτικά, διὰ τὸ καλὸς εἶναι ἔτι ὢν ὡραῖος τυχὼν ἐραστοῦ Κράντορος τοῦ Ἀκαδημαϊκοῦ,

Therefore, after entwining the reasonings and the skepticism of Pyrrhon with the subtle argumentation of Diodorus, a dialectician, he adorned a babbling sort of nonsense with Plato's power of expression and would hold forth and rebut, and was rolled along hither and thither, wherever it fell out; retracting himself, obscure, unstable, yet audacious all the while, knowing nothing at all as he himself admitted, since he was an honest man. Then somehow he would step out like those who have knowledge, and through an illusory façade of arguments he seemed to be versatile. And just as in Homer when it could not be discerned which camp the son of Tydeus was siding with (whether he was allied with the Trojans or the Achaeans), no less inscrutable was Arcesilaus. For it was not in his power ever to utter a consistent or identical argument, nor, I suppose, did he in any way deem such a course worthy of a clever individual. So he was called:

Fearsome sophist, butcher of the untrained.

For just like the Empusae, through the phantom figures of his arguments, through preparation, and through long practice he enchanted, he charmed. He was unable either to know anything himself, or allow others to know. He would frighten and intimidate, and while taking away top honors in sophistry and fraudulent oratory, he would exult over the reproach. He prided himself in a most remarkable way because he did not know what was ugly or beautiful, nor what good is nor what bad is. But however it struck his fancy, after affirming this and then shifting back again, he would overthrow the argument in numerous ways, or as by as many devices as he had prepared. He was, therefore, a hydra cutting himself and being cut by himself, two parts difficult to distinguish from one another and unmindful of what was proper. However he did please his listeners, who along with the listening enjoyed beholding his attractive features. He was, then, most pleasant to hear and to see since men were accustomed to accept his statements as they issued forth from a handsome face and mouth, and not without friendliness in his eyes.

But one should not hear these matters without elaboration, so from the beginning here is the way it fell out. While still a child he met Theophrastus, a gentle man and not unsuited by nature for matters of love. However owing to his beauty which was still in its bloom, he

προσεχώρησε μὲν τούτω, οἷα δὲ τὴν φύσιν οὐκ ἀφυὴς
60 τρεχούσῃ χρησάμενος αὐτῇ ῥᾳδίᾳ γε θερμουργῶς ὑπὸ
φιλονεικίας, μετασχὼν μὲν Διοδώρου εἰς τὰ πεπανουργημένα
πιθάνια ταῦτα τὰ κομψά, ὡμιληκὼς δὲ Πύρρωνι (ὁ δὲ Πύρρων
ἐκ Δημοκρίτου ὥρμητο ἀμόθεν γέ ποθεν), οὕτως μὲν δὴ ἔνθεν
b <κἄνθεν> καταρτυθείς, πλὴν τῆς προσρήσεως, ἐνέμεινε
65 πυρρωνείως τῇ πάντων ἀναιρέσει. Μνασέας γοῦν καὶ
Φιλόμηλος καὶ Τίμων οἱ σκεπτικοὶ σκεπτικὸν αὐτὸν
προσονομάζουσιν, ὥσπερ καὶ αὐτοὶ ἦσαν, ἀναιροῦντα καὶ
αὐτὸν τὸ ἀληθὲς καὶ τὸ ψεῦδος καὶ τὸ πιθανόν.
Λεχθεὶς οὖν ἂν αἰτίᾳ τῶν πυρρωνείων Πυρρώνειος, αἰδοῖ
70 τοῦ ἐραστοῦ ὑπέμεινε λέγεσθαι Ἀκαδημαϊκὸς ἔτι. Ἦν μὲν
τοίνυν Πυρρώνειος, πλὴν τοῦ ὀνόματος· Ἀκαδημαϊκὸς δ' οὐκ
ἦν, πλὴν τὸ λέγεσθαι. Οὐ γὰρ πείθομαι τοῦ Κνιδίου
Διοκλέους φάσκοντος ἐν ταῖς ἐπιγραφομέναις 'Διατριβαῖς'
c Ἀρκεσίλαον φόβῳ τῶν Θεοδωρείων τε καὶ Βίωνος τοῦ
75 σοφιστοῦ ἐπεξιόντων τοῖς φιλοσοφοῦσι καὶ οὐδὲν ὀκνούντων
ἀπὸ παντὸς ἐλέγχειν, αὐτὸν ἐξευλαβηθέντα, ἵνα μὴ πράγματα
ἔχῃ, μηδὲν μὲν δόγμα ὑπειπεῖν φαινόμενον, ὥσπερ δὲ τὸ
μέλαν τὰς σηπίας προβάλλεσθαι πρὸ ἑαυτοῦ τὴν ἐποχήν.
Τοῦτ' οὖν ἐγὼ οὐ πείθομαι. Οἱ δ' οὖν ἔνθεν ἀφορμηθέντες,
80 ὅ τε Ἀρκεσίλαος καὶ Ζήνων, ὑπὸ τοιούτων ἀρωγῶν,
ἀμφοτέροις συμπολεμούντων λόγων, τῆς μὲν ἀρχῆς ὅθεν ἐκ
Πολέμωνος ὡρμήθησαν ἐπιλανθάνονται, διαστάντες δέ γε καὶ
d σφέας αὐτοὺς ἀρτύναντες

σὺν δ' ἔβαλον ῥινούς, σὺν δ' ἔγχεα καὶ μένε' ἀνδρῶν
85 χαλκεοθωρήκων· ἀτὰρ ἀσπίδες ὀμφαλόεσσαι
ἔπληντ' ἀλλήλῃσι, πολὺς δ' ὀρυμαγδὸς ὀρώρει.
Ἀσπὶς ἄρ' ἀσπίδ' ἔρειδε, κόρυς κόρυν, ἄνερα δ' ἀνὴρ
ἐδνοπάλιζεν.
732a Ἔνθα δ' ἅμ' οἰμωγή τε καὶ εὐχωλὴ πέλεν ἀνδρῶν
90 ὀλλύντων τε καὶ ὀλλυμένων

secured Crantor the Academician as a lover and went over to this teacher. But since he was not lacking in cleverness by nature, while it was in full flight he employed it readily, if somewhat recklessly at the promptings of a competitive spirit. He sided with Diodorus in order to learn his persuasive knavery (these familiar subtleties), and after having associated with Pyrrhon, (Pyrrhon issued from Democritus in some way or another), being thus armed on all sides except for the designation, he stood firm as a Pyrrhonian for the overthrow of all things. At any rate the Skeptics Mnaseas, Philomelus, and Timon labeled him a Skeptic just as they were, since he was doing away with the true, the false, and the probable.

Now although by reason of his Pyrrhonism he would have been said to be a Pyrrhonian, out of respect for his lover he still allowed himself to be called an Academic. He was, therefore, a Pyrrhonian except in name; an Academic he was not, except for the designation. For I am not persuaded when Diocles the Cnidian claims in his work entitled *Conversations* that Arcesilaus, through fear of the disciples of Theodorus and Bion the Sophist who were attacking philosophers and not hesitating at all to refute them by any means whatsoever, took heed for himself, and in order to avoid problems appeared to suggest no doctrine; and just as the cuttlefish releases ink he threw the 'suspension' before himself. Now this I do not believe.

In any case, having issued forth from there Arcesilaus and Zeno, accompanied by these kinds of serviceable arguments which fought on behalf of both of them, forgot from whence they had set out at the start—namely from Polemon—and drawing apart and readying themselves for battle:

They clashed shields together and spears, and the might
Of men armored in bronze; and shields with polished centers
      drew near to one another and a great din arose.
Shield pressed against shield, helmet against helmet, and man
      Viciously shook man.
There mingled the scream and the triumphant shout of men
      Killing and being killed.

τῶν Στοϊκῶν· οἱ Ἀκαδημαϊκοὶ γὰρ οὐκ ἐβάλλοντο ὑπ᾽ αὐτῶν, ἀγνοούμενοι ᾗ ἦσαν ἁλῶναι δυνατώτεροι. Ἡλίσκοντο δὲ τῆς βάσεως αὐτοῖς σεισθείσης, εἰ μήτε ἀρχὴν ἔχοιεν μήτε μάχεσθαι ἀφορμήν. Ἡ μὲν δὴ ἀρχὴ ἦν τὸ μὴ πλατωνικὰ
95 λέγοντας αὐτοὺς ἐλέγξαι· τὸ δὲ μηδὲ ἔχειν τινὰ ἀφορμὴν ἦν, εἴπερ μόνον ἕν τι μετέστρεψαν ἀπὸ τοῦ ὅρου τοῦ περὶ τῆς καταληπτικῆς φαντασίας ἀφελόντες. Ὅπερ νῦν μὲν οὐκ ἔστι μηνύειν μοι ἐν καιρῷ, μνησθήσομαι δ᾽ αὐτοῦ αὖθις ἐπὰν
b κατὰ τοῦτο μάλιστα γενέσθαι μέλλω. Διαστάντες δ᾽ οὖν εἰς
100 τὸ φανερὸν ἔβαλλον ἀλλήλους οὐχ οἱ δύο, ἀλλ᾽ ὁ Ἀρκεσίλαος τὸν Ζήνωνα. Ὁ γὰρ Ζήνων εἶχε δή τι τῇ μάχῃ σεμνὸν καὶ βαρὺ καὶ Κηφισοδώρου τοῦ ῥήτορος οὐκ ἄμεινον· ὃς δὴ ὁ Κηφισόδωρος, ἐπειδὴ ὑπ᾽ Ἀριστοτέλους βαλλόμενον ἑαυτῷ τὸν διδάσκαλον Ἰσοκράτην ἑώρα, αὐτοῦ μὲν
105 Ἀριστοτέλους ἦν ἀμαθὴς καὶ ἄπειρος, ὑπὸ δὲ τοῦ καθορᾶν ἔνδοξα τὰ Πλάτωνος ὑπάρχοντα οἰηθεὶς κατὰ Πλάτωνα τὸν
c Ἀριστοτέλην φιλοσοφεῖν, ἐπολέμει μὲν Ἀριστοτέλει, ἔβαλλε δὲ Πλάτωνα καὶ κατηγόρει ἀρξάμενος ἀπὸ τῶν ἰδεῶν, τελευτῶν εἰς τἆλλα, ἃ οὐδ᾽ αὐτὸς ᾔδει, ἀλλὰ τὰ νομιζόμενα
110 ἀμφ᾽ αὐτῶν ἢ λέγεται ὑπονοῶν. Πλὴν οὕτως μὲν ὁ Κηφισόδωρος, ᾧ ἐπολέμει μὴ μαχόμενος, ἐμάχετο ᾧ μὴ πολεμεῖν ἐβούλετο. Ὁ μέντοι Ζήνων καὶ αὐτός, ἐπειδὴ τοῦ Ἀρκεσιλάου μεθίετο, εἰ μὲν μηδὲ Πλάτωνι ἐπολέμει, ἐφιλοσόφει δήπου ἐμοὶ κριτῇ πλείστου ἀξίως, ἕνεκά γε τῆς
115 εἰρήνης ταύτης. Εἰ δ᾽ οὐκ ἀγνοῶν μὲν ἴσως τὰ Ἀρκεσιλάου,
d τὰ μέντοι Πλάτωνος ἀγνοῶν, ὡς ἐξ ὧν αὐτῷ ἀντέγραψεν ἐλέγχεται, [ὅτι] ἐποίησεν ἐναντία καὐτός, μήτε ὃν ᾔδει πλήττων ὅν τε οὐκ ἐχρῆν ἀτιμότατα καὶ αἴσχιστα περιυβρικώς, καὶ ταῦτα πολὺ κάκιον ἢ προσήκει κυνί. Πλὴν
120 διέδειξέ γε μὴν μεγαλοφροσύνη ἀποσχόμενος τοῦ Ἀρκεσιλάου. Ἤτοι γὰρ ἀγνοίᾳ τῶν ἐκείνου ἢ δέει τῶν Στοϊκῶν
πολέμοιο μέγα στόμα πευκεδανοῖο

Of the Stoics, that is. For the Academics were not being hit by them, since they did not know in which way they were most likely to be caught. And they were caught, once their foundation had been shaken, if they did not have either a principle or a base from which to fight. The principle involved proving that they were not using Platonic arguments. They did not have a base if they altered the doctrine of the 'Comprehensible Appearance' by removing even one aspect from its definition. It is not now an opportune time for me to discuss this, but I will mention it again when I am about to deal with this topic.

So, once they separated they let fly at one another openly; not both of them, rather Arcesilaus attacked Zeno. For Zeno possessed a certain solemnity and gravity in conflict, but he was not superior to Cephisodorus the orator. This Cephisodorus, when he saw his own teacher Isocrates being attacked by Aristotle (although with regard to Aristotle he was untutored and unacquainted), since he observed that the doctrines of Plato were in high repute and believing that Aristotle philosophized in accordance with Plato, intended to make war against Aristotle but was really assaulting Plato. He leveled charges, starting from the Ideas and finishing with the rest; doctrines which he himself did not know, but he was conforming to the usual opinions which were in circulation about them. Thus Cephisodorus was not fighting the one he made war against, but was fighting with the one against whom he did not wish to make war.

As for Zeno himself, once he was free of Arcesilaus if he wasn't warring with Plato he philosophized, at least in my judgment, most worthily because of this peaceful disposition. But when he did, though perhaps not ignorant of Arcesilaus' doctrines, surely ignorant of Plato's (as proved by what he has written against him), he too acted in a contradictory fashion: striking not the one he knew but rather the one he should not have, in a most dishonorable, most shameful, and most insolent manner. And this was done much more basely than befits a dog. However he did show quite clearly that it was through magnanimity that he held back from Arcesilaus. For either through ignorance of his teachings or fear of the Stoics he turned away from the "gaping maw of piercing battle" in another

ἀπετρέψατο ἄλλῃ, εἰς Πλάτωνα· ἀλλὰ καὶ περὶ μὲν τῶν
125 Ζήνωνι εἰς Πλάτωνα κακῶς τε καὶ αἰδημόνως οὐδαμῶς
733a νεωτερισθέντων εἰρήσεταί μοι αὖθίς ποτε, ἐὰν φιλοσοφίας
σχολὴν ἀγάγω· μή ποτε μέντοι ἀγάγοιμι σχολὴν τοσαύτην,
τούτου οὖν ἕνεκεν, εἰ μὴ ὑπὸ παιδιᾶς. Τὸν δ᾽ οὖν Ζήνωνα ὁ
Ἀρκεσίλαος ἀντίτεχνον καὶ ἀξιόνικον ὑπάρχοντα θεωρῶν τοὺς
130 παρ᾽ ἐκείνου ἀποφερομένους λόγους καθῄρει καὶ οὐδὲν ᾤκνει.
Καὶ περὶ μὲν τῶν ἄλλων ἃ ἐμεμάχητο ἐκείνῳ οὔτ᾽ ἴσως
εἰπεῖν ἔχω εἴ τε καὶ εἶχον οὐδὲν ἔδει νῦν αὐτῶν μνησθῆναι·
τὸ δὲ δόγμα τοῦτο αὐτοῦ πρώτου εὑρομένου καὐτὸ καὶ τὸ
b ὄνομα βλέπων εὐδοκιμοῦν ἐν ταῖς Ἀθήναις, τὴν
135 καταληπτικὴν φαντασίαν, πάσῃ μηχανῇ ἐχρῆτο ἐπ᾽ αὐτήν.
Ὁ δ᾽ ἐν τῷ ἀσθενεστέρῳ ὢν καὶ ἡσυχίαν ἄγων οὐ δυνάμενος
ἀδικεῖσθαι, Ἀρκεσιλάου μὲν ἀφίετο, πολλὰ ἂν εἰπεῖν ἔχων,
ἀλλ᾽ οὐκ ἤθελε, τάχα δὲ μᾶλλον ἄλλως, πρὸς δὲ τὸν οὐκέτι
ἐν ζῶσιν ὄντα Πλάτωνα ἐσκιομάχει καὶ τὴν ἀπὸ ἁμάξης
140 πομπείαν πᾶσαν κατεθορύβει, λέγων ὡς οὔτ᾽ ἂν τοῦ
Πλάτωνος ἀμυναμένου ὑπερδικεῖν τε αὐτοῦ ἄλλῳ οὐδενὶ
μέλον, εἴ τε μελήσειεν Ἀρκεσιλάῳ, αὐτός γε κερδανεῖν ᾤετο
c ἀποστρεψάμενος ἀφ᾽ ἑαυτοῦ τὸν Ἀρκεσίλαον. Τοῦτο δ᾽ ᾔδει
καὶ Ἀγαθοκλέα τὸν Συρακόσιον ποιήσαντα τὸ σόφισμα ἐπὶ
145 τοὺς Καρχηδονίους. Οἱ Στωϊκοὶ δὲ ὑπήκουον ἐκπεπληγμένοι·
'ἁ μοῦσα γὰρ αὐτοῖς οὐδὲ τότε ἦν φιλόλογος οὐδ᾽ ἐργάτις'
Χαρίτων, ὑφ᾽ ὧν ὁ Ἀρκεσίλαος τὰ μὲν περικρούων, τὰ δ᾽
ὑποτέμνων, ἄλλα δ᾽ ὑποσκελίζων κατεγλωττίζετο αὐτοὺς καὶ
πιθανὸς ἦν. Τοιγαροῦν πρὸς οὓς μὲν ἀντέλεγεν ἡττωμένων, ἐν
150 οἷς δὲ λέγων ἦν καταπεπληγμένων, δεδειγμένον πως τοῖς
d τότε ἀνθρώποις ὑπῆρχε μηδὲν εἶναι μήτ᾽ οὖν ἔπος μήτε
πάθος μήτ᾽ ἔργον ἐν βραχὺ μηδ᾽ ἄχρηστον <ἢ> τοὐναντίον
ὀφθῆναί ποτ᾽ ἄν, εἴ τι μὴ Ἀρκεσιλάῳ δοκεῖ τῷ Πιταναίῳ·
τῷ δ᾽ ἄρα οὐδὲν ἐδόκει οὐδ᾽ ἀπεφαίνετο οὐδὲν μᾶλλον ἢ
155 ῥηματίσκια ταῦτ᾽ εἶναι καὶ φόβους.

direction: towards Plato. But concerning the fabrications which Zeno used against Plato in a wicked and completely disrespectful manner, I will speak again sometime if I find the leisure to philosophize. May I never enjoy such leisure, at least for such a purpose, unless as an amusement.

At any rate when Arcesilaus observed that Zeno was in competition with him and capable of victory, he tried to demolish the arguments issuing from him, and did not hold back at all. And concerning the other matters in which he joined battle with him I am unable to speak, and even if I were there would be no need to mention them now. But regarding this famous doctrine which Zeno had been the first to discover: when Arcesilaus saw that both the doctrine and its name were becoming popular in Athens (that is the doctrine of 'Comprehensible Appearance'), he used every device against it. But the other, being in the weaker position, and since he was holding his peace unable to be injured, let Arcesilaus go, having much that he could say but did not wish to. Rather he quickly did otherwise, and began shadow-boxing with Plato who was no longer among the living, and disturbed the entire procession from his chariot. He said that neither was Plato able to defend himself nor was it a matter of concern for anyone else to plead on his behalf; and if Arcesilaus cared to, he believed that he would benefit in having diverted Arcesilaus away from himself. He was aware that Agathocles the Syracusan had used this device against the Carthaginians.

And the Stoics listened in amazement, "for their Muse was not even then fond of discussion nor a servant" of the Graces, through whom Arcesilaus, while knocking some doctrines down, intercepting some and tripping up others, lashed them with his tongue and was persuasive doing it. That is why the ones against whom he argued were defeated and were amazed by his statements; the fact was that a demonstration had been made to his contemporaries that there was nothing: no utterance, no impression, not one trifling act that would ever be viewed as useless or its opposite unless it was deemed so by Arcesilaus the Pitanean. But then again nothing seemed of value to him, nor did he state anything more than that these things are formulations and fears.

Fr. 26 (3 L.)

(Eus., *Pr.ev.*, XIV, 7, 1-15, p. 734 a-737 a V.;

II, p. 277, 12-281, 8 Mras)

734a Περὶ δὲ Λακύδου βούλομαί τι διηγήσασθαι ἡδύ. Ἦν μὲν δὴ Λακύδης ὑπογλισχότερος καί τινα τρόπον ὁ λεγόμενος
b οἰκονομικός, οὗτος ὁ εὐδοκιμῶν παρὰ τοῖς πολλοῖς, αὐτὸς μὲν ἀνοιγνὺς τὸ ταμεῖον, αὐτὸς δ' ὑποκλείων. Καὶ προηρεῖτο δὲ
5 ὧν ἐδεῖτο καὶ ἄλλα τοιαῦτα ἐποίει πάντα δι' αὐτουργίας, οὔ τί που αὐτάρκειαν ἐπαινῶν οὐδ' ἄλλως πενίᾳ χρώμενος οὐδ' ἀπορίᾳ δούλων, ᾧ γε ὑπῆρχον δοῦλοι ὁποσοιοῦν· τὴν δ' αἰτίαν ἔξεστιν εἰκάζειν. Ἐγὼ δὲ ὃ ὑπεσχόμην τὸ ἡδὺ διηγήσομαι. Ταμιεύων γὰρ αὐτὸς ἑαυτῷ τὴν μὲν κλεῖδα
10 περιφέρειν ἐφ' ἑαυτοῦ οὐκ ᾤετο δεῖν, ἀποκλείσας δὲ
c κατετίθει μὲν ταύτην εἴς τι κοῖλον γραμματεῖον· σημηνάμενος δὲ δακτυλίῳ τὸν μὲν δακτύλιον κατεκύλιε διὰ τοῦ κλείθρου ἔσω εἰς τὸν οἶκον μεθιείς, ὡς δὴ ὕστερον, ἐπειδὴ πάλιν ἐλθὼν ἀνοίξειε τῇ κλειδί, δυνησόμενος ἀνελὼν
15 τὸν δακτύλιον αὖθις μὲν ἀποκλείειν, εἶτα δὲ σημαίνεσθαι, εἶτα δ' ἀναβάλλειν ὀπίσω πάλιν ἔσω τὸν δακτύλιον διὰ τοῦ κλείθρου. Τοῦτο οὖν τὸ σοφὸν οἱ δοῦλοι κατανοήσαντες, ἐπειδὴ προΐοι Λακύδης εἰς περίπατον ἢ ὅποι ἄλλοσε, καὶ αὐτοὶ ἀνοίξαντες ἂν κἄπειτα, ὥς σφιν ἦν θυμός, τὰ μὲν
20 φαγόντες, τὰ δ' ἐμπιόντες, ἄλλα δ' ἀράμενοι ἐκ περιόδου ταῦτα ἐποίουν· ἀπέκλειον μέν, ἐσημαίνοντο δέ, τὸν δακτύλιον πολλὰ τ' αὐτοῦ καταγελάσαντες εἰς τὸν οἶκον διὰ τοῦ
d κλείθρου ἠφίεσαν. Ὁ οὖν Λακύδης πλήρη μὲν καταλιπὼν, κενὰ δ' εὑρισκόμενος τὰ σκεύη ἀπορῶν τῷ γιγνομένῳ, ἐπειδὴ
25 ἤκουσε φιλοσοφεῖσθαι παρὰ τῷ Ἀρκεσιλάῳ τὴν ἀκαταληψίαν, ᾤετο τοῦτ' ἐκεῖν' αὐτῷ συμβαίνειν περὶ τὸ ταμεῖον, ἀρξάμενός τ' ἔνθεν ἐφιλοσόφει παρὰ τῷ Ἀρκεσιλάῳ, μηδὲν μήτε ὁρᾶν μήτε ἀκούειν ἐναργὲς ἢ ὑγιές·

26 (3 L.)

I want to relate something pleasant about Lacydes. Lacydes was somewhat miserly and, after a fashion, the proverbial 'Economist' (the one popular with everyone), opening the storeroom himself and closing it up himself. He would select the things that he needed, and all other such matters he effected through his own effort, not in any way commending self-sufficiency or otherwise suffering from poverty or lack of slaves—indeed he possessed quite a number of them—but one can imagine the reason. For my part, I will narrate the pleasant tale that I promised.

Now although he managed the storeroom himself, he did not feel it necessary to carry the key about on his person, and after closing up he would place it in a hollow writing tablet. After sealing it with his ring he would roll the ring through the keyhole, letting it go inside the room so that later, when he returned and opened up with the key, he would be able after picking up the ring to again close up, then seal, then put the ring once again back inside through the keyhole. Now once the slaves had perceived this bit of ingenuity, when Lacydes went out for a walk or somewhere else, they too would open up. And then according to their desire, after eating some things, drinking up others, and making off with others they would perform the same actions in sequence: they would close up, impress the seal, and with much derisive laughter at his expense they would let the ring fall through the keyhole back into the room.

Now Lacydes, who had left his containers full, upon finding them empty was puzzled by what had transpired. And when he heard that the 'incomprehensibility' doctrine was being discussed in Arcesilaus' circle, he believed that this very thing was happening to himself regarding the storeroom; and starting from that point on he began to study philosophy with Arcesilaus: 'nothing present to sight or hearing is clear or sound.' And once,

καί ποτε ἐπισπασάμενος τῶν προσομιλούντων αὐτῷ τινα εἰς
30 τὴν οἰκίαν ἰσχυρίζετο πρὸς αὐτὸν ὑπερφυῶς, ὡς ἐδόκει, τὴν
ἐποχήν, καὶ ἔφη· 'Τοῦτο μὲν ἀναμφίλεκτον ἐγώ σοι ἔχω
φράσαι, αὐτὸς ἐπ' ἐμαυτοῦ μαθών, οὐκ ἄλλου πειραθείς'.
735a Κἄπειτα ἀρξάμενος περιηγεῖτο τὴν ὅλην τοῦ ταμείου
συμβᾶσαν αὐτῷ πάθην. 'Τί οὖν ἄν', εἶπεν, 'ἔτι Ζήνων λέγοι
35 πρὸς οὕτως ὁμολογουμένην διὰ πάντων φανερὰν μοι ἐν τοῖς
τοιοῖσδ' ἀκαταληψίαν; ὃς γὰρ ἀπέκλεισα μὲν ταῖς ἐμαυτοῦ
χερσίν, αὐτὸς δ' ἐσημηνάμην, αὐτὸς δ' ἀφῆκα μὲν εἴσω τὸν
δακτύλιον, αὖθις δ' ἐλθὼν ἀνοίξας τὸν μὲν δακτύλιον ὁρῶ
ἔνδον, οὐ μέντοι καὶ τἆλλα, πῶς οὐ δικαίως ἀπιστούντως τοῖς
40 πράγμασιν ἔξω; οὐ γάρ πω φήσω, εἰπεῖν, ἔγωγ' ἐπελθόντα
b τινὰ κλέψαι ταῦτα ὑπάρχοντος ἔνδον τοῦ δακτυλίου'. Καὶ ὃς
ἀκούων, ἦν γὰρ ὑβριστής, ἐκδεξάμενος τὸ πᾶν ὡς ἔσχεν
ἀκοῦσαι, μόλις καὶ πρότερον ἑαυτοῦ κρατῶν, ἀπέρρηξε
γέλωτα καὶ μάλα πλατὺν γελῶν τ' ἔτι καὶ καγχάζων
45 διήλεγχεν ἅμα αὐτοῦ τὴν κενοδοξίαν. Ὥστε ἔκτοτε Λακύδης
ἀρξάμενος οὐκέτι μὲν τὸν δακτύλιον ἔσω ἐνέβαλλεν, οὐκέτι
δὲ τοῦ ταμείου ἐχρῆτο ἀκαταληψίᾳ ἀλλὰ κατελάμβανε τὰ
ἀφειμένα καὶ μάτην ἐπεφιλοσοφήκει.
Οὐ μέντοι ἀλλὰ οἵ τε παῖδες φόρτακες ἦσαν καὶ οὐ θατέρα
c 50 ληπτοί, οἷοι δ' οὗτοι οἱ κωμῳδικοί [τε καὶ] Γέται τε καὶ
Δᾶκοι κἀκ τῆς Δακικῆς λαλεῖν στωμυλήθρας
κατεγλωττισμένοι, ἐπεί γε τοῖς Στωϊκοῖς τὰ σοφίσματα
ἤκουσαν, εἴτε καὶ ἄλλως ἐκμαθόντες, εὐθὺ τοῦ τολμήματος
ᾖεσαν καὶ παρελύοντο αὐτοῦ τὴν σφραγῖδα καὶ τοτὲ μὲν
55 ἑτέραν ἀντ' ἐκείνης ὑπετίθεσαν, τοτὲ δ' οὐδ' ἄλλην, διὰ τὸ
οἴεσθαι ἐκείνῳ γε ἀκατάληπτα ἔσεσθαι καὶ οὕτω καὶ ἄλλως.
Ὁ δ' εἰσελθὼν ἐσκοπεῖτο· ἀσήμαντον δὲ τὸ γραμματεῖον
θεωρῶν ἢ σεσημασμένον μέν, σφραγῖδι δ' ἄλλῃ, ἠγανάκτει· τῶν
d δὲ σεσημάνθαι λεγόντων, αὐτοῖς γοῦν τὴν σφραγῖδα ὁρᾶσθαι
60 τὴν αὐτοῦ, ἠκριβολογεῖτ' ἂν καὶ ἀπεδείκνυε· τῶν δ' ἡττωμένων

after calling an acquaintance into the house he started to declaim the 'suspension' to him with a vigor that was preternatural, so it seemed, and said: "I can tell you that this is indisputable, since I have learned it on my own, not by the proof of another!" And then, having gotten a start, he described the entire experience of the storeroom which had befallen him. "What then," he said, "could Zeno still maintain against the incomprehensibility so thoroughly confirmed and manifest to me in such circumstances? For it was I who closed up with my own hands, I myself imprinted the seal, I myself released he ring inside. And, when coming back again and opening up I find the ring within but nothing else, how am I not justified in being suspicious of external reality? For I, at least, will not dare to say that someone came and stole these things while the ring remained inside!" And as the other was listening (for he was an insolent fellow), since he was anticipating the entire outcome while he continued to listen and was scarcely able even earlier to control himself, broke out in laughter, and while still laughing rather rudely and guffawing he at the same time exposed his vacuous reasoning. So starting from that point on Lacydes no longer threw his ring inside and was no longer subject to the 'incomprehensibility' of the storeroom, but began to 'apprehend' the goods which had been set loose. And it was in vain that he had practiced philosophy.

Nevertheless the slaves were veritable knaves and not the kind to be caught one-handed, much like the familiar Getae and Dacians of the comedies who are well equipped even by their own Dacian tongue to deal in glib banter. And after they listened to the sophisms of the Stoics, and otherwise acquired some knowledge, they set straight out for a bit of daring and undid his seal and sometimes set another in place of it, sometimes not even a replacement, because they believed that both this way and that it would be incomprehensible to him. And he, after entering, would make an examination. And when he saw the tablet unsealed, or sealed indeed with another seal, he would become agitated. And when they claimed that it was sealed, or at any rate that they saw his seal, he would specify and demonstrate; and they, defeated by his

τῇ ἀποδείξει φαμένων, εἰ μή τι ἔπεστιν ἡ σφραγίς, αὐτὸν ἴσως ἐπιλελῆσθαι καὶ μὴ σημῆνασθαι, καὶ μὴν αὐτός τ' ἔφη σημηνάμενος μημονεύειν καὶ ἀπεδείκνυε καὶ περιῄει τῷ λόγῳ καὶ ἐδεινολογεῖτο πρὸς αὐτούς, οἰόμενος παίζεσθαι, καὶ
65 προσώμνυεν. Οἱ δ' ὑπολαβόντες τὰς προσβολὰς ἐκείνου αὐτοί γε ᾤοντο ὑπ' αὐτοῦ παίζεσθαι, ἐπεὶ σοφῷ γ' ὄντι δεδόχθαι τῷ Λακύδῃ εἶναι ἀδοξάστῳ ὥστε καὶ ἀμνημονεύτῳ· μνήμην γὰρ εἶναι δόξαν· ἔναγχος γοῦν τοῦ χρόνου ἔφασαν ἀκοῦσαι
736a ταῦτα αὐτοῦ πρὸς τοὺς φίλους. Τοῦ δ' ἀναστρέφοντος αὐτοῖς
70 τὰς ἐπιχειρήσεις καὶ λέγοντος οὐκ ἀκαδημαϊκά, αὐτοὶ φοιτῶντες εἰς Στωϊκῶν τινος τὰ λεκτέα ἑαυτοῖς ἀνεμάνθανον κἀκεῖθεν ἀρξάμενοι ἀντεσοφίστευον καὶ ἦσαν ἀντίτεχνοι κλέπται ἀκαδημαϊκοί· ὁ δὲ στωϊκῶς ἐνεκάλει· οἱ παῖδες δὲ τὰ ἐγκλήματα παρέλυον αὐτῷ ὑπὸ ἀκαταληψίας οὐκ ἄνευ
75 τωθασμῶν τινων. Διατριβαὶ οὖν ἦσαν πάντων ἐκεῖ καὶ λόγοι
b καὶ ἀντιλογίαι· καὶ ἓν οὐδὲν ἐν τῷ μέσῳ κατελείπετο, οὐκ ἀγγεῖον, οὐ τῶν ἐν ἀγγείῳ τιθεμένων, οὐχ ὅσα εἰς οἰκίας κατασκευὴν ἀλλ' ἔστι συντελῆ.

Καὶ ὁ Λακύδης τέως μὲν ἠπόρει, μήτε λυσιτελοῦσαν ἑαυτῷ
80 θεωρῶν τὴν τοῖς ἑαυτοῦ δόγμασι βοήθειαν εἴ τε μὴ ἐξελέγχοι πάντα ἀνατρέψεσθαι ἑαυτῷ δοκῶν, πεσὼν εἰς τἀμήχανον τοὺς γείτονας ἐκεκράγει καὶ τοὺς θεούς, καὶ ἰοὺ ἰοὺ καὶ φεῦ φεῦ καὶ νὴ τοὺς θεοὺς καὶ νὴ τὰς θεὰς ἄλλαι τε ὅσαι ἐν ἀπιστίαις δεινολογουμένων εἰσὶν ἄτεχνοι πίστεις, ταῦτα
c 85 πάντα ἐλέγετο βοῇ ἅμα καὶ ἀξιοπιστίᾳ. Τελευτῶν δέ, ἐπεὶ μάχην εἶχεν ἀντιλεγομένην ἐπὶ τῆς οἰκίας, αὐτὸς μὲν ἂν δήπουθεν ἐστωϊκεύετο πρὸς τοὺς παῖδας, τῶν παίδων δὲ τὰ ἀκαδημαϊκὰ ἰσχυριζομένων, ἵνα μηκέτι πράγματ' ἔχοι, οἰκουρὸς ἦν φίλος τοῦ ταμείου προκαθήμενος. Οὐδὲν δ' εἰς
90 οὐδὲν ὠφελῶν ὑπιδόμενος οἷ τὸ σοφὸν αὐτῷ ἔρχεται, ἀπεκαλύψατο· ' Ἄλλως ', ἔφη, ' ταῦτα, ὦ παῖδες, ἐν ταῖς διατριβαῖς λέγεται ἡμῖν, ἄλλως δὲ ζῶμεν '.

demonstration would say that if the seal was not on it, perhaps he forgot and did not seal it. And he said that of course he remembered sealing it and pointed and went around through the argument and hurled complaints at them in the belief that they made sport with him, and threw in some oaths. They responded to his sallies saying they felt it was they who were being made sport of since Lacydes, a wise man, had decided to be without opinion and thus was also without memory. For memory is an opinion. Just recently at any rate, they said, they had heard him talking in this vein to his friends. And when he began to overturn their line of reasoning, and began to argue in an unacademic fashion, they resorted to one of the Stoics and learned what they should say; and starting from that point on they used counterstrategems and were rival, academic thieves. He leveled charges in a Stoic manner. The slaves dismantled his accusations with 'incomprehensibility" accompanied by jeering remarks. So there were discussions on all topics there, and arguments and counter-arguments. And in the meantime not a single thing was left: not a vessel or anything that might be placed in one—none of those items that contribute to the furnishing of a dwelling.

And Lacydes was at a loss all the while as he contemplated the fact that the aiding force of his own doctrines was profiting him nothing if it did not refute everything, while it seemed to be overturning himself. And lapsing into helplessness he cried out to his neighbors and the gods: "ah me", "alas, alas", and "by the gods", and "by the goddesses", and other artless asseverations of faith which are among those invoked in times of disbelief. All these things he uttered with a loud and sincere cry.

Finally, when he would have a disputatious battle concerning the house he would doubtlessly use Stoic arguments against the slaves; and since the slaves stoutly maintained the Academic doctrines, in order that he might no longer have difficulties he set a friend before the storeroom as a guardian. But being absolutely helpless, and having observed just how far his cleverness reached, he made this admission: "Slaves," he said, "we discuss these matters one way in the schools, we live another way."

d   Ταῦτα μὲν καὶ περὶ τοῦ Λακύδου. Τούτου δὲ γίγνονται ἀκουσταὶ πολλοί, ὧν εἷς ἦν διαφανὴς ὁ Κυρηναῖος
95 Ἀρίστιππος, ἐκ πάντων δ' αὐτοῦ τῶν γνωρίμων τὴν σχολὴν αὐτοῦ διεδέξατο Εὔανδρος καὶ οἱ μετὰ τοῦτον. Μεθ' οὓς Καρνεάδης ὑποδεξάμενος τὴν διατριβὴν τρίτην συνεστήσατο Ἀκαδημίαν, λόγων μὲν οὖν ἀγωγῇ ἐχρήσατο ᾗ καὶ ὁ Ἀρκεσίλαος· καὶ γὰρ αὐτὸς ἐπετήδευε τὴν εἰς ἑκάτερα
100 ἐπιχείρησιν καὶ πάντα ἀνεσκεύαζε τὰ ὑπὸ τῶν ἄλλων λεγόμενα· μόνῳ δ' ἐν τῷ περὶ τῆς ἐποχῆς λόγῳ πρὸς αὐτὸν διέστη, φὰς ἀδύνατον εἶναι ἄνθρωπον ὄντα περὶ ἁπάντων ἐπέχειν· διαφορὰν δ' εἶναι ἀδήλου καὶ ἀκαταλήπτου καὶ
737a πάντα μὲν εἶναι ἀκατάληπτα, οὐ πάντα δ' ἄδηλα. Μετεῖχε δ'
105 οὗτος καὶ τῶν στωϊκῶν λόγων, πρὸς οὓς καὶ ἐριστικῶς ἱστάμενος ἐπὶ πλέον ηὐξήθη, τοῦ φαινομένου τοῖς πολλοῖς πιθανοῦ ἀλλ' οὐ τῆς ἀληθείας στοχαζόμενος· ὅθεν καὶ πολλὴν παρέσχε τοῖς Στωϊκοῖς ἀηδίαν.

Γράφει δ' οὖν καὶ ὁ Νουμήνιος περὶ αὐτοῦ ταῦτα.

This much, then, concerning Lacydes. He had many auditors, one of whom was particularly distinguished, Aristippus the Cyrenean, but out of all his disciples Evandrus and his successors assumed leadership of the school. After them Carneades, in accepting the headship established the third Academy, and employed the same line of reasoning which Arcesilaus had also used. For he too practiced the two-sided attack and ravaged all the statements made by others. He differed with him only in the doctrine of 'suspension', saying that it was impossible for human nature to suspend judgment concerning all things, that there was a difference between 'uncertain' and 'incomprehensible'; and while all things are incomprehensible, not all things are uncertain. He also delved into the Stoic arguments, and when he assumed a combative posture towards them his stature increased all the more, since he was aiming at what appeared plausible to the majority rather than at the truth. That is why he was a source of disgust to the Stoics.

At any rate, this is what Numenius writes about him.

Fr. 27 (4-7 L.)

(Eus., *Pr. ev.*, XIV, 8, 1-15, p.737 b-739 a V.;
II, p. 281. 11-284, 9 Mras)

737b Καρνεάδης δ' ἐκδεξάμενος παρ' Ἡγησίνου χρεὼν φυλάξαι ὅσ' ἀκίνητα καὶ ὅσα κεκινημένα ἦν τούτου μὲν ἡμέλει, εἰς δ' Ἀρκεσίλαον, εἴτ' οὖν ἀμείνω εἴτε καὶ φαυλότερα ἦν, ἐπανενεγκὼν διὰ μακροῦ τὴν μάχην ἀνενέαζε.

5   Καὶ ἑξῆς ἐπιλέγει·

Ἦγε δ' οὖν καὶ οὗτος καὶ ἀπέφερεν ἀντιλογίας τε καὶ στροφὰς λεπτολόγους συνέφερε τῇ μάχῃ ποικίλλων
c ἐξαρνητικός τε καὶ καταφατικός τε ἦν κἀμφοτέρωθεν ἀντιλογικός· εἴ τε που ἔδει τι καὶ θαῦμα ἐχόντων λόγων,
10 ἐξηγείρετο λάβρος οἷον ποταμὸς ῥοώδης, [σφοδρῶς ῥέων,] πάντα καταπιμπλὰς τὰ τῇδε καὶ τἀκεῖθι, καὶ εἰσέπιπτε καὶ συνέσυρε τοὺς ἀκούοντας διὰ θορύβου. Τοιγαροῦν ἀπάγων τοὺς ἄλλους αὐτὸς ἔμενεν ἀνεξαπάτητος, ὃ μὴ προσῆν τῷ Ἀρκεσιλάῳ. Ἐκεῖνος μέν γε περιερχόμενος τῇ φαρμάξει τοὺς
15 συγκορυβαντιῶντας ἔλαθεν ἑαυτὸν πρῶτον ἐξηπατηκὼς μὴ
d ἠσθῆσθαι, πεπεῖσθαι δ' ἀληθῆ εἶναι ἃ λέγει, διὰ τῆς ἀπαξαπάντων ἀναιρέσεως χρημάτων. Κακὸν δ' ἦν ἂν κακῷ ἐπανακείμενον, ὁ Καρνεάδης τῷ Ἀρκεσιλάῳ, μὴ χαλάσας τι σμικρόν, ὑφ'οὗ οὐκ ἄπρακτοι ἔμελλον ἔσεσθαι, κατὰ τὰς ἀπὸ
20 τοῦ πιθανοῦ λεγομένας αὐτῷ θετικάς τε καὶ ἀρνητικὰς φαντασίας τοῦ εἶναι τόδε τι ζῷον ἢ μὴ ζῷον εἶναι. Τοῦτο οὖν ὑπανείς, ὥσπερ οἱ ἀναχάζοντες θῆρες βιαιότερον καὶ μᾶλλον ἑαυτοὺς ἱεῖσιν εἰς τὰς αἰχμὰς καὐτὸς ἐνδοὺς δυνατώτερον ἐπῆλθεν· ἐπεί τε ὑποσταίη τε καὶ εὖ τύχοι, τηνικαῦτα ἤδη
25 καὶ οὗ προυδέδοκτο ἑκὼν ἡμέλει καὶ οὐκ ἐμέμνητο. Τὸ γὰρ
738a ἀληθές τε καὶ τὸ ψεῦδος ἐν τοῖς πράγμασιν ἐνεῖναι συγχωρῶν, ὥσπερ συνεργαζόμενος τῆς ζητήσεως τρόπῳ παλαιστοῦ δεινοῦ λαβὴν δοὺς περιεγίγνετο ἔνθεν. Κατὰ γὰρ

27 (4-7 L.)

Carneades received the school from Hegesinus, and though it was proper that he preserve what was permanent as well as what had been altered in his teachings, he ignored this teacher, and by ascribing what was either excellent or inferior to Arcesilaus, after a long hiatus he renewed the conflict.

And next he adds:

At any rate he would lead up to a point and then retract; while equivocating he would carry contradictions and subtle twists into the conflict; he was denying and affirming and combative from both sides. And if he needed arguments possessing something astonishing, he would rouse himself into a furious state like a turbulent river that floods everything on this side and that, and would burst in and sweep his listeners along in the confusion. So then, while leading the others astray he himself remained undeceived, something which was not characteristic of Arcesilaus. For he, in taking a strong hold on his fellow ecstatics with his sorcery, was unaware of having first beguiled himself not to perceive but to believe that what he said was true, due to the removal of objects altogether.

It would have been evil piled upon evil, Carneades added to Arcesilaus, had he not relented in a small point which his opponents were prepared to turn to their advantage. This involved the presentations designated by him from the 'probable' as those of assent or negation concerning whether something is or is not an animal. So relaxing this aspect somewhat, just as beasts draw back and hurl themselves more forcefully against the spears, so he too by giving in attacked more powerfully. And when he withstood and succeeded, only then did he willingly ignore his former position and not remember it. By conceding that the true and the false are inherent in objects, just as if he were cooperating in the inquiry, he was relinquishing a grip in the manner of a wily wrestler and was prevailing from within. While

τὴν τοῦ πιθανοῦ ῥοπὴν ἑκάτερον παρασχὼν οὐδέτερον εἶπε
30 βεβαίως καταλαμβάνεσθαι. Ἦν γοῦν λῃστὴς καὶ γόης
σοφώτερος. Παραλαβὼν γὰρ ἀληθεῖ μὲν ὅμοιον ψεῦδος,
καταληπτικῇ δὲ φαντασίᾳ καταληπτὸν ὅμοιον καὶ ἀγαγὼν εἰς
b τὰς ἴσας, οὐκ εἴασεν οὔτε τὸ ἀληθὲς εἶναι οὔτε τὸ ψεῦδος, ἢ
οὐ μᾶλλον τὸ ἕτερον τοῦ ἑτέρου ἢ μᾶλλον ἀπὸ τοῦ πιθανοῦ.
35 Ἦν οὖν ὀνείρατα ἀντὶ ὀνειράτων, διὰ τὸ ὁμοίας φαντασίας
ἀληθέσιν εἶναι τὰς ψευδεῖς, ὡς ἀπὸ ᾠοῦ κηρίνου πρὸς τὸ
ἀληθινὸν ᾠόν. Συνέβαινεν οὖν τὰ κακὰ καὶ πλείω. Καὶ μέντοι
λέγων ὁ Καρνεάδης ἐψυχαγώγει καὶ ἠνδραποδίσατο. Ἦν δὲ
κλέπτων μὲν ἀφανής, φαινόμενος δὲ λῃστής, αἱρῶν καὶ δόλῳ
40 καὶ βίᾳ τοὺς καὶ πάνυ σφόδρα παρεσκευασμένους. Πᾶσα γοῦν
Κανρνεάδου διάνοια ἐνίκα καὶ οὐδεμία ἡτισοῦν ἄλλων, ἐπεὶ
καὶ οἷς προσεπολέμει ἦσαν εἰπεῖν ἀδυνατώτεροι.
c Ἀντίπατρος γοῦν ὁ κατ' αὐτὸν γενόμενος ἔμελλε μὲν καὶ
ἀγωνιᾶν τι γράφειν, πρὸς δ' οὖν τοὺς ἀπὸ Καρνεάδου καθ'
45 ἡμέραν ἀποφερομένους λόγους οὔποτ' ἐδημοσίευσεν, οὐκ ἐν
ταῖς διατριβαῖς, οὐκ ἐν τοῖς περιπάτοις οὐδὲν εἶπεν οὐδ'
ἐφθέγξατο οὐδ' ἤκουσέ τις αὐτοῦ, φασίν, οὐδὲ γρῦ·
ἀντιγραφὰς δ' ἐπανετείνετο καὶ γωνίαν λαβὼν βιβλία
κατέλιπε γράψας τοῖς ὕστερον, οὔτε νῦν δυνάμενα καὶ τότε
50 ἦν ἀδυνατώτερα πρὸς οὕτως ἄνδρα ὑπέρμεγαν φανέντα καὶ
d καταδόξαντα εἶναι τοῖς τότε ἀνθώποις τὸν Καρνεάδην. Ὅμως
δέ, καίτοι καὐτὸς ὑπὸ τῆς στωϊκῆς φιλονεικίας εἰς τὸ
φανερὸν κυκῶν, πρός γε τοὺς ἑαυτοῦ ἑταίρους δι' ἀπορρήτων
ὡμολόγει τε καὶ ἠλήθευε καὶ ἀπεφαίνετο ἃ κἂν ἄλλος τῶν
55 ἐπιτυχόντων.

Εἶτα ἑξῆς φησι·

Καρνεάδου δὲ γίγνεται γνώριμος Μέντωρ μὲν πρῶτον, οὐ μὴν
διάδοχος· ἀλλ' ἔτι ζῶν Καρνεάδης ἐπὶ παλλακῇ μοιχὸν

granting each according to the tip of the scale of the 'probable', he asserted that neither was to be grasped with certainty. He was surely a most clever pirate and wizard. For once he accepted falsehood as equivalent to truth and as a mere comprehensible equivalent to a comprehensible appearance, having drawn them into a position of equality he allowed neither the true nor the false; or the one no more than the other or more than the 'probable'. They were dreams in place of dreams, since false appearances were equal to the true, like looking from a wax egg to a real one.

Therefore even more evils occurred. Even as he spoke Carneades was deluding and enslaving. And although he was unnoticed in this thievery, he was a manifest pirate, seizing by treachery and by force even those who were exceedingly well prepared. At any rate Carneades' every notion prevailed and none whatsoever of the others, since he was combating those who were weaker in debate.

It would seem that Antipater his contemporary was intending to write something in private, but he never published anything against the statements which were coming forth from Carneades on a daily basis; not in the schools nor during his walks did he say anything, neither did he utter nor did anyone hear from him, it is said, as much as a single syllable. But he was brandishing the threat of written attacks, and after obtaining a secluded place he wrote and bequeathed books to later generations; writings which have no force now and were less forceful then against a man who appeared to be, and was recognized by his contemporaries as being so over towering as Carneades was. Nevertheless, although he was stirring up confusion to counter the Stoic combativeness, he would confidentially make admissions to his own companions and speak the truth, producing the type of remark that any other chance acquaintance might make.

Then, he says next:

Mentor became the first disciple of Carneades, not however his successor. For Carneades, while he was still alive, after he

εὑρών, οὐχ ὑπὸ πιθανῆς φαντασίας οὐδ ὡς μὴ κατειληφώς, ὡς
60 δὲ μάλιστα πιστεύων τῇ ὄψει καὶ καταλαβὼν παρῃτήσατο τῆς
διατριβῆς. Ὁ δ' ἀποστὰς ἀντεσοφίστευε καὶ ἀντίτεχνος ἦν,
ἐλέγχων αὐτοῦ τὴν ἐν τοῖς λόγοις ἀκαταληψίαν.

739a Καὶ πάλιν ἐπιφέρει λέγων·

Ὁ δὲ Καρνεάδης, οἷον ἀντεστραμμένα φιλοσοφῶν, τοῖς
65 ψεύμασιν ἐκαλλωπίζετο καὶ ὑπ' αὐτοῖς τἀληθῆ ἠφάνιζε.
Παραπετάσμασιν οὖν ἐχρῆτο τοῖς ψεύμασι καὶ ἠλήθευεν
ἔνδον λανθάνων καπηλικώτερον. Ἔπασχεν οὖν πάθημα
ὀσπρίων, ὧν τὰ μὲν κενὰ ἐπιπολάζει τε τῷ ὕδατι καὶ
ὑπερέχει, τὰ χρηστὰ δ' αὐτῶν ἐστι κάτω καὶ ἐν ἀφανεῖ.

70 Ταῦτα καὶ περὶ Καρνεάδου λέγεται. Διάδοχος δ' αὐτοῦ τῆς
διατριβῆς καθίσταται Κλειτόμαχος, μεθ' ὃν Φίλων, οὗ πέρι ὁ
Νουμήνιος μνημονεύει ταῦτα·

Fr. 28 (8 L.)
(Eus., *Pr. ev.*, XIV, 9, 1-4, p. 739 b-d V.;
II, p. 284, 11-285, 3 Mras)

739b Ὁ δὲ Φίλων ἄρα οὗτος ἄρτι μὲν ἐκδεξάμενος τὴν διατριβὴν
ὑπὸ χαρμονῆς ἐξεπέπληκτο καὶ χάριν ἀποδιδοὺς ἐθεράπευε
καὶ τὰ δεδογμένα τῷ Κειτομάχῳ ηὖξε καὶ τοῖς Στωϊκοῖς

ἐκορύσσετο νώροπι χαλκῷ.

5 Ὡς δὲ προϊόντος μὲν τοῦ χρόνου, ἐξιτήλου δ' ὑπὸ
συνηθείας οὔσης αὐτῶν τῆς ἐποχῆς, οὐδὲν μὲν κατὰ ταὐτὰ
ἑαυτῷ ἐνόει, ἡ δὲ τῶν παθημάτων αὐτὸν ἀνέστρεφεν ἐνάργειά
τε καὶ ὁμολογία. Πολλὴν δῆτ' ἔχων ἤδη τὴν διαίσθησιν
ὑπερπεθύμει εὖ ἴσθ' ὅτι τῶν ἐλεγχόντων τυχεῖν, ἵνα μὴ
10 ἐδόκει 'μετὰ νῶτα βαλὼν' αὐτὸς ἑκὼν φεύγειν. Φίλωνος δὲ
γίγνεται ἀκουστὴς Ἀντίοχος, ἑτέρας ἄρξας Ἀκαδημίας.
d Μνησάρχῳ γοῦν τῷ Στωϊκῷ σχολάσας ἐναντία Φίλωνι τῷ
καθηγητῇ ἐφρόνησε μυρία τε ξένα προσῆψε τῇ Ἀκαδημίᾳ.

Ταῦτα καὶ παραπλήσια τούτοις μυρία τῆς Πλάτωνος περὶ
15 διαδοχῆς μνημονεύεται.

discovered him in an act of adultery with his concubine, not by the 'probable appearance' or as not having 'comprehended', but as most certainly trusting his sense of sight and 'comprehending', dismissed him from the school. And upon retiring he began to exchange sophistries with him and was a rival, refuting the 'incomprehensibility' in his statements.

And again he adds:

Carneades, in forming a philosophy from diametrically opposed principles as it were, adorned himself with lies and concealed the truth with them. Thus he used the lies as curtains and spoke the truth within unnoticed, in a rather mercenary fashion. He accordingly underwent the same experience as legumes: those of them that are empty float to the surface of the water and are prominent there, while those that are wholesome remain below in concealment.

These things are said about Carneades. Cleitomachus was made his successor in the school; after him Philo, about whom Numenius mentions the following:

Fr. 28 (8 L.)

Consequently, this Philo, having just received the leadership of the school was stunned with joy, and in rendering gratitude in return he became servile to and magnified the teachings of Cleitomachus; and against the Stoics "he armed himself in flashing bronze." But as time passed and their 'suspension' began to fade through habituation, his thought became inconsistent, and the clearness and correspondence of impressions overturned him. Because he certainly already possessed a great deal of discernment he desired greatly to encounter those who would refute him, so that it would not seem that "after turning tail" he was voluntarily fleeing. Philo had another student, Antiochus, who started another Academy. Since he had studied with the Stoic Mnesarchus his opinions conflicted with those of his master Philo, and he attached countless foreign doctrines to the Academy.

These and numerous other things similar to them are reported about the successors of Plato.

Περὶ ἀφθαρσίας ψυχῆς

Fr. 29 (31 L.)
(Origen., *Contra Celsum*, V, 57; II, p. 60, 5-13 Koteschau;
III, p. 156, 1-9 Borret)

Παράδοξα δὲ πράγματα τοῖς ἀνθρώποις ἐμφαίνεσθαί ποτε καὶ τῶν Ἑλλήνων ἱστόρησαν οὐ μόνον οἱ ὑπονοηθέντες ἂν ὡς μυθοποιοῦντες ἀλλὰ καὶ οἱ ἀνὰ πολὺ ἐπιδειξάμενοι γνησίως φιλοσοφεῖν καὶ φιλαλήθως ἐκτίθεσθαι τὰ εἰς αὐτοὺς
5 φθάσαντα. Τοιαῦτα δ' ἀνέγνωμεν παρὰ τῷ Σολεῖ Χρυσίππῳ, τινὰ δὲ παρὰ Πυθαγόρᾳ, ἤδη δὲ καὶ παρά τισι τῶν νεωτέρων καὶ χθὲς καὶ πρώην γεγενημένων, ὥσπερ παρὰ τῷ Χαιρωνεῖ Πλουτάρχῳ ἐν τοῖς Περὶ ψυχῆς καὶ τῷ Πυθαγορείῳ Νουμηνίῳ ἐν τῷ δευτέρῳ Περὶ ἀφθαρσίας ψυχῆς.

Incertorum operum fragmenta

Fr. 30 (Test. 46 L.)
(Porphyr., *De antro nympharum*, 10; p. 63, 7-24 Nauck;
p. 12, 12-25 West.)

Νύμφας δὲ ναΐδας λέγομεν καὶ τὰς τῶν ὑδάτων προεστώσας δυνάμεις ἰδίως, ἔλεγον δὲ καὶ τὰς εἰς γένεσιν κατιούσας ψυχὰς κοινῶς ἁπάσας. Ἡγοῦντο γὰρ προσιζάνειν τῷ ὕδατι τὰς ψυχὰς θεοπνόῳ ὄντι, ὥς φησιν ὁ Νουμήνιος, διὰ τοῦτο
5 λέγων καὶ τὸν προφήτην εἰρηκέναι ἐμφέρεσθαι ἐπάνω τοῦ ὕδατος θεοῦ πνεῦμα· τούς τε Αἰγυπτίους διὰ τοῦτο τοὺς δαίμονας ἅπαντας οὐχ ἱστάναι ἐπὶ στερεοῦ, ἀλλὰ πάντας ἐπὶ πλοίου, καὶ τὸν Ἥλιον καὶ ἁπλῶς πάντας· οὕστινας εἰδέναι χρὴ τὰς ψυχὰς ἐπιποτωμένας τῷ ὑγρῷ τὰς εἰς γένεσιν
10 κατιούσας· ὅθεν καὶ Ἡράκλειτον ψυχῇσι φάναι τέρψιν μὴ θάνατον ὑγρῇσι γενέσθαι, τέρψιν δ' εἶναι αὐταῖς τὴν εἰς γένεσιν πτῶσιν, καὶ ἀλλαχοῦ δὲ φάναι ζῆν ἡμᾶς τὸν ἐκείνων θάνατον καὶ ζῆν ἐκείνας τὸν ἡμέτερον θάνατον· παρὸ καὶ διεροὺς τοὺς ἐν γενέσει ὄντας καλεῖν τὸν ποιητὴν τοὺς
15 διύγρους τὰς ψυχὰς ἔχοντας. Αἷμά τε γὰρ ταύταις καὶ ὁ δίυγρος γόνος φίλος, ταῖς δὲ τῶν φυτῶν τροφὴ τὸ ὕδωρ.

Concerning The Incorruptibility Of The Soul
29 (31 L.)

That miraculous events sometimes appear among men the Greeks also have reported, not only those who might be suspected of fabricating tales, but also those who have long demonstrated that they philosophize legitimately and that they set out the accounts which have reached them with a concern for the truth. We have read such things in Chrysippus of Soli, and some in Pythagoras; and I have read them in some of those who are more recent and have appeared quite lately, such as Plutarch of Chaeronea in *Concerning the Soul*, and Numenius the Pythagorean in the second book of *Concerning the Incorruptibility of the Soul*.

Fragments From Undesignated Works
30 (Test. 46 L.)

We specifically term the forces presiding over the waters Nymphs and Naiads, but they (the Pythagoreans) give these names also to all souls in general which are descending into generation. For they believe that the souls settle on the water since it is touched by the breath of God, as Numenius says; because of this he adds that the prophet also stated that "a breath of God was carried over the water." And for this reason the Egyptians place all their deities not on solid ground, but rather all are set on a boat, even the Sun and quite simply all of them: it is necessary that they view the souls which are descending into generation hovering over the water.

Whence Heraclitus also says that it is a delight, not death for souls to become moist, and that the fall into generation is a delight for them; and elsewhere he says that we live their death, and they live our death. Therefore the poet calls those in generation wet, since they have moist souls. For both blood and the moist seed are dear to these souls, while water is the nourishment for the souls of plants.

Fr. 31 (Test. 43 L. usque ad 26 ἀθανάτων)

(Porphyr., *o. c.*, 21-24; p. 70, 25-72, 19 Nauck;
p. 22, 2-24, 3 West)

Τοῦ δὴ ἄντρου εἰκόνα καὶ σύμβολόν φησι τοῦ κόσμου φέροντος Νουμήνιος καὶ ὁ τούτου ἑταῖρος Κρόνιος δύο εἶναι ἐν οὐρανῷ ἄκρα, ὧν οὔτε νοτιώτερόν ἐστι τοῦ χειμερινοῦ τροπικοῦ οὔτε βορειότερον τοῦ θερινοῦ. Ἔστι δ' ὁ μὲν
5 θερινὸς κατὰ καρκίνον, ὁ δὲ χειμερινὸς κατ' αἰγόκερων. Καὶ προσγειότατος μὲν ὢν ἡμῖν ὁ καρκίνος εὐλόγως τῇ προσγειοτάτῃ Σελήνῃ ἀπεδόθη, ἀφανοῦς δ' ἔτι ὄντος τοῦ νοτίου πόλου τῷ μακρὰν ἔτι ἀφεστηκότι καὶ ἀνωτάτῳ τῶν
(22) πλανωμένων πάντων ὁ αἰγόκερως ἀπεδόθη. Καὶ ἔχουσί γ'
10 ἐφεξῆς αἱ θέσεις τῶν ζῳδίων, ἀπὸ μὲν καρκίνου εἰς αἰγόκερων· πρῶτα μὲν λέοντα οἶκον Ἡλίου, εἶτα παρθένον Ἑρμοῦ, ζυγὸν δ' Ἀφροδίτης, σκορπίον δ' Ἄρεος, τοξότην Διός, αἰγόκερων Κρόνου· ἀπὸ δ' αἰγόκερω ἔμπαλιν ὑδροχόον Κρόνου, ἰχθύας Διός, Ἄρεος κριόν, ταῦρον Ἀφροδίτης,
15 διδύμους Ἑρμοῦ, καὶ Σελήνης λοιπὸν καρκίνον. Δύο οὖν ταύτας ἔθεντο πύλας καρκίνον καὶ αἰγόκερων οἱ θεολόγοι, Πλάτων δὲ δύο στόμια ἔφη· τούτων δὲ καρκίνον μὲν εἶναι δι' οὗ κατίασιν αἱ ψυχαί, αἰγόκερων δὲ δι' οὗ ἀνίασιν. Ἀλλὰ
(23) καρκίνος μὲν βόρειος καὶ καταβατικός, αἰγόκερως δὲ νότιος
20 καὶ ἀναβατικός. Ἔστι δὲ τὰ μὲν βόρεια ψυχῶν εἰς γένεσιν κατιουσῶν. Καὶ ὀρθῶς καὶ τοῦ ἄντρου αἱ πρὸς βορρᾶν πύλαι καταβαταὶ ἀνθρώποις, τὰ δὲ νότια οὐ θεῶν, ἀλλὰ τῶν εἰς θεοὺς ἀνιουσῶν. Διὰ τὴν αὐτὴν δ' αἰτίαν οὐ θεῶν ἔφη ὁδός, ἀλλ' ἀθανάτων, ὃ κοινὸν καὶ ἐπὶ ψυχῶν ἢ οὐσῶν καθ' αὑτὸ ἢ
25 τῇ οὐσίᾳ ἀθανάτων.

31 (Test. 43 L.)

Seeing that the cave serves as an image and symbol of the world, Numenius and his companion Cronius say that there are two points of extremity in the sky: one which is southernmost in the winter tropic, and the other in the far north, the summer tropic. And the summer tropic is Cancer, while the winter tropic is in Capricorn. And since Cancer is closest to earth and us, it has reasonably been assigned to the moon which is closest to earth; and because the south pole still remains invisible, Capricorn had been assigned to the one which is furthest and highest of all the planets. Now the positions of the Zodiac proceed in order from Cancer to Capricorn. The first is Leo, House of the Sun, then Virgo, House of Mercury; Libra, House of Venus; Scorpio, House of Mars; Sagittarius, House of Jupiter; Capricorn, House of Saturn. From Capricorn in inverse order: Aquarius, House of Saturn; Pisces, House of Jupiter; Aries, House of Mars; Taurus, House of Venus; Gemini, House of Mercury; and Cancer once again, House of the Moon.

Now the theologians call these two, Cancer and Capricorn, gates, while Plato spoke of two 'openings'. And of these two, Cancer is that through which the souls descend; Capricorn, that through which they ascend. So Cancer is northern and associated with descent, Capricorn is southern and associated with ascent. And the north is the area of souls descending into generation. It is also correct that the gates of the cave which are toward the north are places of descent for men, and those toward the south are not for the gods, but for those ascending to the gods. For this reason he says it is not a way of the gods, but of immortals, a term which applies in common to souls which are either in and of themselves or by essence immortal.

Τῶν δύο πυλῶν τούτων μεμνῆσθαι καὶ Παρμενίδην ἐν τῷ Φυσικῷ φησὶ Ῥωμαίους τε καὶ Αἰγυπτίους. Ῥωμαίους μὲν γὰρ τὰ Κρόνια ἑορτάζειν Ἡλίου κατ' αἰγόκερων γενομένου, ἑορτάζειν δὲ τοὺς δούλους ἐλευθέρων σχήματα περιβάλλοντας
30 καὶ πάντων ἀλλήλοις κοινωνούντων, αἰνιξαμένου τοῦ νομοθέτου ὅτι κατὰ ταύτην τοῦ οὐρανοῦ τὴν πύλην οἱ νῦν ὄντες διὰ τὴν γένεσιν δοῦλοι διὰ τῆς κρονικῆς ἑορτῆς καὶ τοῦ ἀνακειμένου Κρόνῳ οἴκου ἐλευθεροῦνται, ἀναβιωσκόμενοι καὶ εἰς αὐτογένεσιν ἀπερχόμενοι. Καταβατικὴ δ' αὐτοῖς ἡ
35 ἀπ' αἰγόκερω ὁδός· διὸ ἰαννούαν εἰπόντες τὴν θύραν καὶ ἰαννουάριον μῆνα τὸν θυραῖον προσεῖπον, ἐν ᾧ Ἥλιος ἀπ' αἰγόκερω πρὸς ἑώαν ἐπάνεισιν ἐπιστρέψας εἰς τὰ βόρεια. Αἰγυπτίοις δ' ἀρχὴ ἔτους οὐχ ὁ ὑδροχόος, ὡς Ῥωμαίοις, ἀλλὰ καρκίνος· πρὸς γὰρ τῷ καρκίνῳ ἡ Σῶθις, ἣν κυνὸς ἀστέρα
40 Ἕλληνες φασί· νουμηνία δ' αὐτοῖς ἡ Σώθεως ἀνατολή, γενέσεως κατάρχουσα τῆς εἰς τὸν κόσμον.

Fr. 32 (Test. 44 L.)

(Porphyr., *o.c.*, 28; p. 75, 11-76, 1 Nauck;
p. 26, 26-28, 6 West)

Λέγει δέ που καὶ Ἡλίου πύλας, σημαίνων καρκίνον τε καὶ αἰγόκερων· ἄχρι γὰρ τούτων πρόεισιν ἀπὸ βορείου ἀνέμου εἰς τὰ νότια κατιὼν κἀκεῖθεν ἐπανιὼν εἰς τὰ βόρεια. Αἰγόκερως δὲ καὶ καρκίνος περὶ τὸν γαλαξίαν τὰ πέρατα
5 αὐτοῦ εἰληχότες, καρκίνος μὲν τὰ βόρεια, αἰγόκερως δὲ τὰ νότια· δῆμος δ' ὀνείρων κατὰ Πυθαγόραν αἱ ψυχαί, ἃς συνάγεσθαι φησὶν εἰς τὸν γαλαξίαν τὸν οὕτω προσαγορευόμενον ἀπὸ τῶν γάλακτι τρεφομένων, ὅταν εἰς γένεσιν πέσωσιν· ὃ καὶ σπένδειν αὐταῖς τοὺς ψυχαγωγοὺς
10 μέλι κεκραμένον γάλακτι ὡς ἂν δι' ἡδονῆς εἰς γένεσιν μεμελετηκυίαις ἔρχεσθαι· αἷς συγκυεῖσθαι τὸ γάλα πέφυκεν.

He says that Parmenides also mentions these two gates in the Physics, as do the Romans and the Egyptians. For the Romans celebrate the Saturnalia when the sun is in Capricorn, and they celebrate by clothing the slaves in the dress of free men and sharing all things in common; the lawgiver implying that those who are now slaves through generation in accordance with this gate of the heavens, will become free men through the Saturnine festival and the House devoted to Saturn by being brought back to life and departing into self-generation. And for them, the path from Capricorn is one of descent. Therefore, having named the door Janus, they also called January the 'month at the door', at which time the sun goes back from Capricorn towards the east, having turned back to the north. With the Egyptians the beginning of the year is not Aquarius, as it is for the Romans, but Cancer. For Sothis, which the Greeks call the Dog Star, is in Cancer, and for them the beginning of the month coincides with the rise of Sothis which rules over generation into the world.

32 (Test. 44 L.)

And he speaks somewhere also of gates of the Sun, indicating Cancer and Capricorn. For the sun progresses as far as these going down from the north wind to the south, and returning from there it passes into the north. Capricorn and Cancer are in the Milky Way and have been assigned to its boundaries: Cancer in the north, Capricorn in the south. And according to Pythagoras the souls are a "people of dreams" which he says are gathered together into the Milky Way, the one so named from those who are nourished by milk when they fall into generation; therefore the conjurers of souls also pour libations to them consisting of milk mixed with honey, signifying that it was for the sake of pleasure that they endeavored to enter into generation. And when they are conceived, milk is also produced as a natural result.

Fr. 33 (Test. 45 L.)

(Porphyr., *o.c.*, 34; p. 79, 19-80, 2 Nauck;
p. 32, 13-21 West)

Οὐ γὰρ ἀπὸ σκοποῦ οἶμαι καὶ τοῖς περὶ Νουμήνιον ἐδόκει Ὀδυσσεὺς εἰκόνα φέρειν Ὁμήρῳ κατὰ τὴν Ὀδύσσειαν τοῦ διὰ τῆς ἐφεξῆς γενέσεως διερχομένου καὶ οὕτως ἀποκαθισταμένου εἰς τοὺς ἔξω παντὸς κλύδωνος καὶ θαλάσσης ἀπείρους·

5   εἰσόκε τοὺς ἀφίκηαι οἳ οὐκ ἴσασι θάλασσαν
    ἀνέρες οὐδέ θ' ἅλεσσι μεμιγμένον εἶδαρ ἔδουσιν.

Πόντος δὲ καὶ θάλασσα καὶ κλύδων καὶ παρὰ Πλάτωνι ἡ ὑλικὴ σύστασις.

Fr. 34 (Test. 47 L.; p. 105, 19-106, 18)

(Macrobius, *Comm. in somnium Scipionis*, I, 12, 1-4;
II, p. 47, 30-48, 22 Willis, 1963)

Descensus vero ipsius, quo anima de caelo in huius vitae inferna delabitur, sic ordo digeritur. Zodiacum ita lacteus circulus obliquae circumflexionis occursu ambiendo complectitur, ut eum qua duo tropica signa Capricornus et Cancer feruntur intersecet.
5   Has solis portas physici vocaverunt, quia in utraque obviante solstitio ulterius solis inhibetur accessio, et fit ei regressus ad zonae viam cuius terminus nunquam relinquit. 2. Per has portas animae de caelo in terras meare et de terris in caelum remeare creduntur. Ideo hominum una, altera deorum vocatur: hominum
10 Cancer, quia per hunc in inferiora descensus est, Capricornus deorum, quia per illum animae in propriae immortalitatis sedem et in deorum numerum revertuntur. 3. Et hoc est quod Homeri divina prudentia in antri Ithacensis descriptione significat. Hinc et Pythagoras putat a lacteo circulo deorsum incipere Ditis
15 imperium, quia animae inde lapsae videntur iam a superis recessisse. Ideo primam nascentibus offerri ait lactis alimoniam,

33 (Test. 45 L.)

For I do not think it irrelevant that for Numenius and his school, Odysseus in the Odyssey also seemed to serve Homer as the symbol of the one passing through successive generation, and thus being restored to those apart from every wave and without experience of the sea:

> Until you reach those who know not the sea,
> Men eating food not mixed with salt.

And the material world is an ocean and sea and wave for Plato also.

34 (Test 47 L.; p. 105, 19-106, 18)

The progression of the descent itself, by which the soul glides downward from heaven into the lower regions of this life, is arranged in the following manner. By completing the circuit of an oblique revolution, the Milky Way encircles the zodiac in such a way that it intersects it where the two tropical signs—Capricorn and Cancer—are displayed. These the natural philosophers have named the 'gates of the sun', because in each of them, at the time of the solstice the further approach of the sun is held back, and it makes its return to the path of the belt of the zodiac, the limits of which it never abandons. It is through these gates that the souls are believed to pass from heaven to earth, and from earth into heaven once again. Therefore one is called that of men, the other that of the gods. Cancer is that of men because the descent is through this into the lower regions; Capricorn is that of the gods because through that one the souls return into the abode of their own immortality and into the company of the gods. And this is what the divine intelligence of Homer signifies in the description of the cave of Ithaca. For this reason Pythagoras too believes that the realm of Pluto starts from the Milky Way downward, because souls which have slipped from there surely appear to have withdrawn from higher realms. Therefore he says that milk is the first food offered to new-borns, because as souls slip into earthly

quia primus eis motus a lacteo incipit in corpora terrena labentibus. Unde et Scipioni de animis beatorum ostenso lacteo dictum est, *hinc profecti huc revertuntur*. 4. Ergo descensurae cum
20 adhuc in Cancro sunt, quoniam illic positae necdum lacteum reliquerunt, adhuc in numero sunt deorum. Cum vero ad Leonem labendo pervenerint, illic condicionis futurae auspicantur exordium.

Fr. 35 (Test. 42 L.)

(Proclus, *In Platonis rem publ.*, II,

p. 128, 26-130, 14; 131, 8-14 Kroll)

Νουμήνιος μὲν γὰρ τὸ κέντρον εἶναί φησιν τοῦτον τοῦ τε κόσμου παντὸς καὶ τῆς γῆς, ὡς μεταξὺ μὲν ὂν τοῦ οὐρανοῦ, μεταξὺ δὲ καὶ τῆς γῆς· ἐν ᾧ καθῆσθαι τοὺς δικαστὰς καὶ παραπέμπειν τὰς μὲν εἰς οὐρανὸν τῶν ψυχῶν, τὰς δ' εἰς τὸν
5 ὑπὸ γῆς τόπον καὶ τοὺς ἐκεῖ ποταμούς· οὐρανὸν μὲν τὴν ἀπλανῆ λέγων καὶ ἐν ταύτῃ δύο χάσματα, τὸν αἰγόκερων καὶ τὸν καρκίνον, τοῦτον μὲν καθόδου χάσμα τῆς εἰς γένεσιν, ἀνόδου δὲ ἐκεῖνον, ποταμοὺς δὲ ὑπὸ γῆς τὰς πλανωμένας (ἀνάγει γὰρ εἰς ταύτας τοὺς ποταμοὺς καὶ αὐτὸν τὸν
10 Τάρταρον)· καὶ ἄλλην πολλὴν ἐπεισάγων τερατολογίαν, πηδήσεις τε ψυχῶν ἀπὸ τῶν τροπικῶν ἐπὶ τὰ ἰσημερινὰ καὶ ἀπὸ τούτων εἰς τὰ τροπικὰ καὶ μεταβάσεις, ἃς αὐτὸς πηδῶν ἐπὶ τὰ πράγματα μεταφέρει, καὶ συρράπτων τὰ πλατωνικὰ ῥήματα τοῖς γενεθλιαλογικοῖς καὶ ταῦτα τοῖς τελεστικοῖς·
15 μαρτυρούμενος τῶν δύο χασμάτων καὶ τὴν Ὁμήρου ποίησιν οὐ μόνον λέγουσαν τὰς μὲν πρὸς βορέαο καταιβατὰς ἀνθρώποισιν ὁδούς, ἐπείπερ ὁ ἥλιος... · τὰς δὲ πρὸς νότου <εἶναι θειοτέρας>, δι' ὧν οὐκ ἔστιν ἀνδράσιν <εἰσελθε>ῖν, ἀθανάτων δὲ μόνον ὁδοὺς αὐτὰς ὑπάρχειν· ὁ γὰρ αἰγόκερως
20 ἀνάγων τὰς ψυχὰς λύει μὲν αὐτῶν τὴν ἐν ἀνδράσι ζωήν, μόνην δὲ τὴν ἀθάνατον εἰσδέχεται καὶ θείαν· οὐ ταῦτα δ' οὖν μόνον, ἀλλὰ καὶ ἡλίου πύλας ὑμνοῦσαν καὶ δῆμον ὀνείρων,

bodies their first movement begins from the Milky Way. Whence it is said by Scipio concerning the blessed souls as he pointed out the Milky Way: "Having fallen from here, they return." Accordingly, when on the verge of descent they are still in Cancer, since being positioned there they have not yet abandoned the Milky Way, they are still in the company of the gods. But when falling they reach Leo, they enter there into the beginning of their future condition.

35 (Test. 42 L.)

For Numenius says that this is the center of the entire universe and of the earth, since it is between the heavens and the earth. Here the judges are seated and send the souls along, some into heaven and some into the region below the earth and the rivers that are there. And equating heaven and the fixed sphere, he says that there are two chasms in it, one Capricorn and one Cancer; the latter is the chasm of descent into generation, the former is that of ascent. And he equates the subterranean rivers with the spheres of the planets, for he draws up both the rivers and Tartarus itself into these spheres. And he brings in a great deal of other marvel talk such as the leaps of the souls from the solstices to the equinoxes and from these to the solstices; and alterations which he, by a leap of his own, transfers to these matters, even stitching the Platonic sayings to astrological lore and this to the teaching of the mysteries. As evidence for the two chasms he cites the poem of Homer which not only states that the paths at the north are paths of descent for men, especially since the sun...but also that those at the south are <more divine>, through which it is not possible for men to pass, but these paths themselves exist only for the immortals. For Capricorn, drawing the souls upwards, dissolves their life as men and accepts within only the immortal and divine. Not only this, then, but the poem also sings of the "gates of the sun and people of the dreams", calling the two

τὰ μὲν δύο τροπικὰ ζῴδια πύλας ἡλίου προσαγορεύσασαν, δῆμον δ' ὀνείρων, ὥς φησιν ἐκεῖνος, τὸν γαλαξίαν. Καὶ γὰρ
25 τὸν Πυθαγόραν δι' ἀπορρήτων "Αιδην τὸν γαλαξίαν καὶ τόπον ψυχῶν ἀποκαλεῖν, ὡς ἐκεῖ συνωθουμένων· διὸ παρά τισιν ἔθνεσιν γάλα σπένδεσθαι τοῖς θεοῖς τοῖς τῶν ψυχῶν καθαρταῖς καὶ τῶν πεσουσῶν εἰς γένεσιν εἶναι γάλα τὴν πρώτην τροφήν. Τὸν δὲ δὴ Πλάτωνα διὰ μὲν τῶν χασμάτων,
30 ὡς εἴρηται, δηλοῦν τὰς δύο πύλας, διὰ δὲ τοῦ φωτός, ὃ δὴ σύνδεσμον εἶναι τοῦ οὐρανοῦ, τὸν γαλαξίαν· εἰς ὃν ἀνιέναι δι' ἡμερῶν δυοκαίδεκα τὰς ψυχὰς ἀπὸ τοῦ τόπου τῶν δικαστῶν· ἦν δὲ ὁ τόπος τὸ κέντρον. Ἐντεῦθεν τοίνυν ἀρχομένην τὴν δυωδεκάδα τελευτᾶν εἰς τὸν οὐρανόν· ἐν ᾗ τὸ
35 κέντρον εἶναι, τὴν γῆν, τὸ ὕδωρ, τὸν ἀέρα, τὰς ἑπτὰ πλανωμένας, αὐτὸν τὸν ἀπλανῆ κύκλον. Εἶναι δ' οὖν τὰ τροπικὰ ζῴδια, τὰ χάσματα τὰ διπλᾶ, τὰς δύο πύλας ὀνόματι διαφέροντα μόνον, καὶ πάλιν τὸν γαλαξίαν, τὸ φῶς τὸ τῇ ἴριδι προσφερές, τὸν δῆμον τὸν ὀνείρων ταὐτόν. Ὀνείροις
40 γὰρ ἀπεικάζειν τὰς ἄνευ σωμάτων ψυχὰς καὶ ἄλλοθι τὸν ποιητήν...

... Ὁ δὲ μόνον τὸν γαλαξίαν ἐκ τῶν ψυχῶν συμπληροῖ τῶν ἐντεῦθεν εἰς οὐρανὸν ἀναβεβηκυιῶν· καὶ ὁ μὲν τὰς εὐδαίμονας οὔ φησι χωρεῖν εἰς τὸν ὑποχθόνιον τόπον, ὁ δὲ
45 ἄγειν ἀναγκάζεται πρῶτον εἰς ἐκεῖνον, εἴπερ πᾶσαν ψυχὴν εἰς τὸν δικαστὴν χωρεῖν πρῶτον δεῖ, ἔπειτα εἰς τὸν ὑπερουράνιον τόπον ἀνελθεῖν, ὅπου γε διάγουσιν αἱ ψυχαὶ εὐδαιμόνως.

Fr. 36 (Test. 48 L.)

(Porphyr., Περὶ τοῦ πῶς ἐμψυχοῦται τὰ ἔμβρυα, p. 34, 20-35, 2 Kalbfleisch in *Abhandlungen...Berlin*, 1895)

Εἰ δὲ δυνάμει ζῷον ὡς τὸ δεδεγμένον τὴν ἕξιν ἢ μᾶλλον ζῷον ἐνεργείᾳ ἦν τὸ ἔμβρυον, δύσκολον μὲν τὸν καιρὸν ἀφορίσαι τῆς εἰσκρίσεως, καὶ πολύ γε τὸ ἀπίθανον ἕξει καὶ πλασματῶδες ὁποῖος ἂν εἶναι ἀφορισθῇ, τοῦ μὲν ὅταν
5 καταβληθῇ τὸ σπέρμα τὸν καιρὸν τοῦτον ἀποδιδόντος

solsticial signs the "the gates of the sun", and calling the Milky Way, as Numenius says, "the people of dreams". For in fact Pythagoras esoterically names the Milky Way 'Hades' and the place of the soul, since they are forced together there. That is why among some nations milk is spilled in offering to the gods who purify souls, and that is why milk is the first food of those falling into generation. So then, as stated before, by the two chasms Plato indicates the two gates; and by the light, which is indeed the bond of the heavens, he signifies the Milky Way. Into this through a period of twelve days the souls ascend from the place of the judges. And this place was the center. Starting from that point, therefore, the dodecade ends in heaven; in it are comprised the earth, the water, the air, the seven planets, even the circle of the fixed stars. So the signs of the solstices, the double chasms, and the two gates differ only in name, and in turn, the Milky Way, the light similar to the rainbow, and the people of dreams are the same thing. For elsewhere the poet likens the souls without bodies to dreams...

(P. 131, 8-14) (Numenius) fills the Milky Way only with souls which have ascended from there into heaven. And while the one (Plato) denies that the blessed pass into the subterranean realm, the other (Numenius) is compelled to lead them first into that realm, since it is required that every soul go to the judge first; then they rise to the realm above heaven, where the souls live in bliss.

36 (Test. 48 L.)

Whether the embryo is a living being potentially, as having received its general configuration, or rather a living being in actuality, it is difficult to determine the time of the soul's entrance. And I suppose it will involve much that is unconvincing and fabricated whatever it has been determined to be. One view defines the time as the moment when the sperm is deposited,

ὡς ἂν μηδ' οἵου τ' ὄντος ἐν τῇ μήτρᾳ γονίμως κρατηθῆναι
μήτι γε ψυχῆς ἔξωθεν τῇ εἰσκρίσει ἑαυτῆς τὴν σύμφυσιν
ἀπεργασαμένης - κἀνταῦθα πολὺς ὁ Νουμήνιος καὶ οἱ τὰς
Πυθαγόρου ὑπονοίας ἐξηγούμενοι, καὶ τὸν παρὰ μὲν τῷ
10 Πλάτωνι ποταμὸν Ἀμέλητα, παρὰ δὲ τῷ Ἡσιόδῳ καὶ τοῖς
Ὀρφικοῖς τὴν Στύγα, παρὰ δὲ τῷ Φερεκύδῃ τὴν ἐκροὴν ἐπὶ
τοῦ σπέρματος ἐκδεχόμενοι, τοῦ δ' ὅταν...

Fr. 37 (Test 49 L.)
(Proclus, *In Timaeum*, I, 76, 30-77, 23 Diehl)

Οἱ δ' εἰς δαιμόνων τινῶν ἐναντίωσιν, ὡς τῶν μὲν
ἀμεινόνων, τῶν δὲ χειρόνων, καὶ τῶν μὲν πλήθει, τῶν δὲ
δυνάμει κρειττόνων, καὶ τῶν μὲν κρατούντων, τῶν δὲ
κρατουμένων, ὥσπερ Ὠριγένης ὑπέλαβεν. Οἱ δ' εἰς ψυχῶν
5 διάστασιν καλλιόνων καὶ τῆς Ἀθηνᾶς τροφίμων καὶ
γενεσιουργῶν ἄλλων, αἳ καὶ τῷ τῆς γενέσεως ἐφόρῳ θεῷ
προσήκουσι. Καὶ ἔστι τῆς ἐξηγήσεως ταύτης προστάτης
Νουμήνιος. Οἱ δὲ καὶ μίξαντες τὴν Ὠριγένους, ὥσπερ
οἴονται, καὶ Νουμηνίου δόξαν ψυχῶν πρὸς δαίμονας
10 ἐναντίωσιν εἶπον, τῶν μὲν δαιμόνων καταγωγῶν ὄντων, τῶν δὲ
ψυχῶν ἀναγομένων· παρ' οἷς ὁ δαίμων τριχῶς· καὶ γὰρ εἶναι
φασι τὸ μὲν θείων δαιμόνων γένος, τὸ δὲ κατὰ σχέσιν, ὃ
μερικαὶ συμπληροῦσι ψυχαὶ δαιμονίας τυχοῦσαι λήξεως, τὸ δὲ
πονηρὸν ἄλλο καὶ λυμαντικὸν τῶν ψυχῶν. Τοὺς οὖν ἐσχάτους
15 δαίμονας τὸν πόλεμον τοῦτον συγκροτεῖν καὶ τὰς ψυχὰς ἐν
τῇ εἰς γένεσιν καθόδῳ· καὶ ἅπερ οἱ παλαιοί, φασι, θεολόγοι
εἰς Ὄσιριν καὶ Τυφῶνα ἀνήγαγον ἢ εἰς Διόνυσον καὶ Τιτᾶνας,
ταῦτα ὁ Πλάτων εἰς Ἀθηναίους καὶ Ἀτλαντίνους ἀναπέμπει
δι' εὐσέβειαν· πρὶν δ' εἰς τὰ στερεὰ σώματα κατελθεῖν,
20 <ἐναντίωσιν> παραδίδωσι τῶν ψυχῶν πρὸς τοὺς ὑλικοὺς
δαίμονας, οὓς τῇ δύσει παρῳκείωσεν· ἐπεὶ καὶ ἡ δύσις, ὡς
ἔλεγον Αἰγύπτιοι, τόπος ἐστὶ δαιμόνων κακωτικῶν· ἐπὶ δὲ
ταύτης ἐστὶ τῆς οἰήσεως ὁ φιλόσοφος Πορφύριος, ὃν καὶ
θαυμάσειεν ἄν τις εἰ ἕτερα λέγοι τῆς Νουμηνίου παραδόσεως.

reasoning that it would not be able to be held fruitfully within the womb without a soul effecting the conjoining by its entrance from outside. And on that subject Numenius has much to say, as do those interpreting the allegorical meanings of Pythagoras who accept that the river Ameles in Plato, the Styx in Hesiod and the Orphics, and the 'efflux' in Pherecydes all refer to the sperm. And another view defines it as the moment when...

37 (Test. 49 L.)

Some interpret it (the myth of the Athenians and the Atlanteans) as an opposition between certain demons, such as between the better and the inferior: some being superior in number, others in might; some conquering, others conquered, as Origen supposed. Others view it as a conflict between souls: the noble souls who are attached to Athena, and others involved in generation, who also belong to the god who presides over generation. And the chief adherent of this exegesis is Numenius. And others, after combining the opinions of Origen and Numenius, as they believe, set forth an opposition between souls and demons: the demons leading downward, the souls being led upward. For them the term 'demon' has three meanings. In fact they say that one type is that of divine demons; another type involves a temporary condition that is filled by some souls which have obtained a demonic station by lot; the other type is evil and harmful to souls. So these last demons wage war with the souls during the descent into generation. And they say that the ancient theologians ascribed such conflicts to Osiris and Typhon, or Dionysius and the titans, while Plato refers these matters back to the Athenians and Atlanteans through piety. They also teach that before they come down into solid bodies there is a conflict between the souls and the material demons which inhabit the west, since the west especially, as the Egyptians used to say, is a place of harmful demons. And the philosopher Porphyry is of this opinion, at whom one would marvel were he to utter something different from the tradition of Numenius.

Fr. 38 (Test. 51 L.)
(Olympiodorus, *In Phaedonem*, p. 84, 21-85, 3 Norvin)

Ὅτι τούτοις χρώμενοι τοῖς κανόσι ῥᾳδίως διελέγξομεν, ὡς οὔτε τἀγαθόν ἐστιν ἡ φρουρά, ὥς τινες, οὔτε ἡ ἡδονή, ὡς Νουμήνιος... Οὕτω δὲ καὶ Πορφύριος προϋπενόησεν ἐν τῷ ὑπομνήματι.

Fr. 39 (Test. 31 L.)
(Proclus, *In Timaeum*, II, 153, 17-25 Diehl)

Τῶν δὲ πρὸ ἡμῶν οἱ μὲν μαθηματικὴν ποιοῦντες τὴν οὐσίαν τῆς ψυχῆς ὡς μέσην τῶν τε φυσικῶν καὶ τῶν ὑπερφυῶν, οἱ μὲν ἀριθμὸν αὐτὴν εἰπόντες ἐκ μονάδος ποιοῦσιν, ὡς ἀμερίστου, καὶ τῆς ἀορίστου δυάδος, ὡς
5 μεριστῆς, οἱ δ' ὡς γεωμετρικὴν ὑπόστασιν οὖσαν ἐκ σημείου καὶ διαστάσεως, τοῦ μὲν ἀμεροῦς, τῆς δὲ μεριστῆς· καὶ τῆς μὲν προτέρας εἰσὶ δόξης οἱ περὶ Ἀρίστανδρον καὶ Νουμήνιον καὶ ἄλλοι πλεῖστοι τῶν ἐξηγητῶν, τῆς δὲ δευτέρας Σευῆρος.

Fr. 40 (Test. 32 L.; cf. test. 20)
(Id., *ibid*, II, 274, 10-14 Diehl)

Θεόδωρος δ' ὁ ἐκ τῆς Ἀσίνης φιλόσοφος, τῶν νουμηνείων λόγων ἐμφορηθείς, καινοπρεπέστερον τοὺς περὶ τῆς ψυχογονίας διέθηκε λόγους, ἀπὸ τῶν γραμμάτων καὶ τῶν χαρακτήρων καὶ τῶν ἀριθμῶν ποιούμενος τὰς ἐπιβολάς.

38 (Test. 51 L.)

Using these cannons we will easily show that the Prison is neither the Good, as some hold, nor pleasure, as Numenius believes...This is what Porphyry also previously surmised in his commentary.

39 (Test. 31 L.)

Among our predecessors, some make the essence of the soul mathematical, as an intermediate between physical realities and those beyond nature; those who say it is a number derive it from the monad, which is indivisible, and the unlimited dyad, which is divisible. Others, claiming that it is a geometrical entity, derive it from the point and extension: the one is indivisible, and the other divisible. Aristander, Numenius and most other exegetes are of the first opinion, while Severus is of the second.

40 (Test. 32 L.)

Theodorus the philosopher from Asine, being filled with the notions of Numenius, made some remarks about the soul in a rather novel way, deriving its conceptions from the letters, the characters and the numbers.

Fr. 41 (Test. 33 L.)

(Iamblichus, Περὶ ψυχῆς, ap. Stob., *Anthol.*, I, 49, 32; p. 365, 5-21 Wachsmuth)

Ἴθι δὴ οὖν ἐπὶ τὴν καθ' αὑτὴν ἀσώματον οὐσίαν ἐπανίωμεν, διακρίνοντες καὶ ἐπ' αὐτῆς ἐν τάξει τὰς περὶ ψυχῆς πάσας δόξας. Εἰσὶ δή τινες οἳ πᾶσαν τὴν τοιαύτην οὐσίαν ὁμοιομερῆ καὶ τὴν αὐτὴν καὶ μίαν ἀποφαίνονται, ὡς καὶ ἐν
5 ὁτῳοῦν αὐτῆς μέρει εἶναι τὰ ὅλα· οἵτινες καὶ ἐν τῇ μεριστῇ ψυχῇ τὸν νοητὸν κόσμον καὶ θεοὺς καὶ δαίμονας καὶ τἀγαθὸν καὶ πάντα τὰ πρεσβύτερα ἐν αὐτῇ ἐνιδρύουσι καὶ ἐν πᾶσιν ὡσαύτως πάντα εἶναι ἀποφαίνονται, οἰκείως μέντοι κατὰ τὴν αὑτῶν οὐσίαν ἐν ἑκάστοις. Καὶ ταύτης τῆς δόξης
10 ἀναμφισβητήτως μέν ἐστι Νουμήνιος, οὐ πάντη δὲ ὁμολογουμένως Πλωτῖνος· ἀστάτως δ' ἐν αὐτῇ φέρεται Ἀμέλιος· Πορφύριος δ' ἐνδοιάζει περὶ αὐτήν, πῇ μὲν διατεταμένως αὐτῆς ἀφιστάμενος, πῇ δὲ συνακολουθῶν αὐτῇ, ὡς παραδοθείσῃ ἄνωθεν. Κατὰ δὲ ταύτην νοῦ καὶ θεῶν καὶ τῶν κρειττόνων
15 γενῶν οὐδὲν ἡ ψυχὴ διενήνοχε κατά γε τὴν ὅλην οὐσίαν.

Fr. 42 (Test. 34 L.)

(Id., *ibid*, I, 49, 67; p.458, 3-4 Wachsmuth)

Ἕνωσιν μὲν οὖν καὶ ταυτότητα ἀδιάκριτον τῆς ψυχῆς πρὸς τὰς ἑαυτῆς ἀρχὰς πρεσβεύειν φαίνεται Νουμήνιος.

Fr. 43 (Test. 35 L.)

(Id., *ibid.*, I, 49, 37; p. 374, 21-375, 1 et 12-18 Wachsmuth)

Ἤδη τοίνυν καὶ ἐν αὐτοῖς τοῖς Πλατωνικοῖς πολλοὶ διαστασιάζουσιν, οἱ μὲν εἰς μίαν σύνταξιν καὶ μίαν ἰδέαν τὰ εἴδη καὶ τὰ μόρια τῆς ζωῆς καὶ τὰ ἐνεργήματα συνάγοντες, ὥσπερ Πλωτῖνός τε καὶ Πορφύριος· οἱ δ' εἰς μάχην ταῦτα
5 κατατείνοντες, ὥσπερ Νουμήνιος· οἱ δ' ἐκ μαχομένων αὐτὰ συναρμόζοντες, ὥσπερ οἱ περὶ Ἀττικὸν καὶ Πλούταρχον... Τῶν δ' αὖ διισταμένων πρὸς τούτους καὶ ἀπὸ τῶν ἔξωθεν προσφυομένων προστιθέντων ὁπωσοῦν τῇ ψυχῇ τὸ κακόν, ἀπὸ μὲν τῆς ὕλης Νουμηνίου καὶ Κρονίου πολλάκις, ἀπὸ δὲ τῶν
10 σωμάτων αὐτῶν τούτων ἔστιν ὅτε καὶ Ἁρποκρατίωνος, ἀπὸ δὲ τῆς φύσεως καὶ τῆς ἀλόγου ψυχῆς Πλωτίνου καὶ Πορφυρίου ὡς τὰ πολλά.

41 (Test. 31 L.)

Come then, let us return to the absolute immaterial essence, examining in sequence also with respect to it all the opinions concerning soul. Now there are some who hold all this kind of essence to be identical in all its parts and one and the same, so that the whole resides in any part whatsoever. These philosophers also set within the separate soul the noetic cosmos, and gods, and demons, and the Good and all the superior levels of being, and assert that all things are equally in all things—conformably, however, in each according to its essence. And Numenius is indisputably of this opinion, but Plotinus is not in total agreement. Amelius subscribes to it with some uncertainty; Porphyry wavers concerning it, at one time resolutely standing away from it, at another following it as if it had been handed down from above. According to this opinion the soul differs in no way from Intellect or gods or the superior types of being, at any rate with respect to its entire essence.

42 (Test. 34 L.)

Numenius appears to support a union and indistinguishable identity of the soul with its own principles.

43 (Test. 35 L.)

Already, therefore, even among the Platonists themselves there are many in disagreement. Some draw the forms and parts of life, as well as its active expressions into one structure and one pattern, as do Plotinus and Porphyry. Others such as Numenius set these elements in pitched battle; others bring them into harmony from a previous state of war, as do Atticus and Plutarch...Again, others are also at variance with these men concerning the exterior accretions which in some way inflict evil on the soul. Numenius and Cronius often derive them from matter; occasionally Harpocration derives them from these bodies themselves; Plotinus and Porphyry for the most part from Nature and the irrational soul.

Fr. 44 (Test. 36 L.)

(Porphyr., Περὶ τῶν τῆς ψυχῆς δυνάμεων,
ap. Stob., *Anthol.*, I, 49, 25a; p. 350, 25-351, 1 Wachsmuth)

Ἄλλοι δέ, ὧν καὶ Νουμήνιος, οὐ τρία μέρη ψυχῆς μιᾶς ἢ δύο γε, τὸ λογικὸν καὶ ἄλογον, ἀλλὰ δύο ψυχὰς ἔχειν ἡμᾶς οἴονται, ὥσπερ καὶ ἄλλα, τὴν μὲν λογικήν, τὴν δ' ἄλογον...

Fr. 45 (Test. 37 L.)

(Id., *ibid.*, I, 49, 25; p. 349, 19-22 Wachsmuth)

Νουμήνιος δὲ τὴν συγκαταθετικὴν δύναμιν παραδεκτικὴν ἐνεργειῶν φήσας εἶναι, σύμπτωμα αὐτῆς φησιν εἶναι τὸ φανταστικόν, οὐ μὴν ἔργον γε καὶ ἀποτέλεσμα, ἀλλὰ παρακολούθημα.

Fr. 46a (Test. 38 L.)

(Olympiodorus, *In Phaedonem*, p. 124, 13-18 Norvin)

Ὅτι οἱ μὲν ἀπὸ τῆς λογικῆς ψυχῆς ἄχρι τῆς ἐμψύχου ἕξεως ἀπαθανατίζουσιν, ὡς Νουμήνιος· οἱ δὲ μέχρι τῆς φύσεως, ὡς Πλωτῖνος ἔνι ὅπου· οἱ δὲ μέχρι τῆς ἀλογίας, ὡς τῶν μὲν παλαιῶν Ξενοκράτης καὶ Σπεύσιππος, τῶν δὲ νεωτέρων
5 Ἰάμβλιχος καὶ Πλούταρχος· οἱ δὲ μέχρι μόνης τῆς λογικῆς, ὡς Πρόκλος καὶ Πορφύριος...

Fr. 46b (Test. 27 a L.)

(Syrianus, *In Aristotelis Metaphysica*, p. 109, 12-14 Kroll)

Νουμηνίῳ μὲν οὖν καὶ Κρονίῳ καὶ Ἀμελίῳ καὶ τὰ νοητὰ καὶ τὰ αἰσθητὰ πάντα μετέχειν ἀρέσκει τῶν ἰδεῶν, Πορφυρίῳ δὲ μόνα τὰ αἰσθητά...

Fr. 46c (Test. 27 b L.)

(Proclus, *In Tim.*, III, 33, 33-34, 3 Diehl)

Εἰ δ', ὡς Ἀμέλιος γράφει καὶ πρὸ Ἀμελίου Νουμήνιος, μέθεξίς ἐστι κἂν τοῖς νοητοῖς, εἶεν ἂν εἰκόνες καὶ ἐν αὐτοῖς.

44 (Test. 36 L.)

Others, one of which is Numenius, believe we do not have three parts of soul, or even one or two, i.e. the rational and irrational, but two souls: as in other respects one rational, the other irrational.

45 (Test. 37 L.)

Numenius, after stating that the function of assent is susceptible to activity, adds that the imagination is an incidental aspect of it, neither action nor effect, rather an attendant circumstance.

46a (Test. 38 L.)

Some, such as Numenius, extend immortality from the rational soul to the state of being ensouled; others, as Plotinus occasionally does, extends it as far as Nature; others such as Xenocrates and Speusippus of the ancients, and Iamblichus and Plutarch of those more recent, as far as the irrational soul; and some extend it only as far as the rational soul, such as Proclus and Porphyry...

46b (Test. 27a L.)

For Numenius, Cronius and Amelius, both the intelligibles as well as all the perceptible objects participate in the Ideas. But for Porphyry, only the perceptibles...

46c (Test. 27b L.)

And if, as Amelius writes, and before Amelius Numenius, there is participation also among the intelligibles, there would also be images within them.

Fr. 47 (Test. 39 L.)

(Io. Philoponus, *In Aristotelis de anima*, p. 9, 35-38 Hayduck,
ap. *Comm. in Arist. gr.*, XV, 1897)

Τῶν δὲ χωριστὴν εἰρηκότων οἱ μὲν πᾶσαν ψυχὴν χωριστὴν σώματος εἰρήκασιν, καὶ τὴν λογικὴν καὶ τὴν ἄλογον καὶ τὴν φυτικήν, οἷος ἦν Νουμήνιος πλανηθεὶς ὑπό τινων ῥησειδίων Πλάτωνος εἰπόντος ἐν Φαίδρῳ· 'πᾶσα ψυχὴ ἀθάνατος'.

Fr. 48 (Test. 40 L.)

(Iamblichus, Περὶ ψυχῆς, ap. Stob. *Anthol.*, I, 49, 40;
p. 380, 6-19 Wachsmuth)

Οἶμαι τοίνυν καὶ τὰ τέλη διάφορα ὄντα καὶ τοὺς τρόπους τῆς καθόδου τῶν ψυχῶν ποιεῖν διαφέροντας. Ἡ μὲν γὰρ ἐπὶ σωτηρίᾳ καὶ καθάρσει καὶ τελειότητι τῶν τῇδε κατιοῦσα ἄχραντον ποιεῖται καὶ τὴν κάθοδον· ἡ δὲ διὰ γυμνασίαν καὶ
5 ἐπανόρθωσιν τῶν οἰκείων ἠθῶν ἐπιστρεφομένη περὶ τὰ σώματα οὐκ ἀπαθής ἐστι παντελῶς, οὐδ' ἀφεῖται ἀπόλυτος καθ' ἑαυτήν· ἡ δ' ἐπὶ δίκῃ καὶ κρίσει δεῦρο κατερχομένη συρομένη πως ἔοικε καὶ συνελαυνομένη.

<Τινὲς δὲ τῶν νεωτέρων οὐχ οὕτως> διακρίνουσιν, οὐκ
10 ἔχοντες δὲ σκοπὸν τῆς διαφορότητος εἰς ταὐτὸ συγχέουσι τὰς ἐνσωματώσεις τῶν ὅλων, κακάς τ' εἶναι πάσας διϊσχυρίζονται καὶ διαφερόντως οἱ περὶ Κρόνιόν τε καὶ Νουμήνιον καὶ Ἁρποκρατίωνα.

Fr. 49 (Test. 41 L.)

(Aeneas Gazaeus, *Theophrastus*, p. 12 Boissonade;
P.G., 85, c. 892 b; p. 12, 1.5-11 M.-E. Colonna [Napoli, 1958])

Πλωτῖνος γοῦν καὶ Ἁρποκρατίων, ἀμέλει καὶ Βοηθὸς καὶ Νουμήνιος τὸν τοῦ Πλάτωνος ἰκτῖνον παραλαβόντες ἰκτῖνον παραδιδόασι, καὶ τὸν λύκον λύκον, καὶ ὄνον τὸν ὄνον, καὶ ὁ πίθηκος αὐτοῖς οὐκ ἄλλο ἢ τοῦτο καὶ ὁ κύκνος οὐκ ἄλλο ἢ
5 κύκνος νομίζεται· καὶ γὰρ πρὸ τοῦ σώματος κακίας ἐμπίμπλασθαι τὴν ψυχὴν δυνατὸν εἶναι λέγουσι καὶ τοῖς ἀλόγοις ἐξεικάζεσθαι· ᾧ γοῦν ὡμοιώθη, κατὰ τοῦτο φέρεται, ἄλλη ἄλλο ζῷον ὑποδῦσα.

47 (Test. 39 L.)

Of those who have stated that (the soul) is separable, some have asserted that all soul is separable from the body: the rational, the irrational, and the vegetative. Such a one was Numenius, led astray by some remarks of Plato who said in the Phaedrus: "All soul is immortal."

48 (Test. 40 L.)

I believe, therefore, that since the ends are different, they also necessitate various manners of descent. For the soul that comes down with a view towards the salvation, purification and perfection of those here causes even the descent to be undefiled. Another, turning towards the corporeal for the sake of the training and correction of its inherent characteristics, is not completely free of passion, nor is it left entirely to itself. And another, descending here for punishment and judgment appears somehow to be dragged and driven along.

But some of those more recent do not make these distinctions, and without having perceived the difference pour the embodiments of all into the same category, and assert strongly that all are evil. And this is especially true of Cronius, Numenius and Harpocration.

49 (Test. 41 L.)

Plotinus and Harpocration, and of course Boethus and Numenius, once having received the kite of Plato hand down a kite, and having received a wolf they hand down a wolf, and having received a mule, they hand down a mule; and the monkey is considered by them to be nothing else than this, and the swan is nothing other than a swan. For before the soul becomes filled with the evil of the body, they say it is capable of resembling irrational creatures. So it assumes a form corresponding to that which it most resembles, each putting on a different living being.

Fr. 50 (Test. 26 L.)

(Proclus, *In Tim.*, III, 196, 12-19 Diehl)

Περὶ δὲ ἁπάντων τῶν κατευθυνόντων τὴν γένεσιν θεῶν λέγωμεν ὡς οὔτε τὴν οὐσίαν ἔχουσι τῇ ὕλῃ συμμεμιγμένην, καθάπερ φασὶν οἱ ἀπὸ τῆς Στοᾶς... οὔτε τὴν μὲν οὐσίαν ἔχουσιν ἀμιγῆ πρὸς τὴν ὕλην τὰς δὲ δυνάμεις καὶ τὰς
5 ἐνεργείας ἀναμεμιγμένας πρὸς αὐτήν, ὡς οἱ περὶ Νουμήνιον λέγουσιν.

Fr. 51 (Test. 28 L.)
(Id., *ibid.*, II, 9, 4-5 Diehl)

Νουμήνιος μὲν οὖν πάντα μεμῖχθαι οἰόμενος οὐδὲν οἴεται εἶναι ἁπλοῦν.

Fr. 52 (Test. 30 L.)

(Calcidius, *In Timaeum*, c. 295-299; p. 297, 7-301, 20 Waszink)

CCXCV. Nunc iam Pythagoricorum dogma recenseatur. Numenius ex Pythagorae magisterio Stoicorum hoc de initiis dogma refellens Pythagorae dogmate, cui concinere dicit dogma platonicum, ait Pythagoram deum quidem singularitatis nomine
5 nominasse, silvam vero duitatis; quam duitatem indeterminatam quidem minime genitam, limitatam vero generatam esse dicere, hoc est, antequam exornaretur quidem formamque et ordinem nancisceretur, sine ortu et generatione, exornatam vero atque illustratam a digestore deo esse generatam, atque ita, quia
10 generationis sit fortuna posterior, inornatum illud minime generatum aequaevum deo, a quo est ordinatum, intellegi debeat. Sed non nullos Pythagoreos vim sententiae non recte assecutos putasse dici etiam illam indeterminatam et immensam duitatem ab unica singularitate institutam recedente a natura sua
15 singularitate et in duitatis habitum migrante—non recte, ut quae erat singularitas esse desineret, quae non erat duitas subsisteret, atque ex deo silva et ex singularitate immensa et indeterminata duitas converteretur; quae opinio ne mediocriter quidem institutis

50 (Test. 26 L.)

And concerning all of the gods that direct the realm of generation, let us say that neither do they have an essence commingled with matter as the Stoics assert, nor do they have an essence unmixed with respect to matter, but powers and activities which are involved with it, as the followers of Numenius say.

51 (Test. 28 L.)

Numenius, then, believing that all things have been mingled, assumes that nothing is simple.

52 (Test. 30 L.)

The teaching of the Pythagoreans must now be reviewed. Numenius, from the school of Pythagoras (with which he says the Platonic doctrine is in harmony), said that Pythagoras gave God the name of Monad, but to matter he gave the name Dyad. This Dyad, he says, when indeterminate is in no way generated, but when limited it is generated; that is, before it was adorned and obtained form and order it was without origin and generation. But once embellished and illumined by the Demiurgic God it is generated; and thus, since the occurrence of generation is subsequent, and when unordered it is in no way generated, it should be considered coeval with God by whom it was brought into order.

But some Pythagoreans, improperly comprehending the force of these notions, suppose even the indeterminate and boundless Dyad to be derived from a single monad as that monad declines from its own nature and passes over into the state of a dyad. Incorrectly, since the monad which existed would cease to be, while the dyad that did not exist would remain. And God would be transformed into matter, and the monad would turn into a boundless and indeterminate dyad—an option which scarcely finds acceptance among educated men.

hominibus competit; denique Stoicos definitam et limitatam silvam esse natura propria, Pythagoram vero infinitam et sine limite dicere, cumque illi quod natura sit immensum non posse ad modum atque ordinem redigi censeant, Pythagoram solius hanc dei fore virtutem ac potentiam asserere, ut quod natura efficere nequeat, deus facile possit, ut qui sit omni virtute potentior atque praestantior, et a quo natura ipsa vires mutuetur.

CCXCVI. Igitur Pythagoras quoque, inquit Numenius, fluidam et sine qualitate silvam esse censet nec tamen, ut Stoici, naturae mediae interque bonorum malorumque viciniam, quod genus illi appellant indifferens, sed plane noxiam. Deum quippe esse—ut etiam Platoni videtur—initium et causam bonorum, silvam malorum, at vero quod ex specie silvaque sit, indifferens, non ergo silvam, sed mundum ex speciei bonitate silvaeque malitia temperatum; denique ex providentia et necessitate progenitum veterum theologorum scitis haberi.

CCXCVII. Silvam igitur informem er carentem qualitate tam Stoici quam Pythagoras consentiunt, sed Pythagoras malignam quoque, Stoici nec bonam nec malam. Dehinc tanquam in progressu viae malis aliquot obviis, perrogati: "Unde igitur mala?" perversitatem seminarium malorum fore causati sunt. Nec expediunt adhuc, unde ipsa perversitas, cum iuxta illos duo sint initia rerum, deus et silva, deus summum et praecellens bonum, silva, ut censent, nec bonum nec malum. Sed Pythagoras assistere veritati miris licet et contra opinionem hominum operantibus asseverationibus non veretur; qui ait existente providentia mala quoque necessario substitisse, propterea quod silva sit et eadem sit malitia praedita. Quod si mundus ex silva, certe factus est de existente olim natura maligna, proptereaque Numenius laudat Heraclitum reprehendentem Homerum, qui optaverit interitum

Finally, the Stoics say that by its own nature matter is definite and limited, but Pythagoras asserts that it is infinite and without limit. And while they are of the opinion that something boundless by nature cannot be brought back into measure and order, Pythagoras maintains that this constitutes the strength and power of God alone: namely, that what nature is unable to effect God can do easily, as befits the one who is more powerful and excellent than any force, and from whom nature itself borrows its powers.

Therefore Pythagoras also, Numenius says, considers matter to be fluid and without quality. He does not however, as the Stoics do, view it as similar to a nature indeterminate between good and evil, a type of thing they label 'indifferent'; rather for him it clearly harmful. For God is (as can also be seen in Plato) the source and cause of good, as matter is of evil. But actually, what consists of form and matter is indifferent; not matter, then, but rather the world which is compounded from the goodness of form and the evil of matter. Finally, it is held by the teachings of ancient theologians that the world is brought forth by providence and necessity.

Thus both the Stoics and Pythagoras agree that matter is formless and without quality, but Pythagoras sees it as evil also; for the Stoics it neither good nor evil. Hence, when evil is encountered, along the way as it were, and they are asked: "Whence therefore is evil?" they answer that perversity is the seed-bed of evil. Nor do they yet explain where the perversity itself has arisen, since according to them there are two principles of things, God and matter: God, the highest and preeminent good; matter, as they believe, neither good nor evil. But Pythagoras is not afraid to assist the truth, even if through surprising and vigorous assertions opposed to the opinion of men. He says that since providence exists, evil too must have persisted because matter exists and it is equipped with malice. For if the world is from matter it was clearly fashioned from the malign nature which was in existence at that time. And therefore Numenius praises Heraclitus for rebuking Homer who wished destruction

ac vastitatem malis vitae, quod non intellegeret mundum sibi deleri placere, siquidem silva, quae malorum fons est, exterminaretur. Platonemque idem Numenius laudat, quod duas mundi animas autemet, unam beneficentissimam, malignam alteram, scilicet silvam, quae, licet incondite fluctuet, tamen, quia intimo proprioque motu movetur, vivat et anima convegetetur necesse est lege eorum omnium quae genuino motu moventur; quae quidem etiam patibilis animae partis, in qua est aliquid corpulentum mortaleque et corporis simile, auctrix est et patrona, sicut rationabilis animae pars auctore utitur ratione ac deo. Porro ex deo et silva factus est iste mundus.

CCXCVIII. Igitur iuxta Platonem mundo bona sua dei tanquam patris liberalitate collata sunt, mala vero matris silvae vitio cohaeserunt. Qua ratione intellegi datur Stoicos frustra causari nescio quam perversitatem, cum quae proveniunt ex motu stellarum provenire dicant. Stellae porro corpora sunt ignesque caelites; omnium quippe corporum silva nutrix, ut etiam quae sidereus motus minus utiliter et improspere turbat originem trahere videantur ex silva, in qua est multa intemperies et improvidus impetus et casus atque ut libet exagitata praesumptio. Itaque si deus eam correxit, ut in Timaeo loquitur Plato, redegitque in ordinem ex incondita et turbulenta iactatione, certe confusa haec intemperies eius casu quodam et improspera sorte habebatur nec ex providentiae consultis salubribus. Ergo iuxta Pythagoram silvae amima neque sine ulla est substantia, ut plerique arbitrantur, et adversatur providentiae consulta eius impugnare gestiens malitiae suae viribus; sed providentia quidem est dei opus et officium, caeca vero fortuitaque temeritas ex prosapia silvae, ut sit evidens iuxta Pythagoram dei silvaeque,

and devastation upon the evils of life, not perceiving that he purposed to destroy the world if in fact matter, which is the source of evil, were to be exterminated. Numenius also praises Plato himself because he posited two world souls: one beneficent, the other malign (clearly matter), which, even though it fluctuates irregularly, because it is moved by interior motion of its own must be alive and activated by a soul, which is the state of all things moved by genuine motion. And it is also the author and patron of the passive part of the soul in which there is everything corporeal and mortal and similar to a body, just as the rational part of the soul claims reason and God as its author. This world, then, has been fashioned from God and matter.

Therefore, according to Plato, the positive aspects of the world are attached to it through the kindness of God as if he were a father, but evil adheres to it through the defect of matter, its mother. Thus it can be understood that the Stoics wrongly give as cause (I don't know what) perversity when they claim that the evil which occurs results from the motion of the stars. Besides, the stars are heavenly bodies and fires, and to be sure, matter is the nurse of all bodies. So that even the events which the motions of the stars disturb to our disadvantage and misfortune can be seen to draw their origin from matter, in which there is much wildness, thoughtless impulse, chance, and, if you will, agitated presumption. For that reason, if God corrects it, as Plato says in the Timaeus, and leads it back into order from a chaotic and turbulent agitation, it clearly received this confused fury through some chance and unfortunate lot, not from the beneficial intentions of providence.

Therefore, according to Pythagoras the soul of matter is not without some substance, as most believe, and it is opposed to providence, desiring to undermine its intentions with the forces of its maliciousness. But providence is the work and function of God, while blind and fortuitous rashness is from the stock of matter; hence it is evident, according to Pythagoras, that the mass

item providentiae fortunaeque coetu cunctae rei molem esse constructam, sed postquam silvae ornatus accesserit, ipsam quidem matrem esse factam corporeorum et nativorum deorum, fortunam vero eius prosperam esse magna ex parte, non tamen usquequaque, quoniam naturale vitium limari omnino nequiret.

CCXCIX. Deus itaque silvam magnifica virtute comebat vitiaque eius omnifariam corrigebat non interficiens, ne natura silvestris funditus interiret, nec vero permittens porrigi dilatarique passim; sed ut manente natura, quae ex incommodo habitu ad prosperitatem devocari commutarique possit, ordinem inordinatae confusioni, modum immoderationi et cultum foeditati coniungens totum statum eius illustrando atque exornando convertit. Denique negat inveniri Numenius—et recte negat—immunem a vitiis usquequaque generatorum fortunam, non in artibus hominum, non in natura, non in corporibus animalium, nec vero in arboribus aut stirpibus, non in frugibus, non in aeris serie nec in aquae tractu, nec in ipso quidem caelo, ubique miscente se providentiae deterioris naturae quasi quodam piaculo. Idemque nudam silvae imaginem demonstrare et velut in lucem destituere studens detractis omnibus singillatim corporibus, quae gremio eius formas invicem mutuantur et invicem mutant, ipsum illud quod ex egestione vacuatum est animo considerari iubet, eamque silvam et necessitatem cognominat; ex qua et deo mundi machinam constitisse deo persuadente, necessitate obsecundante. Haec est Pythagorae de originibus asseveratio.

of the entire cosmos is constructed from a joining of God and matter, as well as providence and chance. But after matter was adorned, she herself became the mother of corporeal and begotten gods; and while her lot is favorable to a great extent, it is not completely so, because her innate defect cannot be totally eliminated.

Thus God adorned matter with a magnificent strength and corrected her defects in every way, while not destroying them lest material nature perish entirely, nor permitting her to spread and expand in every direction. But, while nature stood fast and could thus be called away from a troublesome state to a favorable one and be transformed, by conjoining order to disordered confusion, limit to immoderation, and cultivation to filth, he converted her total state, illuminating and embellishing it. In short, Numenius denies and denies correctly that any condition of generated objects can be found anywhere exempt from defect: not in the arts of man, not in nature, not in the bodies of animals, nor indeed in trees and plants; not in fruits, not in the flow of air or in an expanse of water, nor even in the heaven itself. For everywhere it mingles itself with providence as if it were some stain of an inferior nature.

This same Numenius, striving to present a bare concept of matter, and as it were, set it in the light by individually removing all bodies which one after another borrow their forms from her bosom and interchange them, wishes us to mentally examine the thing itself which has been emptied by abstraction; and this he calls matter and necessity. From this entity and God the fabric of the world was constituted, God persuading and matter obeying. This is the doctrine of Pythagoras concerning origins.

Fr. 53 (33 L.)

(Origenes, *Contra Celsum*, V, 38; II, p. 42, 23-43, 3 Koetschau;
III, p. 116, 29-38 Borret)

Περὶ δὲ Σαράπιδος πολλὴ καὶ διάφωνος ἱστορία, χθὲς καὶ πρώην εἰς μέσον ἐλθόντος κατά τινας μαγγανείας τοῦ βουληθέντος Πτολεμαίου οἱονεὶ ἐπιφανῆ δεῖξαι τοῖς ἐν Ἀλεξανδρείᾳ θεόν. Ἀνέγνωμεν δὲ παρὰ Νουμηνίῳ τῷ
5 Πυθαγορείῳ περὶ τῆς κατασκευῆς αὐτοῦ, ὡς ἄρα πάντων τῶν ὑπὸ φύσεως διοικουμένων μετέχει οὐσίας ζῴων καὶ φυτῶν. ἵνα δόξῃ μετὰ τῶν ἀτελέστων τελετῶν καὶ τῶν καλουσῶν δαίμονας μαγγανειῶν οὐχ ὑπὸ ἀγαλματοποιῶν μόνων κατασκευάζεσθαι θεὸς ἀλλὰ καὶ ὑπὸ μάγων καὶ φαρμακῶν
10 καὶ τῶν ἐπῳδαῖς αὐτῶν κηλουμένων δαιμόνων.

Fr. 54 (38 L.)

(Macrobius, *Saturn.*, I, 17, 65; p. 99, 12-16 Willis)

Ἀπόλλωνα Δέλφιον vocant, quod quae obscura sunt claritudine lucis ostendit ἐκ τοῦ δηλοῦν τὰ ἀφανῆ aut, ut Numenio placet, quasi unum et solum. Ait enim prisca Graecorum lingua δέλφον unum vocari. Unde et frater, inquit, ἀδελφός dicitur quasi iam
5 non unus.

Fr. 55 (39 L.)

(Id., *Comm. in somn. Scipionis*, I, 2, 19; p. 7, 23-8, 3 Willis)

Numenio denique inter philosophos occultorum curiosiori offensam numinum, quod Eleusinia sacra interpretando vulgaverit, somnia prodiderunt, viso sibi ipsas Eleusinias deas habitu meretricio ante apertum lupanar videre prostantes,
5 admirantique et causas non convenientis numinibus turpitudinis consulenti respondisse iratas ab ipso se de adyto pudicitiae suae vi abstractas et passim adeuntibus prostitutas.

53 (33 L.)

Concerning Serapis there is a long and discordant story. It is quite recently that he came into our midst through some subterfuge of Ptolemy who wished to show, as it were, a visible god to those in Alexandria. And we have read in Numenius the Pythagorean about the formation of the god; how he partakes of the essence of all the animals and plants controlled by nature; so that he seems to be established as a god--along with ineffectual rites and the magic formulae that invoke demons--not only by sculptors, but also by magicians, and sorcerers, and the demons held captive by their spells.

54 (38 L.)

They call Apollo the 'Delphian' because he displays what is obscure in the clarity of light ("from the one making the invisible manifest"); or as Numenius believes, as meaning 'one and only'. For he claims that in the ancient Greek language 'one' is designated by 'delphos'. Therefore he also says that brother is indicated by 'adelphos' since it is indeed 'not one'.

55 (39 L.)

Again, dreams disclosed the displeasure of the divinities to Numenius (who among philosophers is rather curious about occult matters), because while interpreting the Eleusinian rites he made them public: it seemed to him that he saw the Eleusinian goddesses themselves, standing in harlots' clothing before an open brothel. And when he marveled at this and demanded the reasons for a disgrace not befitting divinity, they responded in anger that they had been violently dragged away from the sanctuary of their chastity, and had been prostituted everywhere to those coming to them by Numenius himself.

Fr. 56 (34 L.)
(Lydus, *De mensibus*, IV, 53; p. 109, 25-110, 4 Wünsch)

Ὁ Λούκανος ἀδήλου θεοῦ τὸν ἐν Ἱεροσολύμοις ναὸν εἶναι λέγει, ὁ δὲ Νουμήνιος ἀκοινώνητον αὐτὸν καὶ πατέρα πάντων τῶν θεῶν εἶναι λέγει, ἀπαξιοῦντα κοινωνεῖν αὐτῷ τῆς τιμῆς τινα.

Fr. 57 (35 L.)
(Id., *ibid.*, IV, 80; p. 132, 11-15 W.)

Νουμήνιος δ' ὁ Ῥωμαῖος τὸν Ἑρμῆν τὸν προχωρητικὸν λόγον εἶναι βούλεται· οὐδὲ γάρ, φησι, πρότερον βρέφος φθέγξαιτο, πρὶν ἂν τῆς γῆς ἐφάψαιτο, ὥστε Μαῖαν εἰς γῆν καλῶς ἐξελάμβανον οἱ πολλοί.

Fr. 58 (36 L.)
(Id., *ibid.*, IV, 86; p. 135, 13-17 W.)

Ὁ Ἥφαιστος, ὥς φησι Νουμήνιος, γόνιμον πῦρ ἐστιν, ἡ τοῦ ἡλίου ζωογονικὴ θερμότης· διὸ δὴ καὶ χωλὸν ποιοῦσι τὸν Ἥφαιστον, καθ' ὃ χωλεύει καθ' ἑαυτὴν ἡ τοῦ πυρὸς φύσις, ὅταν μὴ συγκεκρότηται τοῖς ἄλλοις.

Fr. 59 (37 L.)
(Id., *ibid.*,; p. 184, 10-13 W.;
inter "fragmenta libris de mensibus falso tributa")

Φασὶ γὰρ τὴν Νέμεσιν τὰ γλαφυρὰ τῶν πραγμάτων εἰς τὸ ἔμπαλιν τρέπειν ταῖς ὑπερβολαῖς τῆς τύχης, ὥς φησι Νουμήνιος, τῷ δ' αὐτῷ τροχῷ τὴν ἰσότητα ἐπάγουσαν.

56 (34 L.)

Lucan says that the temple in Jerusalem belongs to an unknown god, but Numenius argues that he is incommunicable and father of all the gods, who does not deem anyone worthy of the honor of communicating with him.

57 (35 L.)

Numenius the Roman interprets Hermes as the uttered word. For, as he says, an infant does not speak until it touches the earth, so that the majority of men did well when they understood Maia to be the Earth.

58 (36 L.)

Hephaestus, as Numenius says, is productive fire—the generative heat of the sun. Indeed, Hephaestus is also considered to be lame, since the nature of fire is lame by itself when it has not been welded to the other (elements).

59 (37 L.)

For they say that Nemesis turns elegant affairs back in the other direction through the extremities of chance; as Numenius says, bringing in equality by the same wheel.

Fragmentum dubium

Fr. 60

(Porphyr., *De antro nympharum*, 5-6;

p. 59, 1-2 et 60, 1-14 Nauck²; p. 6, 21-22 et 8, 13-23 West.)

[5] Ἄντρα μὲν δὴ ἐπιεικῶς οἱ παλαιοὶ καὶ σπήλαια τῷ κόσμῳ καθιέρουν...

[6] Οὕτω καὶ Πέρσαι τὴν εἰς κάτω κάθοδον τῶν ψυχῶν καὶ πάλιν ἔξοδον μυσταγωγοῦντες τελοῦσι τὸν μύστην,
5 ἐπονομάσαντες σπήλαιον <τὸν> τόπον· πρώτου μέν, ὥς φησιν Εὔβουλος, Ζωροάστρου αὐτοφυὲς σπήλαιον ἐν τοῖς πλησίον ὄρεσι τῆς Περσίδος ἀνθηρὸν καὶ πηγὰς ἔχον ἀνιερώσαντος εἰς τιμὴν τοῦ πάντων ποιητοῦ καὶ πατρὸς Μίθρου, εἰκόνα φέροντος αὐτῷ τοῦ σπηλαίου τοῦ κόσμου, ὃν ὁ Μίθρας
15 ἐδημιούργησε, τῶν δ' ἐντὸς κατὰ συμμέτρους ἀποστάσεις σύμβολα φερόντων τῶν κοσμικῶν στοιχείων καὶ κλιμάτων· μετὰ δὲ τοῦτον τὸν Ζωροάστρην κρατήσαντος καὶ παρὰ τοῖς ἄλλοις, δι' ἄντρων καὶ σπηλαίων εἴτ' οὖν αὐτοφυῶν εἴτε χειροποιήτων τὰς τελετὰς ἀποδιδόναι.

Dubious Fragment

Fr. 60

[5] The ancients would quite appropriately consecrate caves and caverns to the cosmos…

[6] In this fashion also the Persians, while esoterically commemorating the descent of souls below and their going out again, initiate the aspirant, calling the place a cavern. Zoroaster was the first, as Eubulus says, to dedicate a splendid spring-fed natural cavern in the neighboring mountains of Persia in honor of Mithra, the maker and father of all things, since the cavern bore for him the image of the world which Mithra created; and the objects inside, (placed) at measured intervals, bore symbols of the elements and the latitudes of the world. After this Zoroaster, when (the custom) became prevalent among the rest, they performed their initiations in caves or caverns, either natural or man-made.

COMMENTARY

Fr. 1a

l. 3. Εἰς δὲ τοῦτο...: The subject matter of τοῦτο is provided by Origen Fr. 1b: Νουμήνιος, ὅστις...λέγων περὶ τῶν ἐθνῶν ὅσα περὶ τοῦ θεοῦ ὡς ἀσωμάτου διείληφεν. It would appear that much of the first two books of Περὶ τοῦ θεοῦ consisted of a discussion of the technical term ἀσώματος; cf. fr. 4a, l. 27, 31 and note; fr. 6, l. 2, 15 and note; fr. 7, l. 2.

l. 4 ἀναχωρήσασθαι...τοῦ Πυθαγόρου: The traditional catagorization of Numenius as 'Neopythagorean' by some scholars is based to a large extent on statements like this, but such an ascription tends to obscure the essential Middle Platonic character of his thought. For a full discussion of this matter see the notes on Fr. 1b, l. 3.

l. 5. ἐπικαλέσασθαι δὲ τὰ ἔθνη τὰ εὐδοκιμοῦντα...Βραχμᾶνες καὶ Ἰουδαῖοι καὶ Μάγοι καὶ Αἰγύπτιοι: This passage has justly attracted much scholarly attention and inspired a great deal of commentary. Puech employed it as the impetus and focus of his seminal article "Numénius d'Apamée et les théologies orientales au second siècle." On p. 27 he defines the issue: "Ce ne'est pas nous, en effet, qui inventons le problème des influences orientales sur la penseé de Numénius: lui-même nous en signifie la réalité. Le premier livre du Περὶ τἀγαθοῦ (*Du bien*) contient un "appel à l'Orient", un programme défini de syncrétisme..." Festugière translates the fragment and uses it as a set piece at the beginning of the second chapter of *Révélation* Vol. I, entitled "Les prophètes de l'Orient." But since (unlike Puech) he is viewing Numenius from a non-polemical position, Festugière is able to provide a more balanced perspective on the text. He describes it as "ces lignes typiques" (p.

19), and provides a classic interpretation of the theme: "Si toute doctrine prenait d'autant plus d'autorité que'elle revêtait un caractère de révélation et que cette révélation tirait son origine d'un plus lointain passé, ne fallait-il pas remonter, au delà de Pythagore, jusqu'a des sagesses plus proches encore du divin et qui, pour ainsi dire n'avaient plus d'âge." He illustrates the "typical" nature of the motif by cataloguing other instances of its occurrence: Diogenes Laertius (*Prooem.* I, 1): τὸ τῆς φιλοσοφίας ἔργον ἔνιοι φασιν ἀπὸ βαρβάρων ἄρξαι. Γεγενῆσθαι γὰρ παρὰ μὲν Πέρσαις Μάγουσι, παρὰ δὲ βαβυλωνίοις ἢ Ἀσσυρίοις Χαλδαίους, καὶ Γυμνοσοφιστὰς παρ' Ἰνδοῖς; Arnobius (*adv. nat.* IV, 3): Ne nobis fidem habere nolitis, Ægyptios Persas Indos Chaldaeos Armenios interogetis omnesque illos alios, qui interioribus viderunt et cognoverunt haec artibus...; Jerome (Epist. 60, 4. 2) Indus Persa Gothus Ægyptius philosophantur; Augustine (*Civ. Dei*, VIII, 9: sive Platonici...sive Italici...sive aliarum quoque gentium qui sapientes vel philosphi habitui sunt, Atlantici Libyes Ægypti Indi Persae Chaldaei Scythae Galli Hispani aliique reperiuntur qui hoc viderunt. To this list should be added Clement of Alexandria *Stromata* I, 15 *passim*, and Celsus *apud*. Origen, *Contra Celsum*, I, 14: Ἄκουε γὰρ λέγοντος τοῦ Κέλσου ὅτι ἔστιν ἀρχαῖος ἄνωθεν λόγος, περὶ ὃν δὴ ἀεὶ καὶ τὰ ἔθνη τὰ σοφώτατα καὶ πόλεις καὶ ἄνδρες σοφοὶ κατεγένετο. Καὶ οὐκ ἐβουλήθη ἔθνος σοφώτατον εἰπεῖν κἂν παραπλησίως Αἰγυπτίοις καὶ Ἀσσυρίοις καὶ Ἰνδοῖς καὶ Πέρσαις καὶ Ὀδρύσαις καὶ Σαμόθραξι καὶ Ἐλευσινίοις τοὺς Ἰουδαίους. Dörrie (*Vom Transz.*, p. 197) provides an interpretation similar to that of Festugière: "Hinter dem Postulat *veteres sequi* verbirgt sich die Überzeugung, daß in der Gegenwart niemand mehr eine solche Fülle der Erkenntnis besitzen könne." He suggests that the Posidonian concept of a primitive communication with the "Welt-Logos" which is now unachievable lies behind this notion, and no doubt it had a direct influence. But as Festugière points out (*op. cit.* p. 20): "Le mirage oriental avait toujours séduit les imaginations de la Grèce."

Waszink (p. 47) concurs: Nun hat bekanntlich das Streben, die reine Wahrheit in einer entfernten Vergangenheit zu finden, keineswegs mit dem mittleren Platonismus, geschweige denn mit Numenios, angefangen." He too mentions Posidonius as a direct influence on Middle Platonism, but also cites a more fundamental source in the statement of Plato at *Philebus* 16c: Καὶ οἱ μὲν παλαιοί, κρείττονες ἡμῶν καὶ ἐγγυτέρω θεῶν οἰκοῦντες; cf. also the narrative of Critias at *Tim.* 22b relating the Egyptian priest's opinion of Greece: ' ῏Ω Σόλων, Σόλων, ῞Ελληνες ἀεὶ παῖδές ἐστε...Νέοι ἐστε,' εἰπεῖν, 'τὰς ψυχὰς πάντες · οὐδεμίαν γὰρ ἐν αὐταῖς ἔχετε δι' ἀρχαίαν ἀκοὴν παλαιὰν δόξαν οὐδὲ μάθημα χρόνῳ πολιὸν οὐδέν.' (But compare the more positive attitude in *Epinomis* 987d: λάβωμεν δὲ ὡς ὅτιπερ ἂν ῞Ελληνες Βαρβάρων παραλάβωσι, κάλλιον τοῦτο εἰς τέλος ἀπεργάζονται). Another significant passage in this context is the encouragement given by Socrates to Cebes at *Phaedo* 78a: πολλὰ δὲ καὶ τὰ τῶν βαρβάρων γένη, οὓς πάντας χρὴ διερευνᾶσθαι ζητοῦντας τοιοῦτον ἐπῳδόν. Plutarch, considered to be a more "orthodox" Middle Platonist by most scholars, expresses this motif in a text that has some verbal parallels with our fragment. At *De Iside* 45, while leading up to a discussion of a Zoroastrian type of dualism, he says this about the δόξα he is about to introduce:...οὐκ ἐν λόγοις μόνον οὐδ' φήμαις, ἀλλ' ἔν τε τελεταῖς ἔν τε θυσίαις καὶ βαρβάροις καὶ ῞Ελλησι πολλαχοῦ περιφερομένη. Cf. l. 6-7 of this fragment: τὰς τελετάς...τάς τε ἱδρύσεις. Also cf. Maximus of Tyre, XI, 5 (Hobein): ὅτι θεὸς εἷς πάντων βασιλεύς...Ταῦτα καὶ ὁ ῞Ελλην λέγει, καὶ ὁ Βάρβαρος λέγει. A remark by Lewy (p. 314, n. 7) admirably sums up the whole issue: "The orientalism of Numenius is overestimated. The origin of his principal doctrines can be explained by the inner development of Platonic-Pythagorean transcendental philosophy; his frequent references to Oriental doctrines, by his theory of the Oriental origin of the Pythagorean philosophy reflected in Platonism...His principle work, *περὶ τἀγαθοῦ*, was a dialogue which may have resembled those of Plutarch, and offered plentiful opportunities for Oriental and other adornments."

For a thorough discussion of the information about oriental religions that was available to writers during this period, see Festugière (*op. cit.*), Hopfner, *Orient und griechische Philosophie*, Sedlar, *India and the Greek World* and McEvilley, *The Shape of Ancient Thought*.

l. 7. ἱδρύσεις: Dodds' attempt (*N. and A.*, p. 10) to link this term with "the fabrication of magical images" is criticized by Waszink (*P. und N.*, p.46): "Ich diese τελεταί und ἱδρύσεις nicht mit Dodds, auf die Anfertigung von magischen Kultbildern, wie sie im fr. 53 des Numenios zur Sprache commt, beziehen möchte: schon die in der Mitte der Aufzählung erwähnten δόγαμτα genügend m. E. um diese Deutung zu widerraten."

ll. 7-8. Πλάτωνι ὁμολογουμένως: Waszink (*P. und N.*, p.46) points to this phrase as further evidence that the teaching of Plato is fundamental to Numenius' thought.

Fr. 1b

l. 4. ὁ Πυθαγόρειος Νουμήνιος: Numenius has traditionally been categorized as a 'Neopythagorean' by writers both ancient and modern. Leemans (Test. 4.), Puech (p. 45, n.4), and Waszink (*P. und N.* p. 37) provide catalogues of ancient authors who viewed him either as Πυθαγορικός or Πλατωνικός. Clement of Alexandria (*Strom.*, I, 22) calls him Ὁ Πυθαγόρειος, and for Origen also, as in this fragment and fragments 1c, 29 and 53, Numenius is Ὁ Πυθαγόρειος. Eusebius refers to him as Πυθαγορικός (fragments 1a, and 5), or Ὁ Πυθαγόρειος (fr. 24). Longinus (*apud* Porph. *Vita Plotini* 21) lists Numenius as one of the Pythagoreans that Plotinus surpassed in accuracy. Calcidius (fr. 52) employs him as his source for the Pythagorean doctrine of Matter.

But he has also been grouped with Platonists, by other Platonists. In his Περί ψυχῆς (fr. 43), Iamblichus includes him ἐν αὐτοῖς τοῖς Πλατωνικοῖς, and Proclus (*In Remp.*, II, 96, 11) places him at the head of a list of distinguished Platonists: τῶν Πλατωνικῶν οἱ κορυφαῖοι. Νουμήνιος, Ἀλβῖνος, Γάιος, Μάξιμος ὁ Νικαεύς... How then is he to be categorized?

The issue would seem to be a simple one. Indeed, Numenius paints himself in Pythagorean colors by some remarks that are extant in the fragments. As was seen in fr. 1, he feels that it is crucial to go back beyond Plato (ἀναχωρήσασθαι) and examine the teachings of Pythogoras. In fr. 7 he seeks to lend weight to his statements concerning τὸ ὄν by saying that if they do not agree with the teachings of Plato, then they certainly agree with those "of a great, powerful man, such as Pythagoras." In fr. 24, ll. 18-20 he places Plato and Pythagoras on the same level: Καίτοι ἄξιος ἦν αὐτοῖς ὁ Πλάτων, οὐκ ἀμείνων μὲν Πυθαγόρου τοῦ μεγάλου, οὐ μέντοι ἴσως οὐδὲ φλαυρότερος ἐκείνου. At l. 55 he makes Plato himself a Pythogorean: Ὁ δὲ Πλάτων πυθαγόρισας, and goes further to say that Socrates also derived his teachings from the same source. At ll. 67-68 he concludes: ἐάσομεν αὐτὸν (sc. Πλάτων) νῦν ἐφ᾽ ἑαυτοῦ νῦν εἶναι Πυθαγόρειον.

Scholars have reacted to this evidence in varying ways. Zeller (III. 2[4], 235), while recognizing that Numenius characterized himself as a Pythagorean, still felt compelled to include him in his discussion of Middle Platonism because "in seinen Ansichten das platonische fast noch stärker hervortritt als das neupythagoreische." For Puech, Numenius is merely a foreign body attached to the Greek tradition, destroying it from within. Dodds (*N. and A.* V, p. 11) feels that "the main fabric of Numenius' thought is no doubt derived from Neopythagorean tradition (I should call him a Neopythagorean rather than a Middle Platonist)." At *Pagan*, p. 93, he refers to him as " the second-century Pythagorean." Beutler, in his article on Numenius for the Pauly-Wissova (col. 667), takes the opposite view: "Der Kern der Lehren des N. is aber als mittelplatonisch völlig einwandfrei zu bestimmen." Festugière (*Révél.* vol. III, p. 42, n. 1) agrees: "Je m'accorde entièrement avec cet auteur quand il dit...(quotes Beutler). Cf. also vol. IV, p. 131: "dans les fragments conservés, il raisonne, en bon disciple de Platon, d'après la pure méthode argumentative usitée dans les écoles." Martano (p. 84) also adheres to this view: "(senza dimenticare gli apprezzamenti degli antichi che lo ritenevano un pitagorico) appare a noi, sulla base dei frammenti che possediamo, essenzialmente un platonico con vive tinte di pitagorismo." Nilsson (*Greek Piety*, p. 132), refers to Numenius as a "Platonizing Neopythagorean." Van Winden (*Calcidius*, p. 105) takes a somewhat contradictory stance: "Numenius undoubtedly derived much from Plato for the description of Pythagoras' doctrine. The ususal description of Pythagoras' doctrine in Antiquity must owe as much to Plato's system as Plato actually owed to Pythagoras. However, this influence of Plato on Numenius is not yet reason for calling Numenius a Platonist, as Zeller did on the example of Jamblichus and Proclus." Dillon's position is similar (MP, p. 341). In the introduction to his section on Neopythagoreanism, after stressing the heightened interest in Pythagoras which was already exhibited by the immediate successors to Plato, and pointing out that Pythagorean number symbolism was employed by Plutarch, he continues: "But while a greater degree of Pythagorean influence than before now permeates orthodox Platonism, there are also on the fringes of Platonism, in the first and second centuries A.D., men who profess themselves to be Pythagoreans, and these men are in fact sufficiently closely linked with Platonism to require treatement in this work."

    The remarks of van Winden and Dillon point to the source of ambiguity inherent in this issue, *i.e.* the Old Academy took such a great interest in Pythagorean doctrines, an interest that persisted and continued to develop, that by the time of Numenius it becomes difficult to draw the line between 'orthodox' Platonism and Neopythagoreanism. The extensive labors of H.J. Krämer (*Ursprung*, p. 1-111) have brought this problem into sharp focus. His detailed study of the "Strom des Platonismus" that begins with Xenocrates leads him to the conclusion that "die Erscheinung des pythagorisierenden Platonismus von der Alten Akademie selbst ihren Ausgang genommen hat," and that "die geschichtliche Selbstdeutung der Akademie im sinne einer Pythagoras-Nachfolge wird in der Tat durch die angelegentliche Beschäftigung fast aller Platonschüler mit der Geschichte de Pythagoreismus bestätigt (*Ursprung*, p. 53)." His statement (p. 48) that "eine klare Abgrenzung außerordentlich schwierig und nur selten möglich ist," is echoed by two other scholars. Wallis (*Neoplatonism*, p. 32), states: "Neopythagoreanism's metaphysical doctrines are not easlily distinguished from those of Middle Platonism and some of its representatives, like Numenius of Apamea, are indifferently assigned by our sources to both schools." Armstrong (*Plot.* vol. I, p. 40, n. 1), while commenting on Porphyry's *Vita Plotini*, 14, says virtually the same thing: "Cronius and Numenius are usually mentioned together and classed as Pythagoreans, though the boundary between Platonists and Pythagoreans was ill-defined, and Porphyry here quite naturally groups them with the Platonists."

Waszink (*P. und N.*, p. 37-39) thought this issue important enough to interrupt his insightful study of Porphyry's relationship to Numenius in order to discuss it ("Es ist nach meinem Dafürhalten noch immer nich überflüßig, einige Worte der schon in den antiken zeugnissen zum Ausdruck kommenden Frage zu widmen, ob wir Numenios primär als Neupythagoreer zu betrachten haben, wie Dodds annimmt, oder als Vertreter des mittleren Platonismus.") In his discussion he suggests that Numenius' Pythagoreanism consists more of a self-concious stance ("für sein eigenes Bewußtsein") in which the Pythagorean element is exaggerated beyond actual doctrinal content (cf.

Dillon's "men who profess themselves to be Pythagoreans"). His conclusion, which should now be considered normative, harmonizes with the judgements of Beutler, Festugière and Martano: "...in der Praxis wurzelt seine Philosophie doch hauptsächliche im Platonismus, and ganz besonders in der spezifischen, immer als Platondeutung auftretenden, Problematik des mittleren Platonismus."

l. 5. ὅσα περὶ τοῦ θεοῦ ὡς ἀσωμάτου διείληφεν: Cf. fr. 1a, l. 3 and note.

l. 6-8. ἐκατέταξεν αὐτοῖς καὶ τούς Ἰουδαίους...τροπολοῆσαι αὐτοῦς: See notes to fr. 1c.

Fr. 1c

l.1-3 πολλαχοῦ...ἐκτιθέμενον τὰ Μωϋσέως καὶ τῶν προφητῶν...τροπολογοῦντα: This notice by Origen that Numenius often (πολλαχοῦ) allegorized narratives from the Hebrew Bible is one of the most tantalizing reports we have, and makes it all the more regrettable that so little of his writing has survived. Of course it immediately raises the question of whether Numenius was influenced by Philo, and a number of scholars have addressed this issue. In 1860 Möller (p. 107) had already set out the few verbal parallels between the two that can be discerned. He draws attention to Numenius' use of ἑστώς with reference to his First God, a usage that is found frequently in Philo (see notes to fr. 5, l. 25). Numenius' characterization of his Demiurge as διττός recalls Philo's use of the same word to describe his λόγος (see notes to fr. 11, ll. 15-21 and fr. 16, l. 10). Waszink (*P & N* p. 50, n. 4) reviews this short list and adds Numenius' description of the First God as ὁ ὤν in fr. 13 (cf. *Leg. All.* III, 181), and Numenius' use of the concept of προσχρήσις in fr. 22 (cf. *Leg. All.* III, 96. See also fr. 22, l. 2 and note). Other scholars who have detected possible Philonic influene are Zeller (III², p. 237, n. 4), Theiler (*Forschungen*, p. 149), Puech (p. 761), Festugière (*Révélation* III, p.

44, nn. 2-4; IV, p. 40, n. 2), Martano (p. 93) and Krämer (p. 65). Dodds (*Pagan* p. 130, n. 2) states: "Allegorical interpretation of the Old Testament was introduced to the pagan world by Numenius who perhaps drew on Philo." Lewy (p. 314, n. 7) is not convinced: "His knowledge of Philo is no more demonstrable than is that of Plotinus." This is perhaps the controlling opinion on the side of caution, for verbal parallels are few and can often be explained by other sources. However given Numenius' tremendous respect for the Jews and his predilection for allegory, it seems natural to assume that he had some acquaintance with Philo. It will be seen throughout the commentary that the two men share a broad range of Middle Platonic concepts and vocabulary.

Fr. 2

This fragment stands as a small masterpiece in the history of contemplative literature. Festugière (*Révélation* vol. IV, p. 129) refers to it as "ce beau fragment", and chooses "this text of such wondrous beauty" to conclude his *Personal Religion Among the Greeks* (pp. 138-139). Even such a harsh critic of Numenius as Dodds has been forced to recognize its unusual character. In *N. and A.*, p. 17 he says: "Nevertheless, this fragment of Numenius is an impressive piece of writing, and I think Plotinus was familiar with it." In *Pagan*, p. 93, he speaks of a "personal note" in the fragment, and concludes (p. 94): "Plotinus has a good many echoes of this remarkable passage, and I think it is a reasonable assumption that he understood it as a description of mystical union." Dillon (p. 372), like Festugière, translates the fragment in its entirety and describes it as "a vivid poetical elaboration" of Plato *Ep*. VII, 341c.

ll. 1-2. τὴν τοῦ Πλάτωνος διάνοιαν ἑρμηνεύων: Festugière (*op. cit.*) calls attention to these words in a remark no doubt aimed at "l'école orientaliste": "On notera que, dans son introduction à ce beau fragment, Eusebius marque que Numénius se fait ici l'exégète de Platon." Cf. fr. 11, l. 1: Ὁ δὲ Νουμήνιος τὰ Πλάτωνος πρεσβεύων...διερμηνεύει.

ll. 3-5. σημαινομένοις ἔκ τε ὁμοίων ἀπό τε τῶν ἐν τοῖς παρακειμένοις γνωρισμάτων ἐνόντων: This is Numenius' peculiar adumbration for the Greek epistemological commonplace "like is known by like"; cf. Tim., 45c: ἐκπῖπτον ὅμοιον πρὸς ὅμοιον; Philo, De Gig., 9: ἵνα πρὸς τῶν ὁμοίων τὸ ὅμοιον θεωρῆται; Albinus XIV, 2: τῷ ὁμοίῳ τὸ ὅμοιον γνωρίζεται; Plotinus VI. 9. 11: συγγίνεται τῷ ὁμοίῳ τὸ ὅμοιον. The origin of the concept goes back at least to Empedocles, who is quoted by Aristotle at De An., 404b. Aristotle then goes on to say that Plato was guided by this principle when he constructed the World Soul in the Timaeus: τὸν αὐτὸν τρόπον καὶ Πλάτων ἐν τῷ Τιμαίῳ τὴν ψυχὴν ἐκ τῶν στοιχείων ποιεῖ· γινώσκεσθαι γὰρ τῷ ὁμοίῳ τὸ ὅμοιον; cf. Metaph. 1000b: ἡ γνῶσις τοῦ ὁμοίου τῷ ὁμοίῳ. As Cherniss points out (Plutarch, vol. XIII, part 1. p.167, n. e), the Aristotelian interpretation was accepted almost universally by later commentators, i.e. Albinus, loc. cit.; Sextus, Adv. Math., i. 303; Calcidius, Platonis Timaeus, p.100, 8-22 [Waszink]; Proclus, In Platonis Timaeum, ii, p. 135, 23-30 and p. 298, 2-31 [Diehl]. See also Cornford, Plato's Cosmology, pp. 64-65, 94 and 97; Taylor, A Commentary on Plato's Timaeus, p. 133. Here, Numenius is only interested in using the familiar principle to emphasize the stark contrast in the modes of perception needed to apprehend τὰ σώματα on one hand and τἀγαθόν on the other.

ll. 5-6: τἀγαθὸν δὲ οὐδενὸς ἐκ παρακειμένου...οὐδεμία: Cf. Phd. 79a: Οὐκοῦν τούτων μὲν κἂν ἅψαιο κἂν ἴδοις κἂν ταῖς ἄλλαις αἰσθήσεσιν αἴσθοιο, τῶν δὲ κατὰ ταὐτὰ ἐχόντων οὐκ ἔστιν ὅτῳ ποτ' ἄλλῳ ἐπιλάβοιο ἢ τῷ τῆς διανοίας λογισμῷ; Pol. 285e-286a: τοῖς δ' αὖ μεγίστοις οὖσι καὶ τιμιωτάτοις οὐκ ἔστιν εἴδωλον οὐδὲν πρὸς τοὺς ἀνθρώπους εἰργασμένον ἐναργῶς. (This section of the Politicus may well have served as a model for discussions of this type.)

If the notion of τῷ ὁμοίῳ τὸ ὅμοιον γνωρίζεται had become a Platonic commonplace by the second century C.E., its counterpart, the doctrine that the highest level of reality (whether conceived as τἀγαθόν, τὸ ἕν, τὸ ὄν, or ὁ θεός) transcended all human categories and the perceptions associated with them, had also become just as fundamental. It can be seen in Philo, *Leg. All.*, II 1: οὐδὲν δε ὅμοιον θεῷ; *De Opfic.*, 100: (Quoting Philolaus: Ἔστι γὰρ φησίν, ἡγεμὼν...αὐτὸς αὐτῷ ὅμοιος, ἕτερος τῶν ἄλλων; *De Som.*, I, 184: ...ὅτι οὐδενὶ τῶν ἐν γενέσει τὸ ἀγένητον ὅμοιον. It also appears in the *Corpus Hermeticum,* cf. V, 2: ὁ δὲ εἷς ἀγέννητος δηλονότι καὶ ἀφαντασίαστος; IV, 9: τὸ δὲ ἀγαθὸν ἀφανὲς τοῖς φανεροῖς. οὐ γὰρ μορφὴ οὔτε τύπος ἐστὶν αὐτοῦ. διὰ τοῦτο αὐτῷ μὲν ἐστιν ὅμοιον, τοῖς ἄλλοις πᾶσιν ἀνόμοιον. ἀδύνατον γὰρ ἀσώματον σώματι φανῆναι; XI, 5: οὐδὲν γὰρ ὅμοιον τῷ ἀνομοίῳ καὶ μόνῳ καὶ ἑνί; Celsus VI, 63: οὐδ' ἄνθρωπον ἐποίησεν εἰκόνα αὐτοῦ· οὐ γὰρ τοιόσδε ὁ θεὸς οὔτ' ἄλλῳ εἴδει οὐδενὶ ὅμοιος.

l. 7. **οἷον εἴ τις ἐπὶ σκοπῇ καθημένος**: Cf. Plato, *Rep.*, 445c: ὥσπερ ἀπὸ σκοπιᾶς μοι φαίναται; Philo, *Spec. Leg.*, III, 48: μακρόθεν δ' ὡς ἀπὸ σκοπῆς. Festugière (*Révélation, op. cit.*, p. 111, n. 1 and p. 129, n. 3) draws our attention to a passage in Maximus of Tyre, XI, 6 (Hobein): ἡμεῖς δὲ ἆρα οὐ τολμήσομεν ἀναβιβασάμενοι τὸν λογισμὸν εἰς τινα περιωπὴν ἄνω τῆς ψυχῆς περισκέψασθαι τὰ τοῦ θεοῦ ἴχνη.

l. 8. **μίαν, μόνην, ἔρημον**: The phrase is inspired by *Tim.* 34b and its description of οὐρανός as ἕνα μόνον ἔρημον. Cf. *Philebus* 63b (in a different context): Τὸ μόνον καὶ ἔρημον εἰλικρινές. Plotinus uses this type of language in discussions of τὸ ἕν and τἀγαθόν. Cf. V. 3. 10: οὐδὲ γὰρ ἔχει τὸ ἕν πάντη εἰς τί ἐνεργήσει, ἀλλὰ μόνον καὶ ἔρημον ὂν πάντη στήσεται· V. 5. 13: εἰ οὖν μήτε τὸ οὐκ ἀγαθὸν μήτε τὸ ἀγαθὸν ἔχει, οὐδὲν ἔχει. εἰ οὖν 'οὐδὲν ἔχει,' μόνον καὶ ἔρημον τῶν ἄλλων ἐστίν· VI. 7. 25: ὅθεν καὶ τὸ ἔρημον καὶ μόνον μηδὲν ἔχειν ἀγαθόν, ἀλλ' εἶναι ἑτέρως καὶ μειζόνως.

114 *Commentary*

l. 9-10. ὀξὺ δεδορκώς μιᾷ βολῇ κατεῖδε τὴν ναῦν: The phrase as a whole indicates an instantaneous perception. Plato uses the adverb ἐξαίφνης in two famous passages to express the same phenomenon. Dillon (*loc. cit.*) believes that the *Seventh Letter* (341c) is Numenius' model here: ῥητὸν γὰρ οὐδαμῶς ἐστιν ὡς ἄλλα μαθήματα, ἀλλ᾽ ἐκ πολλῆς συνουσίας γιγνομένης περὶ τὸ πρᾶγμα αὐτὸ καὶ τοῦ συζῆν ἐξαίφνης, οἷον ἀπὸ πυρὸς πηδήσαντος ἐξαφθὲν φῶς...; Cf. Plotinus 5. 3. 17: ὅταν ἡ ψυχὴ ἐξαίφνης φῶς λάβῃ. Festugière (*op. cit.*, p 129, n. 5) suggests *Symposium* 210e as an analogue: πρὸς τέλος ἤδη ἰὼν τῶν ἐρωτικῶν ἐξαίφνης κατόψεταί τι θαυμαστὸν τὴν φύσιν καλόν.

ὀξὺ δεδορκώς: The expression recalls the language of *Symp.* 219a: ἥ τοι τῆς διανοίας ὄψις ἄρχεται ὀξὺ βλέπειν ὅταν ἡ τῶν ὀμμάτων τῆς ἀκμῆς λήγειν ἐπιχειρῇ. Cf. Albinus VII, 2: ὀξύτατα διανοίας· Plotinus 5.8.10: ἀλλ᾽ ἔχει τὸ ὀξέως ὁρῶν ἐν αὐτῷ τὸ ὁρώμενον.

μιᾷ βολῇ: Cf. Maximus of Tyre XI. 9a: ὀφθαλμοῦ μὲν γὰρ βολὴ ὀξύτατον, ἀθρόως σπῶσα τὴν αἴσθησιν τοῦ ὁρωμένου. Dodds (*N. and A.*, p. 18) notes that this use of βολή "in the sense of 'a glance'" is rare, and points to its use in Plotinus' early treatise on Beauty (I. 6. 2): Ἔστι (sc. τὸ καλὸν) μὲν γὰρ τι καὶ βολῇ τῇ πρώτῃ αἰσθητὸν γινόμενον. See also Dodd's note (*loc. cit.*) concerning Plotinus' use of βαλεῖν in the sense of ἐπιβαλεῖν.

κατεῖδε: Festugière (*op.cit.*, n. 4) explains the force of the aorist, which he feels is reinforced by μιᾷ βολῇ: "Ce aperception est unique." Des Places (p. 105, n. 3) feels that "l'instantané de la vision explique l'aoriste." The verb is used by Plato in the *Symposium*, 211e in a similar context: ἀλλ᾽ αὐτὸ το θεῖον καλὸν δύναιτο μονοειδὲς κατιδεῖν.

l. 10. δεῖ τινα ἀπελθόντα πόρρω ἀπὸ τῶν αἰσθητῶν: The Platonic belief that the senses present an obstacle to the perception of higher reality receives its classic expression in the *Phaedo*. The section 64a-68b, which presents Socrates' description of the 'true' philosopher's 'rehearsal for death' (see Burnet,

Phaedo, p. 28), provides many examples of this type of language. Perhaps the most representative is 65e-66a: ...μήτε τιν' ὄψιν παρατιθέμενος ἐν τῷ διανοεῖσθαι μήτε ἄλλην αἴσθησιν ἐφέλκων μηδεμίαν...ἀπαλλαγεὶς ὅτι μάλιστα ὀφθαλμῶν τε καὶ ὤτων καὶ ὡς ἔπος εἰπεῖν σύμπαντος τοῦ σώματος, ὡς ταράττοντος καὶ οὐκ ἐῶντος τὴν ψυχὴν κτήσασθαι ἀλήθειαν τε καὶ φρόνησιν ὅταν κοινωνῇ. The *Eleventh Oration* of Maximus of Tyre has several echoes of this passage. Cf. XI, 9d (Hobein): Τὸ δὲ θεῖον αὐτὸ ἀόρατον ὀφθαλμοῖς, ἄρρητον φωνῇ, ἀναφὲς σαρκί, ἀπευθὲς ἀκοῇ. XI, 10b resonates quite closely with the text in Numenius: ἀλλὰ ἀποφράττων μὲν καὶ τὰ ὦτα, ἀποστρέφων δὲ τὰς ὄψεις καὶ τὰς ἄλλας αἰσθήσεις ἔμπαλιν πρὸς ἑαυτόν (sc. τὸ ἀκήρατον ἐκεῖνο φῶς). For Maximus see Festugière *op. cit.*, pp. 111-115. Albinus (X, 5) provides a more clinical version of Numenius' exhortation in his description of the *via negativa*: Ἔσται δὴ πρώτη μὲν αὐτοῦ (sc. ὁ πρῶτος θεός) νόησις ἡ κατὰ ἀφαίρεσιν τούτων, ὅπως καὶ σημεῖον ἐνοήσαμεν κατὰ ἀφαίρεσιν ἀπὸ τοῦ αἰσθητοῦ. Cf. also Philo *Leg. All.* II, 70: ὅτε μὲν γὰρ ἡ αἴσθησις κρατεῖ, ὁ νοῦς ἠνδραπόδισται μηδενὶ προσέχων νοητῷ, ὅτε δὲ ὁ νοῦς κρατεῖ, ἡ αἴσθησις ἄπρακτος θεωρεῖται μηδενὸς ἀντίληψιν ἴσχουσα αἰθητοῦ.

The theme is well represented in the Corpus Hermeticum. In the *Poimandres* (I, 1) the narrator's vision of the divine being is preceded by the necessary bodily state:...κατασχεθεισῶν μου τῶν σωματικῶν αἰθήσεων; cf. CH X, 5-6: ἡ γὰρ γνῶσις αὐτοῦ καὶ θεία σιωπή ἐστι καὶ καταργία πασῶν τῶν αἰσθήσεων...πασῶν τῶν σωματικῶν αἰσθήσεών τε καὶ κινήσεων ἐπιλαθόμενος ἀτρεμεῖ; CH XIII, 10:...τὴν σωματικὴν αἴσθησιν καταλιπών. Plotinus uses a similar expression at 1. 6. 4: ἀναβαίνοντας δεῖ θεάσασθαι καταλιπόντας τὴν αἴσθησιν κάτω περιμένειν. Cf. V. 8. 11: δραμὼν δὲ εἰς τὸ εἴσω ἔχει πᾶν, καὶ ἀφεὶς τὴν αἴσθησιν εἰς τοὐπίσω...εἷς ἐστιν ἐκεῖ. In treatise VI. 9 he lays great emphasis on this doctrine. Cf. VI. 9. 3:...οὔτε πόρρω δεῖ γενέσθαι τῶν περὶ τὰ πρῶτα εἰς τὰ ἔσχατα τῶν πάντων πεσόντα, ἀλλ' ἱέμενον εἰς τὰ πρῶτα ἐπαναγαγεῖν ἑαυτὸν ἀπὸ τῶν αἰσθητῶν ἐσχάτων ὄντων (notice the use of πόρρω); VI. 9. 7: εἰ δὲ τοῦτο, πάντων τῶν ἔξω ἀφεμένην δεῖ ἐπιστραφῆναι πρὸς τὸ εἴσω πάντη, μὴ πρὸς τὶ τῶν ἔξω κεκλίσθαι, ἀλλὰ ἀγνοήσαντα τὰ πάντα καὶ πρὸ τοῦ μὲν τῇ αἰσθήσει. And finally the famous statement at III. 6. 6: ἡ δ' ἀληθινὴ ἐγρήγορσις ἀληθινὴ ἀπὸ σώματος, οὐ μετὰ σώματος, ἀνάστασις.

l. 11. ὁμιλῆσαι τῷ ἀγαθῷ μόνῳ μόνον: Dodds (*N. and A.*, pp. 16-17) describes this phrase as "the best known verbal agreement" between Numenius and Plotinus. He quotes I. 6. 7: ἕως ἄν τις...αὐτῷ μόνῳ αὐτὸ μόνον ἴδῃ; VI. 7. 34: ἵνα δέξηται μόνη μόνον; VI. 9. 11: φυγὴ μόνου πρὸς μόνον. However he cautions that "too much should not be made of this. The phrase itself is a very common one." (See p. 17 for other uses in ancient literature.) He concludes: "Numenius' use of the phrase is relatively common-place and colourless; it was Plotinus who gave it significance by the new metaphysical meaning he attached to μόνος, and magic by the inspired addition of φυγή—'the *escape* of the alone to the Alone'." Cf. Armstrong (*Plotinus*, VII, p. 344, n. 2): "It is a fairly commonplace Greek phrase, generally, but not always, in a religious context. The closest parallel to Plotinus' use of it is in N. fr. 2."

ll. 11-12. ἔνθα μήτε τις ἄνθρωπος μήτε τι ζῶον ἕτερον μηδὲ σῶμα...σμικρόν: Dodds (*N. and A.*, p. 17) points out that "in the same chapter of VI, 7 where he uses the μόνη μόνον formula Plotinus writes οὔτε σώματος ἔτι αἰσθάνεται...οὔτε ἑαυτὴν ἄλλο τι λέγει, οὐκ ἄνθρωπον, οὐ ζῶον, οὐκ ὄν, οὐ πᾶν. The choice of the same series of words, σῶμα, ἄνθρωπος, ζῷον, could easily be coincidence; but it could also be an unconscious echo." It is highly likely that Plotinus' expression is indeed and echo, but it is also likely that Numenius here, as he so often does, echoes and simplifies language from the *Symposium*. Cf. 211a: οὐδ' αὖ φαντασθήσεται αὐτῷ τὸ καλὸν οἷον πρόσοπόν τι οὐδὲ χεῖρες οὐδὲ ἄλλο οὐδὲν ὧν σῶμα μετέχει, οὐδέ τις λόγος οὐδέ τις ἐπιστήμη, οὐδέ που ὂν ἐν ἑτέρῳ τινι, οἷον ἐν ζώῳ ἢ ἐν γῇ ἢ ἐν οὐρανῷ ἢ ἔν τῳ ἄλλω.

l. 13. **ἄφατος καὶ ἀδιήγατος**: The vision is ineffable. Plato(?) had provided the classic expression for this doctrine in his *Seventh Letter*, 341c: ῥητὸν γὰρ οὐδαμῶς ἐστιν, and the term ἄρρητος became the *terminus technicus* throughout the later tradition (Numenius here, as he often does, substitutes his own vocabulary). Cf. Plutarch *De Iside* 383a: τὸ μὴ φατὸν μηδὲ ῥητὸν ἀνθρώποις κάλλος; Albinus X, 3: ὁ πρῶτος θεός...ἄρρητος; X, 4: ἄρρητος δ' ἐστι καὶ νῷ μόνῳ ληπτός; Maximus of Tyre II, 10: ὁ μὲν γὰρ θεός...ἄρρητος φωνῇ; *Corp. Herm.* I, 31: δέξαι λογικὰς θυσίας...ἀνελάλητε, ἄρρητε, σιωπῇ φωνούμενε; Plotinus V. 3. 13: Διὸ καὶ ἄρρητον τῇ ἀληθείᾳ.

ἐρημία θεσπέσιος: Cf. the beautiful passage at Plotinus VI. 9. 11: ἀλλ' ὥσπερ ἁρπασθεὶς ἢ ἐνθουσιάσας ἡσυχῇ ἐν ἐρήμῳ καὶ καταστάσει γεγένηται ἀτρεμεῖ; also VI. 7. 40: ἀλλ' ἔστιν ἔρημον αὐτὸ ἐφ' ἑαυτοῦ.

l. 14. **ἤθη**: Cf. fr. 11, l. 21: το ἴδιον ἦθος (of the δημουργὸς θεός). The term is inspired by *Timaeus* 42e: ὁ μὲν δὴ ἅπαντα ταῦτα διατάξας ἔμενεν ἐν τῷ ἑαυτοῦ κατὰ τρόπον ἤθει. Plotinus paraphrases this passage twice at V. 4. 2.: μένοντος οὖν αὐτοῦ ἐν τῷ οἰκείῳ ἤθει.

ἀγλαΐαι: The word is used mostly by the poets. Plotinus uses it several times: I. 6. 9 (describing virtue) ἕως ἂν ἐκλάμψειέ σοι τῆς ἀρετῆς ἡ θεοειδὴς ἀγλαΐα; III. 8. 11 (describing Νοῦς) ἐν πάσῃ ἀγλαΐᾳ κειμένου; V. 8. 12 (of the contents of the Intelligible realm) τὴν αὐτῶν ἀγλαΐαν ἀσμενίσας; VI. 7. 21 (of Νοῦς and its ζωή) εἶναι δ' αὐτὰ μεστὰ μὲ ἀγλαΐας. The passage which appears to be most directly inspired by Numenius occurs at VI. 9. 4: εἰ δὲ μὴ ἦλθέ τις ἐπὶ το θέαμα, μηδὲ σύνεσιν ἔσχεν ἡ ψυχὴ τῆς ἐκεῖ ἀγλαΐας.

ll. 14-17. αὐτὸ δὲ ἐν εἰρήνῃ, ἐν εὐμενείᾳ...ἐποχούμενον ἐπὶ τῇ οὐσίᾳ: Festugière (*op. cit.*, p. 129, n. 10) makes the following remark about this passage: "Il faut garder, à mon sens, cette suite de courts membres asyndètes...Ces asyndètes sont voules et donnent de la majestè au style." It is this use of asyndeton, as well as some vocabulary items which suggest that the text is an unconscious echo of a poetical passage in the *Symposium*. At 197c-e Agathon concludes his encomium on Ἔρως with a poetic flourish. The section contains the following expressions: οὗτός ἐστιν ὁ ποιῶν εἰρήνην...πραότητα μὲν πορίζων...φιλόδωρος εὐμενείας...ἵλεως ἀγαθός...τρυφῆς, ἁβρότητος πατήρ...ἡγεμὼν κάλλιστος καὶ ἄριστος. Plotinus has a similar echo (without asyndeton) at V. 5. 12: καὶ ἔστι δὲ τὸ μὲν ἤπιον καὶ προσηνὲς καὶ ἁβρότερον.

τὸ ἤρεμον: Cf. *Soph.*, 248e: οὐκ ἂν γενέσθαι περὶ τὸ ἠρεμοῦν. Aristotle (*Metaphysics* 988b), while speaking of the proponents of Forms says: αἴτια μᾶλλαν καὶ τοῦ ἐν ἠρεμίᾳ εἶναι φασιν. See also Philo *De Post.*, 29: τὸ ὄν...τῆς ἑαυτοῦ φύσεως, ἠρεμίας, τῷ σπουδαίῳ μεταδίδωσιν; *Gig.*, 49: στάσις τε καὶ ἠρεμία ἀκλινὴς ἡ παρὰ τὸν ἀκλινῶς ἐστῶτα ἀεὶ θεόν.

τὸ ἡγεμονικόν: The term was used by the Stoics to denote the ruling power of the universe, as well as the rational part of man: cf. Chrysippus *Stoicorum Veterum Fragmenta 2. 186, 192*; Cleanthes I. 112. Numenius' use of it here can only indicate that it had become part of the Platonic vocabulary. Cf. Plutarch *De Iside*, 383a: οὗτος αὐταῖς ἡγεμών ἐστι καὶ βασιλεὺς ὁ θεός.

ἐποχούμενον ἐπὶ τῇ οὐσίᾳ: As Festugière points out (*Révélation*, p. 129, n. 11), the L. S. J. gives meaning 3. of ἐποχέομαι as "metaph., of a higher power, *transcend* the lower" and lists Plotinus I. 1. 8 as the earliest attestation: ὡς ἐποχούμενον τῇ νοητῇ φύσει. Dodds (*N. and A.*, p. 18) feels that the Plotinian text is an echo of this passage and indicates that this 'metaphorical use' does not appear before Numenius. Undoubtedly Numenius is here giving a nice poetic turn to Plato, *Republic* 509b: οὐκ οὐσίας ὄντος τοῦ ἀγαθοῦ, ἀλλ᾽ ἔτι ἐπέκεινα τῆς οὐσίας.

The expression also appears in the *Chaldaean Oracles*, with a somewhat lessened metaphorical quality. Cf. fr. 36: νοῦς πατρὸς ἀρράτοις ἐποχούμενος ἰθυντρῆσιν; see also the hymn provided by Porphyry in *De philosophia ex oraculis*, reproduced by Lewy, p. 10, n. 26: κόσμων ἀμφιδρόμων ἐποχούμενε, δέσποτα, νώτοις αἰθερίοις. Lewy (p. 328, n. 58) sees the image evolving from a combination of the ἐπέκεινα of the *Republic* with the ὑπερουράνιος τόπος of *Phaedrus* 247c.

l. 18. **τοῦ παντὸς ἁμαρτάνει**: Cf. Plato *Phaedrus* 235e: ὡς Λυσίας τοῦ παντὸς ἡμάρτηκεν, and 237c: εἰδέναι δεῖ περὶ οὗ ἂν ᾖ ἡ βουλή, ἢ παντὸς ἁμαρτάνειν ἀνάγκη.

l. 19. **θείας δὲ πρὸς αὐτὸ δεῖ μεθόδου**: The sentiment is also found in *Corp. Herm.* VI, 6: μία γάρ ἐστιν εἰς αὐτὸ ἀποφέρουσα ὁδός, ἡ μετὰ γνώσεως εὐσέβεια.

ll. 19-22. **καὶ ἔστι κράτιστον...ἐκμελετῆσαι μάθημα, τί ἐστι τὸ ὄν**: This concluding part of the fragment seems to resonate with *Rep.* 521c-541b where the various μαθήματα are discussed in terms of a τοῦ ὄντος ἐπάναδον, and which begins with the question: Τί ἂν εἴη, ὦ Γλαύκων, μάθημα ψυχῆς ὁλκὸν ἀπὸ τοῦ γιγνομένου ἐπὶ τὸ ὄν; Albinus (VII) provides a truncated reproduction of this section of the *Republic* that illustrates the way in which Middle Platonism appropriated this material, and is obviously reresentative of the 'Schultradition' from which Numenius was drawing. See note on l. 21 below.

l. 20. **τῶν αἰσθητῶν ἀμελήσαντι, νεανιευσαμένῳ πρὸς τὰ μαθήματα**: Cf. *Rep.* 485d: Ὧι δὴ πρὸς τὰ μαθήματα καὶ πᾶν τὸ τοιοῦτον ἐρρυήκασιν, περὶ τὴν τῆς ψυχῆς οἶμαι ἡδονὴν αὐτῆς καθ᾽ αὑτὴν εἶεν ἄν, τὰς δὲ διὰ τοῦ σώματος ἐκλείποιεν, εἰ μὴ πεπλασμένως ἀλλ᾽ ἀληθῶς φιλόσοφός τις εἴη.

l. 21. **τοὺς ἀριθμοὺς θεασαμένῳ**: Albinus' (VII, 2) description of the study of number provides the context for this phrase: τὸ τε περὶ ἀριθμοὺς μόριον ὂν τοῦ μαθηματικοῦ οὐχ ἣν ἔτυχεν οἰκειότητα ἐμποιεῖ πρὸς τὴν τοῦ ὄντος ἐπάνοδον (cf. *Rep.* 521c above), ἀλλὰ σχεδόν τι τῆς περὶ τὰ αἰσθητὰ πλάνης καὶ ἀγνοίας ἀπαλλάτει ἡμᾶς, συνεργοῦν πρὸς τὴν τῆς οὐσίας γνῶσιν. At VII, 3 he concludes: ἐξ ὧν κατά τινα οἰκείαν ὁδὸν καὶ τὸν ἁπάντων δημιουργὸν ζητήσομεν, μετιόντες ἀπὸ τούτων τῶν μαθημάτων ὥσπερ τινὸς ὑποβάθρας καὶ στοιχείων.

οὕτως ἐμελετῆσαι μάθημα: This rhetorical turn of moving from various μαθήματα to conclude with the ultimate μάθημα is modeled after *Symp.* 211c: καὶ ἀπὸ τῶν μαθημάτων ἐπ' ἐκεῖνο τὸ μάθημα τελευτῆσαι...καὶ γνῷ αὐτὸ τελευτῶν ὃ ἔστι καλόν. Cf. also *Rep.* VI, 505a: ἡ τοῦ ἀγαθοῦ ἰδέα μέγιστον μάθημα.

l. 21. **τὸ ὄν**: Some editors would alter this to τὸ ἕν (see Des Places p. 105, n. 8). Dodds (*N. and A.*, p. 12, n. 1) defends τὸ ὄν by recalling Numenius' use of αὐτοόν in fr. 17 to describe his First God.

Fr. 3

l. 1. **τί δή ἐστι τὸ ὄν**: This appears to resume the conclusion of the previous fragment. Cf. Plutarch, *De E.*, 3923: τί ὂν ὄντως ὄν ἐστι; The question itself is a reprise of *Tim.* 27d: τί τὸ ὂν ἀεί...;

ll. 1-5. **ἆρα ταυτὶ τὰ στοιχεῖα...γενητὰ καὶ παλινάγρετα**: A similar line of argumentation is used by Albinus at X, 8: εἰ σῶμα ἐστιν, ἐξ ὕλης ἂν ὑπάρχοι· ἢ πῦρ ἂν οὖν εἴη ἢ ὕδωρ ἢ γῆ ἢ ἀὴρ ἢ τι ἐκ τούτων...εἰ σῶμά ἐστι, καὶ φθαρτὸς ἔσται καὶ γενητὸς καὶ μεταβλητός.

παλινάγρετα: The L. S. J. cites this passage as a witness to the meaning "*recoverable*, of an element". If the usage is unique to

Numenius, the concept is not. Its origin lies in *Tim.* 42e-43a where Plato describes the creation of the human body by the children of the Demiurge: πυρὸς καὶ γῆς ὕδατος τε καὶ ἀέρος ἀπὸ τοῦ κοσμοῦ δανειζόμενοι μόρια ὡς ἀποδοθησόμεθα πάλιν. Albinus reproduces this in his usual succinct fashion at XVII, 1: οἱ δὴ θεοὶ ἔπλασαν μὲν προηγουμένως τὸν ἄνθρωπον ἐκ γῆς καὶ πυρὸς καὶ ἀέρος καὶ ὕδατος, μοίρας τινὰς δανειζόμενοι εἰς ἀπόδοσιν. Philo expresses the doctrine at *Quis rer. div.* 282: ἕκαστος ἡμῶν συγκριθεὶς ἐκ τῶν τεττάρων καὶ δανεισάμενος ἀφ' ἑκάστης οὐσίας μικρὰ μόρια...ἐκτίνει τὸ δάνειον; and again at *Post. Cain.* 5: αἱ τῶν τετελευτηκότων ἀναστοιχειούμεναι μοῖραι πάλιν εἰς τὰς τοῦ παντὸς δυνάμεις ἐξ ὧν συνέστησαν ἀποκρίνονται, τοῦ δανεισθέντος ἑκάστῳ δανείσματος. Cf. also *Corp. Herm.* 1, 24: ἐν τῇ ἀναλύσει τοῦ σώματος τοῦ ὑλικοῦ...αἱ αἰσθήσεις τοῦ σώματος εἰς τὰς ἑαυτῶν πηγὰς ἐπανέρχονται, μέρη γινόμενοι καὶ πάλιν συνανιστάμεναι εἰς τὰς ἐνεργείας.

l. 6. ἐξ ἀλλήλων γιγνόμενα καὶ ἐπαλλασσόμενα: A reminiscence of Plato's description of the constant transformation of the elements in their 'pre-cosmic' state (*Tim.* 49c), which concludes: κύκλον τε οὕτω διαδιδόντα εἰς ἄλληλα, ὡς φαίνεται, τὴν γένεσιν.

l. 7. μήτε στοιχεῖα ὑπάρχοντα μήτε συλλαβάς: Another glance back at the *Timaeus* (48b) where Plato begins his narrative of "the things which come about due to Necessity." The primordial nature of the elements is clarified in this way: ἕκαστον αὐτῶν λέγομεν ἀρχὰς αὐτὰ τιθέμενοι στοιχεῖα τοῦ παντός, προσῆκον αὐτοῖς οὐδ' ἂν ὡς ἐν συλλαβῆς ἔδεσιν μόνον εἰκότως...ἀπεικασθῆναι. Cornford (p. 161, n. 1) points out that the term στοιχεῖα, which primarily signifies the letters of the alphabet, is used to designate the elements for the first time in *Theaet.* 201e. Philo explains this play on the meanings of στοιχεῖα at *Quis rer. div.*, 282 in an introduction to the passage quoted above: καθάπερ γὰρ ὀνόματα καὶ ῥήματα καὶ τὰ λόγου μέρη πάντα συνέστηκε μὲν ἐκ τῶν τῆς γραμματικῆς στοιχείων, ἀναλύεται δὲ πάλιν εἰς ἔσχατα ἐκεῖνα. Cf. also *Corp. Herm.* I, 10: καὶ κατελείφθη ἄλογα τὰ κατωφερῆ τῆς φύσεως στοιχεῖα.

l. 11. **ποταμὸς γὰρ ἡ ὕλη ῥοώδης καὶ ὀξύρροπος**: Cf. *Chald. Or.* fr. 180: τῆς ὕλης τὸ λάβρον. The imagery is taken from *Tim.* 43a where the children of the Demiurge are depicted inserting the circles of soul into the chaos of the body: τὰς τῆς ἀθανάτου ψυχῆς περιόδους ἐνέδουν εἰς ἐπίρρυτον σῶμα καὶ ἀπόρρυτον. αἱ δ᾽ εἰς ποταμὸν ἐνδεθεῖσαι... Philo uses the same motif in *De Gig.*, 13: ἐκεῖναι δ᾽ ὥσπερ εἰς ποταμὸν τὸ σῶμα καταβᾶσαι ποτὲ μὲν ὑπὸ συρμοῦ δίνης βιαιοτάτης ἁρπασθεῖσαι κατεπόθησαν. Numenius uses this type of imagery again in fr. 27, l. 10 to describe the rhetorical techniques of Carneades: ἐξηγείρατο λάβρος οἷον ποταμὸς ῥοώδης. The ultimate inspiration for this type of language is Heraclitus. Cf. *Cra.* 402a: καὶ ποταμοῦ ῥοῇ ἀπεικάζων τὰ ὄντα λέγει ὡς "δὶς ἐς τὸν αὐτὸν ποταμὸν οὐκ ἂν ἐμβαίης." Plutarch provides a variant of this saying at *De E* 392c. For a full discussion of Middle Platonic teaching concerning the fluidity of ὕλη, see fr. 8, l.5 and notes.

ll. 11-12. **βάθος καὶ πλάτος καὶ μῆκος**: The basic dimensions in which matter can expand. This language apparently played a significant role in the Middle Platonic theological *via negativa*, which is discussed in detail by Krämer, p. 105-107. On p. 107 he quotes Clement of Alexandria *Strom.* V, 11 as the clearest example of this doctrine: ...ἀφελόντες μὲν τοῦ σώματος τὰς φυσικὰς πιότητας, περιελόντες δὲ τὴν εἰς βάθος διάστασιν, εἶτα τὴν εἰς τὸ πλάτος καὶ ἐπὶ τούτοις τὴν εἰς το μῆκος. Cf. VI, 11. As Des Places points out (n. *ad. loc.*), the language appears in Ephesians 3. 18: ἵνα ἐξισχύσητε καταλαβέσθαι σὺν πᾶσιν τοῖς ἁγίοις τί τὸ πλάτος καὶ μῆκος καὶ ὕψος καὶ βάθος. Krämer (p. 247) suggests that the model for the writer of this Deutero-Pauline epistle is a pre-Christian gnostic description of the Pleroma, but the hypothesis has found little acceptance.

ἀόριστος: See note to fr. 4a, l. 3.

Fr. 4a

ll. 2-4. εἰ ἔστιν ἄπειρος ἡ ὕλη, ἀόριστον εἶναι αὐτήν...ἄλογος: Numenius is alluding to the Middle Platonic doctrine which equates ὕλη with the ἀόριστος δύας. Cf. Hermodorus (apud. Simplicius Phys. 248, 2d): τὴν ὕλην ὁ Πλάτων κατὰ τὸ ἄπειρον καὶ ἀόριστον καὶ ὑποτιθέμενος. The equivalence of the terms ἄπειρος and ἀόριστος is demonstrated by two passages from Plutarch. Cf. *De an. proc.* 1012d: ἐκ δὲ τούτων γίγνεσθαι τὸν τοῦ ἑνὸς ὁρίζοντος τὸ πλῆθος καὶ τῇ ἀπειρίᾳ πέρας ἐντιθέντος, ἣν καὶ δυάδα καλοῦσιν ἀόριστον; *Plat. Quaest.* 1002a: οὐ γὰρ ποιεῖ μονὰς ἀριθμόν, ἂν μὴ τῆς ἀπείρου δυάδος ἅψηται. Beutler (col. 669) would see this use of ἄπειρον prefigured in *Phlb.,* 17e; Aristot. *Phys.,* 189a and *Metaphys.* 994a. See also Hager, p. 430.

Variants of the doctrine are found throughout the tradition. Cf. *Tim.* 53a: καὶ τὸ μὲν δὴ πρὸ τούτου πάντα ταῦτ' εἶχεν ἀλόγως καὶ ἀμέτρως; Philo, *De Spec. Leg.* I, 329: οὐ γὰρ θέμις ἀπείρου καὶ πεφυρμένης ψαύειν (sc. ὁ θεός); Albinus, IX, 3: ἄμετρος ὑπάρχει ἡ ὕλη; *Corp. Herm.* I, 10: ἐπήδησεν εὐθὺς ἐκ τῶν κατωφερῶν στοιχείων ὁ τοῦ θεοῦ λόγος...καὶ κατελείφθη ἄλογα τὰ κατωφερῆ τῆς φύσεως στοιχεῖα, ὡς εἶναι ὕλην μόνην. Plotinus employs this terminology while discussing τὸ κακόν (*Ennead* I. 8. 3): Ἤδη γὰρ ἄν τις εἰς ἔννοιαν ἥκοι αὐτοῦ οἷον ἀμετρίαν εἶναι πρὸς μέτρον καὶ ἄπειρον πρὸς πέρας καὶ ἀνείδεον πρὸς εἰδοποιητικὸν καὶ ἀεὶ ἐνδεὲς πρὸς αὔταρκες, ἀεὶ ἀόριστον, οὐδαμῇ ἑστώς.

Although the term ἀόριστος δύας does not appear in the extant verbatim fragments, Numenius does refer to ὕλη in fr. 11 as δύας, and Calcidius (fr. 52) reports this doctrine: ...ait Pythagoram deum quidem singularitas nomine nominasse, silvam vero duitatis; quam duitatem *indeterminatum*...esse dicere. Proclus (fr. 39) tells us that Numenius was among those who held the following doctrine of the soul: οἱ μὲν ἀριθμὸν αὐτὴν εἰπόντες ἐκ μονάδος ποιοῦσιν, ὡς ἀμερίστου, καὶ τῆς ἀορίστου δυάδος, ὡς μεριστῆς. For detailed discussions of the role the ἀόριστος δύας played in later Platonism see Krämer, pp. 25, n. 14; 32, n. 39; 39ff.; 56ff.

l. 5. ἄτακτον: Another image from the *Timaeus*. Cf. 30a: οὕτω δὴ πᾶν ὅσον ἦν ὁρατὸν παραλαβὼν οὐχ ἡσυχίαν ἄγον ἀλλὰ κινούμενον πλημμελῶς καὶ ἀτάκτως, εἰς τάξιν αὐτὸ ἤγαγεν ἐκ τῆς ἀταξίας. Plutarch uses the word in his description of Typhon (Egyptian Seth) at *De Isid.*, 366f.: ἀλλ' ἁπλῶς ὅσον ἐστὶν ἐν τούτοις ἄμετρον καὶ ἄτακτον ὑπερβολαῖς ἢ ἐνδείαις Τυφῶνι προσνέμοντες. At *De an. proc.*, 1014d, he links the term with ἀόριστος: τὴν ἄτακτον καὶ ἀόριστον...ἀρχὴν ἐκείνην. Cf. also *Corp. Herm.* VIII, 3: ὅτε γὰρ ἦν ἀσώματος ἡ ὕλη, ὦ τέκνον, ἄτακτος ἦν.

The terminology of the entire section closely resembles the 'Table of Antitheses' found in Ps-Archytas, fr. 1 (Nolle): τεταγμένα-ἄτακτα, ὁριστά-ἀόριστα, ῥητά-ἄρρητα, λόγον ἔχον-ἄλογον. See Burkert, p. 46, n. 187.

ll. 6-7. **ὅ τι δὲ μὴ ἕστηκεν, οὐκ ἂν εἴη ὄν**: For the Platonists, stability is the essential characteristic of true being. For a full discussion of the important term ἕστηκε see notes to fr. 5, l. 25.

l. 8-9. **ταυτὶ πάντα συνενεχθῆναι τῷ ὄντι ἀθέμιστον εἶναι**: Cf. Philo *op. cit.*: οὐ γὰρ θέμις ἀπείρου καὶ πεφυρμένης ὕλης ψαύειν (*sc.* ὁ θεός).

l. 11-12. **τὴν ὕλην οὔτε αὐτὴν οὔτε τὰ σώματα εἶναι ὄν**: This answers the question posed at fr. 3, ll. 8-9: Σῶμα μὲν ταυτὶ οὕτως οὐκ ἂν εἴη τὸ ὄν. Ἀλλ' ἄρα ταυτὶ μὲν οὔ, ἡ δὲ ὕλη δύναται εἶναι ὄν; Numenius is here distinguishing between the primal, qualityless matter of the ἐκμαγεῖον found at *Tim.*, 50c, and matter that has been shaped and ordered by the Demiurge (cf. *Tim.*, 53a: πρὶν καὶ τὸ πᾶν ἐξ αὐτῶν διακοσμηθὲν γενέσθαι). This distinction is important for Numenius' dualism, which is discussed in the notes to fr. 52. Albinus presents the orthodox Middle Platonic view of primal ὕλη in section VIII. At VIII, 2 he gives a reprise of Plato's description of the ὑποδοχή and ἐκμαγεῖον (Tim. 49a-52b) and states that pure matter (αὐτὴν καθ' αὑτήν) is ἄμορφον...ἄποιον καὶ ἀνείδεον. At VIII, 3 he continues: ἄποιόν τε εἶναι καὶ ἀνείδεον πρὸς ὑποδοχὴν τῶν εἰδῶν· τοιαύτη δ' οὖσα οὔτε σῶμα ἂν εἴη οὔτε ἀσώματον, δυνάμει δὲ σῶμα. This last remark is interesting in several respects. First, it provides a context for Numenius' notion of ὕλη as anterior to σῶμα. Note Albinus' typical use of Aristotelian language: δυνάμει σῶμα. Secondly it shows how pieces of Middle Platonic teaching found its way into the *Corpus Hermeticum*. *Corp. Herm.* VIII has several rather distorted echoes of Albinus' teaching on matter, but the passage which was quoted above (VIII, 3: ὅτε γὰρ ἦν ἀσώματος ἡ ὕλη), must surely arise out of this same milieu.

l.15. τοῦτο οὐδὲν εἰπεῖν ποικίλον: An expression borrowed from the Dialogues. Cf. *Meno*, 75e: τὸ τοιοῦτον βούλομαι λέγειν, οὐδὲν ποικίλον; *Gorg.*, 491d: οὐδὲν ποικίλον ἀλλ' ὥσπερ οἱ πολλοί. A similar rhetorical turn is found at *Phd.*, 72b: οὐδὲν χαλεπόν, ἦ δ' ὅς, ἐννοῆσαι ὃ λέγω.

ll. 15-16. τὰ σώματά ἐστι φύσει τεθνηκότα καὶ νεκρὰ καὶ πεφορημένα: The unstable, impermanent nature of material objects stands in direct contrast to the eternal, unchanging nature of true being. This essential Platonic premise passed into the later tradition and received perhaps even greater emphasis. Cf. *Tim.*, 52a where Plato is describing the realm of 'becoming':...δεύτερον, αἰσθητόν, γεννητόν, πεφορημένον ἀεί, γιγνόμενόν τε ἔν τινι τόπῳ καὶ πάλιν ἐκεῖθεν ἀπολλύμενον; *Phd.*, 91d: ἐπεὶ σῶμά γε ἀεὶ ἀπολλύμενον οὐδὲν παύεται. Philo has a passage that could well have inspired Numenius. In *Leg. All.* III, 69-72, Philo is allegorizing the narrative of Εἵρ (Ηρ LXX) who is made to represent the body. At 69 he says: τὸ σῶμα...καὶ νεκρὸν καὶ τεθνηκὸς αἰεί· μὴ γὰρ ἄλλο τι νοήσῃς ἕκαστον ἡμῶν ποιεῖν ἢ νεκροφορεῖν, τὸ νεκρὸν ἐξ ἑαυτοῦ σῶμα ἐγειρούσης καὶ ἀμοχθὶ φερούσης τῆς ψυχῆς. At 70 he says of Εἵρ: οὐ γὰρ νῦν αὐτὸν ἀπέκτεινεν (sc. ὁ θεός), ἀλλ᾽ ἐξ ἀρχῆς νεκρὸν τὸ σῶμα ἀπειργάσατο. At 72: ὁ φιλόσοφος...τοῦ νεκροῦ ὄντως σώματος ἀλογεῖ. Maximus (XI, 7) has a remote echo of the *Timaeus*: μόγις γὰρ που καὶ τούτοις ἵσταται τὸ σῶμα ὑπὸ τοῦ ἐν τῷ κλύδωνι ἔθους κινούμενόν τε, περιφερομένον. Plotinus warms to the theme, cf. I. 8. 4: Σωμάτων δὲ φύσις, καθόσον μετέχει ὕλης, κακὸν...ἐστέρηταί τε ζωῆς φθείρει τε ἄλληλα φορὰ τε παρ᾽ αὐτῶν ἄτακτος; III. 8. 2: Ὁ μὲν οὖν λόγος ὁ κατὰ τὴν μορφὴν τὴν ὁρωμένην ἔσχατος ἤδη καὶ νεκρός; V. 1. 2: ἔσχε τε ἀξίαν οὐρανὸς ψυχῆς εἰσοικισθείσης ὢν πρὸ ψυχῆς σῶμα νεκρόν. If Numenius had glanced at the New Testament, as Origen (fr. 10) leads us to believe, he might have been struck by Romans, 4. 19: κατενόησεν (sc. Ἀβραάμ) τὸ ἑαυτοῦ σῶμα [ἤδη] νενεκρωμένον.

l. 23-24. σῶμα...παραλυόμενον καὶ σκιδνάμενον: σῶμα, which is merely primal, chaotic matter in ordered form, constantly threatens to disperse and return to its orginal state.

παραλυόμενον: Cf. *Corp. Herm.* VIII, 3: ...τῇ δὲ ἀθανασίᾳ περιβαλὼν τὸ πᾶν σῶμα (sc. ὁ πατήρ), ἵνα μὴ ὕλη καὶ τῆς τούτου συστάσεως θελήσασα ἀποστῆναι διαλυθῇ εἰς τὴν ἑαυτῆς ἀταξίαν.

σκιδνάμενον: Cf. *Tim.*, 37a: ὅταν οὐσίαν σκεδαστὴν ἔχοντός τινος ἐφάπτεται; Plutarch *De an. proc.*, 1023c: χρώμενος ἐπὶ τὴν τῆς ὕλης διαμόρφωσιν, τὸ σκεδαστὸν αὐτῆς καὶ ἀσύνδετον ὁρίζων; *De E.*, 392c: οὐδὲ θνητῆς οὐσίας δὶς ἅψασθαι κατὰ ἕξιν· ἀλλ᾽ ὀξύτητι καὶ τάχει μεταβολῆς σκίδνησι καὶ πάλιν συνάγει. (Some editors would see this passage as a paraphrase of Heraclitus, who is quoted by Plutarch in the lines immediately preceding. For a discussion of the matter see Marcovich, pp. 206-211). Lewy (p. 32, n. 89) quotes a section in Proclus *In Remp.*, II, 126, 14ff., who is in turn quoting a Chaldaen λόγιον which contains the phrase ἀποσκεδάσας τόδε σῶμα. Lewy interprets this in terms of the doctrine of the return of the elements to their source after death (cf. fr. 3, l. 5 παλινάγρετα and note). On p. 277, n. 73, he quotes another passage from Proclus, *In*

Remp., II, 336, 1: τῷ σώματι τω σκιδναμένῳ. Here he takes exception to Kroll for deriving the quotation from the Oracles, and suggests this passage from Numenius as a more likely source. For a later testimony to this concept cf. Nemesius (fr. 4b): Τὰ σώματα τῇ οἰκείᾳ φύσει τρεπτὰ ὄντα καὶ σκεδαστά. It is interesting to note that Plotinus uses this language to describe the nature of Ψυχή and the efforts of Νοῦς to counteract it. Cf. V. 3. 8: τοὐναντίον γὰρ ἐπέστρεψε πρὸς ἑαυτὴν τὴν ψυχήν, καὶ σκίδνασθαι οὐκ ἔιασεν.

ll. 24-25. **χρὴ αὐτὸ ἀπηλλάχθαι τῆς τῶν σωμάτων πάθης**: The language is Platonic. See *Phd.*, 80d-81a, where Socrates is discussing the separation of soul and body at death: οὕτω πεφυκυῖα ἀπαλλαττομένη τοῦ σώματος...ἐὰν μὲν καθαρὰ ἀπαλλάττηται, μηδὲν τοῦ σώματος συνεφέλκουσα...πλάνης καὶ ἀνοίας καὶ φόβων, καὶ ἀγρίων ἐρώτων καὶ τῶν ἄλλων κακῶν τῶν ἀνθρωπείων ἀπηλλαγμένη. Cf. Albinus, X, 1: θεοὶ δὲ ἀπηλλαγμένως τῶν αἰσθητῶν; Maximus, XI, 7: τὸ δε νοητόν, ἀπηλλαγμένον τῆς τούτων ἐπαφῆς; XI, 8: Ἐν ποτέρᾳ δὴ τῶν φύσεων τὸν θεὸν τακτέον; ἆρα οὐκ ἐν τῇ στασιμωτέρᾳ καὶ ἑδραιοτέρα, καὶ ἀπηλλαγμένη τοῦ ῥεύματος τούτου καὶ τῆς μεταβολῆς; At *Tim.*, 52d Plato describes the πάθη of matter before the ordering of the cosmos: τὴν δὲ δὴ γενέσεως τιθήνην ὑγραινομένην καὶ πυρουμένην καὶ τὰς γῆς τε καὶ ἀέρος μορφὰς δεχομένην, καὶ ὅσα ἄλλα τούτοις πάθη συνέπεται πάσχουσαν. There is a passage in Plotinus (VI. 4. 8) that uses the same language and may in fact be an unconscious echo of Numenius: ὃ δέ ἐστι μηδενός σώματος, ἀλλὰ τὸ σῶμα ἐθέλει αὐτοῦ εἶναι, ἀνάγκη τοῦτο τὰ τε ἄλλα πάθη τοῦ σώματος μηδαμῶς αὐτὸ πάσχειν.

ll. 25-26. **ἵνα κἀκείνοις κεκυκημένοις...κατέχῃ**: Cf. Nemesius (fr. 4b, ll. 4-7): τὰ σώματα...δεῖται τοῦ συνέχοντος καὶ συνάγαγοντος καὶ ὥσπερ συσφίγγοντος καὶ συγκρατοῦντος αὐτά. The notion is expressed in mythological terms in fr. 18, ll. 6-8: ὁ δημιουργὸς τὴν ὕλην, τοῦ μήτε διακροῦσαι μήτε ἀποπλαχθῆναι αὐτήν, ἁρμονίᾳ συνδησάμενος. Cf. *Phdr.*, 246b: ψυχὴ πᾶσα παντὸς ἐπιμελεῖται τοῦ ἀψύχου.

l. 27. τὸ ἀσώματον: This important term which has its roots in the Dialogues, and was used by Aristotle, became the *terminus technichus* in Middle Platonism for the concept of incorporeality. For a full discussion of the word see fr. 6 and notes.

l. 28. ἕστηκε καὶ ἔστιν ἀραρυῖα: Once again the stability of immaterial being is emphasized. Cf. fr. 5 and notes. ἀραρυῖα is a poetic equivalent of ἕστηκε, cf. fr. 5, l. 25-26: ἀραρός τε καὶ ἑστηκός.

l. 29. οὔτε γίγνεται οὔτε αὔξεται: Numenius delights in echoing *Symp.* 211a. Cf. fr. 2, ll.11-12 and note; fr. 5, ll. 19-20: οὐδὲ γέγονε μέν, ἐφθάρη δέ, οὐδ' ἐμεγεθύνατο μέν, ἐμειώθη δέ, οὐδὲ μὴν ἐγένετό πω πλεῖον ἢ ἔλασσον; fr. 6, l. 8: τὸ μὴ γεγονέναι μηδὲ φθαρήσεται. The text in Plato reads: οὔτε γιγνόμενον οὔτε ἀπολλύμενον, οὔτε αὐξανόμενον οὔτε φθίνον. For ἐφθάρη and φθαρήσεται, however, cf. Aristotle, *Met.*, 994b: ἀδύνατον τὸ πρῶτον ἀΐδιον ὂν φθαρῆναι.

l. 29-30. οὔτε κίνησιν κινεῖται ἄλλην οὐδεμίαν: In the *Phaedrus* (245c-d) self-motion is set forth as the definitive characteristic of soul. But in later Platonism, under the growing influence of the First Hypothesis of the *Parmenides* and Aristotle's Unmoved Mover, τὸ αὐτὸ κινοῦν gives way to τὶ κινοῦν, αὐτὸ ἀκίνητον (*Metaph.*, 1072b). Movement of any kind is increasingly viewed as a type of change and therefore a basic characteristic of the realm of 'becoming'. See notes to fr. 5, ll. 21-25 for a full discussion of this doctrine.

Fr. 4b

l. 2. τὰ παρὰ Ἀμμωνίου...καὶ Νουμηνίου τοῦ Πυθαγορικοῦ: Dodds (*N. & A.*, p.25) has this to say about the fragment: "The views attributed to 'Ammonius and Numenius' in the second chapter of Nemesius are simply the traditional views common to the two anti-materialist schools, Platonists and Pythagoreans. Ammonius is named as the second founder of

Platonism, Numenius as the leading Pythagorean. The opinions quoted are in no way distinctive of either of them, though no doubt both held them." Des Places included the fragment here because of some similarities with fr. 4a. see his note p. 106. For the Pythagoreanism of Numenius see fr. 1b and notes.

l. 4. σκεδαστά: See notes to fr. 4a, l. 23-24.

l. 5. εἰς ἄπειρον τμητά: Cf. fr. 4a, l. 2-3: εἰ ἔστιν ἄπειρος ἡ ὕλη, ἀόριστον εἶναι αὐτήν.

ll. 6-7 δεῖται τοῦ συνέχοντος...καὶ συκρατοῦντος αὐτά: Cf. fr. 4a, ll. 16-18: ἐπειδὴ τὰ σώματά ἐστι φύσει...πεφορημένα καὶ οὐδ' ἐν ταὐτῷ μένοντα, ἆρ' οὐχὶ τοῦ καθέξοντος αὐτοῖς ἔδει;

l. 11. ἕως ἂν καταντήσωμεν εἰς ἀσώματον: Cf. Plotinus, III. 8. 10: ἕως τις ἐπὶ τὸ ἁπλῶς ἕν ἔλθῃ· τοῦτο δὲ οὐκέτι ἐπ' ἄλλο.

l. 12-13. τονικήν τινα εἶναι κίνησιν περὶ τὰ σώματα: As Des Places points out (*op. cit.*, n. *ad loc.*), this is a reference to the τόνος of Cleanthes. See *Stoicorum veterum fragmenta*, vol. II, p. 149 where this passage constitutes fr. 451. Cf. Philo, *De sacr.* 68 where Philo has God describe the type of motion proper to him: οὐ μεταβατικῶς κινούμενος...ἀλλὰ τονικῇ χρώμενος τῇ κινήσει.

ll. 24. τὰ σώματα τριχῇ διαστατά ἐστιν: Cf. Apollodorus, *Stoicorum veterum fragmenta*, vol. III, 259. Also Philo, *De Opfic.* 49: ὅς (sc. ὁ ἀριθμὸς τρεῖς) ἐκ τῆς ἀσωμάτου καὶ νοητῆς οὐσίας ἤγαγεν εἰς ἔννοιαν ἡμᾶς τριχῇ διαστατοῦ σώματος.

l. 34-36. εἰ δὲ σῶμα ἡ ψυχή...εἰ δ' ἔνδοθεν, ἔμψυχον: A Platonic axiom. Cf. *Phdr.*, 245e: πᾶν γὰρ σῶμα, ᾧ μὲν ἔξωθεν τὸ κινεῖσθαι, ἄψυχον, ᾧ δὲ ἔνδοθεν αὐτῷ ἐξ αὑτοῦ, ἔμψυχον.

ll. 37. ἡ ψυχή, εἰ μὲν τρέφεται, ὑπὸ ἀσωμάτου τρέφεται: Cf. *Phdr.*, 247d: διάνοια...ἁπάσας ψυξῆς...ἰδοῦσα τὸ ὂν ἀγαπᾷ τε καὶ θεωροῦσα τἀληθῆ τρέφεται.

l. 39. Ξενοκράτης οὕτω συνῆγεν: This passage constitutes fr. 66 in Heinze's collection.

Fr. 5

l. 6. τὸ ὂν οὔτε ποτὲ ἦν οὔτε ποτὲ μὴ γένηται: The language originates with Parmenides. Cf. fr. 8: οὐδέ ποτ᾽ ἦν οὐδ᾽ ἔσται. From there it becomes an essential part of the Platonic tradition; cf. Plato Parm., 141e: οὔτε ποτὲ γέγονεν οὔτ᾽ ἐγίγνετο οὔτ᾽ ἦν ποτέ...οὔτ᾽ ἔπειτα γενήσεται οὔτε γενηθήσεται οὔτε ἔσται; Tim., 38a: τὸ δὲ ἀεὶ κατὰ ταὐτὰ ἔχων...οὔτε προσήκει γίγνεσθαι διὰ χρόνου οὐδὲ γενέσθαι ποτὲ οὐδὲ γεγονέναι νῦν οὐδ᾽ εἰς αὖθις ἔσεσθαι; Philo, Quod Deus., 32: ἐν αἰῶνι δὲ οὔτε παρελήλυθεν οὐδὲν οὔτε μέλλει, ἀλλὰ μόνον ὑφέστηκεν; Plutarch, De E., 393a: ὅθεν οὐδ᾽ ὅσιον ἐστιν οὐδ᾽ ἐπὶ τοῦ ὄντος λέγειν ὡς ἦν ἢ ἔσται; Plotinus, III. 7. 3: οὐδὲν αὐτοῦ παρῆλθεν οὐδ᾽ αὖ γενήσεται.

ll. 6-7. ἀλλ᾽ ἔστιν ἀεὶ ἐν χρόνῳ ὁρισμένῳ, τῷ ἐνεστῶτι μόνῳ: The Middle Platonic notion of an eternal present is hinted at by Parmenides (fr. 8): ἐπεὶ νῦν ἔστιν ὁμοῦ πᾶν, ἕν, συνεχές, but is more directly derived from Tim., 37e where Plato is discussing the ἀΐδιον οὐσία: λέγομεν γὰρ δὴ ὡς ἦν ἔστιν τε καὶ ἔσται, τῇ δὲ τὸ ἔστιν μόνον...προσήκει. See Waszink (Studien, p. 42, n.2). Cf. Philo, op. cit.,: μόνον ὑφέστηκεν; Plutarch, De E., 393a: εἷς ὢν ἑνὶ τῷ νῦν τὸ ἀεὶ πεπλήρωκε. Plotinus, V. 1. 4., glosses Tim., 37e: ὁ δὲ νοῦς...ἔστι μόνον, καὶ τὸ 'ἔστιν' ἀεί. He continues: καὶ οὐδαμοῦ τὸ μέλλον...οὐδὲ τὸ παρεληλυθός...ἀλλ᾽ ἐνέστηκεν ἀεί.

l. 7. αἰῶνα: Waszink, op.cit., notes that Numenius' equating of ἐνεστὼς χρόνος with αἰών is 'bemerkenswert'. Once again the source of the language lies in the Timaeus. Cf. Tim., 38a: ἀλλὰ χρόνου ταῦτα αἰῶνα μιμουμένου; 38c: τὸ μὲν γὰρ δὴ παράδειγμα πάντα αἰῶνα ἐστιν ὄν. Cf. Aristotle, Met. 1072b: ὥστε ζωὴ καὶ αἰὼν συνεχὴς καὶ ἀΐδιος ὑπάρχει τῷ θεῷ. Cf. also Philo, Quod Deus., 32: οὐ χρόνος, ἀλλὰ τὸ ἀρχέτυπον τοῦ χρόνου καὶ παράδειγμα αἰὼν ὁ βίος ἐστὶν αὐτοῦ; Plutarch, De E., 393a: ἔστιν ὁ θεός...καὶ ἔστι κατ᾽ οὐδένα χρόνον ἀλλὰ κατὰ τὸν αἰῶνα; Albinus XIV, 6: τὸν χρόνον ἐποίησε...ὡς ἂν εἰκόνα τοῦ αἰῶνος; *Corp. Herm.* XI, 2 nearly elevates αἰών to the level of a divine being: ὁ οὖν αἰὼν ἐν τῷ θεῷ, ὁ δὲ κόσμος ἐν τῷ αἰῶνι...ὁ μὲν αἰὼν ἕστηκε περὶ τὸν θεὸν, ὁ δὲ κόσμος κινεῖται ἐν τῷ αἰῶνι...(3) οὐσία δὲ ὁ αἰών. Cf. Plotinus, V. I. 4: ἐν αἰῶνι πάντα, καὶ ὁ ὄντως αἰών, ὃν μιμεῖται χρόνος.

ll. 12-14. **Οὔκουν εἰκὸς ἐστιν...μηδέπω**: Cf. Plutarch, *De E.*, 393a: οὐδ᾽ ὅσιον ἐστιν οὐδ᾽ ἐπὶ τοῦ ὄντος λέγειν ὡς ἦν ἢ ἔσται.

l. 16. **σχολῇ γ᾽ ἂν ἄλλο τι εἶναι δύναιτο**: The rhetorical turn is borrowed from *Phd.*, 106d: σχολῇ γὰρ ἄν τι ἄλλο φθορὰν μὴ δέχοιτο, εἰ τό γε ἀθάνατον ἀΐδιον ὂν φθορὰν δέξεται.

l. 18. **Τὸ ἄρα ὂν ἀΐδιον τε βέβαιον**: Cf. *Phil.*, 59c: τό τε βέβαιον...περὶ τὰ ἀεὶ κατὰ τὰ αὐτὰ ὡσαύτως; Plutarch, *De E.*, 392e: Τί οὖν ὄντως ὄν ἐστι; τὸ ἀΐδιον καὶ ἀγένητον καὶ ἄφθαρτον; Philo, *De Somn.*, 223: τοσαύτη περὶ τὸ θεῖόν ἐστιν ὑπερβολὴ τοῦ βεβαίου.

l. 19. **Οὐδὲ γέγονε μέν, ἐφθάρη δέ...ἔλασσον**: See fr. 4a, l. 29 and note.

πλεῖον ἢ ἔλασσον: Cf. Philo, *De Sacr.*, 9: θεὸς δὲ ἔλλειψιν ἢ πρόσθεσιν οὐκ ἀνέχεται.

ll. 21-25. **οὐδὲ τοπικῶς κινηθήσεται...οὔτε περὶ τὸ μέσον...κινηθήσεται**: Cf. fr. 4a, l. 29-30: οὔτε κίνησιν κινεῖται ἄλλην οὐδεμίαν. The first section of the fragment removed τὸ ὄν from the flow of Time. Now the highest level of reality must be relieved of all movement in Space. Once again the ultimate source of this concept is Parmenides (fr. 8): αὐτὰρ ἀκίνητον μεγάλων ἐν πείρασι δεσμῶν/ ἔστιν ἄναρχον ἄπαυστον, but the First Hypothesis of the *Parmenides* serves as the model for later Platonism. Cf. *Parm.*, 138c: οὐκ ἄρα κατ᾽ ἀλλοίωσιν γε κινεῖται; 138e-139a: οὔτ᾽ ποι ἰὸν καὶ ἕν τῳ γιγνόμενον χώραν ἀλλάττει...κατὰ πᾶσαν ἄρα κίνησιν τὸ ἓν ἀκίνητον; cf. *Crat.*, 439e: εἰ δὲ ἀεὶ ὡσαύτως ἔχει καὶ τὸ αὐτὸ ἐστι, πῶς ἂν γε μεταβάλλοι ἢ κινοῖτο. The *Timaeus* (40b) provides an important phrase: τὰς δὲ πέντε κινήσεις ἀκίνητον καὶ ἑστός (For ἑστός see below). Aristotle (*Meta.*, 988b), while describing the doctrine of Ideas held by the Platonists says: ἀκινησίας γὰρ αἴτια...φασιν; cf. 1069a: ἄλλη δὲ (sc. οὐσία) ἀκίνητος; and of course 1072b: ἔστι τι κινοῦν αὐτὸ ἀκίνητον. Philo (*De Opfic.*, 100) picks up the refrain: μόνον δ' οὔτε κινοῦν οὔτε κινούμενον ὁ πρεσβύτερος ἄρχων καὶ ἡγεμών. He then goes on to quote Philolaus: ἔστι γὰρ, φησίν, ἡγεμὼν καὶ ἄρχων ἁπάντων θεὸς εἷς ἀεὶ ὤν, μόνιμος, ἀκίνητος; cf. *De Post.*, 28: τὸ ὄν...ἀκίνητόν τε καὶ ἄτρεπτον. Albinus (X, 4) says of his πρῶτος θεός: οὔτε κινεῖ οὔτε κινεῖται. At X, 7 he paraphrases *Parm.*, 138c: μέρη γε μὴν οὐκ ἔχων ἀκίνητος ἂν εἴη κατὰ τόπον καὶ ἀλλοίωσιν. Plutarch (*De an. proc.*, 1023c) distinguishes between ψυχή and ἰδέα in this way: ἡ μὲν γὰρ ἀεικίνητος, ἡ δ' ἀκίνητος; cf. 1024a: τὸ γὰρ νοερὸν...ἀκίνητον. Plotinus (V. 1. 6.) denies motion to the One: παντὶ τῷ κινουμένῳ δεῖ τι εἶναι, πρὸς ὃ κινεῖται· μὴ ὄντος δὲ ἐκείνῳ μηδενὸς μὴ τιμώμεθα αὐτὸ κινεῖσθαι.

οὐδὲ μὲν ὀπίσω...οὔτε περὶ τὸ μέσον...κινηθήσεται: This ennumeration of the seven directions of movement apparently held some importance in certain discussions. Philo supplies essentially the same list at *De Opfic.*, 122 while analyzing the number seven: ἀλλὰ γὰρ καὶ κινήσεις ἑπτὰ εἶναι συμβέβηκε, τὴν ἄνω, τὴν κάτω, τὴν ἐπὶ δεξιά, τὴν ἐπ' εὐώνυμα, τὴν πρόσω, τὴν κατόπιν, τὴν ἐν κύκλῳ. Cf. *All. Leg.*, I, 4.

l. 25-26. **ἑστήξεται...καὶ ἑστηκὸς ἔσται:** Cf. fr. 4a, ll. 6-7: τὸ δὲ ἄτακτον οὐχ ἕστηκεν, ὅ τι δὲ μὴ ἕστηκεν, οὐκ ἂν εἴη ὄν; ll. 28-29: αὕτη γὰρ δὴ φύσεων πασῶν μόνη ἕστηκε; fr. 8, ll. 3-4: μένει δὲ κατὰ τὰ αὐτὰ καὶ ὡσαύτως ἕστηκε; fr. 15, ll. 3: ὁ μὲν πρῶτος θεὸς ἔσται ἑστώς. If being is freed from all movement, the corresponding concept must be that it is 'fixed', stable, and immoveable. A form of the verb ἱστάναι, usually the second perfect, is found in many Middle Platonic texts as a technical term to describe this stability. Often, as here, it appears at the conclusion of a philosophical argument concerned with the concept ἀκίνητος. Michael Williams (*Immoveable*, pp. 39-57) has chronicled the history of this use of the verb within the Platonic tradition to denote Rest. As he points out (p. 39), Plato himself does not often use the term to describe the immutability of the Forms. The common formula which serves this purpose is ὡσαύτως ἀεὶ ἔχει κατὰ ταὐτά (*Phd.*, 78d) or some variant of this phrase. Numenius uses this formula several times, closely connected with a form of ἱστάναι in each instance. It appears at the conclusion of this fragment in close asyndeton with ἑστηκός, and at ll. 3-4 of fr. 8 he strings three important expressions together: μένει δὲ κατὰ τὰ αὐτὰ καὶ ὡσαύτως ἕστηκε. μένει becomes the favorite expression of Plotinus, who seems to prefer it to ἕστηκε although he uses both terms (see below). The Platonic formula ὡσαύτως etc. continued to be a standard item of the Middle Platonic vocabulary, and the use of ἱστάναι took on a life of its own in the later tradition.

When Plato does use the verb in this way it is in dialogues where he is closely scrutinizing his own doctrine of Forms and hence some degree of ambiguity is involved. At *Soph.*, 248e-249a the Stranger calls the very concept into quesion: ὡς ἀληθῶς κίνησιν καὶ ζωὴν καὶ φρόνησιν ἢ ῥᾳδίως πεισθησόμεθα τῷ παντελῶς ὄντι μὴ παρεῖναι...ἀλλὰ σεμνὸν καὶ ἅγιον, νοῦν οὐκ ἔχον, ἀκίνητον ἑστὸς εἶναι; The ambiguity is confirmed at 249d: ἀνάγκη διὰ ταῦτα μήτε τῶν ἓν ἢ καὶ τὰ πολλὰ εἴδη λεγόντων τὸ πᾶν ἑστηκὸς ἀποδέχεσθαι, τῶν τε αὖ πανταχῇ τὸ ὂν κινούντων μηδὲ τὸ παράπαν ἀκούειν. A similar conclusion is reached in the rarified discussions of the *Parmenides*, cf. 139b: τὸ ἓν ἄρα, ὡς ἔοικεν, οὔτε ἕστηκεν οὔτε κινεῖται. (See Williams p. 40 for a discussion of the way in which these ambiguities are resolved within the entire fabric of Plato's thought.) Williams (p. 41) points to an earlier passage in the *Parmenides* that is more positive and which played a significant role in the later tradition. At *Parm.*, 132d, the young Socrates addresses Parmenides in this fashion: ἀλλ' ὦ Παρμενίδη, μάλιστα ἔμοιγε καταφαίνεται ὧδε ἔχειν· τὰ μὲν εἴδη ταῦτα ὥσπερ παραδείγματα ἑστάναι ἐν τῇ φύσει, τὰ τε ἄλλα τούτοις ἐοικέναι καὶ εἶναι ὁμοιώματα. It is characteristic of the later tradition that it ignored the philosophical subtleties and ambiguities of these dialogues, and in the search for a clear, positive doctrine seized on this statement of Socrates. Or as Des Places (p. 49, n. *ad. loc.*) simply puts it: "...les difficultés du *Sophiste* sur le "repos" de l'être semblent perdues de vue."

That this text became a set piece for the later tradition is demonstrated by passages in several writers. Diogenes Laertius (III, 13) quotes an outline of Plato's teaching by Alcimus, a writer from the fourth century B. C. E.: διὸ καὶ φησιν ἐν τῇ φύσει τὰς ἰδέας ἑστάναι καθάπερ παραδείγματα, τὰ δ' ἄλλα ταύταις ἐοικέναι τούτων ὁμοιώματα καθεστῶτα. Williams (p. 42) notes that Stobaeus (*Eclog.*, 1. 12. 6a), in a paragraph describing Plato's doctrine of Forms, quotes the passage from *Parm.*, 132d as his only proof text. Proclus also refers to the use of ἑστάναι in the passage in his commentary on the *Parmenides*. After quoting Lucian (*Vit. auc.* 18), Williams concludes that this use of ἑστάναι was already a part of the Early Academy's vocabulary.

It is with Philo that we first see this usage blossom in typical Middle Platonic fashion. The best example occurs in *De Posteritate Caini* where Philo is inspired into a flurry of this usage by several passages in the Septuagint which also employ the verb ἱστάναι. Cf. *De Post.*, 19: ὁ δὲ θεὸς...ἑστὼς ἔφθακε πάντα; 23: τὸ μὲν οὖν ἀκλινῶς ἑστῶς ὁ θεός ἐστι. At 27 Philo says: Ἀβραὰμ δὲ ὁ σοφὸς ἐπειδὴ ἕστηκε, συνεγγίζει τῷ ἑστῶτι θεῷ. He then quotes Gen. 18. 22, 23: "ἑστὼς ἦν ἔναντι κυρίου..." (The Septuagint reads ἑστηκώς.) At 29 he writes: τὰ κινούμενα κράτει τοῦ ἑστῶτος ἐπέχεται, and at 30 he concludes: οὐ γὰρ στήσεται ὁ θεός, ἀλλ' ἀεὶ ἕστηκεν. His repeated quotation of Deut. 5. 31 (σὺ δὲ αὐτοῦ στῆθι μετ' ἐμοῦ) throughout this section makes it evident that the biblical text serves as the impetus for this showcase of the Platonic usage. The term appears throughout his writing. Cf. *Leg. All.*, II, 83: ἀκλινὴς ἕστηκεν ἀεί; *De Mut.*, 57:

ὡμολόγησε περὶ τοῦ ὄντος, ὅτι πρὸς ἀλήθειαν ἑστὼς ἕν ἦν; De Gig., 49: στάσις τε καὶ ἠρεμία ἀκλιὴς ἡ παρὰ τὸν ἀκλινῶς ἑστῶτα ἀεὶ θεόν.

The terminology finds its way into the *Corpus Hermeticum* as well. *Corp. Herm* II stands as a kind of Hermetic exegesis on *Laws* 893b: Μῶν οὖν οὐκ ἐν χώρᾳ τινὶ τά τε ἑστῶτα ἕστηκεν καὶ τὰ κινούμενα κινεῖται; The Hermetic text elaborates the divine nature of τόπος, and reaches the following conclusion at II, 6: πᾶν δὲ τὸ κινούμενον οὐκ ἐν κινουμένῳ κινεῖται ἀλλ' ἐν ἑστῶτι· καὶ τὸ κινοῦν δὲ ἕστηκεν. At II, 12 it is said that this τόπος is νοῦς...αὐτὸς ἐν ἑαυτῷ ἑστώς. *Corp. Herm.* X, 14 presents this characteristic phrase: τὸ δε ἓν μόνον ἕστηκεν, οὐ κινεῖται. As was mentioned above, *Corp. Herm.* XI, 2 states: ὁ μὲν αἰὼν ἕστηκε περὶ τὸν θεόν. *Corp. Herm.* XVI, 15 uses the term to describe the stability of the logical part of the soul: ὁ δὲ λογικὸν μέρος τῆς ψυχῆς ἀδέσποτον τῶν δαιμόνων ἕστηκεν.

Plotinus' use of the verb is extensive and varied. At I. 8. 3 he uses it to delineate one of the deficiencies of Evil, which is οὐδαμῇ ἑστώς. He describes the static nature of νοῦς at II. 9. 3: ἔστι γὰρ ὡς ἔστι νοῦς ἀεὶ ὡσαύτως ἐνεργείᾳ κείμενος ἑστώσῃ. Cf. V. 3. 10: τὸ ἕν...μόνον καὶ ἔρημον ὂν πάντῃ στήσεται; V.3.12: αὐτὸν δὲ ἐπ' ἄκρῳ τῷ νοητῷ ἑστηκότα βασιλεύειν. He echoes *Parm.* 139b at VI. 9. 3 in an attempt to estblish the utter transcendance of the One: οὐδὲ κινούμενον οὐδ' αὖ ἑστώς...πρὸ κινήσεως, πρὸ στάσεως.

Fr. 6

l. 3. **τοῦ ἀσωμάτου**: Cf. fr. 4a, l. 27: οὐ δοκεῖ ἄλλο τι εἶναι ἢ μόνον γε τὸ ἀσωμάτον, and l. 31: δίκαιον ἐφάνη πρεσβεῦσαι τὸ ἀσωμάτον. This term denoting incorporeality is used sparingly by Plato. Cf. *Phlb.* 64b: κόσμος τι ἀσώματος ἄρξων καλῶς ἐμψύχου σώματος; *Pol.* 286a: τὰ γὰρ ἀσώματα, κάλλιστα ὄντα καὶ μέγιστα; *Soph.* 246b: νοητὰ ἄττα καὶ ἀσώματα εἴδη βιαζόμενοι τὴν ἀληθινὴν οὐσίαν εἶναι. Aristotle greatly expanded the use of the term, but by the time of Philo it used within the Platonic tradition primarily in reference to transcendant levels of reality. Cf. *De Opfic.* 18: ἑκάστῃ τῶν ἀσωμάτων ἰδεῶν τὰς σωματικὰς ἐξομοιῶν οὐσίας; 49: ὃς ἐκ τῆς ἀσωμάτου καὶ νοητῆς οὐσίας ἤγαγεν; *De Cher.* 49: ὁ θεὸς καὶ οἶκός ἀσωμάτων ἰδεῶν ἀσώματος χώρα; *Gig.* 61: κἀκεῖθι ᾤκησαν ἐγγραφθέντες ἀφθάρτον <καὶ> ἀσωμάτων ἰδεῶν πολιτείᾳ. Albinus, much like Numenius in the preceding fragments, provides an involved dialectic that ends in conclusions like the following: (X, 7) οὐ γὰρ ἔσται ἁπλοῦς οὐδὲ ἀρχικός· ὥστε ἀσώματος ἂν εἴη ὁ θεός; (XI, 1): εἰ δὲ αἱ ποιότητες ἀσώματοι, καὶ τὸ δημιουργικὸν τούτων ἀσώματον. At XI, 2 he uses a phrase so similar to that of Numenius at fr. 4a ll. 21-22 (see above) that it appears they are both echoing a standard school dialectic: οὐκ ἄλλο δὲ εὕροιμεν ἂν τοῦτο ἢ ἀσώματον; cf. also XXV, 1. The term appears at *Corp. Herm.* 2, 4: σώματι δὲ ἐναντία φύσις τὸ ἀσώματον...τὸ δὲ ἀσώματον ἢ θεῖόν ἐστι ἢ ὁ θεός.

ll. 5-6. **τὸ ὄνομα αὐτῷ εἶναι...ζητούμενον**: Cf. Aristotle, *Met.* 982b: τὸ ζητούμενον ὄνομα.

ll. 8-15. **τὸ μὴ γεγονέναι μηδὲ φθαρήσεται...τὸ ὂν ἀσώματον**: This section constitutes a suite of expressions that exhibit a dense, interwoven net of Platonic allusions. Each lends a slightly different coloring to the doctrine of the inherent immutability of true Being, the essential premise to the conclusion: τὸ ὂν ἀσώματον.

l. 8. **τὸ μὴ γεγονέναῖ μηδὲ φθαρήσεται**: See fr. 4a, l. 29 and note.

ll. 8-9. **Μήτε κίνησιν μηδεμίαν ἐνδέχεσθαι μήτε μεταβολήν**: This appears to be a conflation of two passages, one Platonic, one Aristotelian. Cf. *Rep.* 381b: πᾶν δὴ τὸ καλῶς ἔχον...ἐλαχίστην μεταβολὴν ὑπ᾽ ἄλλου ἐνδέχεται; and *Met.* 1072b: ἐπεὶ δ᾽ ἔστι τι κινοῦν αὐτὸ ἀκίνητον ὄν...τοῦτο οὐκ ἐνδέχεται ἄλλως ἔχειν οὐδαμῶς. For the concept of ἀκίνητος see fr. 5, ll. 21-25 and notes.

l. 10. **εἶναι δὲ ἁπλοῦν**: Cf. fr. 11, ll.12-13: ὁ θεὸς ὁ μὲν πρῶτος...ἐστιν ἁπλοῦς. The ultimate level of reality has been described as eternal (ἀΐδιον) and motionless (ἀκίνητος, ἕστηκε). Another characteristic is added here that helps define the category of ἀσώματος. The highest level of Being is absolutely simple, beyond all the multiplicity and complexity inherent in the realm of becoming. The seed of the concept appears in the discussion at *Rep.* 380d-382e. Cf. 380d: ἢ ἁπλοῦν τε εἶναι (sc. ὁ θεός) καὶ πάντων ἥκιστα τῆς ἑαυτοῦ ἰδέας ἐκβαίνειν; 381c: ἀδύνατον ἄρα, ἔφην, καὶ θεῷ ἐθέλειν αὐτὸν ἀλλοιοῦν, ἀλλ '...κάλλιστος καὶ ἄριστος ὢν εἰς τὸ δυνατὸν ἕκαστος αὐτῶν μένει ἀεὶ ἁπλῶς ἐν τῇ αὐτοῦ μορφῇ. The discussion concludes with this statement (382e): κομιδῇ ἄρα ὁ θεὸς ἁπλοῦν καὶ ἀληθές. A passage in Aristotle indicates that a more developed form of the teaching may have already existed within the Early Academy. At *Metaph.* 989b he discusses Anaxagoras' doctrine of first principles and appears to be bringing them up to date (ἴσως ἂν φανείη καινοπρεπεστέρως) by placing a Platonic gloss on them. The first part of his interpretation reads thus: συμβαίνει λέγειν αὐτῷ τὰς ἀρχὰς τό τε ἕν (τοῦτο γὰρ ἁπλοῦν καὶ ἀμιγές). Whatever the nature of this passage may be, it appears to have passed into the later Platonic tradition and is echoed by Philo at *Leg. All.* II, 2: ὁ θεὸς μόνος ἐστὶ καὶ ἕν, οὐ σύγκριμα, φύσις ἁπλῆ...ἀμιγὴς ἄλλῳ; Plutarch, *De Isid.* 382d: πρὸς τὸ πρῶτον ἐκεῖνο καὶ ἁπλοῦν ἐξάλλονται; Albinus, X, 1: ἔστι πρῶτα νοητὰ ἁπλᾶ, and X, 7: ἄτοπον δὲ τὸν θεὸν ἐξ ὕλης εἶναι καὶ εἴδους· οὐ γὰρ ἔσται ἁπλοῦς. Maximus (VIII, 6) goes so far as to apply the doctrine to the δαιμόνιον of Socrates: τὸ μὲν γὰρ Σωκράτους δαιμόνιον ἓν καὶ ἁπλοῦν.

But it is Plotinus who seizes on the term, and while using it in his attempt to describe the absolute unity and simplicity of the One, infuses it with a certain majesty. At V. 1. 9 he gives an account of Anaxagoras' teaching that is most likely merely an echo of *Metaph*. 989b: Ἀναξαγόρας δὲ νοῦν καθαρὸν καὶ ἀμιγῆ λέγων ἁπλοῦν καὶ αὐτὸς τίθεται τὸ πρῶτον καὶ χωριστὸν τὸ ἕν. At V. 5. 6, Plotinus expresses doubt that the term 'one' could adequately portray the simplicity of his ultimate principle. In a resigned tone he explains: τάχα γὰρ τοῦτο (*sc*. τὸ ἕν) ἐλέγετο, ἵνα ὁ ζητήσας, ἀρξάμενος ἀπ᾽ αὐτοῦ, ὃ πάντως ἁπλότητός ἐστι σημαντικόν, ἀποφήσῃ καὶ τοῦτο; cf. III. 8. 9: οὐδὲ γάρ, εἰ λέγοιμεν τὸ ἀγαθὸν εἶναι καὶ ἁπλούστατον εἶναι, δῆλον τι καὶ σαφὲς ἐροῦμεν. In a famous passage in his treatise on Beauty (I. 6. 7) he inserts the word into his paraphrase of *Symp*. 211e: ἕως ἄν τις παρελθὼν ἐν τῇ ἀναβάσει πᾶν ὅσον ἀλλότριον τοῦ θεοῦ αὐτῷ μόνῳ αὐτὸ μόνον ἴδῃ εἰλικρινές, ἁπλοῦν, καθαρόν. At III. 8. 9 he sets out the logical premises of the term: τοῦ γὰρ γεννηθέντος πανταχοῦ τὸ γεννῶν ἁπλούστερον. Εἰ οὖν τοῦτο νοῦν ἐγέννησεν, ἁπλούστερον νοῦ δεῖ αὐτὸ εἶναι. At V. 1. 5 Plotinus refers to the One simply as ὁ ἁπλοῦς.

l. 10 **ἀναλλοίωτον:** Cf. *Rep*. 381b-c: Ἀλλ᾽ ἄρα αὐτὸς (*sc*. ὁ θεός) αὑτὸν μεταβάλλοι ἂν καὶ ἀλλοιοῖ; ...ἀδύνατον ἄρα ἔφην, καὶ θεῷ ἐθέλειν αὑτὸν ἀλλοιοῦν; *Parm*. 138c: Οὐκ ἄρα κατ᾽ ἀλλοίωσίν γε κινεῖται; Aristotle, *Metaph*. 1073a: (of the Unmoved Mover) ἀλλὰ μὴν καὶ ὅτι ἀπαθὲς καὶ ἀναλλοίωτον; Albinus, X, 7: (paraphrasing *Parm*. 138c) μέρη γε μὴν οὐκ ἔχων ἀκίνητος ἂν εἴη κατὰ τόπον καὶ ἀλλοίωσιν.

ll. 10-12. **ἐν ἰδέᾳ τῇ αὐτῇ...ἐξίστασθαι...μήθ᾽ ὑφ᾽ ἑτέρου προσαναγκάζεσθαι:** Cf. fr. 8, l. 3: οὐδαμῇ ἐξιστάμενον ἐξ ἑαυτοῦ. The language comes from the same discussion in the *Rebublic* that introduced the term ἁπλοῦν. Cf. *Rep*. 380d: πάντων ἥκιστα τῆς ἑαυτοῦ ἰδέας ἐκβαίνειν...οὐκ ἀνάγκη, εἴπερ τι ἐξίσταιτο τῆς αὑτοῦ ἰδέας, ἢ ὑφ᾽ ἑαυτοῦ μεθίστασθαι ἢ ὑπ᾽ ἄλλου; The *Cratylus* (439d), which Numenius refers to just below, also uses this vocabulary: εἰ δὲ ἀεὶ ὡσαύτως ἔχει καὶ τὸ αὐτό ἐστι, πῶς ἂν τοῦτό γε μεταβάλλοι ἢ μηδὲν ἐξιστάμενον τῆς αὑτοῦ ἰδέας; Cf. the abbreviated paraphrase of Plotinus at VI. 5. 3: Εἰ δὴ τὸ ὂν ὄντως τοῦτο καὶ ὡσαύτως ἔχει καὶ οὐκ ἐξίστασθαι αὐτὸ ἑαυτοῦ...

l. 14. **τὰ ονόματα ὁμοιώσει τῶν πραγμάτων**: Crat. 439d. Philo also has an echo of this passage (*De. Cher.* 56): ὡς αὐτὸ τὸ πρᾶγμα ἐξ ἀνάγκης εὐθὺς εἶναι τοὔνομα καὶ καθ' οὗ τίθεται διαφέρειν μηδέν.

Fr. 7

ll. 5-7. **ταῦτα τοῖς δόγμασι τοῖς Πλάτωνος...οἷου Πυθαγόρου**: Cf. fr. 1b, ll. 3-4 and notes.

l. 8. **φέρ' ἀναμνησθῶ πῶς λέγει**: Numenius claims to be reciting (Timaeus, 27d-28a) from memory, and as Des Places points out (p. 50, n. 2), he cites the text closely except that he omits (with FY, Proclus and Simplicius) the ἀεί found at the beginning of 28a. He also omits the phrase ἀεὶ κατὰ ταὐτὰ ὂν which follows περιληπτόν.

Fr. 8

l. 2. **ἄτρεπτον**: Another term indicating immutability. This use of the word may have been borrowed from Stoicism, cf. Chrysippus, *Stoic.* 2. 158. It appears as an important part of Philo's vocabulary, used in a Platonic sense. Cf. *Leg. All.* I, 51: δεῖ γὰρ ἡγεῖσθαι...αὐτὸν (sc. τὸν θεόν) καὶ ἕνα καὶ ἄφθαρτον καὶ ἄτρεπτον; *Leg. All.* II, 33: ὥσπερ θεοῦ τὸ ἄτρεπτον εἶναι; 89: ἐὰν μάθῃ, ὅτι πάντα τὰ ἄλλα τρέπεται, μόνος δὲ οὗτος ἄτρεπτος ἐστι; *De Cher.* 51: τὸν ἀγένητον καὶ ἄτρεπτον θεόν; *De Post.* 27: ὄντως γὰρ ἀτρέπτῳ ψυχῇ πρὸς τὸν ἄτρεπτον θεὸν μόνη πρόσοδός ἐστι.

l. 3. **ἐξιστάμενον ἐξ ἑαυτοῦ**: See fr. 6, ll. 11-12 and notes.

l. 5. **εἰ τὸ σῶμα ῥεῖ**: Cf. fr. 3, l. 11: ποταμὸς γὰρ ἡ ὕλη and note; fr. 11, l. 17: (of ὕλη) ρεούσης. The image originates, of course, with Heraclitus as reported by Plato himself. Cf. *Crat.* 402a: Λέγει που Ἡράκλειτος ὅτι πάντα χωρεῖ καὶ οὐδὲν μένει; 411b: οὐδὲν αὐτῶν μόνιμον εἶναι οὐδὲ βέβαιον, ἀλλὰ ῥεῖν καὶ φέρεσθαι; 439d: δοκεῖ ταῦτα πάντα ῥεῖν; *Tht.* 182c: κινεῖται καὶ ῥει, ὥς φατε, τὰ πάντα. Plato also uses the language for his own purposes. Cf. *Phd.* 87d: εἰ γὰρ ῥέοι τὸ σῶμα; *Tim.* 43a: ἐπίρρυτον σῶμα καὶ ἀπόρρυτον. Aristotle (*Metaph.* 987a) reports the Heraclitean doctrine that influenced Plato: ὡς ἁπάντων τῶν αἰσθητῶν ἀεὶ ῥεόντων.

The fluidity of Matter was an essential aspect of Xenocrates' teaching. Cf. fr. 28 (Heinze): Ξενοκράτης συνεστάναι τὸ πᾶν ἐκ τοῦ ἑνὸς καὶ τοῦ ἀενάου, ἀέναον τὴν ὕλην αἰνιττόμενος διὰ τοῦ πλήθους. Albinus (XI, 2) echoes the passages from the Dialogues: παθητὰ γὰρ τὰ σώματα καὶ ῥευστά. Cf. Maximus II, 10: κρείττων (*sc.* ὁ θεός) ...πάσης ῥεούσης φύσεως. Plotinus makes extensive use of the doctrine. In an interesting passage at V. 1. 9, he claims that Heraclitus subscribed to the doctrine of the One: Ἡράκλειτος δὲ τὸ ἓν οἶδεν ἀίδιον καὶ νοητόν· τὰ γὰρ σώματα γίγνεται ἀεὶ καὶ ῥέοντα. Cf. V. 6. 6: τὰ δὲ ῥεῖ καὶ οὐ μένει, ὅσα ἐν αἰσθήσει; IV. 7. 3: οὐδ' ἂν εἴη σῶμα οὐδὲν ψυχικῆς δυνάμεως οὐκ οὔσης. ῥεῖ γάρ, καὶ ἐν φορᾷ αὐτοῦ ἡ φύσις; III. 6. 6: Μαρτυρεῖ δὲ καὶ ἡ γένεσις αὐτῶν (*sc.* τῶν σωμάτων) καὶ ἡ ῥοὴ καὶ ἡ φθορά.

l. 6. **ὑπὸ τῆς εὐθὺ μεταβολῆς:** Cf. Plutarch, *De E* 392b: ἀλλ' ὀξύτητι καὶ τάχει μεταβολῆς 'σκίδνησι καὶ πάλιν συνάγει'...

ἀποδιδράσκει: Cf. Plotinus, I. 8. 4: φεύγει τε οὐσίαν ἀεὶ ῥέοντα.

l. 7. **ἀόριστον:** See notes to fr. 4a, l. 3.

l. 14. **'Τί γάρ ἐστι Πλάτων ἢ Μωσῆς ἀττικίζων';:** Gager (pp. 66-68) sets out the history of this sentence (cf. also Beutler col. 666, and Stern, vol. 2, pp. 206-216). It's earliest occurrence appears in Clement *Strom.* I, 22, 150. 4 as a direct quotation from Numenius. Eusebius quotes this passage from Clement at 9, 6, 9 in an effort to show that pagan writers were acquainted with the teachings of the Jews. The present fragment is the next use of it. It appears again in Book 2 of Theodoret's *Graecorum Affectionum Curatio*, and is probably a quotation from Eusebius (see Gager p. 66, n. 121). Theodoret (2. 114) goes a step further though, and adds that Plato σεσύληκεν ἐκ τῆς Μωυσῆς θεολογίας. The saying again appears in Hesychius of Miletus (*Fragmenta Historicum Graecorum* 171) who follows the tone of Theodoret's σεσύληκεν: "Numenius the Apamean...questioned the thought of Plato because he stole what he said about god and the cosmos from the books of Moses. Therefore he said, 'What is Plato...?'" The saying's last appearance occurs in the Suidas (s. v. Νουμήνιος) which is nearly a verbatim reproduction of Hesychius.

As Gager points out on p. 67, the authenticity of the saying has been called into question. Dodds (*N & A*, p. 6) was struck by the formulation of the remark which seems to emphasize the position of Moses: "...we might urge that instead of describing Plato as 'Moses talking Attic' Numenius *ought* to have described Moses as 'Plato talking Hebrew'. Puech (p. 32) says that this formulation as well as Eusebius' curious manner of introducing the saying (l. 12: εἰκότως δῆτα εἰς αὐτὸν ἐκεῖνο τὸ λόγιον περιφέρεται) led Schürer (*Geschichte*, III, p. 627) and Reinach (*Textes*, p. 175, n. 2) to view it as a Jewish oral tradition. But he reiterates the fact that Clement presents the saying as a direct quotation, and as Gager (*op. cit.*) suggests, the chronological proximity of Clement to Numenius (approximately 50 years) must outweigh Eusebius' odd ambivalence.

Assuming that the saying is authentic, what aspect of Plato's philosophy could Numenius have been referring to? Merlan (*Cambridge History*, p. 100) gives a reasonable conjecture: the apparent equivalence in Numenius' mind of the Platonic τὸ ὄν and the ὁ ὤν of the Septuagint; cf. fr. 13 and notes.

Fr. 9

1. 2. Ἰαννῆς καὶ Ἰαμβρῆς: Origen refers to this text at *Contra Celsum* IV, 51 (fr. 10a): Ἐκτίθεται (sc. Νουμήνιος) καὶ τὴν περὶ Μωϋσέως καὶ Ἰαννοῦ καὶ Ἰαμβροῦ ἱστορίαν. The reference is, of course, to the story of the magical contest at Exod. 7:11-13. However the inclusion of the Egyptian magicians' names lends added interest to this fragment, since they are not provided by the biblical narrative. Gager (pp. 137-140) provides an excellent commentary on this issue. He tells us that the earliest reference to the magicians is found in the Damascus Document from Qumran which mentions "Jannes and his brother whom Belial raised up in the time of Moses and Aaron." The most well-known reference is found in 2 Timothy 3:8 where it is merely stated: Ἰάννης καὶ Ἰαμβρῆς ἀνέστησαν Μωϋσεῖ. Pliny the Elder seems to have had access to a garbled version of this tradition, for in Book 30 of his *Natural History* he groups Jannes along with Moses while describing an ancient magical tradition. Apuleius may have been using Pliny as a source when he presents a list of magicians that includes Moses and Johannes (a variant of Jannes) in chapter 90 of his *Apology*. There is also a pseudepigraphic book entitled *Jannes and Jambres*, of which only fragments exist; see *OTP* 2:427-442.

It would appear from the phrase τὰ δ' ἑξῆς at the beginning of the fragment that Numenius is providing a catalogue of famous magicians from the past, and the focus here is on the Egyptians. Moses, although he is praised for being "very powerful at prayer", is simply introduced as antagonist to the Egyptian priests, who succeed in repelling his plagues. Dodds (*N & A*, p. 6), comments on this fact while refuting Puech's hypothesis that Numenius was a Jew: "And would any Jew, orthodox or not, allow that the Pharaoh's magicians, Iannes and Iambres, were a match for Moses?" Waszink (*P & N*, p. 49) views Numenius' mention of the Egyptians' names as proof that his

Commentary 143

knowledge of Jewish traditions extended well beyond the opening verses of Genesis.

l. 7. ὁ Μουσαῖος: Hadas (p. 74 and n. 6) Gager (p. 139) and Des Places (p. 52 n. 3) point out that this form of Moses' name is found elsewhere only in the Jewish apologist Artapanus (*apud* Alexander Polyhistor, cited by Eusebius *P. E.*, 9. 27. 3). Gager interprets the situation thus: "In Artapanus it obviously represents an attempt to identify Moses with Musaeus, the teacher of Orpheus, but it seems unlikely that Numenius had the same intention. In his case it is probably a simple adjustment of the orthography to common Greek name."

Fr. 10

l. 1-2. ἐκτίθεται καὶ περὶ τοῦ 'Ιησοῦ ἱστορίαν: This is the only reference we have to Numenius' knowledge of Christianity. Whether Numenius was allegorizing a passage from writings or an oral tradition remains unclear. However it is not implausible, considering his knowledge of the Septuagint (see fr. 1c and note), that he had also done some reading in Christian texts.

ll. 4-5. ἐκτίθεται καὶ τὴν περὶ Μωϋσεως...ἱστορίαν: See fr. 9 and note.

Fr. 11

ll. 4-5. θεοῦ πέρι πρώτου καὶ δευτέρου: According to Krämer (p. 37-38), the first example, and presumably the origin of the use of ordinal numbers to designate levels of being is found in the teachings of Xenocrates. Cf. fr. 15: ἥντινα προσαγορεύει καὶ Ζῆνα περιττὸν καὶ νοῦν, ὅστις ἐστὶν αὐτῷ πρῶτος θεός.

l. 5. χρὴ πρότερον διελέσθαι ἕκαστα ἐν τάξει: This rather verbose preamble on the importance of definition appears to be modeled after *Phdr*. 237c: Περὶ παντός, ὦ παῖ, μία ἀρχὴ τοῖς μέλλουσι καλῶς βουλεύεσθαι· εἰδέναι δεῖ περὶ οὗ ἂ ἦ ἡ βουλή, ἢ παντὸς ἁμαρτάνειν ἀνάγκη.

l. 9-10. **μὴ δὴ πάθωμεν ἡμεῖς ταὐτόν**: Cf. *Phdr*. 237c: ἐγὼ οὖν καὶ σὺ μὴ πάθωμεν ὃ ἄλλοις ἐπιτιμῶμεν.

ll. 10. **θεὸν δὲ προσκαλεσάμενοι**: Cf. Plotinus V. 1. 6: ὧδε οὖν λεγέσθω θεὸν αὐτὸν ἐπικαλεσαμένοις.

ll. 12-13: **ὁ θεὸς μέντοι ὁ πρῶτος**: The πρῶτος θεός of Xenocrates (see above), or at least the terminology he initiated, became a fixture of the later tradition. Plutarch (*De Isid.* 372e) says of Isis: ἔχει δὲ σύμφυτον ἔρωτα τοῦ πρώτου καὶ κυριωτάτου πάντων; cf. 382d: πρὸς τὸ πρῶτον ἐκεῖνο καὶ ἁπλοῦν...ἐξάλλονται. It can be seen in Moderatus (*apud.* Simplicius *In Phys.* A 7, 230. 34 sqq., Diels): οὗτος γὰρ (*sc.* Μοδέρατος) κατὰ τοὺς Πυθαγορείους τὸ μὲν πρῶτον ἓν ὑπὲρ τὸ εἶναι καὶ πᾶσαν οὐσίαν ἀποφαίνεται.

Albinus (X. 3) employs a list of epithets to describe his First God: ὁ πρῶτος θεὸς ἀΐδιος ἐστιν, ἄρρητος, αὐτοτελής, τουτέστιν ἀπροσδεής, ἀειτελὴς τουτέστιν ἀεὶ τέλειος, παντελὴς τουτέστι πάντη τέλειος; cf. the *primus deus* of Apuleius (De Platone 194). It appears in the *Chaldean Oracles* (fr. 5.) πῦρ ἐπέκεινα τὸ πρῶτον, and the *Corpus Hermeticum* (2, 5): νοητὸς γὰρ πρῶτος ὁ θεός ἐστιν ἡμῖν. Plotinus uses the term while admonishing the Gnostics for their endless multiplication of divine principles. At II. 9. 6 he suggests the proper course to be taken: δέον ἐκεῖ τὸ ὡς ὅτι μάλιστα ὀλίγον εἰς ἀριθμὸν διώκειν καὶ τῷ μετὰ τὸ πρῶτον τὰ πάντα ἀποδιδόντας ἀπηλλάχθαι. Just below this he lists the doctrines that the Gnostics claim to have received from Plato: ψυχῆς ἀθανασίαν, νοητὸν κόσμον, θεὸν τὸν πρῶτον. Ennead V. 4 derives its title from the term and naturally abounds in this kind of language; cf. V. 4. 1: εἴ τι ἔστι μετὰ τὸ πρῶτον, ἀνάγκη ἐξ ἐκείνου εἶναι, τὸ τελεώτατον καὶ τὸ πρῶτον ἀγαθόν.

ll. 13-14. ἐν ἑαυτοῦ ὤν ἐστιν ἁπλοῦς, διὰ τὸ ἑαυτῷ συγγιγνόμενος διόλου μή ποτε εἶναι διαίρετος: Just as τὸ ὄν in fr. 8, l. 3 is described as οὐδαμῶς οὐδαμῇ ἐξιστάμενον ἐξ ἑαυτοῦ, so too the πρῶτος θεός remains perfectly simple and indivisible by remaining concentrated in his own self-contemplation. Plutarch (*De An Proc.* 1024c) uses the phrase ἐφ᾽ ἑαυτοῦ to express the same concept: ὁ δὲ νοῦς αὐτὸς μὲν ἐφ᾽ ἑαυτοῦ μόνιμος ἦν καὶ ἀκίνητος. Cf. Plotinus V. 3. 12: δεῖ μὲν γάρ τι πρὸ πάντων εἶναι ἁπλοῦν, τοῦτο καὶ πάντων ἕτερον τῶν μετ᾽ αὐτό, ἐφ᾽ ἑαυτοῦ ὄν. The *Chaldean Oracles* have a more poetic version, cf. fr. 3: ὁ πατὴρ ἥρπασσεν ἑαυτόν. See Festugiére *Révélation*, vol. III, p. 54.

ll. 14-15. ὁ θεὸς μέντοι ὁ δεύτερος: The Second God of Numenius is one of the most interesting and original facets of his teaching. The δεύτερος θεός that appears in Middle Platonism is foreshadowed in the famous passage of (?)Plato's Second Letter 312e: περὶ τὸν πάντων βασιλέα πάντ᾽ ἐστὶ καὶ ἐκείνου ἕνεκα πάντα, καὶ ἐκεῖνο αἴτιον ἁπάντων τῶν καλῶν· δεύτερον δὲ πέρι τὰ δεύτερα, καὶ τρίτον πέρι τὰ τρίτα. Merlan (*Drei anm.*, pp. 138-139) sees Numenius making direct use of this passage in the formulation of his doctrine, and no doubt he was familiar with it. However there were some preparatory steps within the tradition that made the inclusion of a δεύτερος θεός logical. The extant fragments of Xenocrates' do not specifically name a δεύτερος θεός, but his Dyad, or World Soul which is named after his πρῶτος θεός would naturally be viewed as such. The introduction by Eudorus of Alexandria of a second One was a decisive step in this direction. Cf. *apud* Simplicius *in Phys.* 181. 27 sqq. (where Eudorus claims to be describing 'Pythagorean' doctrines): ὡς μὲν ἀρχὴ τὸ ἕν, ὡς δὲ στοιχεῖα τὸ ἕν καὶ ἡ ἀόριστος δυάς, ἀρχαὶ ἄμφω ἓν ὄντα πάλιν· καὶ δῆλον ὅτι ἄλλο μέν ἐστιν ἓν ἡ ἀρχὴ τῶν πάντων, ἄλλο δὲ ἓν τὸ τῇ δυάδι ἀντικείμενον, ὃ καὶ μονάδα καλοῦσιν. Dörrie (*Eudorus* p. 32) sees this as "nichts als ein Referat"; Dillon however (p.119, with n. 1) thinks it "perverse" to hold this view, and continues:

"By that reckoning, Antiochus must be taken simply as a faithful reporter of Old Academic doctrine, and indeed Philo as an accurate interpreter of the philosophy of Moses." Whatever the case may be, the doctrine of a first principal characterized only by its absolute transcendence, with another set of principles below it was introduced into the tradition. Dillon (p. 128) would take Philo as evidence that Eudorus' first One, which he called ὁ ὑπεράνω θεός, was completely devoid of attributes. Several statements made in *Legum Allegoria* II support this interpretation. Cf. *Leg. All.* II, 1: μόνος δὲ καὶ καθ' αὑτὸν εἷς ὢν ὁ θεός, οὐδὲν δὲ ὅμοιον θεῷ; 2: ὁ θεὸς μόνος ἐστὶ καὶ ἕν,...φύσις ἁπλῆ. At 3, after a series of attribute denying remarks, he concludes with something that sounds like an echo of a passage from Eudorus: τέτακται οὖν ὁ θεὸς κατὰ τὸ ἓν καὶ τὴν μονάδα, μᾶλλον δὲ ἡ μονὰς κατὰ τὸν ἕνα θεόν. It is with Philo, and his doctrine of the Λόγος as a subordinate deity, that we also see the emergence of the δεύτερος θεός. Cf. *Leg. All.* II, 86: τὸ δὲ γενικώτατόν ἐστιν ὁ θεός, καὶ δεύτερος ὁ θεοῦ λόγος.

Another step was taken by Moderatus. In a text that was partially quoted above (see note to ll. 12-13), he distinguishes three separate 'Ones': τὸ μὲν πρῶτον ἓν ὑπὲρ τὸ εἶναι καὶ πᾶσαν οὐσίαν ἀποφαίνεται, τὸ δὲ δεύτερον ἕν, ὅπερ ἐστὶ τὸ ὄντως ὂν καὶ νοητόν, τὰ εἴδη φησὶν εἶναι, τὸ δὲ τρίτον, ὅπερ ἐστὶ τὸ ψυχικόν. In his landmark article "The *Parmenides* of Plato and the Neoplatonic 'One'", Dodds discerned in this text a commentary on the first three hypotheses of that dialogue (see especially pp. 137-138). It is probably safe to say also that there was some influence from the Second Letter. A text from Plotinus actually draws the two together. At V. 1. 8 he quotes the familiar passage from the Second Letter, and a few lines below he expressly interprets the *Parmenides* in a way that seems to echo Moderatus: ὁ δὲ παρὰ Πλάτωνι Παρμενίδης ἀκριβέστερον λέγων διαιρεῖ ἀπ' ἀλλήλων τὸ πρῶτον ἕν, ὃ κυριώτερον ἕν, καὶ δεύτερον ἓν πολλὰ λέγων, καὶ τρίτον ἓν καὶ πολλά. Armstrong, in a note to this passage, suggests that the interpretation may be Neo-Pythagorean and points to the article by Dodds.

The language of Moderatus helped set the stage for the emergence of the δεύτερος θεός. Albinus is another step along the way, but as Dörrie (*Eudorus* p. 34) and Dillon (p. 128) point out, he seems to be more directly influenced by Eudorus. Dörrie sees the ὑπεράνω θεός of Eudorus appearing in Albinus as his ὑπερουράνιος θεός, and Dillon thinks that Albinus' description of the πρῶτος θεός is also dependent on Eudorus' first One. The ὑπερουράνιος θεός appears at XXVIII, 3 in Albinus' discussion of the Platonic τέλος, which appears to have been redefined by Eudorus to comprise the doctrine of the ὁμοίωσις θεῷ found in the *Theaetetus*, 176b (see Dillon p. 122). For Albinus, however, it is first necessary to ascertain which god is the goal of this ὁμοίωσις. He makes the following distinction: τὸ τέλος εἴη ἂν τὸ ἐξομοιωθῆναι θεῷ, θεῷ δηλονότι τῷ ἐπουρανίῳ, μὴ τῷ μὰ Δία ὑπερουρανίῳ, ὃς οὐκ ἀρετὴν ἔχει, ἀμείνων δ' ἐστὶ ταύτης. Here Albinus is ranging a secondary god beneath his supreme god, which he elsewhere describes as πρῶτος θεός or πρῶτος νοῦς. In order to determine what ἐπουράνιος θεός signifies, it is necessary to examine several interesting passages that are primarily concerned with describing the πρῶτος θεός. At X, 2 Albinus says of this deity: αἴτιος ὑπάρχων τοῦ ἀεὶ ἐνεργεῖν τῷ νῷ τοῦ σύμπαντος οὐρανοῦ. After a few lines inspired by Aristotle's *Metaph.* 1072a he concludes: οὕτω γε δὴ καὶ οὗτος ὁ νοῦς κινήσει τὸν νοῦν τοῦ σύμπαντος οὐρανοῦ. So although Albinus does not use the term δεύτερος, he is indeed placing a second νοῦς below his primary god. At X, 3 this νοῦς τοῦ σύμπαντος οὐρανοῦ is identified with the World Soul of the *Timaeus*: πατὴρ δέ ἐστι τῷ αἴτιος εἶναι πάντων καὶ κοσμεῖν τὸν οὐράνιον νοῦν καὶ τὴν ψυχὴν τοῦ κόσμου. With the expression of this relationship, we are very close to Numenius' δεύτερος θεός, as will be seen below.

Also closely related to Numenius is *Chald. Or.* fr. 7: Πάντα γὰρ ἐξετέλεσσε πατὴρ καὶ νῷ παρέδωκε δευτέρῳ, ὃν πρῶτον κληΐζετε πᾶν γένος ἀνδρῶν (on this passage see fr. 17 and notes). This Second Nous is also referred as δὶς ἐπέκεινα in fr. 169 (see Lewy p. 9, n. 23 and p. 114, n. 187). Cf. also the ἕτερος νοῦς δημιουργός of the *Poimandres* (*Corp. Herm.* I, 9). Later Plotinus (V. 5. 3) will be able to make the following remark about his Νοῦς: καὶ θεὸς αὕτη ἡ φύσις, καὶ θεὸς δεύτερος προφαίνων ἑαυτὸν πρὶν ὁρᾶν ἐκεῖνον.

l. 15. **καὶ τρίτος ἐστὶν εἷς**: See fr. 21, l. 4 and note.

ll. 15-21. **συμφερόμενος δὲ τῇ ὕλῃ...ἐπορεξάμενος τῆς ὕλης**: Dillon (p. 7) has made it clear that the Demiurge of the *Timaeus* underwent a major transformation in the later tradition. As a result of the introduction of an absolutely transcendent first principle, a πρῶτος θεός not directly involved in the creation of the cosmos, the active principle, or Demiurge assumed the role of a δεύτερος θεός (see above). Dillon also makes the important observation that this subordinate Demiurge was "always liable to conflation with the World Soul in its rational aspect", and this conflation is exactly what we see happening in the δεύτερος θεός of Numenius. It is clearly seen in fr. 15 where the following distinction is made: ὁ μὲν οὖν πρῶτος περὶ τὰ νοητά, ὁ δὲ δεύτερος περὶ τὰ νοητὰ καὶ αἰσθητά. Cf. Philo *De vita Mos.* II, 127 where the λόγος is described in the same manner: διττὸς γὰρ ὁ λόγος ἔν τε τῷ παντὶ καὶ ἐν ἀνθρώπου φύσει· κατὰ μὲν τὸ πᾶν ὅ τε περὶ τῶν ἀσωμάτων καὶ παραδειγματικῶν ἰδεῶν, ἐξ ὧν ὁ νοητὸς ἐπάγη κόσμος, καὶ ὁ περὶ τῶν ὁρατῶν, ἃ δὴ μιμήματα καὶ ἀπεικονίσματα τῶν ἰδεῶν ἐκείνων ἐστίν, ἐξ ὧν ὁ αἰσθητὸς οὗτος ἀπετελεῖτο. A similar expression is found in *Chald. Or.* fr. 8:...δυὰς παρὰ τῷδε κάθηται· ἀμφότερον ἔχει, νῷ μὲν κατέχειν τὰ νοητά, αἴσθησιν δ' ἐπάγειν κόσμοις. This double orientation of the Demiurge (cf. fr. 16, l. 10: ὁ γὰρ δεύτερος διττὸς ὤν; Plotinus V. 3. 3: μέσον δυνάμεως διττῆς, χείρονος καὶ βελτίονος, χείρονος μὲν τῆς αἰσθήσεως. βελτίονος δὲ τοῦ νοῦ) is an echo of *Tim.* 37b where it is said that the World Soul can be either πρὸς τὰ κατὰ ταὐτὰ ἔχοντα ἀεί or περὶ τὸ αἰσθητόν. Krämer (pp. 72-75) argues strongly for the identification of Demiurge-World Soul in Numenius and the *Chaldean Oracles*, and suggests that it may have Gnostic coloring. He adduces a description of the Valentinian Demiurge found in Hippol. *Ref.* VI, 33 that exhibits the same dual 'above and below' orientation. Whether or not this aspect of Numenius' δεύτερος θεός is influenced by Valentinian Gnosticism is questionable. But as one moves further through this passage it becomes obvious that some flavor of Gnosticism has played a role in its formation.

l. 16. **ὕλῃ δυάδι οὔσῃ**: See fr. 4a ll. 2-3 and note.

ἑνοῖ μὲν αὐτήν, σχίζεται δὲ ὑπ' αὐτῆς: Note the ambivalent nature of the action. Matter is unified by the influence of the Demiurge and creation becomes possible, but the deity is somehow damaged or lessened as a result. Compare the superior position of the πρῶτος θεός in l. 14: μή ποτε εἶναι διαίρετος.

l. 17. **ἐπιθυμητικὸν ἦθος ἐχούσης**: Cf. the σύμφυτος ἐπιθυμία of *Pol.* 272e. Festugière (*Herm. Tris.* p. 24, n. 60) calls attention to this passage in reference to *Poimandres* 24: καὶ τὸ ἦθος τῷ δαίμονι ἀνενέργητον παραδίδως. He interprets thus: "Il y a des passions qui viennent de la ὕλη et autres qui sont dues aux astres."

ῥεούσης: See fr. 8 l. 5 and note.

ll. 17-18. **τῷ οὖν μὴ εἶναι πρὸς τῷ νοητῷ (ἦν γὰρ ἂν πρὸς ἑαυτῷ)**: Numenius emphasizes that the proper orientation for the δεύτερος θεός is towards the noetic realm. Once again his condition is contrasted with that of the πρῶτος θεός who is described as ἐν ἑαυτοῦ ὤν. Cf. Plotinus V. 1. 6: (of the One) ἐπιστραφέντος ἀεὶ ἐκείνου πρὸς αὐτό; I. 1. 9: (of the Soul) ἀτρεμήσει οὖν οὐδὲν ἡ ψυχὴ πρὸς ἑαυτὴν καὶ ἐν ἑαυτῇ.

ll. 18-19. **διὰ τὸ τὴν ὕλην βλέπειν**: The perfect concentration of the Demiurge is disrupted by a glance towards matter. For Numenius' doctrine of a pre-existent ὕλη see fr. 52 and notes. Plotinus adopts this kind of language to describe the deficiencies of spiritual entities. In I. 8. 4 he contrasts the perfect soul with a lesser one: ἡ μὲν οὖν τελεία καὶ πρὸς νοῦν νεύουσα ψυχὴ ἀεὶ καθαρὰ καὶ ὕλην ἀπέστραπται...ἡ δὲ μὴ μείνασα τοῦτο, ἀλλ' ἐξ αὐτῆς προελθοῦσα...σκότος ὁρᾷ καὶ ἔχει ἤδη ὕλην βλέπουσα εἰς ὃ μὴ βλέπει. At VI. 9. 2 Plotinus seems to be echoing and responding to this fragment while describing the proper activity of Nous: τὸν νοῦν ἀνάγκη ἐν τῷ νοεῖν εἶναι καὶ τόν γε ἄριστον καὶ τὸν οὐ πρὸς τὸ ἔξω βλέπουσα νοεῖν τὸ πρὸ αὐτοῦ· εἰς αὐτὸν γὰρ ἐπιστρέφων εἰς ἀρχὴν ἐπιστρέφει.

l. 19. ταύτης ἐπιμελούμενος: The phrase serves to characterize Numenius' Demiurge as a World Soul. Cf. *Phdr.* 246b: ψυχὴ πᾶσα παντὸς ἐπιμελεῖται τοῦ ἀψύχου; *Leg.* 897c: δῆλον ὡς τὴν ἀρίστην ψυχὴν φατέον ἐπιμελεῖσθαι τοῦ κοσμοῦ παντός.

ἀπερίοπτος ἑαυτοῦ γίγνεται: Plotinus describes the souls that incline towards bodies in a similar way at IV. 3. 17: ἀμελήσαντες αὐτῶν ἔλαθον.

l. 20. ἅπτεται τοῦ αἰσθητοῦ: An activity of the World Soul. Cf. *Tim.* 37a: ὅταν μὲν περὶ τὸ αἰσθητὸν γίγνηται.

l. 21. ἀνάγει τε ἔτι εἰς τὸ ἴδιον ἦθος: This appears to be a rough paraphrase of *Leg.* 897c which was partially quoted above: καὶ ἄγειν αὐτόν τὴν τοιαύτην ὁδὸν ἐκείνην. There is an interesting passage in *Corp. Herm.* 16, 5 that, although it is setting forth a solar theology, uses language so similar to Numenius that dependence in one direction or the other must be suspected: οὕτω γὰρ οὐρανὸν καὶ γῆν συνδεῖ ὁ δημιουργός, λέγω δὴ ὁ ἥλιος, τὴν μὲν οὐσίαν κατάγων, τὴν δὲ ὕλην ἀνάγων καὶ περὶ αὐτὸν καὶ εἰς αὐτὸν τὰ πάντα ἕλκων. For ἦθος see fr. 2, l. 14 and note.

l. 21. ἐπορεξάμενος τῆς ὕλης: This 'desire of the Demiurge' is one of the most Gnostic elements of Numenius' philosophy. Cf. fr. 18, ll. 11-12 where it is said of the Demiurge: λαμβάνει...τὸ δ' ὁρμητικὸν ἀπὸ τῆς ἐφέσεως. Cf. Plotinus' account in IV. 8. 7 of the manner in which Soul becomes involved in the lower levels of reality: ...εἰ μὴ μετὰ τοῦ αὐτῆς ἀσφαλοῦς διακοσμοῖ, προθυμίᾳ δὲ πλείονι εἰς τὸ εἴσω δύοιτο μὴ μείνασα ὅλη μεθ' ὅλης. In passages where he describes the declension of Nous away from the One as a type of 'fall' he comes very close to the language of Numenius. Cf. III. 8. 8: ἀλλ' ἀρξάμενος ὡς ἐν οὐχ ὡς ἤρξατο ἔμεινεν, ἀλλ' ἔλαθεν ἑαυτὸν πολὺς γενόμενος, οἷον βεβαρημένος, καὶ ἐξείλιξεν αὐτὸν πάντα ἔχειν θέλων.

Fr. 12

l. 2. οὔτε δημιουργεῖν ἐστι χρεὼν τὸν πρῶτον: Another indication of the ultimate transcendence of the First god. Cf. ἀργόν below l. 12. The πρῶτος θεός of Albinus (also called πατήρ; see below) similarly entrusts creation to a second οὐράνιος νοῦς. At X. 3 it is said of this second Nous: ὃς κοσμηθεὶς ὑπὸ τοῦ πατρὸς διακοσμεῖ σύμπασιν φύσιν ἐν τῷδε τῷ κόσμῳ. Tractate X of the *Corpus Hermeticum* also has a πατὴρ θεός who does not create directly. At X, 3 the following reason is given: οὐ γὰρ ἐρῶ, ὦ Τάτ, ποιοῦντι· ὁ γὰρ ποίων ἐλλιπής ἐστι πολλῷ χρόνῳ, ἐν ᾧ ὁτὲ μὲν ποιεῖ, ὁτὲ δὲ οὐ ποιεῖ. Cf. *Poimandres* 9 where the πατὴρ θεός entrusts creation to a ἕτερος νοῦς δημιουργός. So too, the system of the *Chaldean Oracles* absolves the first principle of creative activity in the material realm. Cf. fr. 5:

> ...οὐ γὰρ ἐς ὕλην
> πῦρ ἐπέκεινα τὸ πρῶτον ἑὴν δύναμιν κατακλείει
> ἔργοις ἀλλὰ νόῳ· νοῦ γὰρ νόος ἐστὶν ὁ κόσμου
> τεχνίτης πυρίου.

Celsus (*apud* Origen *Contra Celsum* VI, 61) demonstrates how a Middle Platonist who shared Numenius' view might view the creation narrative in Genesis: οὐ θέμις τὸν πρῶτον θεὸν κάμνειν οὔτε χειρουργεῖν οὔτε κελεύειν. Cf. also *De Mundo* 397b.

ll. 2-3. πατέρα τὸν πρῶτον θεόν: A common designation for the highest god in Middle Platonism which has Platonic models. Cf. *Tim.* 27c and 41a (of the Demiurge), *Ep.* VI 323d. For other Middle Platonic use see Xenocrates fr. 15; Philo *De Opfic.* 144; Albinus X, 3; Maximus XI, 8 and 11; *Chald. Or.* fr. 3 and 7; *Corp. Herm.* X, 1-3.

l. 12. ἀργὸν εἶναι ἔργων συμπάντων: Cf. l. 2 above. Armstrong (*Architecture* p. 12) thinks that the statement is Aristotelian in spirit. Interestingly enough, *Corp. Herm.* XI, 5 contains a polemic against this teaching. Whether it is aimed at Numenius himself or some other common source is difficult to tell: οὐ γὰρ ἀργος ὁ θεός, ἐπεὶ πάντα ἂν ἦν ἀργά· ἅπαντα γὰρ πλήρη τοῦ θεοῦ. ἀλλ᾽ οὐδὲ ἐν τῷ κόσμῳ ἐστὶν ἀργία οὐδαμοῦ. The theme is repeated at XI, 13: εἰ δὲ μήτε ἀργός ἐστι, τέλειος δέ, ἄρα πάντα ποιεῖ. Dodds (*N. & A.*, p. 7) and Des Places (p. 54, n. 3) call attention to the *hebes deus* of Marcion (Tertullian, *Adv. Marc.* V, 19) in this context. Cf. also Plotinus' use of ἀνενέργητον at V. 6. 6. Beutler (col. 669) suggests that the Platonist Origen's ὅτι μόνος ποιητὴς ὁ βασιλεύς could have been directed at Numenius.

l. 13. βασιλέα: Another common designation for the πρῶτος θεός in the Middle Platonic tradition. It is most likely inspired by the famous passage in the Second Letter 312e: περὶ τὸν πάντων βασιλέα πάντ᾽ ἐστὶ καὶ ἐκείνου ἕνεκα πάντα, καὶ ἐκεῖνο αἴτιον ἁπάντων τῶν καλῶν. Cf. also *Phlb.* 28c; *Leg.* 904a; Xenocrates fr. 15; Maximus XI, 5; Plutarch *De Isid.* 383a. Plotinus quotes the Second Letter at I. 8. 2 and VI. 7. 42. Cf. II. 9. 9: τὸν μέγαν τὸν ἐκεῖ βασιλέα; the extended metaphor in V. 5. 3 culminating in the expression βασιλεὺς βασιλέως καὶ βασιλέων; V. 3. 12: αὐτὸν δὲ ἐπ᾽ ἄκρῳ τῷ νοητῷ ἑστηκότα βασιλεύειν ἐπ᾽ αὐτοῦ.

ll.13-14. ἡγεμονεῖν δι' οὐρανοῦ ἰόντα: An echo of *Phdr.* 247b: ὁ μὲν δὴ μέγας ἡγεμὼν ἐν οὐρανῷ Ζεύς...πρῶτος πορεύται. The influence of 246b may also be present: ψυχὴ πᾶσα...πάντα δὲ οὐρανὸν περιπολεῖ. Cf. Xenocrates fr. 15: τὴν μὲν ὡς ἄρρενα πατρὸς ἔχουσιν τάξιν ἐν οὐρανῷ βασιλεύουσαν.

ll. 14-15. κάτω τοῦ νοῦ πεμπομένου...πᾶσι τοῖς συντεταγμένοις: The notion of νοῦς being reserved for an elite group is not common in the Platonic tradition. Beutler (col. 670) attributes it to the "weitverbreitete Gedanke von der ἐπιτηδειότης des Aufnehmenden." It is well established in the Hermetic writings and has affinities with certain Gnostic teachings.

There are several passages in the *Timaeus* that might have served as an impetus to this doctrine. At 51d Plato draws several distinctions between νοῦς and δόξα ἀληθής, concluding at 51e: τοῦ μὲν πάντα ἄνδρα μετέχειν φατέον, νοῦ δὲ θεοῦς, ἀνθρώπων δὲ γένος βραχύ τι. And at 90a the "highest form of soul" is portrayed as a δαίμων which is given to men. Plato is using figurative language here, but as happened so often, poetic language was taken over by segments of the tradition as literal doctrine. Dillon (p. 213) suggests that the doctrine of νοῦς as a separate entity was furthered by Aristotle *De. An.* III 5: οὗτος ὁ νοῦς χωριστὸς καὶ ἀπαθῆς καὶ ἀμιγής...χωρισθεὶς δ' ἐστὶ μόνον τουθ' ὅπερ ἐστί, καὶ τοῦτο μόνον ἀθάνατον καὶ ἀΐδιον. The concept is fully established in Plutarch's *De Genio Socratis*. Beutler (*op. cit.*) points to 589c of this text as an example of the notion of "der ἐπιτηδειότης des Aufnehmenden." There it is said that a particular class of περιττοὶ ἄνδρες are capable of receiving the thoughts of higher beings (τὸ νοηθὲν ὑπὸ τῶν ἀμεινόνων). Dillon (p. 212) calls attention to 591 d-e where during a discussion inspired by *Tim.* 90a a distinction is made between the part of the soul that submerges itself in the body and that which remains outside (ἔξω τὸ καθαρώτατον). At 591e the narrator concludes: τὸ μὲν οὖν ὑποβρύχιον ἐν τῷ σώματι φερόμενον ψυχὴ λέγεται· τὸ δὲ φθορᾶς λειφθὲν οἱ πολλοὶ νοῦν καλοῦντες ἐντὸς εἶναι νομίζουσιν αὐτῶν...οἱ δὲ ορθῶς ὑπονοοῦντες ὡς ἐκτὸν ὄντα δαίμονα προσαγορεύουσι.

This text in Plutarch, then, contains the two elements that will merge into the doctrine being examined here: 1) the notion of a spiritual elite, and 2) a conception of νοῦς as a separate entity. The fully developed teaching of a νοῦς that is the manifestation of a divine being bestowed upon a select group of individuals emerges clearly in the *Corpus Hermeticum*. Dillon (p. 213) suggests that Plutarch may have indeed have been influenced by Hermetic concepts and points to Tractate X as a likely source. At section 21 of this text the imagery of *Tim.* 90a is taken over in part, and νοῦς is described as a δαίμων in the service of God who punishes the wicked and aids the virtuous. After a description of the punishments it inflicts on the impious, another form of action is presented: εἰς δὲ τὴν εὐσεβῆ ψυχὴν ὁ νοῦς ἐμβὰς ὁδηγεῖ αὐτὴν ἐπὶ τὸ τῆς γνώσεως φῶς. At the beginning of 22 it is said: διό, ὦ τέκνον, εὐχαριστοῦντα τῷ θεῷ δεῖ εὔχεσθαι καλοῦ τοῦ νοῦ τυχεῖν. Further, at the end of 23, Tat appears confused by this doctrine and his father responds: οἴει οὖν ὦ τέκνον, ὅτι πᾶσα ψυχὴ νοῦν ἔχει τὸν ἀγαθόν; He then distinguishes once again between νοῦς as ἀγαθὸς δαίμων and the punishing force, which he describes in language similar to what we have in Numenius: τοῦ καταπεμπομένου ὑπὸ τῆς Δίκης. Section 24 continues to portray the condition of ψυχή without νοῦς, emphasizing the fact that νοῦς abandons the torpid soul: ἡ δὲ τοιαύτη ψυχή ὦ τέκνον, νοῦν οὐκ ἔχει.

All of this is reminiscent of the familiar section of the *Poimandres* (22-23) where the narrator also expresses surprise at this doctrine: οὐ πάντες γὰρ ἄνθρωποι νοῦν ἔχουσιν; Poimandres responds with some impatience: εὐφήμει, ὦ οὗτος, λαλῶν· παραγίνομαι αὐτὸς ἐγὼ ὁ Νοῦς τοῖς ὁσίοις καὶ ἀγαθοῖς...τοῖς δὲ ἀνοήτοις καὶ κακοῖς...πόρρωθεν εἰμι. There is a punishing δαίμων here also, which does not receive the status of νοῦς. Dillon (p. 391) views both of these tractates as possible influences on Plutarch and explains his reasoning: "It seems more likely that this concept of the *nous* as a faculty, or entity, operative only in a select few, is an alien concept working its influence on Plutarch, rather than a Platonist concept that is being reshaped by the Hermetics." If this holds true for Plutarch, it must certainly be even more likely in the case of Numenius. Dillon (p. 371), while not being emphatic, suggests the possibility in his remarks on this fragment: "This selective participation in intellect is reminiscent of the separable intellect which we met in Plutarch, and even more of the *nous* of *Poimandres*, ch. 22, which is present only to the elect." Surprisingly, Dillon refrains from discussing another Tractate from the *Corpus Hermeticum* that expressly deals with this theme in language that is similar to that of Numenius. At IV, 3 the premise of the doctrine is announced: τὸν μὲν οὖν λόγον, ὦ Τάτ, ἐν πᾶσι τοῖς ἀνθρώποις ἐμέρισε, τὸν δὲ νοῦν οὐκέτι. The doctrine produces the familiar surprise in the student: διὰ τί οὖν ὦ πάτερ, οὐ πᾶσιν ἐμέρισε τὸν νοῦν ὁ θεός; After explaining that God wanted νοῦς to be a kind of ἆθλον within the soul, Hermes describes the method of its dispersal in IV, 4: κρατῆρα μέγαν πληρώσας τούτου κατέπεμψε. God is then called τὸν καταπέμψαντα τὸν κρατῆρα. The results of partaking in νοῦς are then spelled out: ὅσοι...ἐβαπτίσαντο τοῦ νοός, οὗτοι μετέσχον τῆς γνώσεως καὶ τέλειοι ἐγένετο ἄνθρωποι, τὸν νοῦν δεξάμενοι. Cf. Plotinus III. 8. 9: ἢ οὐκ ἔστιν, ὅπου μὴ ἔστιν, οἷς ἐστι μετέχειν αὐτοῦ.

l. 15. ἐν διεξόδῳ: Cf. *Phdr.* 247a: πολλαί...διέξοδοι ἐντὸς οὐρανοῦ.

ll. 16-20. Βλέποντος...πρὸς ἡμῶν ἕκαστον...εὐδαίμονος: Witt (p. 131, n. 6) and Dillon (p. 371) refer to the *Politicus*-Myth as the model for this section.

l. 16. ἐπεστραμμένου πρὸς ἡμῶν ἕκαστον: The verb ἐπιστρέφειν is normally used in the tradition to describe the action of Soul in its turning away from lower realms toward higher levels of reality. Plutarch uses this language while discussing the influence of νοῦς upon the World Soul at *De An. Proc.* 1024d: ὁ δὲ νοῦς...ἐγγενόμενος τῇ ψυχῇ καὶ κρατήσας εἰς ἑαυτὸν ἐπιστρέφει. Albinus' πρῶτος θεός performs a similar action upon the 'sleeping' World Soul at X, 3: τὴν ψυχὴν τοῦ κόσμου ἐπεγείρας καὶ εἰς ἑαυτὸν ἐπιστρέψας; and XIV, 3: ἐγείρων καὶ ἐπιστρέφων πρὸς αὐτὸν τόν τε νοῦν αὐτῆς. Cf. Maximus X, 3: ἄλλο τι ἢ τὴν σχολὴν τῆς ψυχῆς τοῦ ἀγαθοῦ ἀνδρὸς ἀπὸ τῶν τοῦ σώματος ἡδονῶν καὶ παθήματων, ὅταν ἀπαλλαγεῖσα τοῦ περὶ ἐκεῖνο ταράχου, καὶ ἐπιστρέψασα εἰς ἑαυτὴν τὸν νοῦν, ἔμπαλιν ἐντυγχάνει τῷ ἀληθεῖ αὐτῷ, ἀφεμένη τῶν εἰδώλων; Plotinus (V. 8. 11) uses the verb in reference to the orientation of the individual soul during contemplation: εἰ δ᾽ ἐπιστραφείη εἰς δύο, καθαρὸς μένων ἐφεξῆς ἐστιν αὐτῷ ὥστε αὐτῷ παρεῖναι ἐκείνως πάλιν, εἰ πάλιν ἐπ᾽ αὐτὸν στρέφοι. ἐν δὲ τῇ ἐπιστροφῇ κέρδος...ἔχει.

ll. 18-19. **μεταστρέφοντος δὲ εἰς τὴν ἑαυτοῦ περιωπὴν τοῦ θεοῦ**: The image is drawn from *Pol.* 272e: τότε δὴ τοῦ παντὸς ὁ μὲν κυβερνήτης...εἰς τὴν αὐτοῦ περιωπὴν ἀπέστη.

Fr. 13

l. 2. **γεωργῷ**: Cf. *Phdr.* 276b: ὁ νοῦν ἔχων γεωργός, ὧν σπερμάτων κήδοιτο; Philo *Leg. All.* I 47: καθάπερ ἀγαθὸς γεωργός (of the the human νοῦς); *Corp. Herm.* IX, 6: ὥσπερ ἀγαθὸς ζωῆς γεωργός (see below); XIV, 10: ἴδε γεωργὸν σπέρμα καταβάλλοντα εἰς τὴν γῆν; see Puech's note in *Corpus Hermeticum* I, p. 104, n. 24.

φυτεύοντα: Cf. *Tim.* 42a: ὁπότε δὴ σώμασιν ἐμφυτευθεῖεν (sc. αἱ ψυχαῖ) ἐξ ἀνάγκης; Philo *Leg. All.* I, 48: πρέπει τῷ θεῷ φυτεύειν...ἐν ψυχῇ τὰς ἀρετάς; 49: θεοῦ δὲ σπείροντος καὶ φυτεύοντος ἐν ψυχῇ τὰ καλά, ὁ λέγων νοῦς ὅτι "ἐγὼ φυτεύω" ἀσεβεῖ. οὐ φυτεύσεις οὖν, ὅταν ὁ θεὸς φυτουργῇ; Maximus XI,

7: ὁ δὲ (sc. νοῦς) τῇ πάσῃ ψυχῇ ἐμπεφυτευμένος; *Corp. Herm.* XIV, 10: ἴδε τὸν αὐτὸν ἄμβελον φυτεύοντα.

l. 3. **ἀνὰ τὸν αὐτὸν λόγον**: Des Places (p. 55 n. *ad. loc.*) uses the parallel usage at *Phd.* 110d to support the reading of the Bologne (O) manuscript. He then calls attention to the expression two lines preceding, ἀνὰ λόγον τὰ φυόμενα φύεσθαι, and makes the likely suggestion that this grouping of words exerted an unconscious influence on Numenius.

l. 4. **Ὁ μὲν γε ὢν σπέρμα πάσης ψυχῆς σπείρει**: Beutler (col. 670) misinterprets the passage: "der erste ist σπέρμα πάσης ψυχῆς." As Krämer points out (p. 83, n. 213): "Die Abtrennung ὁ μὲν γε ὢν σπέρμα ist wegen des folgenden σπείρει unmöglich." He adopts Festugière's interpretation (*Révélation* vol. III, p. 44, n. 2) of ὤν without predicate derived from Philo's usage, cf. *Leg. All.* III, 181: χρεῖος γὰρ οὐδενός ἐστιν ὁ ὤν (see Krämer's note for other examples). Krämer sees the model for this in the Septuagint version of Exodus 3:14: ἐγώ εἰμι ὁ ὤν, which is quoted by Philo at *De Somn.* I, 231 and *De Mut.* 11, and could have been appropriated by Numenius either through Philo or the general Alexandrian-Jewish tradition. Cf. fr. 1c and notes. Dodds on the other hand (*N. & A.*, p. 15) feels that the ὤν "must have some predicate" and states that Festugière's interpretation of ὁ ὤν as a 'Hebraism' cannot be defended. He suggests in turn that the text is corrupt and proposes the emendation ὁ μέν γε α ' ὤν (= πρῶτος ὤν); cf. fr. 16, l. 10. Whittaker (*Moses*, passim) has devoted an entire article to the refutation of Dodds' position. Krämer also rejects it, and Waszink (*P. und A.*, p. 51, n. 4) terms it: "unwahrscheinlich Deutung und Konjectur von Dodds."

σπείρει: The image of divine 'sowing' derives from Plato. Cf. *Phd.* 83d: ὥστε ταχὺ πάλιν πίπτειν εἰς ἄλλο σῶμα καὶ ὥσπερ σπειρομένη ἐμφύεσθαι; *Tim.* 41e: δέοι δὲ σπαρείσας αὐτὰς εἰς τὰ προσήκοντα ἑκάσταις ἕκαστα ὄργανα χρόνων φῦναι; 42d: διαθεσμοθετήσας δὲ πάντα αὐτοῖς ταῦτα ἵνα τῆς ἔπειτα εἴη κακίας ἑκάστων ἀναίτιος, ἔσπειρεν τοὺς μὲν εἰς γῆν, τοὺς δὲ εἰς σελήνην, τοὺς δ᾽ εἰς τἆλλα ὅσα ὄργανα χρόνου· τὸ δὲ μετὰ τὸν σπόρον... Cf. Philo, *De Cher.* 44: τίς οὖν ὁ σπείρων ἐν αὐταῖς τὰ καλὰ πλὴν ὁ πατήρ; *Leg. All* I, 49: θεοῦ δὲ σπείροντος καὶ φυτεύοντος ἐν ψυχῇ τὰ καλά. It appears along with the image of the γεωργός in the texts from the *Corpus Hermeticum* cited above; cf. IX, 6: ἵνα πάντα παρ᾽ ἑαυτῷ ἀπὸ τοῦ θεοῦ λαβών, τὰ σπέρματα φυλάττων ἐν ἑαυτῷ πάντα ποιῇ ἐνεργῶς; XIV, 10: ἴδε γεωργὸν σπέρμα καταβάλλοντα εἰς τὴν γῆν...οὕτω καὶ ὁ θεὸς ἐν μὲν οὐρανῷ ἀθανασίαν σπείρει. Cf. also John 4:37: ὁ λόγος ἐστὶν ἀληθινὸς ὅτι ἄλλος ἐστὶν ὁ σπείρων καὶ ἄλλος ὁ θερίζων.

l. 5. **ὁ νομοθέτης**: The epithet has been labeled 'biblical' due to James 4:12: εἷς ἐστιν ὁ νομοθέτης καὶ κριτὴς ὁ δυνάμενος σῶσαι καὶ ἀπολέσαι (see Des Places, p. 108 n. 3). Beutler (col. 670 and *Gnomon* XVI, 1940, p. 112) states that the term had a place in Middle Platonism. (Festugière, III, p. 44, n. 2 quotes Beutler's opinion). The closest parallel is Albinus, XVI, 2 where he is summarizing *Tim.* 41e-42d: ὁ τῶν ὅλων δημιουργός...εἶπεν αὐταῖς νομοθέτου τρόπον. Thillet (in Des Places' note) views that section of the *Timaeus* as the origin for the metaphorical use of the term. He cites the use of νόμους at 41e and διαθεσμοθετήσας at 42d (see above). Plotinus applies the title to his Νοῦς at V. 9. 5, and in a note to the passage Armstrong suggests that Plotinus is influenced by Numenius' usage. He apparently thinks the term has a biblical flavor since he suggests that Numenius may be "consciously" attempting to identify his Demiurge with the God of the Jews through its use.

l. 6. **διανέμει**: Another echo from *Tim.* 41e: συστήσας δὲ τὸ πᾶν διεῖλεν ψυχὰς ἰσαρίθμους τοῖς ἄστροις, ἔνειμέν θ᾽ ἑκάστην πρὸς ἕκαστον. Cf. Plutarch, *De Iside* 377b: τὸν μὲν διδόντα τὰς ἀρχάς, τὴν δ᾽ ὑποδεχομένην καὶ διανέμουσαν; *Corp. Herm.* X, 7: ἀπὸ μιᾶ ψυχῆς τῆς τοῦ παντὸς πᾶσαι αἱ ψυχαί εἰσιν...ὥσπερ ἀπονενεμημέναι.

l. 7. τὰ ἐκεῖθεν προκαταβεβλημένα: Krämer (p. 69, n. 171) and following him Des Places (p. 109, n. 5) see this as an allusion to the Valentinian concept of the προβολή. Cf. Hippolytus, *Refut.* VI 29, 37-38.

Fr. 14

ll. 11-14. ἐξαφθέντα ἀφ᾽ ἑτέρου λύχνου...τοιοῦτον τὸ χρῆμα ἐστι τὸ τῆς ἐπιστήμης: Philo (*De Gig.* 25 uses the same image to illustrate the nature of ἐπιστήμη: ἀλλ᾽ οἷα γένοιτ᾽ ἂν ἀπὸ πυρός, ὅ, κἂν μυρίας δᾷδας ἐξάψῃ, μένει μηδ᾽ ὁτιοῦν ἐλλατωθέν ἐν ὁμοίῳ. τοιαύτη τις ἐστι καὶ τῆς ἐπιστήμης ἡ φύσις. τοὺς γὰρ φοιτητὰς καὶ γνωρίμους ἀποφήνασα ἐμπείρους πάντας κατ᾽ οὐδὲν μέρος ἐλλατοῦνται. Numenius' statement several lines above this section that the bestower of knowledge also benefits from the transfer finds a parallel in the continuation of the Philonic text: πολλάκις δὲ καὶ πρὸς τὸ ἄμεινον ἐπιδίδωσιν...αἱ γὰρ συνεχεῖς πρὸς ἑτέρους ὁμιλίαι μελέτην καὶ ἄσκησιν ἐμποιοῦσαι ὁλόκληρον τελειότητα ἐργάζονται. Cf. Numenius' more concise προσώνησε τῇ περὶ ὧν ἠπίστατο ἀναμνήσει. Although the concept and imagery is identical, the different nuances of language suggest that Philo and Numenius are drawing from a philosophical commonplace. Witt (*Classical Quarterly*, XXV, 1931, p. 200, n. 8) argues that it can be traced back to Posidonius. Dodds (*Proclus*, p. 214) also sees it as a product of the Middle Stoa. Dodds (*N & A*, p. 23) also cites this concept of 'undiminished giving' as one of the two "main structural laws or postulates of Neoplatonism...explicitly formulated by Numenius." He says further that the concept "implies non-reciprocating causal relations, so that the cause is never dissipated among its effects. This is cardinal for Plotinus, who like Numenius uses the illustration of communicated knowledge (IV. 9. 5; III. 9. 2)...It is not original with Numenius; I have argued elsewhere that it is a product of the Middle Stoa. But

Numenius states it more clearly and in a more generalized form than anyone else before Plotinus."

l. 17. ἕξις: Cf. Theat. 197b: ἐπιστήμης που ἕξιν φασὶν αὐτὸ εἶναι.

Fr. 15

l. 2. βίοι: Cf. fr. 12, l. 20: τὸν δὲ νοῦν ζῆν βίου ἐπαυρόμενον εὐδαίμονος; Phdr. 248a: καὶ οὗτος μὲν θεῶν βίος; Philo *Quod Deus* 32: αἰὼν ὁ βίος ἐστὶν αὐτοῦ (sc. τοῦ θεοῦ).

l. 3. ἑστώς: See fr. 5, ll. 25-26 and notes.

ll. 3-5. **ὁ δὲ δεύτερος περὶ τὰ νοητὰ καὶ αἰσθητά**: See fr. 11, 14-17 and notes.

l. 8. **στάσιν φημὶ εἶναι κίνησιν σύμφυτον**: The language ultimately drives from *Soph*. 250-c: τρίτον ἄρα τι παρὰ ταῦτα τὸ ὂν ἐν τῇ ψυχῇ τιθείς, ὡς ὑπ' ἐκείνου τήν τε στάσιν καὶ τὴν κίνησιν περιεχομένην...κινδυνεύομεν ὡς ἀληθῶς τρίτον ἀπομαντεύεσθαι τι τὸ ὄν, ὅταν κίνησιν καὶ στάσιν εἶναι λέγωμεν. But as was the case with the *Parmenides*, the language was appropriated by the tradition stripped of the dialectical complexities it was carrying, underwent other influences, especially Peripatetic, and ultimately took on a life of its own. In this case, the phraseology of the *Sophist* is infused with touches from Aristotle's Unmoved Mover; cf. *Metaph*. 1072a: ἔστι τι ὃ οὐ κινούμενον κινεῖ, ἀΐδιον, καὶ οὐσία καὶ ἐνέργεια οὖσα (see Krämer (p. 70 and p. 114, n. 307; Des Places p. 110, n. 4). Krämer (*op. cit.*) links this passage in Numenius closely with Albinus' description of his πρῶτος θεός at X, 2 which is cast in Aristotelian terms: ἐνεργεῖ δὲ ἀκίνητος...καὶ ὡς τὸ ὀρεκτὸν κινεῖ τὴν ὄρεξιν ἀκίνητον ὑπάρχον.

There are parallels in the *Corpus Hermeticum* that come even closer to Numenius. Cf. II, 8: πᾶσα οὖν κίνησις ἐν στάσει καὶ ὑπὸ στάσεως κινεῖται. In his note to this passage (*Corpus*

Hermeticum I, p. 40, n. 15) Festugière quotes the second half of our fragment, interpreting (as does Krämer) the κίνησιν σύμφυτον in terms of the Aristotelian ἐνέργεια. *Corp. Herm.* X, 11 uses similar language: ἡ δὲ νοητὴ στάσις κινεῖ τὴν ὑλικὴν κίνησιν τὸν τρόπον τοῦτον. XI, 17 begins with the μὴ θαυμάσῃς admonition employed by Numenius and concludes: τοῦτο γὰρ...ὥσπερ κίνησίς ἐστι τοῦ θεοῦ, κινεῖν τὰ πάντα καὶ ζωοποιεῖν. In a completely different context XII, 17 applies the contradictory terms to ἡ γῆ: ἀλλὰ καὶ πολυκίνητος μόνη ἥδε καὶ στασίμη.

ll. 9-10. **ἡ σωτηρία ἀναχεῖται εἰς τὰ ὅλα**: Krämer (p. 179, n. 183) points to *Metaph.* 1091b as the source for this use of σωτηρία: θαυμαστὸν δ᾽ εἰ τῷ πρώτῳ καὶ ἀϊδίῳ καὶ αὐταρκεστάτῳ τοῦτ᾽ αὐτὸ πρῶτον οὐχ ὡς ἀγαθὸν ὑπάρχει τὸ αὔταρκες καὶ ἡ σωτηρία. Cf. *De Mundo* 397b: ἀρχαῖος μὲν οὖν τις λόγος καὶ πάτριός ἐστι πᾶσιν ἀνθρώποις ὡς ἐκ θεοῦ καὶ διὰ θεοῦ ἡμῖν συνέστηκεν, οὐδεμία δὲ φύσις αὐτὴ καθ᾽ ἑαυτὴν ἐστιν αὐτάρκης, ἐρημωθεῖσα τῆς ἐκ τούτου σωτηρίας; Maximus XI, 12: βασιλέα δὲ αὐτὸν δὴ τὸν μέγαν...παρέχοντα τοῖς πειθομένοις σωτηρίαν ὑπάρχουσαν ἐν αὐτῷ; *Corp. Herm.* II, 12: Νοῦς...ἑστώς...καὶ σωτήριος τῶν ὄντων; Plotinus VI. 7. 23: ἀλλὰ τί νῦν ποιεῖ (sc. τὸ ἀγαθόν); ἢ᾽ καὶ νῦν σώζει ἐκεῖνα.

Fr. 16

l. 2. **Εἰ δ᾽ ἔστι μὲν νοητὸν ἡ οὐσία καὶ ἡ ἰδέα**: Cf. *Corp. Herm.* XVI, 6: εἰ δέ τίς ἐστι καὶ νοητὴ οὐσία...; Philo *De Opfic.* 49: ὃς (sc. ὁ ἀριθμὸς τρεῖς) ἐκ τῆς ἀσωμάτου καὶ νοητῆς οὐσίας ἤγαγεν; Albinus XIV, 2: Λέγων οὖν εἶναι τινα νοητὴν οὐσίαν.

l. 3. **πρεσβύτερον**: A common term to denote ontological priority. Cf. *Tim.* 34c: οὐ γὰρ ἂν ἀρχεσθαι πρεσβύτερον ὑπὸ νεωτέρου συνέρξας εἴασεν; Philo *De Opfic.* 100: μόνον δ᾽ οὔτε κινοῦν οὔτε κινούμενον ὁ πρεσβύτερος ἄρχων καὶ ἡγεμών;

Plotinus V. 5. 12: τὸ δὲ (sc. ἀγαθόν) πρεσβύτερον οὐ χρόνῳ, ἀλλὰ τῷ ἀληθεῖ.

αἴτιον εἶναι ὁ νοῦς: Albinus presents a similar, more detailed *via eminentiae* that also leads to the final αἴτιον. At X, 2 the following progression is presented: ἐπεὶ δὲ ψυχῆς νοῦς ἀμείνων, νοῦ δὲ τοῦ ἐν δυνάμει ὁ κατ' ἐνέργειαν πάντα νοῶν καὶ ἅμα καὶ ἀεί, τούτου δὲ καλλίων ὁ αἴτιος τούτου καὶ ὅπερ ἂν ἔτι ἀνωτέρω τούτων ὑφέστηκεν. οὗτος ἂν εἴη ὁ πρῶτος θεός, αἴτιον ὑπάρχων τοῦ ἀεὶ ἐνεργεῖν τῷ νῷ τοῦ σύμπαντος οὐρανοῦ. Albinus also refers to his πρῶτος θεός as οὗτος ὁ νοῦς several lines later and calls it νοῦν τὸν πρῶτον at XXVII, 1. As Krämer points out (p. 41), this use of νοῦς to denote the highest god is not present in Plato and he states that it must be viewed as an innovation of Xenocrates. Indeed in fr. 15 (Heinze) it is reported that he called his first principle Ζῆνα καὶ περιττὸν καὶ νοῦν, ὅστις ἐστὶν αὐτῷ πρῶτος θεός.

Albinus, in his usual fashion, surrounds his use of νοῦς with Aristotelian concepts and undoubtedly Aristotle's portrayal of the Prime Mover was readily assimilated by later Platonists (see Dillon, p. 13) Still, it is inaccurate to label a thinker like Numenius an 'Aristotelianizing Platonist', as Armstrong does (*Architecture*, p. 7), simply because he conceives of his First God as νοῦς. Festugière (*Révélation*, IV, p. 127) downplays Numenius' use of the term: "Si Numénius l'appelle aussi Intellect c'est en vertu d'une inconsequence de langage que nous avons déjà notée plus haut (pp. 112s.) à propos de Maxime de Tyr; et cette inconsequence vient elle- même de la contamination, alors usuelle, entre le platonisme et l'aristotélisme en matière de théologie." Dillon (p. xv) expresses a similar opinion concerning Middle Platonic terminology: "Indeed our enthusiasm for ferreting out 'Aristotelianisms' and 'Stoicisms'…tends rather to lead to false view of the situation. In fact a wide range of terms and concepts had already by the beginning of the first century B. C. become virtually common currency, and in later times there was really no sense of their ultimate provenance." *Corp. Herm.* II, 14 goes a step beyond both Numenius and Albinus: ὁ οὖν θεὸς οὐ νοῦς ἐστιν, αἴτιος δὲ τοῦ <νοῦν> εἶναι.

l. 3-4. **οὗτος μόνος εὕρηται ὢν τὸ ἀγαθόν**: The concept of the ultimate transcendant principle as the sole source of good was fairly widespread. Cf. Philo *De. Mut. Nom.* 7: ἐζήτει (sc. Μωυσῆς) τὸν τριπόθητον καὶ μόνον ἀγαθὸν τηλαυγῶς ἰδεῖν; Mark 10:18: ὁ δὲ Ἰησοῦς εἶπεν αὐτῷ: τί με λέγεις ἀγαθόν; οὐδεὶς ἀγαθὸς εἰ μὴ εἷς θεός. It finds emphatic expression in the *Corpus Hermeticum,* couched in language that is very similar to that of Numenius. Cf. II, 14: οὔτε γὰρ τῶν ἄλλων λεγομένων θεῶν οὔτε ἀνθρώπων οὔτε δαιμόνων τις δύναται...ἀγαθὸς εἶναι ἢ μόνος ὁ θεός...(15) μὴ οὖν εἴπῃς ἄλλο τι ἀγαθὸν ἐπεὶ ἀσεβεῖς, ἢ ἄλλο τί ποτε τὸν θεὸν ἢ μόνον τὸ ἀγαθόν. Tractate VI bears the title: Ὅτι ἐν μόνῳ τῷ θεῷ τὸ ἀγαθόν ἐστιν, ἀλλαχόθι δὲ οὐδαμοῦ, and the first line reads: Τὸ ἀγαθὸν ὦ Ἀσκληπιέ, ἐν οὐδενί ἐστιν, εἰ μὴ ἐν μόνῳ τῷ θεῷ, μᾶλλον δὲ τὸ ἀγαθὸν αὐτός ἐσιν ὁ θεὸς ἀεί. Plotinus picks up the refrain at II. 9. 1: ὅταν λέγωμεν τὸ ἕν, καὶ ὅταν λέγωμεν τἀγαθόν, τὴν αὐτὴν δεῖ νομίζειν τὴν φύσιν καὶ μίαν λέγειν.

ll. 4-5: **ὁ μὲν δημιουργὸς θεός ἐστι γενέσεως**: The Demiurge's control over the realm of becoming preserves the complete transcendence of the First God.

l. 5. **τὸ ἀγαθὸν οὐσίας εἶναι ἀρχή**: This way of emphasizing the transcendence of the First Principle is adopted by Plotinus. Cf. I. 8. 6: ἀλλ' εἰ οὐσία τἀγαθόν, πῶς ἐστιν αὐτῷ τι ἐναντίον· ἢ τῷ ἐπέκεινα οὐσίας; V. 5. 11: τὸ δὲ πρῶτον ἀρχὴ τοῦ εἶναι καὶ κυριώτερον αὖ τῆς οὐσίας; VI. 7. 16: οὕτως καὶ ἡ τοῦ ἀγαθοῦ φύσις αἰτία οὐσίας καὶ νοῦ οὖσα. The language originates with Aristotle, cf. *Metaph.* 1003b: εἰ οὖν τοῦτ' ἐστὶν ἡ οὐσία, τῶν οὐσιῶν ἂν δέοι τὰς ἀρχὰς καὶ τὰς αἰτίας ἔχειν τὸν φιλόσοφον.

ll. 6-8. **ἀνάλογον δὲ τούτῳ μὲν ὁ δημιουργὸς θεός...εἰκὼν αὐτῆς ἐστι καὶ μίμημα**: The entire section is modeled after portions of the *Timaeus*. Cf. *Tim*. 29b: ...πᾶσα ἀνάγκη τόνδε τὸν κόσμον εἰκόνα τινὸς εἶναι...ὧδε οὖν περὶ τε εἰκόνος καὶ περὶ τοῦ παραδείγματος αὐτῆς διοριστέον...(29c) ὄντος δὲ εἰκόνος εἰκότας ἀνὰ λόγον τε ἐκείνων ὄντας· ὅτιπερ πρὸς γένεσιν οὐσία, τοῦτο πρὸς πίστιν ἀλήθεια. If Numenius had read Paul, 2 Cor. 4:4 might have attracted his attention: ὅς (*sc*. Χριστός) ἐστιν εἰκὼν τοῦ θεοῦ. Cf. also Collosians 1:15; Gen. 1:27.

ll. 7-8. μιμητής...μίμημα: More imagery from the *Timaeus*. Cf. *Tim*. 41c (from the Address to the Gods): ...μιμούμενοι τὴν ἐμὴν δύναμιν περὶ τὴν ὑμετέραν γένεσιν; 42e (the gods' response): ...μιμούμενοι τὸν σφέτερον δημιουργόν; 46c: μιμούμενοι τὰς τοῦ θεοῦ πάντως ἀπλανεῖς οὔσας; 48e: μίμημα δὲ παραδείγματος δεύτερον, γένεσιν ἔχον καὶ ὁρατόν; 50c: (of material objects): τῶν ὄντων ἀεὶ μιμήματα. Plotinus also uses this language, cf. II. 9. 2: θετέον, ἀλλ᾽ ἕνα νοῦν τὸν αὐτὸν ὡσαύτως ἔχοντα, ἀκλινῆ πανταχῇ, μιμούμενον τὸν πατέρα καθ᾽ ὅσον δίον τε αὐτῷ. Cf. also the Deutero-Pauline literature, Ephesians 5:1: Γίνεσθε οὖν μιμηταὶ τοῦ θεοῦ ὡς τέκνα ἀγαπητά.

l. 10. Ὁ γὰρ δεύτερος διττὸς ὤν: Cf. fr. 11, l. 16 where it is said that the Demiurge is 'divided' (σχίζεται) by his creative contact with matter. Perhaps the original impetus for this type of language lies in *Rep*. 439d where Plato begins to distinguish the parts of the soul: ἀξιώσομεν αὐτὰ διττά τε καὶ ἕτερα ἀλλήλων εἶναι, τὸ μὲν ᾧ λογίζεται λογιστικόν...τὸ δέ...ἀλόγιστόν τε καὶ ἐπιθυματικόν; Philo uses the word in a different way to describe his Λόγος, cf. *De Vita Moses* 127: διττὸς γὰρ ὁ λόγος ἔν τε τῷ παντὶ καὶ ἐν ἀνθρώπου φύσει. Several scholars are inclined to see Numenius' usage as a borrowing from Philo (see notes to fr. 1c), but a passage from Albinus seems to indicate that Numenius was in part transferring a set of common Middle-Platonic ethical categories to his Demiurge. At II, 1 Albinus makes a distinction between the theoretical and practical ways of living: διττοῦ δ᾽ ὄντος τοῦ βίου, τοῦ μὲν θεωρητικοῦ τοῦ δὲ πρακτικοῦ. Since Numenius divides the Demiurge's nature into the creative and contemplative (l. 12: ἔπειτα θεωρητικὸς ὅλως; cf. fr. 18, ll. 11-12: λαμβάνει τε τὸν μὲν κριτικὸν ἀπὸ τῆς θεωρίας) it would appear that here he is making the life of the Demiurge conform to these categories, while implying shades of meaning borrowed from the *Republic*. Plotinus (V. 8. 7) uses the word in his description of the Soul to emphasize its bi-directional orientation: διττῆς δὲ φύσεως ταύτης οὔσης, νοητῆς, τῆς δὲ αἰσθητῆς. This meaning too is surely contained in Numenius' use of the word.

l. 11. **αὐτοποιεῖ τήν τε ἰδέαν ἑαυτοῦ**: A curious phrase with respect to a secondary deity. In the *Chaldean Oracles* the god Aion is characterized as αὐτοφυής (see Lewy, p. 101, n. 145), and in *Corp. Herm.* XVI, 19 it is said: πάντα οὖν ποιῶν (sc. ὁ θεός), ἑαυτὸν ποιεῖ. Perhaps the closest approximation to what Numenius is saying here is the later Neo-Platonic concept of the αὐθυπόστατον, which Dodds (*Proclus* p. 224) describes as "not 'self-caused' in the sense of being an independent ἀρχή, but 'hypostatizes itself' or determines the particular potentiality which shall be actualized in it."

l. 12. **ἔπειτα θεωρητικὸς ὅλως**: Dodds (*N. & A.* p. 16) feels that ἔπειτα here is "meaningless", and that the phrase θεωρητικὸς ὅλως applies "more naturally" to the First God. He points out that Scott "brutally altered ἔπειτα to ἐπεί and added ὁ πρῶτος at the end of the sentence." Dodds' solution is to read ἐπεὶ ὁ α΄ θεωρητικὸς ὅλως (cf. a similar conjecture for fr. 13). However the phrase should be read with the somewhat obscure conclusion to fr. 12 which in turn is inspired by the *Politicus* myth and its system of cosmic cycles. If Numenius did indeed subscribe to such a doctrine of cycles, ἔπειτα makes perfect sense as does θεωρητικὸς ὅλως as applied to the Second God. At any rate, aside from Dillon's appropriation (p. 369, n. 1), Dodds' conjecture has received little acceptance by other scholars.

166 *Commentary*

ll. 14-16. δημιουργὸς ἀγαθός...ὁ καλὸς κόσμος: These phrases indicate that although Numenius may have been influenced by contemporary Gnostic currents, his view of the Cosmos remained firmly within the Platonic tradition. Cf. Merlan, *Drei An.* p. 139, n. 3 and Beutler, col. 672.

Fr. 17

Norden (pp. 72-73), who felt that Numenius' distinction of πρῶτος θεός and δεύτερος θεός was taken directly from the system of Valentinus, provides the following remarkable commentary on this fragment (p. 73): "Platon ist es also, der den in Unkenntnis des höchsten Gottes dahin wandelnden Menschen dessen Erkenntnis vermittelt: Numenius hat auf Platon das Amt des christlichen Gottessohnes, eben diese Erkenntnis zu vermitteln, einfach übertragen, und ihm dabei eine ῥῆσις an die ἄνθρωποι in den Mund gelegt, die sich...anlehnt an soteriologische ῥήσεις orientalischer Wanderpropheten im Dienste einer Propaganda der wahren γνῶσις θεοῦ, und die uns gerade auch für die Gnostiker bezeugt ist." These remarks have prompted strong responses from Festugière, Lewy and Dodds. Festugière (*Révélation* vol. IV, p. 130) quotes the statement in full and concludes: "Il suffit de lire, non pas ce seul fr. 26 (L.), mais toute la suite des extraits du π. τἀγαθοῦ, pour reconnaître la fantaisie de cette assertion" He points out that the prophetic style was common in Greece from Parmenides on, and then devotes several pages to refuting the 'orientaliste' position of Norden (cf. notes to fr. 1a).

Lewy (p. 319, n. 25) first summarizes Norden's position and then concludes that "this derivation is open to serious objections." He emphasizes Norden's failure to take into account the developments within Platonism that led to the distinction between First and Second Gods (cf. notes to fr. 11), as well as his failure to recognize Valentinus' "receptivity to the Platonism of his time." Lewy agrees with Festugière's position concerning the essential Greek nature of the prophetic exhortation and points to Lucretius' hymns to Epicurus as an analogue. Cf. also Epictetus' *Discourses*.

Dodds (*Proclus*, pp. 310-313) devotes an entire appendix to an examination of Norden's position, especially with respect to Plotinus, but his conclusions can be applied to Numenius as well. He makes the important point (p. 311) that the characteristic Platonic doctrine of the unknowability of God differs from that found in Gnosticism since it maintains that while the divine is inaccessible to the common human intellect, it can be grasped in an *unio mystica* that is completely ineffable (cf. Festugière *op. cit.*, pp. 131-132). He quotes two Platonic texts to illustrate this, the first *Parm.* 142a: οὐδ' ὀνομάζεται ἄρα οὐδὲ λέγεται οὐδὲ δοξάζεται οὐδὲ γιγνώσκεται, οὐδέ τι τῶν ὄντων αὐτοῦ αἰσθάνεται. Dodds states that this text was understood to refer to the supreme God by the Neopythagorean school of the first century C. E., and "probably" by the Old Academy itself. The second text that he adduces is the famous passage from the Seventh Letter 341c-d (see notes to fr. 2, l. 9). Dodds quotes part of fr. 2 in note 3 of p. 310 and remarks: "There is some reason to believe that Numenius was acquainted with the Gnosis (Norden p. 109) but he was also acquainted with Plato." Indeed, a close examination of fr. 2 indicates that the *unio mystica* is central to the unknowability of God, and his expression of it stands squarely with the Middle-Platonic tradition.

A closely related issue raised by this fragment turns on the similarity of its style and content with fr. 7 of the *Chaldean Oracles* which reads: Πάντα γὰρ ἐξετέλεσσε πατὴρ καὶ νῷ παρέδωκε δευτέρῳ ὃν πρῶτον κληΐζετε πᾶν γένος ἀνδῶν. The parallel was first noticed by Kroll (14, 1) but Lewy was the first to seriously address the question of priority. On p. 320 he says: "The similarity of the stylistic formulation is, in fact, striking, and makes plausible the supposition that the authors of the Chaldæn Oracles depend directly on Numenius." In n. 27 to this paragraph he asserts that "a reversal of the relation between Numenius and the Chaldæans is out of the question" because Numenius displays no knowledge of them and does and does not list them among the 'nations of reknown' whose doctrines support those of Plato (see fr. 1a and notes). Beutler (col. 671) takes a similar position, based on Dodds' Appendix (see above): "...die verblüffende Ähnlichkeit in der Formulierung des N. mit den or. ch. uns nicht zur Annahme einer Abhängigkeit des N. von den or. chald. zwingt". Waszink (*P. und N.*, pp. 43-44) concurs: "...schliesse ich mich der mehr üblichen Ansicht an, wonach der Verfasser der chaldäischen Orakel aus Numenios schöpft." Dodds (*N. & A.*, pp. 10-11) questions Lewy's reasoning and views Numenius as a possible "missing link" between the *Oracles* and Porphyry.

l. 2. ᾔδει ὁ Πλάτων: Festugière (*op. cit.*, p. 128, n. 3) suggests that Numenius is alluding to a text such as *Tim.* 28c, *Epist.* VII, 341c, or *Epist.* II, 312e.

ll. 3-4. πρῶτον νοῦν, ὅστις καλεῖται αὐτοόν: Cf. Albinus 27, 1: ὅπερ θεόν τε καὶ νοῦν τὸν πρῶτον προσαγορεύσαι ἄν τις. Krämer (p. 109) places this characterization of the First God with the ground of being (αὐτοόν) directly within the Xenocratic tradition. Thillet (Des Places, p. 111, n. 2) points out that the word αὐτοόν is also found in Alexander of Aphrodisias *In Arist. Metaph.*, 125, 15.

l. 4. ἀγνοούμενον: See the discussion of Norden's position above.

l. 5. Ὦ ἄνθρωποι: Festugière (*op. cit.*, p. 130) suggests an analogue in *Prot.* 337e: ὦ ἄνδρες, ἔφη, οἱ παρόντες. This is dismissed by Dodds (*N. & A.*, p. 11, n. 1) because "the speaker there addresses not mankind but the assembled company." A parallel closer in tone and content is found at *Corp. Herm.* 1, 27: Ὦ λαοί, ἄνδρες γηγενεῖς, οἱ μέθῃ καὶ ὕπνῳ ἑαυτοὺς ἐκδεδωκότες καὶ τῇ ἀγνωσίᾳ τοῦ θεοῦ, νήψατε.

l. 6. τοπάζετε: The word emphasizes the imprecise nature of opinions concerning the gods.

l. 7. πρεσβύτερος: Cf. fr. 16, l. 3.

Fr. 18

ll. 2-3. Κυβερνήτης...τοῖς οἴαξι διϊθύνει τὴν ναῦν: Numenius is here putting a poetic touch on the metaphor that was used often within the Platonic tradition. At *Republic* 488a-489b Plato uses the parable of ὁ ἀληθινὸς κυβερνήτης to describe the plight of οἱ ἀληθινοῖ φιλοσόφοι. The myth of the *Politicus*, which influenced the conclusion of fr. 12, is obviously the primary model for Numenius here, cf. *Pol.* 272e: τότε δὴ τοῦ παντὸς ὁ μὲν κυβερνήτης, οἷον πηδαλίων οἴακος ἀφεμένος, εἰς τὴν αὑτοῦ περιωπὴν ἀπέστη. Cf. also Plato's use of the verb διακυβερνᾶν at *Phlb.* 28d and *Tim.* 42e. This image would be used repeatedly by later writers. Philo employs it at *Leg. All.* III, 223 to describe the way νοῦς controls the whole man: ναῦς εὐθυδρομεῖ μέν, ἡνίκα τῶν οἰάκων λαβόμενος ὁ κυβερνήτης ἀκολούθως πηδαλιουχεῖ...οὕτως ἐπειδὰν μὲν ὁ τῆς ψυχῆς ἡνίοχος ἢ κυβερνήτης ὁ νοῦς ἄρχῃ τοῦ ζῴου ὅλου. Cf. *De. Opfic.* 46, describing the power of the creator: οἷα γὰρ ἡνίοχος ἡνιῶν, ἢ κυβερνήτης οἰάκων ἐνειλημμένος, ἄγει ᾗ ἂ ἐθέλῃ κατὰ νόμον καὶ δίκην ἕκαστα. Plutarch (*De. Isid.* 369c) uses the metaphor to deny that there is single controlling force in the universe: οὔθ' εἷς ἐστιν ὁ κρατῶν καὶ κατευθύνων ὥσπερ οἴαξιν. Like Philo, Plutarch uses the image to describe the mind, cf. *Plat. Quaest.* 1008a: ὥσπερ κυβερνήτην ἐνιδρύσασα (sc. ἡ φύσις) τῇ κεφαλῇ τὸν λογισμόν. He also echoes Plato's use of διακυβερνᾶν at *De. proc. an.* 1026e. It appears in Plotinus at IV. 3. 17 in a description of the way souls attend to bodies: ὥσπερ χειμαζομένων πλοίων κυβερνῆται.

l. 7. τοῦ μήτε διακροῦσαι μήτε ἀποπλαγχθῆναι: The L. S. J. cites this passage as the sole witness for the intransitive use of διακρούειν in the sense of 'break away' or 'escape'. Cf. Numenius' descriptions of σῶμα in fr. 4a, ll. 23-24 and fr. 8, ll. 5-6.

l. 8. ἁρμονίᾳ συνδησάμενος: The ultimate source is Plato's description of the circles of the World Soul in *Tim*. 34c-36e. At 36e it is said of the Soul: αὐτὴ δὲ ἀόρατος μέν, λογισμοῦ δὲ μετέχουσα καὶ ἁρμονίας ψυχή. Numenius' use of ἁρμονία is paralleled in the *Poimandres*. At ch. 14 of that tractate an action of Ἄνθρωπος is described: ὁ τοῦ τῶν θνητῶν κόσμου καὶ τῶν ἀλόγων ζώων ἔχων πᾶσαν ἐξουσίαν διὰ τῆς ἁρμονίας παρέκυψεν. In his note to this passage Festugière says: "Je prends ἁρμονία au sens concret (<<charpente, armature>>)" and points to this use by Numenius to support his interpretation. Dillon (p. 370) suggests that Numenius could be using the term "with a consciousness of its Hermetic significance."

ll. 11-12. λαμβάνει τε τὸ μὲν κριτικὸν ἀπὸ τῆς θεωρίας, τὸ δ' ὁρμητικὸν ἀπὸ τῆς ἐφέσεως: Another reference to the divided (διττός) nature of the Demiurge. See fr. 44 where Porphyry reports that Numenius held a similar doctrine of two distinct souls in man, ἡ λογική and ἡ ἄλογον.

τὸ μὲν κριτικὸν ἀπὸ τῆς θεωρίας: Cf. fr. 16, l. 12: ἔπειτα θεωρητικὸς ὅλως.

τὸ δ' ὁρμητκὸν ἀπο τῆς ἐφέσεως: Cf. fr. 11, 21: ἐπορεξάμενος τῆς ὕλης. The language for the whole passage originates in Plato's doctrine of the tri-partite soul which is set out in the fourth book of the *Republic* (cf. *Tim*. 89e and Diogenes Laertius III, 67). There (440e) the parts are determined to be τὸ λογιστικόν, τὸ θυμοειδές and τὸ ἐπιθυμητικόν. An interesting passage from Albinus (25, 7) gives some indication of how this doctrine operated in a Middle Platonic milieu: καὶ ἡ θεῶν δὲ ψυχὴ κέκτηται καὶ αὐτὴ τό τε κριτικόν...καὶ μὴν τὸ ὁρμητικόν τε...καὶ τὸ οἰκειωτικόν. He goes on to say that in incarnated human souls ἡ οἰκειωτική becomes equivalent to τὸ ἐπιθυμητικόν, and ἡ ὁρμητική becomes τὸ θυμοειδές. It would appear from this that Numenius is diverging from the tradition represented by Albinus since his derivation of τὸ ὁρμητικὸν ἀπὸ τῆς ἐφέσεως would be equivalent to τὸ ἐπιθυμητικόν of Plato. For an analysis of this passage from Albinus see Witt, p. 85. (Strangely enough, he misreads this fragment and in n. 6 attributes Numenius' description of the Demiurge to the First God.)

Fr. 19

l. 2. μετέχει δὲ αὐτοῦ τὰ μετίσχοντα: Numenius shifts to the Platonic technical language normally used to describe the 'participation' of particulars with their forms. Cf. *Parm.* 132d-e: τὸ δὲ ὅμοιον τῷ ὁμοίῳ ἆρ' οὐ μεγάλη ἀνάγκη ἑνὸς τοῦ αὐτοῦ μετέχειν;...οὗ δ' ἂν τὰ ὅμοια μετέχοντα ὅμοια ᾖ, οὐκ ἐκεῖνο ἔσται αὐτὸ τὸ εἶδος; Aristotle *Metaph.* 990b: κατὰ δὲ τὸ ἀναγκαῖον καὶ τὰς δόξας τὰς περὶ αὐτῶν, εἰ ἔστι μεθεκτὰ τὰ εἴδη, τῶν οὐσιῶν ἀναγκαῖον ἰδέας εἶναι μόνον· οὐ γὰρ κατὰ συμβεβηκὸς μετέχονται, ἀλλὰ δεῖ ταύτῃ ἑκάστου μετέχειν.

ll. 2-3. ἐν μόνῳ τῷ φρονεῖν: Cf. Albinus X, 4: ἄρρητος δ' ἐστὶ νῷ μόνῳ ληπτός.

l. 3. συμβάσεως: Plotinus' use of the word is more technical and is used in negative terms to emphasize the transcendence of the One. Cf. V. 4. 1: εἰ γὰρ μὴ ἁπλοῦν ἔσται συμβάσεως ἔξω πάσης...οὐκ ἂν ἀρχὴ εἴη; VI. 8. 14: τὸ ὄντως καὶ τὸ πρῶτον, ἀμιγὲς τύχαις καὶ αὐτομάτῳ καὶ συμβάσει.

ll. 4-5. τὸ φρονεῖν...μόνῳ τῷ πρώτῳ: Cf. Romans 16. 27: μόνῳ σοφῷ θεῷ.

ll. 5-6. ὑφ' οὗ οὖν τὰ ἄλλα ἀποχραίνεται καὶ ἀγαθοῦται: Cf. Philo *De Dec.* 81: ὅς ἐστι τὸ πρῶτον ἀγαθὸν καὶ τελεώτατον, ἀφ' οὗ τρόπον πηγῆς ἄρδεται τῷ κόσμῳ καὶ τοῖς ἐν αὐτῷ τὰ ἐπὶ μέρους ἀγαθά.

l. 6. μόνον μόνῳ: Cf. fr. 2, l. 11 and notes. Des Places (p. 112, n. 2) feels that this instance of the phrase doesn't have the same valence as that in fr. 2 but the difference is nearly indistinguishable.

ll. 7-9. εἰ γὰρ ἀγαθός ἐστιν ὁ δεύτερος...παρὰ δὲ τοῦ πρώτου: Cf. fr. 16, ll. 3-4: οὗτος μόνος εὕρηται ὢν τὸ ἀγαθόν.

ll. 11-12. ὁ Πλάτων ἐκ συλλογισμοῦ...τὸ ἀγαθὸν ὅτι ἐστὶν ἕν: Merlan (*Drei An*. p. 144) says that there can be no doubt that Numenius is here quoting from Aristoxenus' (*Harm. El.* II, 30) report about Plato's lecture 'On the Good.' According to this source Plato arrived at the famous conclusion: καὶ τὸ πέρας ὅτι ἀγαθόν ἐστιν ἕν. Merlan goes on to point out that the word πέρας, which probably is intended to indicate the end of the lecture, was taken by Numenius to denote the final term of a syllogism. Hence the puzzling phrase ἐκ συλλογισμοῦ. Merlan defends Numenius' interpretation by reminding us that since the time of Aristotle the term for the 'Schlußsatz' was συμπέρασμα.

l. 12. τῷ ὀξὺ βλέποντι: Cf. fr. 2, l. 9: ὀξὺ δεδορκώς.

τὸ ἀγαθὸν ὅτι ἐστὶν ἕν: It is easy to see how Numenius might have interpreted Matthew 19:17: τί με ἐρωτᾷς περὶ τοῦ ἀγαθοῦ; εἷς ἐστιν ὁ ἀγαθός.

Fr. 20

l. 2. ταῦτα δ' οὕτως ἔχοντα: Cf. *Corp. Herm.* IV, 8: τούτων δὲ οὕτως ἐχόντων, ὦ Τάτ...

l. 3. τὸν κυκλικόν: Numenius here implies that the 'common' conception of the Demiurge as 'good' needs further clarification, which he immediately provides.

l. 4. ἐν Τιμαίῳ εἰπών· "Ἀγαθὸς ἦν": *Tim.* 29e. Cf. Albinus XXII, 1, without direct citation of the *Timaeus*: διότι ἀγαθὸς ἦν.

ἐν δὲ τῇ Πολιτείᾳ: *Rep.* VI, 508e; VII, 517b.

ll. 5-6. τοῦ δημιουργοῦ ἰδέαν οὖσαν τὸ ἀγαθόν: This would appear to conflict with the statement made at fr. 16, ll. 10-11: ὁ γὰρ δεύτερος...αὐτοποιεῖ τήν τε ἰδέαν ἑαυτοῦ.

ll. 6-7. ἀγαθὸς μετουσίᾳ τοῦ πρώτου: Cf. fr. 19, ll. 8-9.

l. 7. τοῦ πρώτου τε καὶ μόνου: Cf. Philo *De Post.* 183: ζηλώσας τὸν θεοῦ τοῦ πρώτου καὶ μόνου ζῆλον. This use of καὶ μόνος also appears in the Hermetic literature, cf. *Corp. Herm.* IV, 8: ἵνα πρὸς τὸν ἕνα καὶ μόνον σπεύσωμεν; V, 2: εὖξαι πρῶτον τῷ κυρίῳ καὶ πατρὶ καὶ μόνῳ; X, 14: ἡ δὲ ἀρχὴ ἐκ τοῦ ἑνὸς καὶ μόνου. Plotinus has a similar expression at VI. 7. 1: τὸ μόνον καὶ ἓν καὶ ἁπλῶς.

Fr. 21

l. 1. πατέρα: Cf. fr. 12, l. 3 and note.

l. 2. ποιητήν: The term comes from the famous passage at *Tim.* 28c: τὸν μὲν ποιητὴν καὶ πατέρα τοῦδε τοῦ παντὸς εὑρεῖν τε ἔργον. Cf. *Corp. Herm.* XIV, 4: θεὸν μὲν διὰ τὴν δύναμιν, ποιητὴν δὲ διὰ τὴν ἐνέργειαν, πατέρα διὰ τὸ ἀγαθόν.

ll. 3-5. ὁ γὰρ κόσμος...τὸ δὲ δημιουργούμενον ὁ τρίτος: This report by Proclus flies in the face of statements made by Numenius himself in fr. 11 and 16. There it is clear that the Demiurge is indeed διττός, but as Dillon points out (p. 367), the division is not between the First and Second Gods, but between the Second and Third. Cf. fr. 11, ll. 14-15: ὁ θεὸς μέντοι ὁ δεύτερος καὶ τρίτος ἐστὶν εἷς· συμφερόμενος δὲ τῇ ὕλῃ δυάδι οὔσῃ ἑνοῖ μὲν αὐτήν, σχίζεται δὲ ὑπ' αὐτῆς. This apparent misreading on the part of Proclus has naturally perplexed students of Numenius. Beutler (col. 672) is openly suspicious: Man muß daher dem Zeugnis fr [21] das vom κόσμος als dritten

Gott spricht, mit Argwohn gegenüberstehen; es scheint eine Vergröberung der Lehre des N. vorzuliegen. Festugière (*Révélation*, vol. IV, p. 124) tries to find a way out of the difficulty by interpreting the Third God not as the concrete world, but rather the world as it exists in the mind of the Demiurge. He suggests (p. 123) that Proclus may have read the *Timaeus* into Numenius' own statements: "il est possible que Proclus dintingue le monde intelligible (Vivant en soi), l'Intellect démiurgique, le monde qui lui-même est dieu." Dodds (*N. & A.*, pp. 14-15), interpreting with the help of fr. 22 (see below), gives the following convoluted and not totally satisfying explanation: "The objective correlate of the Third God is the physical cosmos which 'imitates' the second οὐσία but is itself γένεσις; hence Numenius could apply the term ποίημα to the Third God." Cf. Krämer pp. 81-82. Merlan (*op. cit.*, p. 140, n. 2) is not so optimistic: " Es ist schwer anzunehmen, daß der den 'oberen' Demiurgen mit dem überdemiurgischen Gott verwechselt hat, aber ich sehe keinen Ausweg." Dillon (*op. cit.*) gives the definitive verdict: "Proclus is in error in this passage."

l. 6. προστραγῳδῶν: Indicating an exaggerated, pompous style. Cf. Des Places p. 113 n. *ad. loc.*; Dillon (*op. cit.*) translates: "dramatic bombast."

ll. 6-7. πάππον, ἔγγονον, ἀπόγονον: The series was probably inspired by *Tim.* 50d: καὶ δὴ καὶ προσεικάσαι πρέπει τὸ μὲν δεχόμενον μητρί, τὸ δ᾽ ὅθεν πατρί, τὴν δὲ μεταξὺ τούτων φύσιν ἐκγόνῳ. Cf. Albinus XVI, 1: τοῖς ἐκγόνοις αὐτοῦ θεοῖς ἐπέταξε τὴν τούτων ποίησιν.

ll. 7-8. οὐκ ὀρθῶς τἀγαθὸν συναριθμεῖ τοῖσδε τοῖς αἰτίοις: Proclus feels that Numenius has threatened the absolute transcendence of The Good by bringing it into a connection of any kind with lower entities. Cf. *in. Tim.*, III, p. 103. 28.

Fr. 22

l. 1. τὸ 'ὅ ἐστι ζῷον': *Tim.* 39e.

l. 2. ἐν προσχρήσει τοῦ δευτέρου νοεῖν: The concept of the a spiritual entity 'using' a lower was already established in the Dialogues. It began with the idea that the soul 'uses' the body. In the *Alcibiades* the image of the 'tool' is brought in, with the implication that the body is the soul's tool; cf. 129c: ὥσπερ σκυτοτόμος τέμνει που τομεῖ καὶ σμίλῃ καὶ ἄλλοις ὀργάνοις...(129e) ἔχεις μὲν οὖν, ὅτι γε τὸ τῷ σώματι χρωμένον...ἢ οὖν ἄλλο τι χρῆται αὐτῷ ἢ ψυχή (cf. Plotinus I. 1. 1: ἢ γὰρ ψυχῆς, ἢ χρωμένης ψυχῆς σώματι); this is simply assumed at *Phd.* 79c: ...ἡ ψυχή, ὅταν μὲν τῷ σώματι προσχρῆται εἰς τὸ σκοπεῖν τι...The *Timaeus* provides several examples of this language that were probably most influential in establishing the concept; cf. 28a: ὁ δημιουργὸς πρὸς το κατὰ ταὐτὰ ἔχον βλέπων ἀεί, τοιούτῳ τινὶ προσχρώμενος παραδείγματι; 46c: ταῦτ' οὖν πάντα ἔστιν τῶν συναιτίων οἷς θεὸς ὑπηρετοῦσιν χρῆται τὴν τοῦ ἀρίστου κατὰ τὸ δυνατὸν ἰδέαν ἀποτελῶν; 68e: ὁ τοῦ καλλίστου τε καὶ ἀρίστου δημιουργὸς χρώμενος μὲν ταῖς περὶ ταῦτα αἰτίαις ὑπηρετούσαις. Philo has an echo of this at *Quod Deus Immut.* 57: δίδωσι δὲ λόγῳ χρώμενος ὑπηρέτῃ δωρεῶν ᾧ καὶ τὸν κόσμον εἰργάζετο. (Cf. a distant echo in *Corp. Herm.* X, 17: ἡ δὲ ψυχὴ καὶ αὐτὴ θεία τις οὖσα καθάπερ ὑπηρέτῃ τῷ πνεύματι χρῆται.) Indeed, within the development of the Philonic λόγος, the doctrine as employed by Numenius appears in a fully developed form, complete with the tool imagery of the *Alcibiades*; cf. *All. Leg.* III, 96: σκιὰ θεοῦ δὲ ὁ λόγος αὐτοῦ ἔστιν, ᾧ καθάπερ ὀργάνῳ προσχρησάμενος ἐκοσμοποίει. (Cf. the Hermetic analogue at *Corp. Herm.* X, 18: δημιουργὸς γὰρ ὢν ὁ νοῦς τῶν πάντων, ὀργάνῳ τῷ πυρὶ πρὸς τὴν δημιουργίαν χρῆται.) This text caught Waszink's attention (*P. und N.*, p. 51, n. 4; cf. fr. 1c and notes): "Schliesslich möchte ich die Frage erheben, ob der für Numenios so wichtige Begriff der πρόσχρησις nicht auch durch

Philon veranlasst oder doch wenigstens beeinglusst worden ist." It would seem that Philo's use of the concept grew out of a natural Middle-Platonic development, and while Numenius needn't have been completely dependent on Philo for his own usage, the possibility of Philonic influence is conceivable.

Although the background of this doctrine is clear, the exact interpretation of Numenius' use of it has been a matter of intricate scholarly discussion. Scott (II, p. 86, n. 8) threw up his hands in despair, referring to this fragment as an "an obscure passage" and concluding: "But I do not know what can be meant by ἐν προσχρήσει τοῦ δευτέρου ('making use of the second νοῦς in addition'?) and ἐν προσχρήσει τοῦ τρίτου." Festugière (*op. cit.* p. 124 and n. 1) cites Proclus' critique of Numenius' position (103. 33: οὐκ οὕτω δὲ διῄρηται νῦν ὑπὸ τοῦ Πλάτωνος, ὥστε ἕτερον μὲν εἶναι τὸν νοοῦντα νοῦν, ἕτερον δὲ τὸν διανοούμενον) as evidence for reading διανοούμενον as a passive, and thinks Numenius is making a distinction, not found in Plato, between activities and causes. Thus he derives the following series: 1) Intelligible World; 2) Thought thinking (pensée pensante) *i. e.* the Demiurgic thought; 3) the thought Thought (pensée pensée) *i. e.* the sensible world as it exists in the mind of the Demiurge; 4) the concrete world.

Dodds (*op. cit.* pp. 13-14 and n. 1), though citing the same text in Proclus, arrives at a different conclusion. He argues that the passive use of the verb διανοέω is "exceedingly rare", reads it in the middle sense and convincingly interprets Proclus' phrase thus: "νοῦς διανοούμενος as opposed to νοῦς νοῶν surely means 'νοῦς exercising διάνοια', and corresponds to Plato's phrase (νοῦς) διενοήθη." He then concludes that the three Gods each have their own level of mental activity, but feels that "the distinctions are blurred by the concept of πρόσχρησις." For Dodds, it is the characteristic act of the Second God to νοεῖν and the First God can do so only by invoking the assistance of the Second. Hence the First God is actually positioned beyond mental activity, if in a somewhat compromised manner. The Second God, in turn, can abandon νόησις (cf. fr. 11, ll. 17-18) and employ διάνοια, but only through the assistance of the Third God which is in fact the part of him that is split off when he comes into contact with matter and begins creating the Cosmos. Hence the Third God (or lower half of the Second), exercising only διάνοια corresponds to the Plotinian World Soul. Dodds interpretation adequately clarifies the matter and reveals that Numenius' use of the concept was indeed quite similar to that of Philo.

Fr. 23

ll. 5-8. καὶ κατηγόρει ἐχούσῃ στάσεις μὲν πρὸς ἀλλήλους...καὶ ἄλλα τοιαῦτα: Immediately before introducing this fragment Eusebius had quoted *Euthyphro* 5e-6c, which provides the models for Numenius' remarks. Des Places (p. 61, n. 1) wonders whether Eusebius might be slipping the enumerations of a Christian apologist such as Athenagoras or Justin into his quotation of Numenius. But it is typical of Numenius' style to embellish and dramatize.

ll. 11-12. ἐπεὶ δὲ ζῆν οὐκ ἂν προείλατο μᾶλλον ἢ ἀληθεύειν: Like his master Socrates. Cf. *Apol.* 38e: ἀλλὰ πολὺ μᾶλλον αἱροῦμαι ἀπολογησάμενος τεθνάναι ἢ ἐκείνως ζῆν; Xenophon *Mem.* IV, 4: προείλατο μᾶλλον τοῖς νόμοις ἐμμένων ἀποθανεῖν ἢ παρανομῶν ζῆν.

Fragments 24-28: see Introduction.

Fr. 29

l. 1. παράδοξα δὲ πράγματα: Cf. Eusebius' concluding remark to fr. 9: διὰ δὴ τούτων ὁ Νουμήνιος καὶ τοῖς ὑπὸ Μωσέως ἐπιτελέσθαι παραδόξοις θαύμασι...μαρτυρεῖ.

ll. 3-5. οἱ...ἐπιδειξάμενοι γνησίως φιλοσοφεῖν: Another indication of Origen's respect for Numenius. Cf. the comparison to Celsus in fr. 1b: διὰ πολλῶν δείξας εἶναι ἐλλογιμώτατος καὶ βασανίσας δόγαμτα...ὁ Πυθαγόρειος Νουμήνιος.

ll. 7-8. παρὰ τῷ Χαιρωνεῖ Πλουτάρχῳ ἐν τοῖς Περὶ ψυχῆς: Des Places (p. 116, n. *ad. loc.*) notes that the fragments attributed to Themistius by Stobaeus have been restored to Plutarch by D. Wyttenbach. They are nn. 177-178 in the collections of F. H. Sandbach (Plutarchus, *Moralia*, VII Leipzig, 1967; *Plutarch's Moralia*, XV, in the Loeb edition.)

Fr. 30

l. 5. τὸν προφήτην: The third extant reference to Moses by Numenius; cf. fr. 8 and 9.

ll. 5-6. ἐμφέρεσθαι ἐπάνω τοῦ ὕδατος θεοῦ πνεῦμα: Genesis 1:2. Gager (p. 65, n. 119) points out that the only deviation from the Septuagint text is the prefix ἐμ φέρεσθαι. He suggests that it is a "stylistic alteration" on Numenius' part. Des Places (p. 118, n. *ad. loc.*) notes that the words θεοῦ πνεῦμα in the Genesis text are combined in Numenius' use of θεοπνόῳ just above (l. 4). This word is rare and late—L. S. J. gives this fragment as a witness. It also appears in *Corp. Herm.* I, 30: θεόπνους γενόμενος τῆς ἀληθείας ἦλθον, and Gager (*op. cit.*, n. 120) praises Festugière's translation ("rempli du souffle divin" for retaining the literal meaning of the two components. He suggests that this literal meaning should also be read in this fragment.

ll. 6-8. τούς τε Αἰγυπτίους...πάντας ἐπὶ πλοίου, καὶ τὸν Ἥλιον: Cf. Plutarch *De Iside* 364c: Ἥλιον δὲ καὶ σελήνην οὐχ ἅρμασιν ἀλλὰ πλοίοις ὀχήμασι χρωμένους περιπλεῖν φασιν.

ll. 10-11. Ἡράκλειτον ψυχῇσι φάναι τέρψιν μὴ θάνατον ὑγρῇσι γενέσθαι: A puzzling rendition of the famous fragment (36 DK,

66 Marcovich) preserved by Clement (*Strom.* VI, 17, 1-2) and Eusebius (*Praep. Ev.* X, 2, 6) which reads:

ψυχῆσιν θάνατος ὕδωρ γενέσθαι,

ὕδατι δὲ θάνατος γῆν γενέσθαι·

ἐκ γῆς δὲ ὕδωρ γίνεται,

ἐξ ὕδατος δὲ ψυχή.

Philo also preserves the first two lines at *De Aet. Mund.* 111. Diels tried to solve the puzzle by conjecturing ἢ θάνατον which is adopted by Marcovich (p. 354). However it seems that Porphyry is revising Heraclitus here for the sake of argument.

ll. 12-13. ἀλλαχοῦ δὲ φάναι ζῆν ἡμᾶς τὸν ἐκείνων θάνατον καὶ ζῆν ἐκείνας τὸν ἡμέτερον θάνατον: Cf. fr. 62 DK, 47 Marcovich:

ἀθάνατοι θνητοί, θνητοὶ ἀθάνατοι,

ζῶντες τὸν ἐκείνων θάνατον,

τὸν δὲ ἐκείνων βίον τεθνεῶτες.

Cf. Philo's version at *Leg. All.* I, 108: εὖ καὶ ὁ Ἡράκλειτος κατὰ τοῦτο Μωυσέως ἀκολουθήσας τῷ δόγματι, φησὶ γάρ· 'Ζῶμεν τὸν ἐκείνων θάνατον, τεθνήκαμεν δὲ τὸν ἐκείνων βίον'. Euripides paraphrased the concept; cf. (with Des Places p. 118, n. *ad. loc.*) fr. 638 Nauck[2], cited by Plato, *Gorg.* 492e:

τίς δ' οἶδεν, εἰ τὸ ζῆν μέν ἐστι κατθανεῖν,

τὸ κατθανεῖν δὲ ζῆν;

Cf. (with Dodds, *Gorgias*, p. 300, n. *ad. loc.*) Euripides' *Phrixus* (fr. 833):

τὶς δὲ οἶδεν εἰ ζῆν τοῦθ' ὃ κέκληται θανεῖν,

τὸ ζῆν δὲ θνήσκειν ἐστί;

Fr. 31

l. 1. **τοῦ δὴ ἄντρου**: The point of departure for the preceding fragment, this fragment and the next five fragments lies in the description in the *Odyssey* of the 'Cave of the Nymphs' (13, 109-112):

...δύω δέ τέ οἱ θύραι εἰσίν,

αἱ μὲν πρὸς Βορέαο καταιβαταὶ ἀνθρώποισιν,

αἱ δ' αὖ πρὸς Νότου εἰσι θεώτεραι· οὐδέ τι κείνῃ

ἄνδρες ἐσέρχονται, ἀλλ' ἀθανάτων ἐστιν.

εἰκόνα καὶ σύμβολον φησι τοῦ κόσμου: We know from Origen (fr. 1b and 1c) that Numenius had a penchant for allegorization. This interpretation of the Homeric passage is the only extended example left to us. Cf. fr. 57.

l. 2. **Νουμήνιος καὶ ὁ τούτου ἑταῖρος Κρόνιος**: Numenius is occasionally mentioned in association with this shadowy figure (cf. fr. 46b and 48), and he is included by Porphyry in the list of Platonists whose works were read in Plotinus' school (*Vita Plotini*, 14). That is all we know about him. Des Places (p. 118, n. *ad. loc.*) suggests that ἑταῖρος be translated as 'disciple' or 'colleague'. It is fairly clear from the prominence of Numenius in later antiquity that Cronius could only have been a student or lesser associate. Perhaps his role was similar to that played by Porphyry in the Plotinian circle.

ll. 4-5. **ὁ μὲν...κατὰ καρκίνον, ὁ δέ...κατὰ αἰγόκερων**: De Ley (p. 20 and n. 1), following the doubts expressed by Leemans (p. 102, n. 19) views this section as a "digression on the *thema mundi*" which is lacking in Proclus (fr. 35) and Macrobius (fr. 34) and which "does not belong to the quotation proper...neither is its doctrine Numenian." Elferink (p. 7) sees no difficulty in attributing the doctrine to Numenius.

ll. 15-16. **δύο...πύλας**: *Illiad* 5. 646; 9. 156. Cf. fr. 32, l. 1.

l. 16. οἱ θεολόγοι: A term usually applied to the Presocratic cosmologists. Cf. Aristotle *Metaph*. 1000a: οἱ μὲν περὶ Ἡσίοδον καὶ πάντες ὅσοι θεολόγοι.

l. 17. Πλάτων δὲ δύο στόμια ἔφη: A reference to the Myth of Er, *Rep.* 615d: ἐγγὺς τοῦ στομίου ἦμεν μέλλοντες ἀνιέναι. This in turn refers back to 614c: τόπον...ἐν ᾧ τῆς τε γῆς δύ' χάσματα. Cf. fr. 35, l. 6.: ἐν ταύτῃ δύο χάσματα.

ll. 17-18. τούτων δὲ καρκίνον μὲν εἶναι δι' οὗ κατίασιν αἱ ψυχαί, αἰγόκερων δὲ δι' οὗ ἀνίασιν: Cf. fr. 34, ll. 9-12: hominum Cancer, quia per hunc in inferior descensus est, Capricornus deorum quia per illum animae...reveruntur; fr. 35, ll. 6-8: ...λέγων καὶ ἐν ταύτῃ δύο χάσματα, τὸν αἰγόκερων καὶ τὸν καρκίνον, τοῦτον μὲν καθόδου χάσμα τῆς εἰς γένεσιν, ἀνόδου δὲ ἐκεῖνον.

l. 26. τῶν δύο πυλῶν τούτων μεμνῆσθαι καὶ Παρμενίδην: A free interpretation of Parmenides fr. 1, l. 11 (Sextus *adv. math.* VII, III and Simplicius *de caelo* 557, 25):

ἔνθα πύλαι Νυκτός τε καὶ Ἤματός εἰσι κελεύθων

l. 27. φησί: Des Places here retains the reading of Vaticanus which attributes the end of ch. 23 and the beginning of ch. 24 directly to Numenius. See Des Places p. 118 and note *ad. loc.*

Fr. 32

l. 1. λέγει δέ που καὶ Ἡλίου πύλας: Cf. fr. 31, l. 15-16. The Homeric passage that Porphyry has in mind here is *Odyssey* 24, 12: ἧδε παρ' Ἠελίοιο πύλας καὶ δῆμον ὀνείρων. See δῆμος ὀνείρων below, l. 6. In the passage Hermes is leading the souls of the slaughtered suitors into the underworld. The 'Gates of the Sun' represent the extreme West where it was thought that the sun disappeared into the subterranean passage leading back to the East. See Stanford vol. II, p. 412, n. *ad. loc.*

ll. 2-6. ἄχρι γὰρ τούτων πρόεισιν...αἰγόκερως δὲ τὰ νότια: A description of the sun's ecliptic. See Trouillard's note *ad. loc.* in Des Places p. 118.

l. 6. δῆμος δ' ὀνείρων κατὰ Πυθαγόραν αἱ ψυχαί: The authenticity of the final book of the *Odyssey* has been questioned since Aristarchus (see Stanford *op. cit.*, p. 404, n. to 23, 296). Burkert (p. 279, n. 10) mentions several scholars who view various sections of the epic to be Pythagorean forgeries, and Carcopino (*Apôtres* p. 202, n. 7; p. 208, n. 128) claims that the beginning of ch. 24, with the mention of δῆμος ὀνείρων is just such a forgery. He suggests the Orphic Onomacritus as the likely forger. Whatever the case may be, the expression was important to the Pythagoreans, and Porphyry is using a gloss from the school.

ll. 8-9. ὅταν εἰς γένεσιν πέσωσιν: The image is inspired by *Phaedr.* 248c-d: βαρυνθεῖσα δὲ πτερορρυήσῃ τε καὶ ἐπὶ τὴν γῆν πέσῃ...ἐν τῇ πρώτῃ γενέσει.

l. 9. τοὺς ψυχαγωγούς: An epithet applied to Hermes, who leads souls to the underworld; cf. the passage from the *Odyssey* cited above. In this context however, the term applies to necromancers or conjurers of souls. See L. S. J., meaning II.

l. 10. μέλι κεκραμένον γάλακτι: Cf. Odysseus' offering to the dead at 11, 26-27:

ἀμφ' αὐτῷ δὲ χοὴν χεόμην πᾶσιν νεκύεσσι,
πρῶτα μελικρήτῳ...

Fr. 33

l. 2. εἰκόνα: For Numenius' allegorical interpretation of the *Odyssey* see (with Des Places p. 84, n. 2, and Elsas p. 29) Carcopino *op. cit.* pp. 201ff. See also Dodds *Pagan* p. 101, n. 1.

ll. 5-6. εἰσόκε...ἔδουσιν: *Odyssey* 11, 122-123.

ll. 7-8. πόντος...καὶ κλύδων...ἡ ὑλικὴ σύστασις: Cf. fr. 3, l. 11: ποταμὸς γὰρ ἡ ὕλη. For πόντος cf. *Pol.* 273d: ἄπειρον ὄντα πόντον; for κλύδων cf. Maximus XI, 7: μόγις γάρ που καὶ τούτοις ἵσταται τὸ σῶμα ὑπὸ τοῦ ἐν τῷ κλύδωνι ἔθους κινούμενόν τε, καὶ...σειόμενον. For the Middle Platonic doctrine of the fluidity of matter see notes to fr. 8, ll. 5-6.

Fr. 34

Macrobius' survey (*Commentarii in Somnium Scipionis*, I, 10, 7-12) of the allegorical interpretations of the Underworld and its punishments, of which this fragment is a portion, along with the scholarly search for his sources which it inspired, opens a window into a major chapter in the study of the religions of Late Antiquity. De Ley (p. 7) and Elferink (p. 5) point out that this section In Macrobius turns on his attempt to elucidate a sentence in Cicero which reads: *Vestra vero quae dicitur esse vita mors est* (*Somn. Scip.*, 3, 2; cf. fr. 30, ll. 12-13). In so doing he is led to bring in the interpretaions of the *Platonici*, who are divided into three sects. The third sect, which he describes as *quorum sectae amicior est ratio*, is characterized by their transferal of the Underworld to the planetary spheres, and as De Ley puts it, this interpretation "is supplemented with a description of the soul's descent towards embodiment. This *descensus animae* is one of the rare elaborated statements on that 'metaphysical' subject which the Ancients have left us."

The problem of the origin of this *descensus*, and Numenius' role in it, has led to protracted debate. It is generally agreed that Macrobius was using Porphyry as his direct source (Beutler col. 676; Festugière, *Révélation* vol. III, p. 42, n. 2), whether it be his commentary on the *Timaeus* (Elferink p. 40), or the commentary on the *Republic* (Leemans, p. 40, n. 3; De Ley, p. 23). It is also well known that Porphyry often used Numenius as a source; cf. fr. 30, 31, 33 and the famous remark of Proclus at l. 24-25 of fr. 37: ὁ φιλόσοφος Πορφύριος, ὃν καὶ θαυμάσειεν ἄν τις εἰ ἕτερα λέγοι τῆς Νουμηνίου παραδόσεως. The influence of Numenius is assured at I, 12, 1-4 where the gates of Capricorn and Cancer are described, since both Porphyry (fr. 31) and Proclus (fr. 35) mention the same description, with Proclus attributing it directly to Numenius. And since these paragraphs serve as the introduction to the *descensus* proper which constitutes the remainder of the chapter, it has been assumed that Numenius lies behind the entire account.

Franz Cumont was the first to make this assumption. Heavily influenced by the theories set forth by Bousset in his *Die Himmelreise der Seele* and *Hauptprobleme der Gnosis* (see Culianu pp. 29-30) he accepted the "Chaldean" origin of the doctrine, and on the basis of this text in Macrobius credited Numenius with its introduction into philosophic circles. A classic expression of his position is found in *After Life in Roman Paganism*, p. 107: "This doctrine is certainly of Chaldeo-Persian origin, and was spread in the first century especially by the mysteries of Mithras. Then, in the second century, the Pythagorean Numenius introduced it into philosophic speculation. Man's soul was held to descend from the height of heaven to this sublunary world, passing through the planetary spheres, and thus at birth it acquired the dispositions and the qualities peculiar to each of these stars. After death it went back to its celestial home by the same path. Then as it traversed the zones of the sky, it divested itself of the passions and faculties which it had acquired during its descent to earth, as it were of garments." Cf. *Lux Perpetua*, pp. 187-188; *Astrology Among the Greeks and Romans*, p. 108; *The Mysteries of Mithra*, p. 145.

Leemans followed Cumont's speculations and included the entire *descensus* with its ὄχημα doctrine in his collection of Numenius' fragments (see the extracts from Leeman's letter to J. Bidez reproduced in De Ley, pp. 8-10 for a full presentation of his line of reasoning). Beutler (*Gnomon*, 16 (1940), pp. 111-115, and

RE, col. 677) objected to this on the grounds that the description of the descent through the spheres at I, 12, 5ff. includes a 'geometrical' definition of soul, whereas we are told by Proclus (see fr. 39) that Numenius viewed the soul as number. Festugière (*op. cit*) expressed full agreement with Beutler. Waszink (*P. und. N.*, p. 77) took exception to Leeman's contention (p. 94, n. to 12ff.) that Numenius possessed the fully developed doctrine of the ὄχημα found in later Neoplatonism, but granted him the Middle Platonic version current at the time (see below). Nevertheless he sides with Beutler (cf. *Studien*, p. 13, n. 1) in denying direct Numenian influence on Porphyry in this regard. Theiler (*Ammonius und Porphyrios*, p. 122) also expresses some doubt: "In der Schwebe muss bleiben, ob Numenios diese lehre vom ὄχημα anwandte, wie Leemans annahm." Elferink (*Descente*, pp. 40-41), a student of Waszink, and who devoted a monograph to the subject, ultimately agrees with Beutler and his teacher.

Dodds on the other hand (*N. and. A.*, pp. 8-9) defends the position of Leemans: "I am convinced that Beutler is mistaken about this, not only because the passage forms a continuous piece of exposition with no perceptible break in thought, but because doctrines and expressions attested as Numenian appear throughout its length." At p. 9, n. 1 he attacks Beutler's only major objection, the geometrical definition of the soul: "But 12, 5 is not a definition; it is merely a metaphorical description of the soul's transition from unity to multiplicity, which is symbolized by the figure of the cone." Mazza (*Studi arnobiani*, pp. 136-137) agrees with Dodds, and De Vogel includes the *descensus* in *Greek Philosophy* III, pp. 431-433, and attributes it to Numenius. De Ley, a student of Leemans' who also devoted an entire monograph to the question, attacks several of Leemans' and Dodds' arguments but ultimately agrees with them: "I think we have removed...all serious objections against the attribution to Numenius of the central theme of the chapter, *viz.* the ὄχημα theory (p. 51)"; "...as for its contents c. 12 reproduces Numenius' eschatology probably fairly faithfully (p. 65)." He is supported by Flamant (*Macrobe* pp. 525-65). Des Places implicitly follows Beutler by including only the unquestioned lines from Macrobius in the fragment. But at p. 116, n. 3 while reviewing the scholarly debate, he admits: "Leemans, que je n'ai pas suivi jusque-la, avait peut-être raison de le citer en entire comme 'Test. 47'." Culianu (p. 12) adopts an agnostic position: "Some scholars claim that the whole doctrine was known by Numenius of Apamea, who transmitted it to Porphyry...This might be true, but there is no decisive evidence either for, or against this assumption." Wallis (p. 35) says that the passage "is probably based on Numenius." Dillon (p. 376) tacitly accepts the ascription.

This complex debate, on which much philological and exegetical ingenuity has been expended, revolves around the issue of direct attribution to Numenius through Porphyry. But stepping back a bit, perhaps two more general questions should be asked with regard to the important subject of Numenius' eschatology: Given the significance of this doctrine at the time, could Numenius have *possibly* been unaware of it, and if he was aware of it, could he *possibly* have rejected it? If we examine the extensive diffusion of the doctrine, I believe the answers will become self-evident.

The origin of the theory has not been agreed upon. Culianu (pp. 16-31) provides a thorough survey of the scholarly discussion from the nineteenth century to the present, from which two major trends emerge. The first, that of the "religiongeschichtliche Schule", is represented by Bousset (*Himmelreise*), who argued for the Iranian/Babylonian origin of the doctrine. The second attempts to view the later doctrine as an inner development within the Greek tradition. This 'school' in turn is divided between two theories, the *shamanistic*, which is represented by Rhode (*Psyche*), Meuli (*Scythica*), Dodds (*The Greeks and the Irrational*), and Cornford (*Principium Sapientiae*), and the *Pythagorean*. The latter, while not definitively solving the problem, has generally produced more interesting and useful insights. The theory of Pythagorean origins gained momentum with Delatte's *Études sur la literature pythagoricienne*. Culianu (p. 27) summarizes his position thus: "Delatte assigns the celestial eschatology of Late Antiquity to an uninterrupted Pythagorean underground tradition. The descensus/ascensus of the soul, with its variants, would belong to this long tradition." Rougier (*L'origine astronomique de la croyance pythagoricienne en l'immortaltité celeste des âmes*) saw the origin of the doctrine in Pythagorean astronomical notions. Boyance (*Études sur le Songe de Scipion*) generally agreed with him but emphasized the role of Plato's immediate disciples in formulating the celestial eschatology. Cumont (see above) agreed that the celestial eschatology formed a part of Pythogoreanism, but conforming to the influence of Bousset believed that it had been inherited from "Chaldaean" sources. He also viewed Posidonius as the great synthesizer who blended these elements and transmitted the new mixture to later thinkers (*Afterlife* pp. 27-28) Burkert (*Lore and Science* pp. 362-368) gives an admirable synopsis of the entire question, emphasizing the fact that the doctrine developed slowly over time and grew by assimilating a wide variety of elements from diverse sources. A balanced appraisal would conclude that each of the theories mentioned makes a contribution to the question, but none can stand alone.

Leaving the questions of origins aside, it is important to underscore the diffusion of the doctrine. As Culianu (p. 11) puts it: "Under one form or another, the mythology of the embodiment of the soul...represented one of the major cultural constants of Late Antiquity, from Basilides to Hierocles." At the heart of the theory lies the notion that mind cannot come into direct contact with matter. It must be shielded and mediated by soul. As de Ley (p. 53) points out, the seed of this concept was present already in the *Timaeus*, cf. 30b: νοῦν δ' αὖ χωρὶς ψυχῆς ἀδύνατον παραγενέσθαι τῳ. διὰ δὴ τὸν λογισμὸν τόνδε νοῦν μὲν ἐν ψυχῃ, ψυχὴν δ᾽ ἐν σώματι συνιστὰς τὸ πᾶν συνετεκταίνετο. In Tractate X, 16-17 of the *Corpus Hermeticum* this concept is employed with the common later motif of 'vestments': ἡ σύνθεσις τῶν ἐνδυμάτων τούτων, ὦ τέκνον, ἐν σώματι γηίνῳ γίνεται· ἀδύνατον γὰρ τὸν νοῦν ἐν γηίνῳ σώματι γυμνὸν αὐτὸν καθ᾽ ἑαυτὸν ἑδράσαι...ἔλαβεν οὖν ὥσπερ περιβόλαιον τὴν ψυχήν, ἡ δὲ ψυχὴ καὶ αὐτὴ θεία τις οὖσα καθάπερ ὑπηρέται τῷ πνεύματι χρῆται. Cf. the χιτῶνα at Ch. 18 of this text and in Proclus *Elements* prop. 209. Macrobius has *indumenta* at I, 11.

This Hermetic text reflects the passage from the *Timaeus* faithfully in that there is no mention of a descent, and the 'garments' are viewed merely as a necessary aspect of embodiment (but cf. X, 16: ὁ δὲ νοῦς καθαρὸς γενόμενος τῶν ἐνδυμάτων). Indeed, the descent as portrayed by Macrobius (ch. 12) follows the 'positive' view of the process. As the soul descends it receives the following qualities from the planets (Macrobius fortunately provides the Greek terms from his source): Saturn -- λογιστικόν et θεωρητικόν; Jupiter -- πρακτικόν; Mars – θυμικόν; Sun – αἰσθητικόν et φανταστικόν; Venus – ἐπιθυμητικόν; Mercury – ἑρμηνευτικόν; Moon – φυτικόν. These qualities are what Jonas (p. 158) describes as "the empirical character of man, comprising all the faculties and propensities by which man relates himself to the world of nature and society." At this point the *descensus* remains within the "astrological range of ideas...In an affirmative cosmology these are useful gifts which fit man for his earthly existence" (p. 157). Jonas suggests Servius *In Aen.* XI. 51 and the *Kore Kosmou* as further examples of the positive view. Cf. Bousett, *Die Lehren*, p. 735, who stresses the fact that this purely astrological and positive view is the oldest layer of the doctrine.

But in more negative cosmologies such as later Platonism, Hermeticism and Gnosticism the *descensus* and its results come to be seen in a tragic light. Here its aspect as 'Fall' is emphasized, and the necessary 'envelopments' or 'garments' come to be viewed as foreign 'appendages' or 'accretions'. The classic expression of this in Numenius' era is found in the *Poimandres*. In ch. 13 it is merely stated that Ἄνθρωπος, once having entered the realm of creation, partakes in the characteristics of each of the 'governors' (διοικητές = planets): ἕκαστος δὲ μετεδίδου τῆς ἰδίας τάξεως· καὶ καταμαθὼν τὴν τούτων οὐσίαν καὶ μεταλαβὼν τῆς αὐτῶν φύσεως ἠβουλήθη ἀναρρῆξαι τὴν περιφέρειαν τῶν κύκλων. So far, this appears to be a positive process, the acquisition of power on the part of Ἄνθρωπος. Bousett (*op. cit.*) labels this "eine Inkongruenz". It is not until ch. 24 with the description of the ἄνοδος that we learn what was inherited in each planetary sphere: καὶ τῇ πρώτῃ ζώνῃ δίδωσι τὴν αὐξητικὴν ἐνέργειαν καὶ τὴν μειωτικήν (= the φυτικόν of Macrobius), καὶ τῇ δευτέρᾳ τὴν μηχανὴν τῶν κακῶν, δόλον ἀνενέργητον, καὶ τῇ τρίτῃ τὴν ἐπιθυμητικὴν ἀπάτην ἀνενέργητον (the simple ἐπιθυμητικόν of Macrobius has here become a 'deception'), καὶ τῇ τετάρτῃ τὴν ἀρχοντικὴν προφανίαν ἀπλεονέκτητον, καὶ τῇ πέμπτῃ τὸ θράσος τὸ ἀνόσιον καὶ τῆς τόλμης τὴν προπέτειαν (a negative transformation of Macrobius' θυμικόν), καὶ τῇ ἕκτῃ τὰς ἀφορμὰς τὰς κακὰς τοῦ πλούτου ἀνενεργήτους, καὶ τῇ ἑβδόμῃ ζώνῃ τὸ ἐνεδρεῦον ψευδός. That this passage from the *Poimandres* represents an Hermetic commonplace is indicated by a text in Arnobius (*Adv. nat.* II, 16: see Jonas p. 157), who claims to be reporting an Hermetic teaching: " While we slide and hasten downwards to the human bodies, there attach themselves to us from the cosmic spheres the causes by which we become ever worse (trans. Jonas.)"

The concept of 'attachments' or 'accretions' is central to the doctrine, and it provides further evidence that Numenius held it himself. Iamblichus (Περὶ ψυχῆς, *apud* Stob., *Anthol.*, I, 49, 37 = fr. 43) reports that there was a debate among the Platonists concerning the origin of the 'appendages' of the soul, and Numenius (along with Cronius) is said to derive them from matter itself: ἀπὸ τῶν ἔξωθεν προσφυομένων προστιθέντων ὁπωσοῦν τῇ ψυχῇ τὸ κακόν, ἀπὸ μὲν τῆς ὕλης Νουμηνίου καὶ Κρονίου πολλάκις. The use of πολλάκις indicates that Numenius was emphatic about this concept. De Ley (p. 51) cogently adduces this text to support his view that Numenius adhered to the theory of the *descensus*. He continues his persuasive line of reasoning (p. 52) by pointing to fr. 49 where Numenius is grouped with Plotinus and several other Platonists who believed that the soul could be filled with evil before entering the body: πρὸ τοῦ σώματος κακίας ἐμπίμπλασθαι τὴν ψυχὴν δύνατον εἶναι λέγουσι. This would indicate that the acquisition of τὰ προσφυομένα, from which evil comes, begins immediately upon entering the material cosmos through the gate of Cancer.

Another related piece of evidence is provided by fr. 44 where we are told by Porphyry that Numenius held the doctrine of two separate souls, the λογική and the ἄλογον. Dodds (*op.cit.,* p. 7) seized upon this testimony as a clear indication of 'oriental' influence on Numenius. He says that "before Numenius the doctrine is not stated in this radical form, so far as I am aware, anywhere in the native Greek tradition." He suggests several analogues in the Hermetic and Gnostic traditions. Iamblichus (*De Myst.* 8, 6) provides the Hermetic teaching: δύο γὰρ ἔχει ψυχάς, ὡς ταὐτά φησι τὰ γράμματα, ὁ ἄνθρωπος, καὶ ἡ μὲν ἐστιν ἀπὸ τοῦ πρώτου νοητοῦ...ἡ δὲ ἐνδιδομένη ἐκ τῆς τῶν οὐρανίων περιφορᾶς.

One Gnostic parallel is the well known reference to Basilides in Clement *Stromata* 2, 20, 113. There Basilides is also said to view the passions as 'appendages': Οἱ δὲ ἀμφὶ τὸν Βασιλείδην προσαρτήματα τὰ πάθη καλεῖν εἰώθασι, πνεύματα <τε> τινα ταῦτα κατ᾿ οὐσίαν ὑπάρχειν προσηρτημένα τῇ λογικῇ ψυχῇ. We can gather that this assemblage of accreted spirits actually constituted a second soul from the title of his son Isidorus' book Περὶ προσφυοῦς ψυχῆς. Clement makes the following comment about Isidorus: Δύο γὰρ δὴ ψυχὰς ὑποτίθεται καὶ οὗτος ἐν ἡμῖν, καθάπερ οἱ Πυθαγόρειοι; cf. Bardasanes (Ephraem. *Hymn*. 53, p. 553e) and his teaching that man has "a soul from the seven", and the ἀντίμιμον πνεῦμα of the *Pistis Sophia* and *Apocryphon of John*. Clement may have had Numenius in mind when mentioning the 'Pythagoreans'; cf. Lewy p. 504, n. 29. Dodds (*op. cit.*), De ley (p. 53) and Dillon (p. 376) all associate the Numenian doctrine of the two souls with that of τὰ προσφυόμενα and the *descensus*. Dodds and Mazza (p. 136) cite Macrobius' use of the term *incrementa* as a reflection of Numenius' προσφυόμενα, and both see it as further evidence for attributing Macrobius' *descensus* to Numenius (see Des Places p. 122, n. 3)

Evidence for the doctrine within the Middle Platonic tradition is scarce. Culianu (pp. 46-47) believes he has found traces of the *descensus* in Plutarch's myth of Aridaeus-Thespesius (*De Sera* 565b) where colors are assigned to the several vices. He speculates that Plutarch was using "some work of the Hermetic *vulgata*" similar to the *Panaretos* as his source, where vices and colors are associated with each planet. Celsus' interpretation of the Mithraic Ladder at *Contra Cels.* VI, 22 provides another rare testimony: Αἰνίττεται ταῦτα καὶ ὁ Περσῶν λόγος, καὶ ἡ τοῦ Μίθρου τελετή, <ἣ> παρ' αὐτοῖς ἐστιν. ἔστι γάρ τι ἐν αὐτῇ σύμβολον τῶν δύο τῶν ἐν οὐρανῷ περιόδων, τῆς τε ἀπλανοῦς καὶ τῆς εἰς τοὺς πλανήτας αὖ νενεμημένης, καὶ τῆς δι' αὐτῶν τῆς ψυχῆς διεξόδου. The question as to whether Celsus correctly interpreted the symbol is a matter of scholarly debate which need not concern us here. The fact that he did read it in this fashion serves to show that he was aware of the doctrine. Plotinus knew it, as evidenced by I. 6. 7: τεῦξις δὲ αὐτοῦ (*sc.* τοῦ ἀγαθοῦ) ἀναβαίνουσι πρὸς ἄνω καὶ ἐπιστραφεῖσι καὶ ἀποδυομένοις ἃ καταβαίνοντες ἠμφιέσμεθα; cf. IV. 3. 15. For the later Neoplatonic elaborations of the doctrine see Dodds *Proclus*, Appendix II, 318-321.

It would appear that the doctrine exercised most influence in Hermetic/Gnostic circles. (Boussett, *op. cit.*, p. 737, and Culianu, *Ordine*, p. 109, see Hermeticism as the source for the final pessimistic transformation of the astrological lore.) Indeed, the entire Gnostic portrayal of the planetary Archons and the γνῶσις requisite to pass them constitutes the extreme negative development of the doctrine (see Culianu, pp. 48-49).

In view of all of this, even if we do not ascribe the passage in Macrobius directly to Numenius, it would seem overly conservative to deny him possession of the *descensus* doctrine. And it is most probable that his version of it, as suggested by Dodds and Dillon, followed the Hermetic/Gnostic model.

l. 5. **Has solis portas physici vocaverunt:** Cf. fr. 31, ll. 15-16: δύο οὖν ταύτας ἔθεντο πύλας...οἱ θεολόγοι; fr. 32, l. 1: λέγει δέ που καὶ Ἡλίου πύλας. See note *ad. loc.*

ll. 9-12. **Ideo hominum una...reveruntur:** Cf. fr. 31, ll. 17-18.

ll. 12-13. **hoc est quod Homeri...in antri Ithacensis...significant:** See. fr. 31, l. 1 and note.

ll. 14-15. **a lacteo circulo deorsum incipere Ditis imperium:** The transferal of the Underworld to areas above the earth was a central aspect of the *descensus* doctrine. In ch. 11 Macrobius describes the teaching of a third group of Platonists thus: *hi enim caelum, quod* ἀπλανής *sphaera vocitatur partem unam, septem vero sphaeras, quae vagae vocantur, et quod inter illas ac terram est terramque ipsam alteram partem esse voluerunt.* In his note *ad. loc.*, Leemans explains that the term 'alteram partem' refers to Tartarus. Cf. fr. 35, ll. 8-9 where Proclus states that Numenius raised the Underworld to the realm of the planets: ἀνάγει γὰρ εἰς ταύτας τοὺς ποταμοὺς καὶ αὐτὸν τὸν Τάρταρον. See De Ley, p. 21.

l. 19. *hinc profecti huc reveruntur:* Dream of Scipio 3, 1.

Fr. 35

Proclus is discussing what obviously must have been a Numenian commentary on the Myth of Er, *Rep.* 614b-621d.

l. 1. τὸ κέντρον εἶναι φησιν τοῦτον: Numenius is referring to the τόπον τινά δαιμόνιον of *Rep.* 614c.

l. 3. τούς δικαστάς: Cf. *Rep.* 614c: δικαστὰς δὲ μεταχὺ τούτων (*sc.* χασμάτων) καθῆσαι.

l. 6. δύο χάσματα: Cf. *Rep.* 614c: ἐν ᾧ (*sc.* τόπῳ) τῆς γῆς δύ᾽ εἶναι χάσματα ἐχομένω ἀλλήλοιν καὶ τοῦ οὐρανοῦ αὖ ἐν τῷ ἄνω ἄλλα καταντικρύ.

ll. 6-8. τὸν αἰγόκερων καὶ τὸν καρκίνον...ἀνόδου δὲ ἐκεῖνον: Cf. fr. 31, ll. 17-18; fr. 34, ll. 9-11.

ll. 9-10. ἀνάγει γὰρ εἰς ταύτας τοὺς ποταμοὺς καὶ αὐτὸν τὸν Τάρταρον: The main thrust for Numenius' commentary appears to have been the transferal of the Underworld into the planetary spheres; see notes to fr. 34. Culianu (p. 45) points out that Plutarch had elevated the rivers of the Underworld in the myth of *De genio* 590f: δύο δὲ αὐτὴν (*sc.* τὴν θάλασσαν) ἔχειν ἀναστομώσεις, πυρὸς ἐμβάλλοντας ἐναντίους ποταμοὺς δεχομένας. Cf. also the description of the Styx immediately following. For Plato's description of the rivers of Hades see *Phd.* 112-113c.

l. 10. τερατολογίαν: The word is an expression of contempt in Proclus; cf. the ironic tone of Socrates at *Phdr.* 229d: ...πλήθη τε καὶ ἀτοπίαι τερατολόγων τινῶν φύσεων. See also (with Des Places, p. 86, n. *ad. loc.*) Puech p. 43 and n. 4.

l. 11. πηδήσεις: Another derisive remark by Proclus, but cf. the myth of Aridaeus/Thespesius in Plutarch *De Sera* 564a: ἀλλὰ τὰς μὲν (*sc.* ψυχάς) ἐκπηδᾶν ἐλαφρότητι θαυμαστῇ.

ll. 13-14. συρράπτων τὰ πλατωνικὰ ῥήματα...τοῖς τελεστικοῖς: This was the synthesizing agenda which Numenius felt was necessary for the pursuit of truth. Cf. fr. 1a, l. 6: προσφερόμενον αὐτῶν τὰς τελετάς.

ll. 15-19: μαρτυρόμενος τῶν δύο χασμάτων...ὑπάρχειν: Cf. fr. 31-32 and notes.

l. 20. λύει μὲν αὐτῶν τὴν ἐν ἀνδράσι ζωήν: Cf. *Pomandres* ch. 24: ἐν τῇ ἀναλύσει τοῦ σώματος τοῦ ὑλικοῦ.

ll. 22-26. καὶ ἡλίου πύλας ὑμνοῦσαν...συνωθουμένων: Cf. fr. 31-32 and notes.

ll. 26-28. γάλα σπένδεσθαι...τὴν πρώτην τροφήν: Cf. fr. 32, ll. 9-10; fr. 34, ll. 16-17.

ll. 29-30. τοῦ φωτός, ὃ δὴ σύδεσμον εἶναι τοῦ οὐρανοῦ: Cf. *Rep.* 616b-c: καὶ ἰδεῖν αὐτόθι κατὰ μέσον τὸ φῶς ἐκ τοῦ οὐρανοῦ τὰ ἄκρα αὐτοῦ τῶν δεσμῶν τεταμένα—εἶναι γὰρ τοῦτο τὸ φῶς σύνδεσμον τοῦ οὐρανοῦ.

ll. 36-37. τὸ φῶς τὸ ἴριδι προσφερές: Cf. *Rep.* 616b: εὐθύ, οἷον κίονα, μάλιστα τῇ ἴριδι προσφερῆ.

ll. 38-39. ἀπεικάζειν τὰς ἄνευ σωμάτων ψυχάς...τὸν ποιητήν: Cf. (with Des Places p. 87, n. *ad. loc.*) *Odyssey* 11, 207: τρὶς δέ μοι ἐκ χειρῶν σκιῇ εἴκελον ἢ καὶ ὀνείρῳ ἔπτατ᾽...; 222: ψυχὴ δ᾽ ἠΰτ᾽ ὄνειρος ἀποπταμένη πεπότηται.

l. 47. τὸν ὑπερουράνιον τόπον: Cf. *Phdr.* 247c.

Fr. 36

l. 3. εἰσκρίσεως: Festugière (vol. III, p. 267, n. 1) mentions the quasi-technical nature of the term, comparing this instance with Albinus XXV, 6: τῷ δὲ ἀθανάτους εἶναι τὰς ψυχὰς λόγῳ ἠκολούθησε τὸ εἰσκρίνεσθαι αὐτὰς τοῖς σώμασι, παρεμφυομένας ταῖς τῶν ἐμβρύων διαπλαστικαῖς φύσεσι.

ll. 9-10. τὸν παρὰ μὲν τῷ Πλάτωνι ποταμὸν ᾿Αμέλητα: Cf. *Rep.* X, 621a.

ll. 10-11. παρὰ δὲ τῷ ῾Ησιόδῳ καὶ τοῖς ᾿Ορφικοῖς τὴν Στύγα: Cf. Hesiod *Theogony*, 361; *Orphicorum fragmenta*, fr. 49, v. 26.

l. 11. παρὰ δὲ τῷ Φερεκύδῃ τὴν ἐκροὴν: For a discussion of the theories concerning Pherecydes' ἐκροή, see *KR*, p. 59, n. 1.

Fr. 37

The context of the fragment is a review of the allegorical interpretations of the battle between the inhabitants of Atlantis and Athens, which is related by Critias in *Tim.* 24d-25d.

l. 4. ᾿Ωριγένης: Origen the Platonist, not the Christian; see Lewy, p. 505. Des Places' note *ad. loc.* in which he quotes the Christian Origen's *Contra Celsum* VI, 42 leads one to wonder if he could have confused the two.

ll. 4-7. εἰς ψυχῶν διάστασιν...προσήκουσι: Lewy (p. 503-504) provides a persuasive interpretation of Numenius' doctrine. He first makes the sound assumption that Numenius saw Athene, according to a common allegory, as Reason. (Cf. *Crat.* 407b: οἱ πολλοὶ ἐξηγούμενοι τὸν ποιητήν φασι τὴν ᾿Αθηνᾶν αὐτὸν νοῦν τε καὶ διάνοιαν πεποιηκέναι.) From this he deduces that the "principal motif" of Numenius' allegory was the conflict between souls devoted to Reason and those concerned only with the material realm, and notes that this opposition agrees with Numenius' teaching of two antagonistic human souls. (Cf. fr. 43, ll. 4-5 and note; fr. 44 and note.) He concludes: "We may consequently presume that Numenius explained the war between Athens and Atlantis as the struggle between the λογικαί and the ἄλογοι ψυχαί and the victory of the former as the triumph of reason over the passions." In n. 29 to p. 504 Lewy tells us that Zeller III², p. 239) was the first to draw a relationship between Numenius' interpretation of the war and his two-soul theory. Dillon (p. 378) surmises that the 'agents of generation' (γενεσιουργοί) "sound very much like material daemons, engaged in ensnaring souls into incarnation." He admits that due to the nature of the evidence, this conjecture must remain somewhat tentative.

l. 6. τῷ τῆς γενέσεως ἐφόρῳ θεῷ: Poseidon. See Lewy p. 503; Dillon *op. cit.*

ll. 8-9. οἱ δὲ μίξαντες τὴν Ὠριγένους...καὶ Νουμηνίου δόξαν: Proclus is referring to the doctrine of Porphyry. See l. 24 below and Lewy *op. cit.*

ll. 13-14. τὸ δὲ πονηρὸν ἄλλο καὶ λυμαντικὸν τῶν ψυχῶν: Cf. *Corp. Herm.* XVI, 13: ὑπὸ τούτῳ δὲ ἐτάγη ὁ τῶν δαιμόνων χορός, μᾶλλον δὲ χοροί· πολλοὶ γὰρ οὗτοι καὶ ποικίλοι...ἀγαθοὶ καὶ κακοὶ ὄντες τὰς φύσεις. 15: γενόμενον γὰρ ἡμῶν ἕκαστον καὶ ψυχωθέντα παραλαμβάνουσι δαίμονες οἱ κατ᾽ ἐκείνην στιγμὴν τῆς γενέσεως.

ll. 16-17. οἱ παλαιοί...εἰς Ὄσιριν καὶ Τυφῶνα ἀνήγαγον ἢ εἰς Διόνυσον καὶ Τιτᾶνας: Cf. Celsus *apud* Origen *Contra Cels.* VI, 42 (quoted by Des Places, see note to l. 3 above):

...the ancients hint at a sort of divine war...And Pherecydes, who was far earlier than Heraclitus, relates a myth of an army drawn up in battle against another army, and says that Kronos was leader of the one and Ophioneus of the other; he tells of their challenges and their contests, and that they made agreements that whichever of the two fell into Ogenus should be the vanquished party, while the party which drove the other out and conquered should possess the heaven...this is also the meaning contained in the mysteries which affirm that the Titans and Giants fought the gods, and in the mysteries of the Egyptians which tell of Typhon and Horus and Osiris (trans. Chadwick).

Commentary 197

This text merely provides another general view of the thought world in which these discussions took place. Plutarch, however, presents an interpretation of Osiris-Typhon (Egyptian Seth) that resonates quite closely with Lewy's reading of Numenius' allegory. Cf. *De Iside* 371a-b: ἐν μὲν οὖν τῇ ψυχῇ νοῦς καὶ λόγος ὁ τῶν ἀρίστων πάντων ἡγεμὼν καὶ κύριος Ὄσιρίς...Τυφὼν δὲ τῆς ψυχῆς τὸ παθητικὸν καὶ τιτανικὸν καὶ ἄλογον καὶ ἔμπληκτον.

ll. 18-19. ταῦτα ὁ Πλάτων...ἀναπέμπει δι' εὐσέβειαν: Cf. *Euthyphro* 5c-6c where Socrates, who has been accused of ἀσεβεία, questions Euthyphro about τὸ εὐσεβές. At 6b Socrates tries to steer his interlocutor towards a true notion of εὐσέβεια by asking: Καὶ πόλεμον ἆρα ἡγῇ εἶναι τῷ ὄντι ἐν τοῖς θεοῖς πρὸς ἀλλήλους, καὶ ἔχθρας γε δεινὰς καὶ μάχας καὶ ἄλλα τοιαῦτα πολλά, οἷα λέγεταί τε ὑπὸ τῶν ποιητῶν; the issue is raised again with emphasis in *Rep.* II, 377e-378c: πρῶτον μέν, ἦν δ' ἐγώ, τὸ μέγιστον καὶ περὶ τῶν μεγίστων ψεῦδος ὁ εἰπὼν οὐ καλῶς ἐψεύσατο ὡς Οὐρανός τε ἠργάσατο ἅ φησι δρᾶσαι αὐτὸν Ἡσίοδος, ὅ τε αὖ Κρόνος ὡς ἐτιμωρήσατο αὐτόν...(378b-c): οὐδέ γε ἦν δ' ἐγώ, τὸ παράπαν ὡς θεοὶ θεοῖς πολεμοῦσί τε καὶ ἐπιβουλεύουσι καὶ μάχονται...πολλοῦ δεῖ γιγαντομαχίας τε μυθολογητέον αὐτοῖς καὶ ποικιλτέον. Here Proclus is saying that Plato exercised εὐσέβεια by removing these narratives from the divine realm. For Numenius' interpretation of the *Euthyphro* see fr. 23.

ll. 24-25. Πορφύριος, ὃν καὶ θαυμάσειεν ἄν τις εἰ ἕτερα λέγοι τῆς Νουμηνίου παραδόσεως: Lewy (*op. cit.*, p. 503, n. 23) states that this "mordant remark on Porphyry" originated with Iamblichus. Waszink (*P. und. N.*, p. 36) follows Lewy: "Wie nun aber Lewy richtig vermutet hat, ist dieser Satz nicht das Eigentum des Proklos, sondern vielmehr dem Numenios und Porphyrios feindlich gesinnten Jamblichos zuzuschreiben"

Fr. 38

l. 2. ἡ φρουρά: Cf. Phd. 62b: ὁ μὲν οὖν ἐν ἀπορρήτοις λεγόμενος περὶ αὐτῶν λόγος, ὡς ἔν τινι φρουρᾷ ἐσμεν οἱ ἄνθρωποι καὶ οὐ δεῖ ἑαυτὸν ἐκ ταύτης λύειν οὐδ᾽ ἀποδιδράσκειν, μέγας τέ τίς μοι φαίνεται.

ll. 2-3. οὔτε ἡ ἡδονή, ὡς Νουήνιος: In light of fr. 2, ll. 16-17 it is difficult to conceive just what this notice could be referring to. Des Places (p. 121, n. *ad. loc.*) connects this fragment with fr. 32, l. 10 where it is suggested that souls fall into γένεσις through a desire for pleasure (δι᾽ ἡδονῆς).

Fr. 39

This is the notice that led Beutler (col. 677) to reject Numenius as the source for Macrobius' description of the soul's descent through the planetary spheres (fr. 34; see introductory note to that fragment; for detailed and opposing analyses of the way in which these definitions of soul apply to Macrobius and the ascertainment of his sources, see Elferink pp. 8-28 and De Ley's critique pp. 27-50.) Both the 'arithmetic' and the 'geometric' definitions of soul arise from interpretations of *Tim.* 35aff. which begins: τῆς ἀμερίστου καὶ ἀεὶ κατὰ ταὐτὰ ἐχούσης οὐσίας καὶ τῆς αὖ περὶ τὰ σώματα γιγνομένης μεριστῆς τρίτον ἐξ ἀμφοῖν ἐν μέσῳ συνεκεράσατο οὐσίας εἶδος.

l. 3. οἱ μὲν ἀριθμὸν εἰπόντες: The definition of soul as number can be traced back to Xenocrates. Cf. Plutarch *De an. proc.* 1012d (fr. 68 Heinze): τοὺς μὲν Ξενοκράτης προσηγάγετο, τῆς ψυχῆς τὴν οὐσίαν ἀριθμὸν αὐτὸν ὑφ᾽ ἑαυτοῦ κινούμενον ἀποφηνάμενος. Krämer (p. 76) views Numenius' adherence to this definition as an "Erneuerung altakademischer Lehre."

l. 5. οἱ δ' ὡς γεωμετρικὴν ὑπόστασιν: The 'geometrical' definition goes back to Speusippus (attested by Iamblichus *De Anima, apud.* Stob. I 363, 26 Wachs = fr. 40 Lang): ἐν ἰδέα δὲ τοῦ πάντη διαστατοῦ Σπεύσιππυς (sc. αὐτὴν ἀφωρίσατο). See Krämer (p. 209, n. 48) for the path of influence exerted by this doctrine.

Fr. 40

l. 1. Θεόδωρος: Theodorus of Asine was a student and eventual rival of Iamblichus who united various strands of the Neoplatonic tradition (see Wallis p. 95). Unlike his master he retained Plotinus' doctrine of an unfallen portion of the soul, a stance in which he also agreed with Numenius, cf. fr. 42.

Fr. 41

ll. 4. ὁμοιομερῆ...ὡς καὶ ἐν ὁτῳοῦν αὐτῆς μέρει εἶναι τὰ ὅλα: The language is that of Anaxagoras; cf. Simplicius *Phys.* 164, 26: καὶ οὕτως ἂν εἴη ἐν παντὶ πάντα· οὐδὲ χωρὶς ἔστιν εἶναι, ἀλλὰ πάντα παντὸς μοῖραν μετέχει; 164, 23: ἐν παντὶ παντὸς μοῖρα ἔνεστι (cited in *KR*, pp. 375-376). Ross (I, p. 132) says that the word ὁμοιομερῆ was most likely invented by Aristotle but was mistakenly attributed to Anaxagoras by later doxographers through a misunderstanding of *Metaph.* 984a: Ἀναξαγόρας...ἅπαντα τὰ ὁμοιομερῆ, καθάπερ ὕδωρ ἢ πῦρ, οὕτω γίγνεσθαι καὶ ἀπόλλυσθαί φησι. Ross defines the word as meaning "things whose parts are similar to one another and to the whole things"; cf. Festugière III, p. 184, n. 2. Plato illustrates the concept at *Prot.* 329d: ὥσπερ τὰ τοῦ χρυσοῦ μόρια οὐδὲν διαφέρει τὰ ἕτερα τῶν ἑτέρων, ἀλλήλων καὶ τοῦ ὅλου. In this doctrine of Numenius, the physical concept of Anaxagoras has simply been transferred to the metaphysical realm, emphasizing the utter self-consistency of the ἀσώματον οὐσία.

ll. 6-7. τὸν νοητὸν κόσμον...ἐν αὐτῇ ἐνιδρύουσι: Cf. Plotinus III. 4. 3: ἔστι γὰρ καὶ πολλὰ ἡ ψυχὴ καὶ πάντα καὶ τὰ ἄνω καὶ τὰ κάτω αὖ μέχρι πάσης ζωῆς, καὶ ἐσμὲν ἕκαστος κόσμος νοητός. Armstrong (*Plotinus* VI, p. 340, n. 1) says that Plotinus' "clearest explanation" for this passage lies in VI. 5. 7, 1-9 which concludes: ὄντων δὲ καὶ τῶν ἄλλων, οὐ μόνον ἡμῶν, ἐκεῖνα (sc. τὰ νοητά) πάντες ἐσμὲν ἐκεῖνα. ὁμοῦ ἄρα ὄντες μετὰ πάντων ἐσμὲν ἐκεῖνα· πάντα ἄρα ἐσμὲν ἕν. The later Neoplatonists would have none of it. See *e. g.* Armstrong *Plotinus* III, p. 150, n. 1

ll. 7-8. ἐν πᾶσιν ὡσαύτως πάντα εἶναι: A somewhat more comprehensive statement than that in ll. 7-8. Every immaterial entity is contained in every other. Cf. *Corp. Herm.* XIII, 2: τὸ πᾶν ἐν παντί; Plotinus V. 8. 4: καὶ γὰρ ἔχει πᾶς πάντα ἐν αὐτῷ καὶ αὖ ὁρᾷ ἐν ἄλλῳ πάντα, ὥστε πανταχοῦ καὶ πᾶν πᾶν καὶ ἕκαστον πᾶν καὶ ἄπειρος ἡ αἴγλη. The concept appears as Proposition 103 in Proclus' *Elements*: Πάντα ἐν πᾶσιν.

ll. 8-9. οἰκέως μέντοι κατὰ τὴν οὐσίαν ἐν ἑκάστοις: Cf. Proclus *loc. cit.*: οἰκείως δὲ ἐν ἑκάστῳ. Plotinus expresses the concept at I. 8. 2: τὸ γοῦν μεταλαμβάνον οὐχ ὁμοῦ πάντων, ἀλλ' ὅτου δύναται μεταλαμβάνει. Dodds (*Elements* p. 254) notes that Syrianus ascribed the general principle that "all things are in all things, but each after its own fashion" to 'the Pythagoreans'.

l. 10. ἀναμφισβητήτως μέν ἐστι Νουμήνιος: A most valuable statement by Iamblichus, since the verbatim fragments of Numenius provide no hint of this important doctrine. Dodds (*N. & A.*, p. 23) states that it is one of "the main structural laws or postulates of Neoplatonism...explicitly formulated by Numenius". See Dodds *op. cit.* for a discussion of the manner in which the principle was employed by later Neoplatonists.

Fr. 42

l. 1. **ἕνωσιν:** Cf. the Hermetic expressions at *Corp. Herm.* I, 6: τὸ ἐν σοὶ βλέπον καὶ ἀκοῦον, λόγος κυρίου, ὁ δὲ νοῦς πατὴρ θεός. οὐ γὰρ διίστανται ἀπ' ἀλλήλων· ἕνωσις γὰρ τούτων ἐστὶν ἡ ζωή; XII, 1: ὁ νοῦς οὖν οὐκ ἔστιν ἀποτετμημένος τῆς οὐσιότητος τοῦ θεοῦ, ἀλλ' ὥσπερ ἡπλομένος καθάπερ τὸ τοῦ ἡλίου φῶς.

Festugière (*op. cit.* p. 47) emphasizes the fact that Iamblichus' reference to this doctrine appears in his section on eschatology, and therefore assumes it applies only to the soul "remontée au ciel". Dodds (*op. cit.* p. 22, n. 1), while saying that Plotinus took over "this very important article of faith from Numenius", rightly points to fr. 41 and 14 as evidence against Festugière's interpretation. Indeed, this concept of "indistinguishable identity (ταὐτότητα ἀδιάκριτον)" with divine principles constitutes a logical extension of the doctrine πάντα ἐν πᾶσιν. But the decisive factor here is the important role played by the concept in the thought of Plotinus and the manner in which he understands it, which is clearly not eschatological. Cf. IV. 8. 8: οὐ πᾶσα οὐδ' ἡμετέρα ψυχὴ ἔδυ, ἀλλ' ἔστι τι αὐτῆς ἐν τῷ νοητῷ ἀεί; II. 9. 2: ὁτὲ δὲ τὸ χεῖρον αὐτῆς καθελκυσθὲν συνεφελκύσασθαι τὸ μέσον· τὸ γὰρ πᾶν αὐτῆς οὐκ ἦν θέμις καθελκύσαι. In *Ennead* VI he twice uses the Hermetic formulation; VI. 4. 14: οὐδὲ γὰρ οὐδὲ νῦν ἀποτετμήμεθα; VI. 9. 9: οὐ γὰρ ἀποτετμήμεθα οὐδὲ χωρίς ἐσμεν.

Fr. 43

l. 2. **εἰς μίαν σύνταξιν καὶ μίαν ἰδέαν τὰ εἴδη...τῆς ζωῆς...συνάγοντες:** Festugière (*Révélation* III, p. 207, n. 4) says that the 'parts of life' being referred to here are the rational and irrational elements of soul, the παθητικόν and the λογιστικόν; cf. Aristotle *Magna Moralia* I, 1, 1182a, 24: Πλάτων διείλετο τὴν ψυχὴν εἴς τε τὸ λόγον ἔχον καὶ εἰς τὸ ἄλογον ὀρθῶς (cf. fr. 44 and notes). He points out that Albinus also insisted on the disharmony between the two aspects of soul and quotes XXIV, 2: ἕτερα ὄντα τῇ φύσει τό τε παθητικὸν καὶ τὸ λογιστικὸν καὶ τόποις ὀφείλει κεχωρίσθαι. εὑρίσκεται γὰρ μαχόμενα ἀλλήλοις. Cf. also (with Festugière) the Hermetic text in Stobaeus *Exc.* II, B 5, 4-6: χαλεπὴ (sc. ὁδός) ψυχῇ ὁδεῦσαι ἐν σώματι οὔσῃ. πρῶτον μὲν γὰρ αὐτὴν ἑαυτῇ πολεμῆσαι δεῖ καὶ διάστασιν μεγάλην ποιῆσαι...ἑνὸς γὰρ γίγνεται πρὸς δύο ἡ σύστασις, τοῦ μὲν φεύγοντος τῶν δὲ καθελκόντων κάτω, καὶ ἔρις καὶ μάχη πολλὴ πρὸς ἄλληλα τούτων γίγνεται.

While this battle between the parts of the individual human soul is no doubt the main focus of Iamblichus' discussion, it is important to observe that a dualism on a larger scale lies in the background. At l. 5 where Numenius is listed among those who portray the elements of life as warring entities, there can be little doubt that the reference also implies his doctrine of preexistent matter unremittingly hostile to the efforts of God (see fr. 52 and notes). Festugière admits as much by quoting from that fragment. If any question remains it is laid to rest by Iamblichus' mention of Plutarch and his tendency to depict hostile entities coming into some kind of concord. A text from *Quaest. Plat.* shows clearly that the poles of the dualism are body and soul on a cosmic scale, and that they are 'fitted together' (Iamblichus may have been inspired to use the verb συναρμόζω by Plutarch himself); cf. 1001b: δυεῖν ὄντων ἐξ ὧν ὁ κόσμος συνέστηκε, σώματος καὶ ψυχῆς, τὸ μὲν οὐκ ἐγέννησε θεὸς ἀλλά, τῆς ὕλης παρασχομένης, ἐμόρφωσε καὶ συνήρμοσε. Cf. also (with Cherniss *Plutarch* p. 33, n. e) *De An. Proc.* 1014 b-c: τὴν δὲ οὐσίαν καὶ ὕλην...ἐμπαρασχεῖν...ἔταξε καὶ διεκόσμησε καὶ συνήρμοσε. For the association of Plutarch and Atticus see Festugière *op. cit.* p. 208, n. 3.

ll. 7-8. ἀπὸ τῶν ἔξωθεν προσφυομένων προστιθέντων...τῇ ψυχῇ τὸ κακόν: Plato provides the seed for this doctrine at *Tim.* 42c: ...συνεπισπώμενος τὸν πολὺν ὄχλον καὶ ὕστερον προσφύντα ἐκ πυρὸς καὶ ὕδατος καὶ ἀέρος καὶ γῆς, θορυβώδη καὶ ἄλογον ὄντα. Cf. (with Cornford p. 144, n. 2) the image of the sea encrusted Glaucus at *Rep.* 611d and the phrase ἄλλα δὲ προσπεφυκέναι. Albinus (XVI, 2) expands on the doctrine: ὅτι τὰ πάθη ἀπὸ σώματος προσφύσεται θνητά· πρῶτα μὲν αἰσθήσεις, ἔπειτα δὲ ἡδονὴ καὶ λύπη, φόβος τε καὶ θυμός...τέλος δὲ αὐταῖς τῶν πόνων ἔσται τὸ νικῆσαι μὲν τὰ προσφύντα, εἰς δὲ τὴν οἰκείαν ἕξιν ἐλθεῖν.

προστιθέντων: Jonas (p. 159, n. 13) points out that this simple image underwent a profound transformation in later antiquity. Especially in the Hermetic and Gnostic milieus the notion of 'accretions; to the soul became a central aspect of the doctrine of the soul's descent into the material realm and its eventual return through the heavens (for a thorough discussion of this see the introductory note to fr. 34). At I. 1. 12 Plotinus employs his version of the doctrine in a commentary on the Glaucus image. The verb προστίθημι is uses throughout the passage. Cf. l. 8: ὁ δ' ἁμαρτεῖν διδοὺς συμπλέκει μὲν καὶ προστίθησιν αὐτῇ καὶ ἄλλο εἶδος τὸ τὰ δεινὰ ἔχον πάθη. At l. 15, after quoting the the image of Glaucus, he paraphrases Plato thus: δεῖ δὲ περικρούσαντας τὰ προστιθέντα, εἴπερ τις ἐθέλει τὴν φύσιν, φησίν ἰδεῖν. A mention of 'ascent' follows: ἡ δὲ ἀναχώρησις καὶ ὁ χωρισμὸς οὐ μόνον τοῦδε σώματος, ἀλλὰ καὶ ἅπαντος τοῦ προστεθέντος. Καὶ γὰρ ἐν τῇ γενέσει ἡ προσθήκη. Finally the 'descent' is set forth: τὸ δὲ πῶς ἡ γένεσις, εἴρηται, ὅτι καταβαινούσης, ἄλλου του ἀπ' αὐτῆς γινομένου τοῦ καταβαίνοντος ἐν τῇ νεύσει.

Fr. 44

l. 1. τρία μέρη ψυχῆς: The tripartite soul was well established in the dialogues. Cf. *Rep.* 439d where a preliminary distinction is made between τὸ λογιστικὸν τῆς ψυχῆς and τὸ ἀλόγιστικόν τε καὶ ἐπιθημητικόν. At 441a the third member is added: οὕτως καὶ ἐν ψυχῇ τρίτον τοῦτό ἐστι τὸ θυμοειδές. The *Phaedrus* myth clothes the doctrine in allegory, cf. 253c: καθάπερ ἐν ἀρχῇ τοῦδε τοῦ μύθου τριχῇ διείλομεν ψυχὴν ἑκάστην, ἱππομόρφω μὲν δύο τινὲ εἴδη, ἡνιοχικὸν δὲ εἶδος τρίτον. At *Tim.* 89e the commonplace nature of the doctrine is expressed: καθάπερ εἴπομεν πολλάκις, ὅτι τρία τριχῇ ψυχῆς ἐν ἡμῖν εἴδη κατῴκισται. Cf. Albinus XXIV, 1: τριμερής ἐστιν ἡ ψυχή; Philo *Leg. All.* I, 70: νοτέον οὖν ἐστιν ἡμῶν τριμερὴς ἡ ψυχὴ καὶ ἔχει μέρος τὸ μὲν λογικόν, τὸ δὲ θυμικόν, τὸ δὲ ἐπιθυμητικόν.

l. 2. δύο γε, τὸ λογικὸν καὶ ἄλογον: Despite the acceptance of the tripartite doctrine of soul, there is in the later tradition a tendency also to revert to a division similar to that made at *Rep.* 439d (see above). Dillon (p. 174) calls this "the normal bipartite division of the soul." Philo provides several instances of this, cf. *Spec. Leg.* I, 333: ...τὴν ὅλην ψυχὴν ἐκ λογικοῦ καὶ ἀλόγου μέρους συνεστῶσαν· καὶ οἱ μὲν τὸ λογικόν, ὃ δὴ νοῦς ἐστι, διεκληρώσαντο, οἱ δὲ τὸ ἄλογον, ὅπερ εἰς τὰς αἰσθήσεις τέμνεται; *Leg. All.* II, 6: τὸ ἡγεμονικὸν τῆς ψυχῆς πρεσβύτερον τῆς ὅλης εἶναι, τὸ δὲ ἄλογον νεώτερον...τὸ δὲ ἄλογον αἴσθησίς ἐστι καὶ τὰ ταύτης ἔκγονα πάθη. Cf. Plutarch *De virt. mor.* 3, 441ff, where the distinction λογιστικόν-ἄλογον is made. Albinus (XXIV, 1) says that the soul is tripartite κατὰ τὰς δυνάμεις, but then adds: φύσει δὲ χωρίζεται τὸ παθητικὸν καὶ λογιστικόν. The bipartite soul appears at *Corp. Herm.* XVI, 15 in a discussion of the χοροὶ δαιμόνων: οὗτοι οὖν εἰς τὰ δύο μέρη τῆς ψυχῆς δύντες διὰ τοῦ σώματος στοβοῦσιν αὐτήν...τὸ δὲ λογικὸν μέρος τῆς ψυχῆς ἀδέσποτον τῶν δαιμόνων ἕστηκεν.

δύο ψυχάς: Krämer (p. 73) thinks that the two soul doctrine of Numenius corresponds to the splitting of his δεύτερος θεός into a second and third. More to the point is Hager's observation (p. 84, followed by Wazsink, *P. und. N.*, p. 76) that once the concept of two opposed World Souls is accepted (see fr. 52 and notes), it is natural to apply this cosmic division to humans, the microcosm. Plutarch, whose dualism resembles that of Numenius, came close to this distinction between νοῦς and ψυχή (see Dillon, p. 211-213), but as Dodds (*N. & A.*, p. 7) points out, "before Numenius the doctrine is not stated in this radical form...anywhere in the native Greek tradition."

The notion of corresponding macrocosmic/microcosmic dualism no doubt plays a role here. Dillon (p. 376), however, thinks "there is a magical or astrological component in this theory as well." He is referring to Numenius' teaching concerning the soul's descent and its acquisition of 'accretions'. See introductory note to fr. 34.

Fr. 45

Beutler (col. 677) appropriately refers to this fragment as "ein nicht ganz verständliches Zeugnis über N.' Erkenntnistheorie." As he points out, although the vocabulary is Stoic, the way in which it is used reveals that this notice is part of Numenius' anti-Stoic polemic (see fr. 4b and notes). The Stoic epistemology had posited the following series (see Rist *Stoic.*, p. 140): (a) bare sensation (αἰσθήσεις), (b) perception through acceptation of αἰσθήσεις (φαντασία), and (c) recognition of perception through an act of assent (συγκατάθεσις). Numenius is attacking this system by removing φαντασία from its primary role to that of an incidental. But that is about all one can say concerning his position in this matter. Beutler concludes: "Wie N. seine Lehre begründet hat, ist nicht auszumachen."

Fr. 46a

ll. 1-2. ἀπὸ τῆς λογικῆς ψυχῆς ἄχρι τῆς ἐμψύχου ἕξεως ἀπαθανατίζουσιν: Dillon (p. 377) reacts to this passage thus: "Rather mysteriously, Numenius admits the irrational soul some kind of immortality..." However Beutler (col. 676) provides a satisfactory delineation of the logic behind Numenius' position: "Da N. die Hyle mit ihrer Seele als ewig ansetze und die ἄλογος ψυχή aus der Hyle stammen ließ (s. Chalc. p. 326, 17ff...) mußte für ihn jedes seelische Verhalten unsterblich sein." We also learn from fr. 47 that Numenius was led to this position by his reading of *Phdr*. 345c: πᾶσα ψυχὴ ἀθάνατος.

ἄχρι τῆς ἐμψύχου ἕξεως: This rather odd phrase is clarified by the notice in fr. 47 where the following distinction between types of 'separable' (hence immortal) souls is made: τὴν λογικὴν καὶ τὴν ἄλογον καὶ τὴν φυτικήν (cf. the μέχρι τῆς φύσεως attributed to Plotinus in l. 2).

Albinus (XXV, 5), though tentative, followed a more conservative Platonic line in denying immortality to irrational souls: ὅτι μὲν οὖν αἱ λογικαὶ ψυχαὶ ἀθάνατοι ὑπάρχουσι κατὰ τὸν ἄνδρα τοῦτον (=Πλάτωνας) βεβαιώσαιτ' ἄν τις· εἰ δὲ καὶ αἱ ἄλογοι, τοῦτο τῶν ἀμφισβητουμένων ὑπάρχει. πιθανὸν γὰρ τὰς ἀλόγους ψυχάς...θνητάς τε καὶ φθαρτὰς ὑπάρχειν.

l. 4. Ξενόκρατες καὶ Σπεύσιππος: Dillon (p. 17, n. 1) calls this "a bothersome late doxographic report to the effect that both Speusippus and Xenocrates accorded immortality to both the rational and irrational soul." He feels however that the nature of the evidence allows no further speculation on their position.

l. 5. Πλούταρχος: Plutarch of Athens, the first Neoplatonic head of the Academy (see Wallis p. 138).

Fr. 46b

ll. 1-2. τὰ νοητά...μετέχειν ἀρέσκει τῶν ἰδέων: It is not clear just how Numenius might have distinguished τὰ νοητά from αἱ ἰδέαι. Proclus' notice in fr. 46c makes more sense by speaking only of μέθεξίς ἐν τοῖς νοητοῖς. It still remains a curious doctrine, perhaps best read in connection with his belief ἐν πᾶσιν πάντα εἶναι (fr. 41, ll. 7-8) and πάντα μεμῖχθαι (fr. 51).

Fr. 46c

See note to fr. 46b.

Fr. 47

See fr. 46a and notes.

Fr. 48

ll. 1-2. τὰ τέλη διάφορα ὄντα...τῆς καθόδου τῶν ψυχῶν: For a discussion of this passage and Iamblichus' doctrine of the 'reasons' for the descent of souls, see Festugière *Révélation* vol. III, pp. 69-73. Albinus (XXV, 6) provides several causes for incarnation: ἢ βουλήσει θεῶν ἢ δι' ἀκολασίαν ἢ διὰ φιλοσωματίαν.

l. 11. κακὰς τ' εἶναι πάσας: This phrase was incredibly misinterpreted by Lévêque and Wachsmuth (II, 291, 293, 296) who felt that τὰς ψυχάς was to be understood here, and taking διαφερόντως in conjunction with the phrase rendered it ("omnes animas malas esse) *sed diverso modo*" (see Festugière *op. cit.*, p. 222, n. 6). This was corrected by Leemans (p. 66, n. 3) and, following him, Festugière. The phrase of course refers to τὰς ἐνσωματώσεις, and διαφερόντως is to be taken with οἱ περὶ Κρόνιον κτλ. as its position in the sentence clearly indicates. Festugière's *notamment*, (followed by Des Places) renders it nicely. Given Numenius' general dualism and pessimistic view of matter, the doctrine reported here would seem to be a natural one. Leemans (*op. cit.*) links it more specifically to fr. 43 and Numenius' concept of evil 'accretions' applied to the soul by matter, a situation which obviously involves every incarnation. This extreme pessimism regarding the descent of souls is another of Numenius' 'Gnostic' traits (see Dillon p. 377).

Fr. 49

The Platonic doctrine of transmigration into the bodies of animals finds expression in several dialogues. At *Phd.* 81d-82b it is stated at the beginning that souls of the dead wander about until they are bound to a body through their desire for corporeality. Then Socrates says: ἐνδοῦνται δέ, ὥσπερ εἰκός, εἰς τοιαῦτα ἤθη ὁποῖ' ἄττ' ἂν καὶ μεμελητηκυῖαι τύχωσιν ἐν τῷ βίῳ; cf. *Phdr.* 249b: ἔνθα καὶ εἰς θηρίου βίον ἀνθρωπίνη ψυχὴ ἀφικνεῖται; *Tim.* 42c: κατὰ τὴν ὁμοιότητα τῆς τοῦ τρόπου γενέσεως εἴς τινα τοιαύτην ἀεὶ μεταβαλοῖ θήρειον φύσιν. Albinus (XXV, 6), like Numenius, adhered to the early Platonic tradition: διαμείβειν (sc. τὰς ψυχάς) πολλὰ σώματα καὶ ἀνθρώπινα καὶ οὐκ ἀνθρώπινα. *Corp. Herm.* X, 19 contains a polemic against the teaching: ἄλλο γὰρ σῶμα οὐ χωρεῖ ἀνθρωπίνην ψυχήν, οὐδὲ θέμις ἐστὶν εἰς ἀλόγου ζῴου σῶμα ψυχὴν ἀνθρωπίνην καταπεσεῖν. θεοῦ γὰρ νόμος οὗτος, φυλάσσειν ψυχὴν ἀνθρωπίνην ἀπὸ τῆς τοσαύτης ὕβρεως. Wallis (p. 113) says that the interpretation of the doctrine posed "a problem where the school's internal disputes came to a head." Later Neoplatonists such as Iamblichus and Proclus denied that the human soul could inhabit the body of an animal (Wallis p. 120).

ll. 2-3. τὸν τοῦ Πλάτωνος ἰκτῖνον παραλαβόντες...καὶ τὸν λύκον λύκον: Cf. Phd. 82a: τοὺς δέ γε ἀδικίας τε καὶ τυραννίδας καὶ ἁρπαγὰς προτετιμηκότας εἰς τὰ τῶν λύκων...καὶ ἰκτίνων γένη.

l. 3. καὶ ὄνον τὸν ὄνον: Cf. Phd. 81e: οἷον τοὺς γαστριμαργίας τε καὶ ὕβρεις καὶ φιλοποσίας μεμελετηκότας καὶ μὴ διηυλαβημένους εἰς τὰ τῶν ὄνον γένη.

l. 4. ὁ πίθικος: Cf. Rep. 620c: πόρρω δ' ἐν ὑστάτοις ἰδεῖν τὴν τοῦ γελωτοποιοῦ Θερσίτου πίθηκον ἐνδυομένην.

ὁ κύκνος: Cf. Rep. 620a: ἰδεῖν μὲν γὰρ ψυχὴν ἔφη τὴν ποτε Ὀρφέως γενομένην κύκνου βίον αἱρουμένην.

ll. 5-6. πρὸ τοῦ σώματος κακίας ἐμπίμπλασθαι...λέγουσι: De Ley (p. 52) uses this statement to support his argument that Numenius held the doctrine of the *descensus/ascensus* of the soul. See introductory note to fr. 34.

ll. 7-8. ᾧ γοῦν ὡμοιώθη, κατὰ τοῦτο φέρεται...ὑποδῦσα: Cf. Phd. 81e and Tim. 42c quoted above. Des Places (p. 123, n. *ad. loc.*) points out that Aeneas is here giving a rough quotation of Plotinus IV. 3. 12: ἐκεῖ γάρ, ᾧ ἂν ὁμοιωθεῖσα ᾖ, φέρεται, ἡ μὲν εἰς ἄνθρωπον, ἡ δὲ εἰς ζῷον ἄλλη ἄλλο.

Fr. 50

l. 1. τῶν κατευθυνόντων τὴν γένεσιν θεῶν: See the descriptions of the Demiurge in fr. 16, ll. 4-5: ὁ μὲν δημιουργὸς θεός ἐστι γενέσεως, and fr. 18, l. 3 where it is said that the Demiurge τὴν ἁρμονίαν δ' ἰθύνει. Cf. also fr. 37, l. 6 where mention is made of ὁ τῆς γενέσεως ἔφορος θεός.

ll. 3-5. τὴν μὲν οὐσίαν ἀμιγῆ πρὸς τὴν ὕλην...τὰς ἐνεργείας ἀναμεμιγμένας: A reference to the 'split' nature of Numenius' Demiurge. Cf. fr. 11, ll. 15-16 and fr. 16, l. 10.

Fr. 51

l. 1. πάντα μεμῖχθαι: Cf. fr. 52, ll. 90-91: *Denique negat inveniri Numenius...immune a vitiis usquequaque generatorum fortunam*. It was commonplace within the tradition that all things inhabiting the realm of becoming are characterized by a mixture of good and evil. Its direct origin lies in the *Timaeus* where the role of ἀνάγκη in the creation of the cosmos is described. Cf. *Tim*. 48a: μεμειγμένη γὰρ οὖν ἡ τοῦδε κόσμου γένεσις ἐξ ἀνάγκης τε καὶ νοῦ συστάσεως ἐγεννήθη. *Laws* X 906a contributed to the theme: συγκεχωρήκαμεν ἡμῖν αὐτοῖς εἶναι μὲν τὸν οὐρανὸν πολλῶν μεστὸν ἀγαθῶν, εἶναι δὲ καὶ τῶν ἐναντίων. Cf. Philo *De Opfic*. 31: εἰλικρινὲς γὰρ οὐδὲν τῶν ἐν αἰσθήσει; 73: τὰ δὲ τῆς μικτῆς ἐστι φύσεως. Two passages in Plutarch's *De Iside* sound very close to what Proclus is reporting for Numenius, cf. 369c: ἀλλὰ πολλὰ καὶ μεμειγμένα κακοῖς καὶ ἀγαθοῖς, μᾶλλον δὲ μηδέν, ὡς ἁπλῶς εἰπεῖν, ἄκρατον; 371a echoes the passage from the *Timaeus*: μεμειγμένη γὰρ ἡ τοῦδε τοῦ κόσμου γένεσις καὶ σύστασις ἐξ ἐναντίων. Plotinus subscribes to the doctrine, cf. V. 8. 7: ἀλλ᾽ οὖν ἐκεῖθεν ἦν σύμπαντα ταῦτα, καὶ καλλιόνως ἐκεῖ· τὰ γὰρ τῇδε καὶ μέμικται καὶ οὐκ ἐκεῖνα μέμικται.

Fr. 52

l. 2. **Numenius ex Pythagorae magisterio:** van Winden (p. 104) raises the question whether Calcidius is here translating Numenius literally or giving a free rendering of Neo-Pythagorean ideas. He gives three indications that point toward a close translation: (a) Calcidius makes frequent use of *oratio oblique*, (b) Numenius' name is mentioned four times, and (c) the style of the passage differs from Calcidius' normal manner of expression, while exhibiting traits that are found in the writing of Numenius, i. e. the use of images, mannered construction and excessive use of synonyms. Beutler (col. 672) also noticed this: "...der Bericht des Chalcidius zeigt die Eigentümlichkeit des numenianischen

Stils: Häufung von Synonyms, und ware unschwer ins Griechische umzustetzen."

ll. 2-3. **Stoicorum hoc de initiis dogma refellens:** For the thrust of the anti-Stoic polemic see Krämer p. 77 and n. 198.

ll. 3-4. **cui concinere dicit dogma platonicum:** van Winden (p. 105) provides a realistic evaluation of this statement: "Numenius undoubtedly derived much from Plato for the description of Pythagoras' doctrine. The usual description of Pythagoras' doctrine in Antiquity must owe as much to Plato's system as Plato actually owed to Pythagoras." See notes to fr. 1b.

ll. 4-5. **deum quidem singularitas...silvam vero duitas...indeterminatum:** The common Middle Platonic distinction between the μονάς and ἀόριστος δύας. These exact terms do not appear in the extant verbatim fragments, but traces of their meaning can be found. For μονάς cf. the descriptions of τὸ ὄν and ὁ πρῶτος θεός as 'simple' (ἁπλοῦς) in fr. 6, l. 10; fr. 11, l. 13; cf. also the conclusion of fr. 19: τὸ ἀγαθὸν...ἐστὶν ἕν. The ἀόριστος δύας is also much in evidence. Numenius uses the term ἀόριστος to describe ὕλη several times (fr. 3, l. 12; fr. 4a, l. 3), and in fr. 11, ll. 15-16 he states that matter is a dyad: συμφερομένος (sc. ὁ δεύτερος) δὲ τῇ ὕλῃ δυάδι οὔσῃ...σχίζεται ὑπ' αὐτῆς. These scattered references are confirmed by Proclus (*In Timaeum* II, 153=fr. 39) who tells us that Numenius was among those who held the following doctrine of soul: οἱ μὲν ἀριθμὸν αὐτὴν (sc. τὴν ψυχήν) εἰπόντες ἐκ μονάδος ποιοῦσιν...καὶ τῆς ἀορίστου δυάδος. See also fr. 4a, l. 3 and note.

ll. 5-9. **minime genitam...esse generatum:** Numenius' position is primarily inspired by several passages in the *Timaeus*, especially 30a: οὕτω δὴ πᾶν ὅσον ἦν ὁρατὸν παραλαβὼν (sc. ὁ δημιουργός) οὐχ ἡσυχίαν ἄγον ἀλλὰ κινούμενον πλημμελῶς καὶ ἀτάκτως, εἰς τάξιν αὐτὸ ἤγαγεν ἐκ τῆς ἀταξίας; cf. Plato's description of ἡ τιθήνην γενέσεως at 52d-53c, where a chaotic sea of elements swirls about, πρὶν καὶ τὸ πᾶν ἐξ αὐτῶν διακοσμηθὲν γενέσθαι (cf. *antequam exornaretur*). *Politicus* 273b also contributed to the formation of this doctrine: τούτων δὲ αὐτῷ τὸ σωματοειδὲς τῆς συγκράσεως αἴτιον, τὸ τῆς πάλαι ποτὲ φύσεως σύντροφον, ὅτι πολλῆς ἦν μετέχον ἀταξίας πρὶν εἰς τὸν νῦν κόσμον ἀφικέσθαι. Plutarch and Atticus held a view similar to Numenius, cf. Plutarch *De Proc. An.*, 1014b: τὴν δ' οὐσίαν καὶ ὕλην, ἐξ ἧς γέγονεν, οὐ γενομένην ἀλλὰ ὑποκειμένην ἀεὶ τῷ δημιουργῷ εἰς διάθεσιν καὶ τάξιν αὐτῆς; Atticus (Proclus, *In Timaeum* I, 283, 27-30=fr. 20 Des Places): ὅς φησι τὸ μὲν 'πλημμελῶς καὶ ἀτάκτως κινούμενον' εἶναι ἀγένητον, τὸ δὲ κόσμον ἀπὸ χρόνου γεννητόν. Cf. also Albinus, IX, 1: ἀρχικὸν λόγον ἐπεχούσης τῆς ὕλης; Apuleius *De Plat.* 191: *materium vero inprocreabilem incorruptamque commemorate*. For a general discussion see (with Leemans) Baeumker pp. 143ff.

l. 9. **a digestore deo:** ὁ δημιουργός. Cf. Apuleius *De Plat.* 191: *deus artifex*; 198: *a fabricatore deo*.

l. 11. **aequaevum deo:** Along with Plutarch and Atticus, Numenius posits a radical dualism of two eternally co-existing, diametrically opposed principles. Cf. Aristotle's report at *Metaph.* 986b that the Pythagoreans taught ὅτι τἀναντία ἀρχαὶ τῶν ὄντων.

ll. 12-15. **sed non nullos Pythagoreos...in duitatis migrante:** There were two branches of Pythagoreanism involved in what Dillon (p. 373) calls "an age old controversy." One was monistic, the other dualistic. Beutler (col. 673) points out that this 'Schulunterschied' is reported by Sextus Empiricus VII, 258-284 who refers to both teachings. Leemans (p. 92) quotes a report in Diogenes Laertius (VIII, 25) saying that Alexander Polyhistor found the exact teaching here refuted by Numenius in some Pythagorean memoirs (ὑπομνήματα): ἀρχὴν μὲν ἁπάντων μονάδα· ἐκ δὲ τῆς μονάδος ἀόριστον δυάδα ὡς ἂν ὕλην τῇ μονάδι αἰτίῳ ὄντι ὑποστῆναι. Leemans (*op. cit.*) claims that the dualistic teaching constitutes the older stratum of Pythagoreanism, while the monistic doctrine shows traces of

Posidonian influence. See Krämer p. 78, n. 198 for a discussion of possible origins of the monistic teaching. Dillon (*op. cit.*, n. 1) makes the cogent observation that a similar opposition existed among the Gnostics. The monistic school was represented by the Valentinians who derived matter from a gradual differentiation from the Godhead, while the Manichaeans adhered to the Persian doctrine of two co-eternal antagonistic principles.

ll. 20-21. **infinitam et sine limite:** ἄπειρος Cf. fr. 4a, ll. 2-3.

l. 26. **fluidem:** Cf. fr. 3, l. 11; fr. 8, l. 5 and notes. Leemans (*op. cit.*) points to an older analogue in Xenocrates, fr. 28: οἱ ἀπὸ Πυθαγόρου τρεπτὴν καὶ ἀλλοιωτὴν καὶ μεταβλητὴν καὶ ῥευστήν...τὴν ὕλην.

l. 27. **sine qualitate:** The concept is derived from the description of the 'receptacle of becoming' at *Tim*. 50b-c: δέχεταί τε γὰρ ἀεὶ τὰ πάντα, καὶ μορφὴν οὐδεμίαν ποτὲ οὐδενὶ τῶν εἰσιόντων ὁμοίαν εἴληφεν οὐδαμῇ οὐδαμῶς. Cf. Albinus' version (VIII, 2): αὐτὴν δὲ καθ᾽ αὑτὴν ἄμορφόν τε ὑπάρχειν καὶ ἄποιον.

l. 29. **sed plane noxiam:** Leemans (*op. cit.*) suggests that Numenius is responding to a statement of Chrysippus (*apud* Plutarch *De comm. notit.*, 1076c-d): οὐ γὰρ ἥ γε ὕλη τὸ κακὸν ἐξ ἑαυτῆς παρέσχηκεν· ἄποιος γάρ ἐστι καὶ πάσας ὅσας δέχεται διαφορὰς ὑπὸ τοῦ κινοῦντος αὐτὴν καὶ σχηματίζοντος ἔσχε.

ll. 29-30. **Deum...initium et causam bonorum:** Cf. the classic statement at *Rep*. 379c: οὐδ᾽ ἄρα ἦν δ᾽ ἐγώ, ὁ θεός, ἐπειδὴ ἀγαθός, πάντων ἂν εἴη αἴτιος...ἀλλὰ ὀλίγων μὲν τοῖς ἀνθρώποις αἴτιος, πολλῶν δὲ ἀναίτιος· πολὺ γὰρ ἐλάττω τἀγαθὰ τῶν κακῶν ἡμῖν, καὶ τῶν μὲν ἀγαθῶν οὐδένα ἄλλον αἰτιατέον, τῶν δὲ κακῶν ἄλλ᾽ ἄττα δεῖ ζητεῖν τὰ αἴτια, ἀλλ᾽ οὐ τὸν θεόν. Maximus has an essay (41) entitled Τοῦ θεοῦ τὰ ἀγαθὰ ποιοῦντος, πόθεν τὰ κακά. See Witt, p. 121.

ll. 30-31. **silvam malorum** Cf. the Platonic teaching reported by Aristotle at *Metaph*. 988a: ἔτι δὲ τὴν τοῦ εὖ καὶ τοῦ κακῶς αἰτίαν τοῖς στοιχείοις (i.e. τὸ ἕν and ἡ δυάς) ἀπέδωκεν; Celsus (apud Origen Contra Cels., IV, 65): ἐκ θεοῦ οὐκ ἔστι κακά, ὕλῃ δὲ πρόσκειται καὶ τοῖς θνητοῖς ἐμπολιτεύεται.

l. 34. **ex providentia et necessitae:** Des Places (p. 124, n. 6) shows that in Calcidius *providentia* is interchangeable with *intelligentia*. Thus this phrase echoes the conjunction of νοῦς--ἀνάγκη at *Tim.* 47e-48a: μεμειγμένη γὰρ οὖν ἡ τοῦδε τοῦ κόσμου γένεσις ἐξ ἀνάγκης τε καὶ νοῦ συστάσεως ἐγεννήθη. Cf. *Theaet.* 176a: ἀλλ᾽ οὔτ᾽ ἀπολέσθαι τὰ κακὰ δυνατόν, ὦ Θεόδωρε--ὑπεναντίον γάρ τι τῷ ἀγαθῷ ἀεὶ εἶναι ἀνάγκη.

veterum theologorum: Leemans (*op. cit.*, p. 93) mentions the classic θεολόγοι: Moses, Orpheus, Pythagoras, Pherecydes and Homer. But the phrase is better read in the context of τὰ ἔθνη τὰ εὐδοκιμοῦντα in fr. 1a. See notes *ad. loc.* Interestingly enough, Plutarch makes the same sort of appeal when introducing his own doctrine of radical dualism. Cf. *De Iside* 369b: διὸ καὶ παμπάλαιος αὕτη κάτεισιν ἐκ θεολόγων...δόξα... οὐκ ἐν λόγοις μόνον οὐδ᾽ φήμαις, ἀλλ᾽ ἔν τε τελεταῖς ἔν τε θυσίαις καὶ βαρβάροις καὶ Ἕλλησι πολλαχοῦ περιφερομένη.

ll. 38-39. **Unde igitur mala?:** Cf. the titles to Maximus *Diss.* 41, 9 (see above) and Plotinus I. 8. *Περὶ τοῦ τίνα καὶ πόθεν τὰ κακά*.

ll. 44-46. **existente providentia...et eadem sit militia praedita:** The argument implies the necessity of opposites. Cf. (with van Winden, p. 113) Plotinus I. 8. 6 (referring to *Theaet.* 176a quoted above): τὰ γὰρ κακὰ εἶναι ἀνάγκῃ, ἐπείπερ τοὐναντίον τι δεῖ εἶναι τῷ ἀγαθῷ.

ll. 48-51. **Numenius laudat Heraclitum reprehendentem Homerum...exterminaretur:** Aristotle (*Eth. Eud.*, 1235a) is the oldest source for this type of remark: οἱ δὲ τὰ ἐναντία φίλα· καὶ Ἡράκλειτος ἐπιτιμᾷ τῷ ποιήσαντι 'ὡς ἔρις ἔκ τε θεῶν καὶ ἀνθρώπων ἀπόλοιτο' (*Il.* 18, 107)· οὐ γὰρ ἂν εἶναι ἁρμονίαν μὴ ὄντος ὀξέος καὶ βαρέος, οὐδὲ τὰ ζῷα ἄνευ θήλεος καὶ ἄρρενος ἐναντίων ὄντων. Numenius most likely drew his inspiration from Plutarch *De Iside* 370d: Ἡράκλειτος μὲν γὰρ ἄντικρυς πόλεμον ὀνομάζεται 'πατέρα καὶ βασιλέα καὶ κύριον πάντων,' καὶ τὸν μὲν Ὅμηρον εὐχόμενον 'ἔκ τε θεῶν ἔριν ἔκ τ᾽ ἀνθρώπων ἀπολέσθαι' λανθάνειν, φησί, τῇ πάντων γενέσει καταρώμενον, ἐκ μάχης καὶ ἀντιπαθείας τὴν γένεσιν ἐχόντων. The full Heraclitean text (DK 53; Marcovich 29) that Plutarch is abbreviating reads:

> πόλεμος
>
> πάντων μὲν πατήρ ἐστι, πάντων δὲ βασιλεύς,
>
> καὶ τοὺς μὲν θεοὺς ἔδειξε τοὺς δὲ ἀνθρώπους,
>
> τοὺς μὲν δούλους ἐποίησε τοὺς δὲ ἐλευθέρους.

Marcovich (p. 133) adduces our text as a testimony to fr. 28 (80 DK) which is preserved by Celsus (*apud* Origen, *Conta Cels.* VI, 42):

> εἰδέ<ναι> χρή
>
> τὸν πόλεμον ἐόντα ξυνόν
>
> καὶ δίκην ἔριν
>
> καὶ γινόμενα πάντα κατ᾽ ἔριν καὶ χρεών.

See (with Des Places, p. 97, n. 9) the other *testimonia* collected in Marcovich, pp. 133-149.

ll. 51-53. **Platonemque idem Numenius laudat, quod duas mundi animas autumnet...scilicet silvam:** The 'proof' text for a Platonic doctrine of the evil world soul occurs at *Leg.* X, 896e: μίαν ἢ πλείους; πλείους· ἐγὼ ὑπὲρ σφῶν ἀποκρινοῦμαι. δυοῖν μέν γέ που ἔλαττον μηδὲν τιθῶμεν, τῆς τε εὐεργέτιδος καὶ τῆς τἀναντία δυναμένης ἐξεργάζεσθαι. Plutarch and Atticus join Numenius in taking this passage literally, cf. Plutarch *De proc. an.* 1014d: τὴν ἄτακτον καὶ ἀόριστον αὐτοκίνητον δὲ καὶ κινητικὴν ἀρχὴν ἐκείνην, ἣν πολλαχοῦ μὲν ἀνάγκην ἐν δὲ τοῖς Νόμοις ἄντικρυς ψυχὴν ἄτακτον εἴρηκε καὶ κακοποιόν;

De Iside 307ff.: ἐν δὲ τοῖς Νόμοις…οὐ δι᾿ αἰνιγμῶν οὐδὲ συμβολικῶς, ἀλλὰ κυρίοις ὀνόμασιν οὐ μιᾷ ψυχῇ φησι κινεῖσθαι τὸν κόσμον, ἀλλὰ πλείοσιν ἴσως, δυοῖν δὲ πάντως οὐκ ἐλάττοσιν, ὧν τὴν μὲν ἀγαθουργὸν εἶναι, τὴν δ᾿ ἐναντίαν ταύτῃ καὶ τῶν ἐναντίων δημιουργόν.

Cherniss (*Plutarch*, vol. XIII, part 1, p. 187, n. *f*) states that Atticus derived his teaching from Plutarch, cf. Proclus, *In Timaeum* I, 391 (=fr. 26 Des Places): οἳ (sc. οἱ περὶ ᾿Αττικόν) καὶ τὴν ὕλην ὑπὸ ἀγενήτου φασὶ κινουμένην ψυχῆς, ἀλόγου δὲ καὶ κακεργέτιδος, 'πλημμελῶς καὶ ἀτάκτως' φέρεσθαι. Chernis views this literal interpretation of the *Laws* passage as a misreading; see the bibliography he provides in the note and cf. Waszink, *P. und N.*, p. 68 and n. 1.

l. 53. **scilicet silvam:** Beutler (*op. cit.*) and Theiler (*Entretiens* III, p. 74) proposed reading *silvae* here, but van Winden (pp. 113-114) successfully refutes this conjecture and is followed by Waszink (*op. cit.*, pp. 68-69). Beutler and Waszink point out that Numenius' identification of the evil world soul with matter sets his doctrine apart from that of Plutarch. See *De proc. an.* 1015e, (partially quoted above) where Plutarch makes a clear distinction between matter and the evil soul. This is also reflected in the separation of Isis-Typhon in *De Iside*. Waszink is correct in associating Plutarch's evil soul with the ἀνάγκη of the *Timaeus*.

ll. 53-55. **quia intimo propioque motu movetur…moventur:** This statement is based on the Platonic axiom that soul is the cause of all self-movement, cf. *Phdr.* 245e *passim*. Cf. also *Epinomis* 988d-e: τῆς φορᾶς πάσης καὶ κινήσεως ψυχὴν αἰτίαν εἶναι θαῦμα οὐδέν, τὴν δ᾿ ἐπὶ τἀγαθὸν φορὰν καὶ κίνησιν τῆς ἀρίστης ψυχῆς εἶναι, τὴν δ᾿ ἐπὶ τοὐναντίον ἐναντίαν; Atticus (fr. 23 Des Places): εἰ δ᾿ ἄτακτος ἡ κίνησις, ἀπὸ ἀτάκτου ψυχῆς.

l. 56. **patibilis animae partis:** van Winden (p. 14) observes that Calcidius has here altered Numenius' doctrine of two distinct human souls to accord with his own, more orthodox position of a unified soul composed of parts. For both doctrines see fr. 44 and notes.

ll. 60-61. **dei tanquam patris:** Cf. (with Leemans) *Tim.* 50d.

ll. 61-62. **mala vero matris silvae vitio cohaeserunt:** Cf. *Pol.* 273b-c: παρὰ μὲν γὰρ τοῦ συνθέντος πάντα καλὰ κέκτηται· παρὰ δὲ τῆς ἔμπροσθεν ἕξεως, ὅσα χαλεπὰ καὶ ἄδικα.

l. 63. **Stoicos:** the doctrine here attributed to the Stoics by Numenius has few parallels. For a full discussion see van Winden, pp. 115-116.

l. 65. **omnium quippe corporum silva nutrix:** A reference to ἡ τιθήνην τῆς γενέσεως in *Tim.* 49a; 52d.

ll. 69-70. **si deus correxit, ut Timaeo loquitur Plato...iactatione:** Cf. *Tim.* 30a quoted above in notes to ll. 8-9.

ll. 73-74. **ut plerique arbitrantur:** Leemans (*op. cit.*, p. 95) interprets this as a glance at the Lyceum and the doctrine that matter is mere potentiality, cf. Aristotle *De an.*, II, 412a: ἔστι δ᾽ ἡ μὲν ὕλη δύναμις.

ll. 74-75. **et adversatur providentiae consulta...suae viribus:** See the texts describing the evil world soul quoted above.

malitiae suae viribus: van Winden (p. 117) makes the important observation that *militia* refers to more than the mere disorganization of matter. He points to *vires* as signifying a force of will constantly striving to maintain the original chaos. Cf. Witt (p. 121): "But none of these Platonists endows matter with that Satanic spirit which Numenius seems to attribute to it."

l. 80. **corporeorum et nativorum deorum:** Cf. with Leemans, p. 96: *Tim.* 40d: τὰ περὶ θεῶν ὁρατῶν καὶ γεηηντῶν; explained by Eusebius *Pr. Ev.*, XV, 22, 825d: θεοὺς ὁρατούς, ἥλιον, καὶ σελήνην καὶ τοὺς λιοποὺς ἀστέρας.

l. 82. **quoniam natural vitium limari omnino nequiret:** Cf. *Theat.* 176a: οὔτ᾽ ἀπολέσθαι τὰ κακὰ δυνατόν; *Tim.* 30a:

βουληθεὶς γὰρ ὁ θεὸς ἀγαθὰ μὲν πάντα, φλαῦρον δὲ μηδὲν εἶναι κατὰ δύναμιν; 48a: τὰ πλεῖστα ἐπὶ τὸ βέλτιστον ἄγειν.

ll. 84-85. **non interficiens, ne natura silvestris funditus interiret:** Cf. ll. 48-51.

l. 85. **nec vero permittens porrigi dilatarique passim:** This is an echo of fr. 18, ll. 6-8.

ll. 90-96. **negat inveniri Numenius...immunem a vitiis...piaculo:** Cf. fr. 51 and notes.

nec in ipso quidem caelo: Cf. fr. 50 and note.

ll. 96-101. **idemque nudam silvae imaginem demonstrare...eamque silvam et necessitam cognominat:** Numenius suggests the technique of ἀφαίρεσις. Cf. Albinus X, 5: ἔσται δὴ πρώτη μὲν αὐτοῦ (sc. τοῦ θεοῦ) νόησις ἡ κατὰ ἀφαίρεσιν τούτων, ὅπως καὶ σημεῖον ἐνοήσαμεν κατὰ ἀφαίρεσιν ἀπὸ τοῦ αἰσθητοῦ.

l. 103. **obsecundante:** van Winden (p. 120) sees a contradiction in the use of this verb in light of what Numenius has said about the recalcitrance of matter. He suspects that it may be an interpolation on the part of Calcidius to soften the doctrine. But it is more likely that Numenius is here reverting (albeit inconsistently) to the mode of expression found at *Tim.* 48a: δι' ἀνάγκης ἡττωμένης ὑπὸ πειθοῦς.

Fr. 53

l. 1. περὶ δὲ Σαράπιδος πολλὴ καὶ διάφωνος ἱστορία: Origen may be referring to Clement *Protr.* 48 where three different accounts of the origin of Sarapis are provided. The first relates that the statue, an image of Pluto, was a gift from the people of Sinope to Ptolemy Philadelphius. Plutarch *De Idide* 28-30 361f-362e gives a much embellished version of this account, stating that Ptolemy Soter saw the colossal statue in a dream and that it ordered him to transfer it from Sinope to Alexandria. Both he and Clement indicate that the name is a combination of Osiris and Apis. Tacitus *Histories* IV, 83-84 also provides a detailed version of the story. For scholarly theories about the origin of the cult see (with Chadwick p. 295, n. 2) Cook, *Zeus* I, p. 188; Wilcken, *Urkunden der Ptolemäerzeit* I, pp. 82ff.; Nock, *Conversion*, pp. 35ff.; Jouguet, "Les premieres Ptolémées et l'Hellénisation de Sarapis", in *Homages à J. Bidez et à F. Cumont*, pp. 159-166.

l. 3. Πτολεμαίου: Ptolemy I Soter, c. 367-283 B. C. E.

ll. 5-6. πάντων τῶν...ζῴων καὶ φύτων: Cf. (with Chadwick *op. cit.*) Aelius Aristides *Orat.* XLV (8), 32: προέστηκε (sc. Σάραπις) δὲ καὶ πάντων ζῴων γενέσεως καὶ τροφῆς. There are traces of the god Dionysius who was assimilated into the figure of Sarapis; cf. the equation of Plutarch at *De Iside* 362b: βέλτιον δὲ τὸν Ὄσιριν εἰς ταὐτὸ συνάγειν τῷ Διονύσῳ, τῷ τ' Ὀσίριδι τὸν Σάραπιν.

ll. 7-10. ἵνα δόξῃ...κηλουμένων δαιμόνων: As Chadwick (*op. cit.*, n. 3) points out, an image of deity had to be composed of the proper materials (see the story of Bryaxis in Clement *op. cit.*), and spells were necessary to compel the god to inhabit the statue. He quotes Proclus *On the Priestly Art* (ed. Bidez, in *Catalogue des Manuscrits Alchimiques Grecs* VI, pp. 150ff.): καὶ ἀγάλματα πολλάκις κατασκευάζουσι σύμμικτα καὶ θυμιάματα, φυράσαντες εἰς ἓν τὰ μερισθέντα συνθήματα καὶ ποιήσαντες τέχνῃ ὁποῖον κατ' οὐσίαν τὸ περιληπτικὸν καθ' ἕνωσιν τῶν πλειόνων δυνάμεων; Porphyry *de Abst.* II, 49: "...the priest of any of the gods is skilled in the technique of setting up images"; and Iamblichus *de Myst.* V, 23: "It is not that we must abhor all matter, but only that which is alien to the gods; that which has affinities with them we should choose out, because it is suitable to be used for buildings of the gods and for setting up images and also for the performances of the sacrifices." Dodds (*N. and A.*, p. 10) wanted to connect this notice in Origen with the ἱδρύσεις of fr. 1a, l. 7. see note *ad. loc.*

Fr. 54

ll. 1-3. Ἀπόλλωνα...aut ut Numenio placet, quasi unum et solum: Plutarch (*De Iside* 381f) informs us that this doctrine was Pythagorean in origin: οἱ δὲ Πυθαγόρειοι καὶ ἀριθμοὺς καὶ σχήματα θεῶν ἐκόσμησαν προσηγορίαις...τὸ δὲ ἓν Ἀπόλλωνα πλήθους ἀποφάσει καὶ δι᾽ ἁπλότητα τῆς μονάδος. Cf. 393b: Ἀπόλλων μὲν γὰρ οἷον ἀρνούμενος τὰ πολλὰ καὶ τὸ πλῆθος ἀποφάσκων ἐστίν...ὡς εἷς καὶ μόνος. Plotinus refers to the teaching at V. 5. 6: τάχα δὲ καὶ τὸ 'ἕν' ὄνομα τοῦτο ἄρσιν ἔχει πρὸς τὰ πολλά. ὅθεν καὶ Ἀπόλλωνα οἱ Πυθαγορικοὶ συμβολικῶς πρὸς ἀλλήλους ἐσήμαινον ἀποφάσει τῶν πολλῶν.

unum et solum: Cf. fr. 20, ll. 6-7: τοῦ πρώτου καὶ μόνου; *Corp. Herm.* IV, 8: ἵνα πρὸς τὸν ἕνα καὶ μόνον σπεύσωμεν; X, 14: ἡ δὲ ἀρχὴ ἐκ τοῦ ἑνὸς καὶ μόνου; Plotinus VI. 7. 1: τὸ μόνον καὶ ἕν καὶ ἁπλῶς.

ll. 4-5. frater, inquit, ἀδελφός dicitur quasi iam non unus: The etymology rests on a presumed alpha privative (Des Places p. 100, n. 1). See also Whittaker in *Class. Quart.*, 1969, p. 187 and n. 2-19.

Fr. 55

l. 1. occultorum curiosiori: This phrase has been used by scholars who feel the need to berate Numenius; cf. Dodds' damning criticism in *N. and A.*, p. 11: "But because he was, as Macrobius says, *occultorum curiosior*, he welcomed all the superstitions of his time, whatever their origin, and thereby contributed to the eventual degradation of Greek philosophical thought." This type of polemic is obsolete and has been left behind by more recent scholarship.

ll. 2-3. quod Eleusinia acra interpretando vulgaverit: The strict rule of secrecy imposed on the initiates of the Eleusinian

Mysteries is implicit in the Homeric *Hymn to Demeter*, cf. ll. 478-479:

σεμνά (sc. ὄργια), τά τ' οὔ πως ἔστι παρεξ[ίμ]εν [οὔτε πυθέσθαι,]

οὔτ' ἀχέειν· μέγα γάρ τι θεῶν σέβας ἰσχάνει αὐδήν.

For a thorough discussion of the matter see Mylonas pp. 224-229. He mentions the notorious case of Alcibiades (p. 224) who imitated the rites while intoxicated. As Mylonas tells us "he was condemned *in absentia*, his property was confiscated, all the priests and priestesses were called upon to pronounce curses upon him; and this in spite of his popularity and the fact that shortly before his conviction he had been entrusted with one of the most important military missions ever undertaken by Athens, the Sicilian expedition." Cf. Plutarch, *Alcibiades*, 19-22; Thucydides, VI, 27-28, and 60; Xenophon, *Hellenica* I, 4, 14.

On p. 225 Mylonas notes that even in the second century C. E. the prohibition remained strong enough to prevent Pausanius from describing the buildings in the precincts sacred to Demeter; cf. *Peri. Hell.* I, 38, 7 and I, 14, 3. If Numenius were indeed residing in Alexandria, as seems likely, he may have felt immune from the prohibition. However this fragment remains a curious notice, and it is difficult to tell how much credence to give it, or even determine Macrobius' source. Burkert (*Cults*, p. 85) adds to the confusion by interpreting the fragment this way: "Numenius once felt he had betrayed the secret of Eleusis through philosophy." Mylonas rightly ignores the fragment in his discussion, marveling instead (p. 226) "that the basic and important substance of the sacred rites was never disclosed."

Fr. 56

l. 1. ὁ Λούκανος ἀδήλου θεοῦ τὸν ἐν Ἱεροσολύμοις ναόν: De Places (p. 125, n. ad. loc.) cites *Pharsalia* 2, 592-593: *dedita sacris/incerti Iudaea dei*. Cf. Gager, p. 22, n. 19.

l. 2. ἀκοινώτητον: Cf. (with Des Places) Wisdom 14:21 τὸ ἀκοινώτατον ὄνομα λίθοις καὶ ξύλοις περιέθεσαν. Perhaps another instance of Numenius' knowledge of Jewish writings. See fr. 9 and note.

Fr. 57

l. 1. Νουμήιος δ' ὁ Ῥομαῖος: A puzzling reference. Dodds (*N. and A.*, p. 6) sees it as a "mere blunder" or an indication that perhaps Numenius taught at Rome, but there is little else in the tradition surrounding Numenius that would support this conjecture. Beutler (col. 664) views the notice as "unkontrollierbar".

ll. 1-2. τὸν Ἑρμῆν τὸν προχωρητικὸν λόγον: Another instance of Numenius' tendency to allegorize. The L. S. J. gives this as the only instance of προχωρητικός and defines it as an equivalent of προφορικός.

ll. 2-3. οὐδὲ γὰρ, φησι, πρότερον βρέφος φθέγξαιτο, πρὶν ἂν τῆς γῆς ἐφάψαιτο: De Places (p. 125, n. ad. loc.) cites Macrobius *Saturn.* I, 12, 20: *Vox nascenti homini terrae contact datur*.

ll. 3-4. ὥστε Μαῖαν εἰς γῆν: According to Greek mythology Maia was the daughter of Atlas and mother of Hermes by Zeus, cf. Hesiod, *Theog.*, 938. The name itself means 'mother'. Des Places (*op. cit.*) mentions in this connection the shortened Aeolic and Doric form μᾶ for μῆτερ, which appears in the phrase μᾶ γᾶ = μῆτερ γῆ. See L. S. J.

Elsas (p. 15) interprets the fragment thus: "Numenius...der Hermes den hervortretenden Logos nennt und seine Mutter Maia als Prinzip characterisiert, durch das dieser Hervorgang sinnenfällig wird."

Fr. 58

Another example of Numenian allegory, but the notice does not allow us to determine how he arrived at it or what his purpose was. Des Places' citing of *Il.* I, 600 in this context provides little illumination.

Fr. 59

l. 1. **Νέμεσιν:** This fragment is an indication of the broad spectrum of topics that Numenius addressed and suggests that if his works had been preserved, we would have an invaluable commentary on Greek mythology at our disposal.

Fr. 60

ll. 3-4. **τὴν εἰς κάτω κάθοδον τῶν ψυχῶν καὶ πάλιν ἔχοδον:** For the doctrine of the *descensus/ascensus* of the soul, see the introductory note to fr. 34. For another description of the Persian (*i. e.* Mithraic) mysteries by a Platonist see Celsus *apud* Origen *Contra Cels.* VI, 22. Origen introduces this section by saying: ὁ Κέλσος...ἐκτίθεται τινα καὶ περσικὰ μυστήρια.

l. 6. **Εὔβουλος:** Cumont (*Mysteries*, p. 82 and note †) cites Porphyry (*De Abstin.* II, 56; IV, 16) as mentioning that Eubulus had published 'Mithraic Researches' in several books.

l. 8-9. **εἰκόνα φέροντος:** Des Places (p. 102) says that the appearance of this formula at *De antro nympharum* 70, 25-71 = fr. 31 in conjunction with Numenius' name leads one to believe that the present fragment reflects Numenian teaching. He adds that the entire tractate may depend on Numenius.

BIBLIOGRAPHY

I.   Primary Sources

Albinus. *Epitome*. Trans. and ed. Pierre Louis. Paris: Les Belles Letters, 1945.

Apuleius Madaurensis. *Opuscules Philosophiques*. Trans. and ed. Jean Beaujeu. Paris: Les Belles Lettres, 1973.

Aristotle, *Metaphysica*. Ed. W. Jaeger. Oxford: Clarendon Press, 1957.

Atticus. *Fragments*. Trans. and ed. Édouard Des Places. Paris: Les Belles Lettres, 1977.

Clement of Alexandria. *Les Stromates II*. Trans. and ed. Cl. Mondésert Sources Chrétiennes no. 38. Paris: Les Éditions du Cerf, 1954.

Corpus Hermeticum. 4 vols. Trans. A.-J. Festugière. Ed. A. D. Nock. Paris: Les Belles Lettres, 1954-1960; rpt. 1972-1973.

Diogenes Laertius. *Lives*. 2 vols. Trans. and ed. R. D. Hicks. Loeb Classical Library. Cambridge (MA): Harvard University Press, 1925.

Eusebius of Caesarea. *Praeparatio Evangelica*. 2 vols. Ed. C. Mras G. C. S., 43. Berlin, 1954-1956.

Hermetica. 4 vols. Trans. and ed. W. Scott. Oxford: Clarendon Press, 1924-1936.

Heraclitus. *Editio Maior*. Ed. M. Marcovich. Merida: The Los Andes University Press, 1967.

Homer. Opera. 5 vols. Ed. Thomas W. Allen. Oxford: Clarendon Press, 1902-1912.

Maximus of Tyre. *Philosophoumena*. Ed. H. Hobein. Leipzig: B. G. Teubner, 1910.

Novum Testamentum Graece. Ed. Eberhard Nestle, Erwin Nestle, Kurt Aland and Barbara Aland. Stuttgart: Deutsche Bibelstiftung, 1979.

Numenius. *Fragments*. Trans. and ed. Édouard Des Places. Paris: Les Belles Lettres, 1973.

Numenius van Apamea. Ed. E.-A. Leemans. MAB, Classe de Lettres 27,1937.

Oracles Chadaïques. Trans. and ed. Édouard Des Places. Paris: Les Belle Lettres, 1971.

Origen. *Contre Celse*. Vol. 1. Trans. and ed. Marcel Borret. Sources Chrétiennes no. 132. Paris: Les Éditions du Cerf, 1967.

Philo. Vols. 1-10. Trans. and ed. F. H. Colson and G. H. Whitaker. Loeb Classical Library. Cambridge (MA): Harvard University Press, 1929-1962.

Plato. *Opera*. 5 vols. Ed. John Burnett. Oxford: Clarendon Press, 1900-1907.

Plotinus. *Opera*. 3 vols. Ed. Paul Henry and Hans-Rudolph Schwyzer. Oxford: Clarendon Press, 1964-1982.

Plotinus. 7 vols. Trans. and ed. A. H. Armstrong. Loeb Classical Library. Cambridge (MA): Harvard University Press, 1966-1988.

Plutarch. *Moralia*. 16 vols. Loeb Classical Library. Cambridge (MA): Harvard University Press, 1936-1976.

Proclus. *The Elements of Theology*. Trans. and ed. E. R. Dodds. Oxford: Clarendon Press, 1963.

Septuaginta. Ed. Alfred Rahlfs. Stuttgart: Deutsche Bibelstiftung, 1935.

Xenocrates. ed. Richard Heinze. Leipzig: B. G. Teubner, 1982.

II. Secondary Literature

Armstrong, A. H. *The Architecture of the Intelligible Universe in the Philosophy of Plotinus*. Cambridge: Cambridge University Press, 1940 (Reprint: Amsterdam: A.M. Hakkert, 1967).

Arnou, R. *Le désir de dieu dans la philosophie de Plotin*. Librairie Félix Alcan, [1921?], Rome: Presses de l'Universite Gregorienne, 1967².

Baeumker, Clemens. *Das Problem der Materie in der griechischen Philosophie*. Frankfurt: Minerva GMBH, 1963 (=Münster 1890).

Beutler, R. "Numenios." *Pauly-Wissowa*, Suppl. VII, col. 664-678.

Bluck, R. S. "The Second Platonic Epistle." *Phronesis* 5 1960, pp. 104-151.

Bousset, Wilhelm. (Rev.) "Die Lehren de Hermes Trismegistos." *Göttingische Gelehrte Anzeigen*, XII, 1914, pp. 697-755.

------*Die Himmelreise der Seele*. (repr.) Darmstadt: Wissenschaftliche Buchgesellschaft, 1960.

Bréhier, E. *La Philosophie de Plotin*. Paris: Bibliothèque d'Histoire de la Philosophie, 1961².

Burkert, W. *Lore and Science in Ancient Pythangoreanism* (tr. E. L. Minar). Cambridge (MA): Harvard University Press, 1972.

------*Ancient Mystery Cults*. Cambridge (MA): Harvard University Press, 1987.

Carcopino, J. *De Pythagore aux Apôtres*. Etudes sur la conversion du Monde Romain. Paris, 1956.

Chadwick, Henry. Origen: *Contra Celsum*. Cambridge: Cambridge University Press, 1953.

Cornford, F. M. Plato's Cosmology. London: Routledge & Kegan Paul, Ltd., 1937

------*Principium Sapientiae. The Origins of Greek Philosphical Thought*. Cambridge 1952

Culianu, Ioan. *Psychanodia I*. Leiden: E.J. Brill, 1983

Cumont, F. *Astrology and Religion Among the Greeks and Romans*. New York: G.P. Putnam's and Sons, 1912 (repr. New York: Dover, 1960)

------*Lux Perpetua*. Paris: 1949

-----*The Mysteries of Mithra* (trans. Thomas J. McCormack). New York: Open Court, 1903.

de Vogel, C.J. "A la recherche des étapes entre Platon et le Néoplatonisme." *Mnemosyne* IV, 7, 1954, pp.111-122.

De Ley, Herman. *Macrobius and Numenius*. Brussells: Latomus, 1972.

Delatte, A. *Etudes sur la literature pythagoricienne*. Paris, 1915

Dillon, John. *The Middle Platonists*. London: Duckworth, 1977

Dodds, E.R. *The Greeks and the Irrational*. Berkeley: University of California Press, 1963

------"Numenius and Ammonius." *Entretiens Sur l' Antiquité Classique*. V: *Les sources de Plotin*. Vandoeuvres-Genéve, 21-29 Août 1957. Genéve: Fondation Hardt, 1960, pp. 3-32.

------*Pagan and Christian in an Age of Anxiety*. Cambridge: Cambridge University Press 1965 (Repriint: New York: W.W. Norton & Company, 1970).

-----"*The Parmenides* of Plato and the Origin of the Neoplatonic One." *Classical Quarterly*, 22,1928, pp. 129-142.

Dörrie, Heinrich. "Der Platoniker Eudorus Von Alexandreia." *Hermes* 79, pp. 25-39.

-----"Die Frage nach dem Transzendenten im Mittelplatonismus." *Entretiens sur l'Antiquité Classique*. V: *Les Sources de Plotin*. Vandoeuvres-Genéve, 21-29 Août 1957. Genéve: Fondation Hardt, 1960, pp. 193-223.

------"Die Schuletradition im Mittelplatonismus und Porphyrios." *Entretiens sur l'Antiquité Classique,* XII: *Porphyre.* Vandoeuvres-Genéve, 30 Août – 5 Septembre, 1965. Genéve: Fondation Hardt, 1966, pp. 3-25.

Elferink, M. A. *La Descente de l'Âme d'apres Macrobe.* Leiden: E.J. Brill, 1968

Elsas, Christoph. *Neuplatonische und gnostische Weltablehnung in der Schule Plotins.* Berlin: Walter de Gruyter, 1975.

Festugiére, A. J. *La Révélation d'Hermès Trismégiste.* 4 vol. Paris: Etudes Bibliques, 1949-54.

------*Personal Religion Among the Greeks.* Berkeley: University of California Press, 1954

Finamore, John F. *Iamblichus and the Theory of the Vehicle of the soul.* Chico: Scholar's Press, 1985

Flamant, J. *Macrobe et le néo-platonisme latin, à fin du IV^{e}siècle.* Leiden: E. J. Brill, 1977.

Gager, John G. *Moses in Greco-Roman Paganism.* Nashville: Abingdon Press, 1972.

Hadas, Moses. *Hellenistic Culture: Fusion and Diffusion.* New York: Columbia University Press, 1959.

Hadot, P. *Porphyre et Victorinus.* Paris: Études Augustiniennes, 1968.

Hager, F. P. "Die Materie und das Böse im antiken Platonismus." *Museum Helveticum 19,* 1962, pp. 73-103.

Hopfner, T. *Orient und griechische Philosophie.* Leipzig: ("Beihefte zum Alten Orient", Heft 4) 1925.

Jonas, Hans. *The Gnostic Religion.* Boston: Beacon Press, 1963[2].

Jones, R. M. "The Ideas as the Thoughts of God." *Classical Philology* 21, 317-326.

------*The Platonism of Plutarch.* London: Garland Publishing, 1980.

Krämer, H. J. *Der Ursprung der Geistmetaphysik.* Amsterdam: Verlag P. Schippers, 1964.

Lewy, H. *Chaldaean Oracles and Theurgy.* Cairo: Institut Francais d' Archéologie Orientale, 1956 (Paris: Études Augustiniennes, 1978).

Loenen, J. H. "Albinus' Metaphysics. An Attempt at Rehabilitation." *Mnemosyne* IV 9, 1956, pp. 296-319; IV 10, 1957, pp. 35-56.

Majercik, Ruth M. *Julian the Theurgist: the Chaldean Oracles, Text, Translation and Commentary.* Leiden: E. J. Brill, 1989.

Martano, Giuseppe. *Numenio d' Apamea.* Naples: Biblioteca del Giornale Italiano di Filologia. 1960. (^{1}Rome, 1941).

Mazza, M. "Studi Arnobiani I: La dottrina dei 'viri novi' nel second libro dell' *Adversus Nationes* di Arnobio." *Helikon* 3, 1 (1963), pp. 111-169.

Merlan, Philip. "Drei Anmerkungen zu Numenius." *Philologus* 106, 1962, pp. 137-145.

------*From Platonism to Neoplatonism.* The Hague, 1960^2

------"Greek Philosophy from Plato to Plotinus" in *The Cambridge History of Later Greek and Early Medieval Philosophy.* Cambridge: Cambridge University Press, 1967, pp. 14-137.

Meuli, K. "Scythica". *Hermes,* 70 (1935), 121-76.

Möller, E.W. *Geschichte der Kosmologie in der griechischen Kirche bis auf Origenes.* Halle: Julius Fricke, 1860 (Graz: Akademische Druck-u. Verlagsanstalt, 1977).

Mylonas, George E. *Eleusis and the Eleusinian Mysteries.* Princeton: Princeton University Press, 1961.

Nilsson, Martin P. *Geschichte der griechischen Religion.* 2 vol. München: Beck, 1955-1961^2.

Norden, E. *Agnostos Theos. Untersuchungen zur Formengeschichte religöser Rede.* Stuttgart: 1956^4.

Pearson, Birger. *Gnosticism, Judaism, and Egyptian Christianity.* Minneapolis: Fortress Press, 1990.

Peterson, E. "Herkunft und Bedeutung der μόνος πρὸς μόνον Formel bei Plotin." *Philologus* 88, 1932, pp. 30-

Pétrement, Simone. *Le Dualisme chez Platon, les Gnostiques et les manichéens.* Paris: Presses Universitaries de France (Bibliotéque de Philosophie Contemporaine), 1947.

Puech, G. C. "Numénius d'Apamée et les theologies orientales au second siècle." *Annuaire de l'Institut de Philologie et d'Histoire Orientales et Slaves,* 2, 1934 (Mélanges Bidez), pp. 745-778.

Rist, John M. *Plotinus: The Road to Reality.* Cambridge: Cambridge University Press, 1967.

------*Stoic Philosophy.* Cambridge: Cambridge University Press, 1969.

Ross, W. D. *Aristotle's Metaphysics.* (2 vol.) Oxford University Press, 1958.

Rudolph, Kurt. *Gnosis: The Nature and History of Gnosticism.* San Francisco: Harper and Row, 1987.

Runia, David T. *Philo of Alexandria and the Timaeus of Plato.* Leiden: E. J. Brill, 1986.

Schwyzer, H. R. "Plotinos." *Pauly-Wissowa,* XXI, 1951, col. 471-592.

Sedlar, Jean W. *India and the Greek World: A Study in the Transmission of Culture.* Totowa: Rowan and Littlefield, 1980.

Stanford, W. B. *The Odyssey of Homer.* (2 vol.) London: Macmillan Press, 1947.

Stern, Menahem. *Greek and Latin Authors on Jews and Judaism.* Jerusalem: Israel Academy of Sciences and Humanities, 1974-1984.

Theiler, Willy. *Die Vorbereitung des Neuplatonismus.* Berlin: Weidmannsche Buchhandlung, 1930 (Problemata 1).

Turcan, R. *Mithras platonicus. Recherches sur l'hellénisation philosophique de Mithra.* Leiden: E.J. Brill, 1975.

Wallis, R. T. *Neoplatonism.* London: Duckworth, 1972.

Waszink J.-H. *Studien zum Timaioskommentar des Calcidius.* Leiden: E. J. Brill, 1964

------"Porphyrios und Numenios." *Entretiens sur l'Antiquité Classique,* XII: *Porphyre.* Vandoeuvres-Genéve, 30 Août – 5 Septembre, 1965. Genéve: Fondation Hardt, 1966, pp. 35-78.

Whittaker, John. "Moses Atticizing." *Phoenix* XXI, 1967, pp. 196-201.

Williams, Michael Allen. *The Immovable Race: A Gnostic Designation and the Theme of Stability in Late Antiquity.* Leiden: E. J. Brill, 1985.

van Winden, J. C. M. *Calcidius On Matter: His Doctrines and Sources.* Leiden: E. J. Brill, 1959.

Witt, R. E. *Albinus and the History of Middle Platonism.* Cambridge: Cambridge University Press, 1937.

Zintzen, C. "Die Wertung von Mystik und Magie in der neuplatonischen Philosophie." *Rheinisches Museum für Philologie,* NF 108, 1965, pp. 71-100.

Subject Index

Academics and Plato, 37
Agathocles, 51
Alone incorporeal, 9
Alone, the, 5
Ameilius, 83-85
Ammonius, 11
Analogies, 5
Antiochus, 65
Antipater, 63
Antisthenes, 39
Apollo, 95
Arcesilaus, 43-53, 59
Aristander, 81
Aristippus, 39, 59
Aristotle, 41, 49
    accords with Plato, 49
Assent and soul, 85
Astrological lore attached to Plato, 75
Athena, 79
Atlantis, interpreted, 79
Atticus, 83
Being
    and eternity, 15-19
    and intellect and reason, 19
    and mathematics, 5
    and matter, 7
    and the elements, 7
    and the Good, 29
    as incorporeal, 17
    not spatial nor becoming, 15
    stable and fixed, 15-17
    without beginning, 17
Bion, 47
Blood dear to souls in generation, 67
Body
    and extension, 13
    and movement, 13
    and soul, 13
    divisible and mutable, 11
    dependence on Zeus, 9

Boethus, 87
Brahmans, 3
Breath of God, 67
Cancer, tropic of, 69, 73-75
Capricorn, tropic of, 69, 73-75
Carneades, 59-65
Cave as analogy for the world, 69
Caves consecrated, 101
Celsus, 3
Cephisodorus, 49
Chance, 99
Chrysippus, 67
Cleitomachus, 65
Complexity, 89
Cosmos and essence, 29
Cosmos and soul, 83
Crantor, 43, 47
Crates, 43
Cronius, 69, 83-87
Defects inherent in material things, 95
Delphian Apollo, 95
Demiurge, 25
    and the First God, 25
    and unordered matter, 89
    as helmsman, 31
    contemplates ideas, 31
Demons and souls, 79
Descent of the soul, theories, 87
Diocles, 47
Diodorus, 43-47
Dionysius, 79
Discursive Intellect and the Third God, 35
Divine gifts, 27
Dodecade, 77
Dog star, 71
Dyad and matter, 23
Dyad, Pythagorean matter, 89
Egypt and Moses, 19

Egyptians 3
   solar boat, 67
   teachings, 79
Elements, 7, 77
Eleusinian rites disclosed, 95
Embryo, 77
Epicureans free from faction, 39
Epops, 5
Equinoxes, 75-77
Eretrian school, 39
Essence and Cosmos, 29
Essence, immaterial, 83
Eternity and being, 15-19
Evandrus, 59
Evil, its source, 91
Extension and body, 13
Extension and soul, 13
Father - the First God, 25
Father, Maker, Product, 33
First God and the Second, 23, 27-35
First God
   and the Second, and movement, 27
   as Father, 25
   the Living Being, 35
   unknown to mankind, 29
Future, present and past, 15
Gates of the Sun, 69-77
Generation 'wet', 67
Geometrical soul, 81
Gifts, divine, 27
God
   and matter as two principles, 91-95
   named Monad, 89
   incorporeal, 3
Gods, mundane, 89
Good, the, 5
   above essence, 5
   book concerning the, 3-5, 19
   participated through intellect, 31
   and Being, 29
   and Intellect, 29
   and the Demiurge 29, 33
   in the Timaeus and Republic, 33
Harpocration, 83, 87

Hephaestus, 99
Heraclitus, 91
   and his school, 43
   and 'moist souls', 67
Hermes, 99
Homer, 45, 73, 91
   and two paths, 75
Iamblichus, 85
Images among intelligibles, 85
Imagination and soul, 85
Immaterial essence, 83
Immortality, its extent in souls, 85
Incorporeal, 9
   as being, 17
Intellect
   and being, 19
   and the Good, 29
   the Second God, 35
Intelligibles and images, 85
Irrational creatures and soul, 87
Irrational soul and immortality, 85-87
Isocrates, 49
Jambres (Egyptian) 19-21
Jannes (Egyptian) 19-21
Janus, 71
Jerusalem, 99
Jesus, 21
Jews, 3, 19
Judgment of souls, 77
King, the First God, 25
Lacydes, 53-59
Living Being - the First God, 35
Lucan, 99
Magi, 3
Magic, 95
Maia, 99
Material things and intrinsic defects, 95
Mathematical soul, 81
Matter 7-9
   and being, 7-9
   and God as two principles, 91-95
   and necessity, 95
   and providence, 93-95

Matter
    and the Dyad, 23, 89
    as mother of corporeal Gods, 95
    as unknowable and unlimited, 9
    harmful, 91-93
    without quality, 91
    movement and force, 11
Megarian school, 39
Menedemus, 43
Mentor, 63
Milk and honey libations, 71
Milky way, 71-77
Miracles, 67
Mithra, 101
Mnaseas, 47
Mnesarchus, 65
Moist seed and soul in generation, 67
Monad, Pythagorean God, 89
Moses, 5, 19-21
Myths and Plato, 35
Naiads, 67
Name similar to the named, 17
Nations, their initiations, dogmas and rituals, 3
Nature and immortality, 85
Nature and parts of the soul, 83-85
Necessity
    and matter, 95
    and Providence, 91
New Year, 71
Number, Concerning, 5
Nymphs, 67
Ocean, as material world, 73
Odysseus, 73
Origen, 79
Osiris, 79
Parmenides, 71
Past, present and future, 15
People of dreams, 71, 75-77
Persian initiations, 101
Perversity as the source of evil, 91
Philo, 65
Philomelus, 47
Place, Concerning, 5

Planetary houses, 69
Planets, 77
Plato
    and later philosophers, 39-45
    and Pythagoras, 37, 41, 89
    and the Academics, 37-39
    and theological myths, 35
    and two world souls, 93
Plotinus, 11, 83, 85, 87
Plutarch, 67, 85
Pluto and the milky way, 73
Polemon, 37, 43, 47
Porphyry, 79-85
Present, past and future, 15
Principles of the soul, 83
Prison, its meaning, 81
Prometheus, 27
Providence
    and matter, 93-95
    and necessity, 91
Ptolemy, 95
Pyrrhon, 43-47
Pythagoras 3, 17, 37, 67
    and Plato, 37, 41, 89
Pythagorean doctrines, 67, 71-73, 77-79, 89-91, 95
Pythagorean misconceptions of the Dyad, 89
Ritual and caves, 101
Rivers as symbols, 79
Saturn, 71
Saturnalia, 71
Scipio, 75
Second God and the First, 23, 27, 31-35
Second God, Intellect, 35
Serapis, 97
Severus, 81
Simplicity, its non-existence, 89
Socrates
    and Pythagoras, 39
    and Pythagorean teachings, 41
    and the three Gods, 39
    death, 35

Solstices, 75-77
Sothis (dog star), 71
Soul
    and assent, 85
    and body, 13
    and demons, 79
    and extension, 13
    and immortality, 85, 87
    and irrational creatures, 87
    and movement, 13
    and the cosmos, 83
    and imagination, 85
    and its principles, 83
    as giving body adherence, 11
    derived from letters, etc. 81
    descending, 67, 71
    entry into the embryo, 77-79
    incorruptibility, 67
    intermediate, 81
    is body, disputed, 11
    judged, 77
    mathematical, 81
    parts, theories of, 83-85
    purpose of descent, 87
    relations to other things, 83
    separable, 87
    various descents, 87
Speech, human, 99

Sperm, symbolised, 79
Speusippus, 37, 85
Stars,
    as harmful, 93
    influence of, 93
Stilpon, 43
Stoics, 11, 47, 51, 59, 63-65, 91
    doctrine of harmful stars, 93
    factionalism, 39
Tartarus, 75
Theodorus, 47, 81
Theological myths and Plato, 35
Theophrastus, 43-45
Third God and the Second, 23, 33-35
Third God, Discursive Intellect, 35
Timon, 43, 47
Titans, 79
Tropics, 69
Typhon, 79
Unknown God, 99
Unordered matter and the Demiurge, 89
Water, and descending souls, 67
World souls, dyadic, 93
Xenocrates, 13, 37, 43, 85
Zeno, 41, 43, 49, 51
Zodiac, 69, 73
Zoroaster, 101

INDEX VERBORVM AB EVSEBIO SERVATORVM

Omittuntur articuli; interiectiones (ὦ...); particulae ἄν, γάρ, γε, δέ, ἤ (ἤτοι), καί, μέν, οὐ (οὐδέ, οὔτε), μή (μηδέ, μήτε), τε; praepositiones, verbum εἶναι. Recensentur tantum exempla ab Eusebio in *Praeparatione evangelica* deprompta; non autem verba citationum aliorum auctorum, ut Homeri, Platonis..., neque ea (minoribus typis composita) quibus Eusebius fragmenta introducit vel concludit. Crassiore numero indicatur fragmentum; ceteris, lineae.

Cj. = e coniectura.
V. l. = varia lectio.

ἀβέλτερος 19, 7
ἀβρύνεσθαι 25, 45
Ἀγαθοκλῆς 25, 144
ἀγαθός 16, 9, 15; 19, 8, 10 (bis); 20, 6, 10; 25, 46; τἀγαθόν (τὸ ἀγαθόν) 2, 5, 11, 14, 13, 17; 16, 4, 5; 19, 3, 10, 13; 20, 5, 6, 10 (bis? cj.)
ἀγαθοῦν 19, 6
ἀγανακτεῖν 26, 58
ἀγαπώντως 24, 38
ἀγγεῖον 26, 77 (bis)
ἄγειν 25, 127 (bis), 136; 27, 6, 32
ἀγένητος 7, 13
ἀγλαΐα 2, 14
ἀγνοεῖν 6, 3; 17, 4; 24, 53; 25, 34, 35, 92, 115, 116
ἄγνοια 24, 14; 25, 121
ἄγνωστος 4 a, 4 (bis)
ἀγωγή 26, 98
ἀγωνιᾶν 27, 44
ᾄδειν 25, 19
ἀδελφιδοῦς 24, 5
ἀδελφός 23, 8 (bis)
ἄδηλος 26, 103, 114
ἀδιήγητος 2, 13
ἀδικεῖν 25, 137
ἀδόξαστος 26, 67
ἀδύνατος 3, 10; 5, 15; 26, 102; 27, 42, 50
ἀεί 5, 7, 18, 26; 24, 8, 32, 54
ἀηδία 26, 108
ἀθέμιστος 4 a, 9
Ἀθῆναι 25, 134
Ἀθηναῖοι 23, 5, 10, 14
Αἰγύπτιοι 1 a, 9; 9, 2, 6
Αἴγυπτος 9, 4, 8
αἰδημόνως 25, 125
ἀΐδιος 5, 18; 7, 14; 8, 2; 15, 9
αἰδώς 25, 69
αἰθήρ 18, 4
αἱρεῖν 12, 10; 27, 39
αἴρειν 26, 20

αἰσθάνεσθαι 27, 16
αἰσθητόν, τό 2, 6; 11, 20; τὰ αἰσθητά 2, 10, 16, 20; 15, 5
αἰσχρός 25, 45, 118
αἰτία 6, 7; 23, 10; 24, 14, 60; 25, 70; 26, 8
αἴτιον, τό 14, 16; 16, 3; 24, 50
αἴτιος 24, 22, 42
αἰχμή 27, 23
αἰών 5, 8
ἀκαδημαϊκός adj. 26, 73; subst. m. 25, 58, 70, 71, 91; subst. n. pl. 26, 70, 88
Ἀκαδημία 24, 66; 26, 98; 28, 11, 13
ἀκατάληπτος 26, 56, 104 (bis)
ἀκαταληψία 26, 26, 36, 47, 74; 27, 62
ἀκίνητος 27, 2
ἀκούειν 12, 12; 15, 6; 25, 50, 52, 55; 26, 25, 28, 43, 44, 68; 27, 12, 47
ἀκουστής 26, 94; 28, 11
ἀκρόασις 25, 51
ἀκριβολογεῖσθαι 26, 60
ἀκροβολισμός 12, 18
ἀλαζών 23, 14
ἀλήθεια 26, 107
ἀληθεύειν 23, 12 (bis); 27, 54, 66
ἀληθής 24, 33; 27, 16, 36; τὸ ἀληθές 25, 68; 27, 26, 31, 33; τἀληθῆ 27, 65
ἀληθινός 27, 37
ἀλιάς 2, 7
ἁλίσκεσθαι 25, 92 (bis)
ἀλλά 2, 6, 12; 3, 1, 8, 10; 4 a, 10; 5, 6, 25; 6, 6; 7, 6; 14, 12, 17; 17, 6; 24, 29, 62; 25, 1, 46, 55, 100, 109, 124, 138; 26, 47, 49, 107; 27, 58
ἀλλαχοῦ 24, 49

ἄλλη 25, 124; ἄλλη καὶ ἄλλη 20, 2
ἀλλήλων... 3, 6; 23, 6; 24, 28, 32, 42; 25, 10, 11, 49, 100
ἄλλος 3, 2; 4 a, 13, 27, 30; 5, 16, 21; 6, 8; 19, 2, 5; 23, 8, 15; 24, 11(bis), 14, 50, 54; 25, 42, 109, 131, 141, 148; 26, 5, 20, 32, 39, 56, 58, 78, 83, 100; 27, 13, 41, 54
ἄλλοσε 26, 18
ἄλλοτε 24, 54
ἄλλως 11, 7; 19, 4, 10; 25, 138; 26, 6, 54, 56, 91, 92
ἄλογος 4 a, 3, 4
ἅλωσις 12, 10
ἅμα 4 a, 16; 24, 61; 25, 12, 30; 26, 45, 85
ἀμαθής 25, 105
ἅμαξα 25, 139
ἁμαρτάνειν 2, 18
ἀμείνων 24, 19; 25, 102; 27, 3
ἀμελεῖν 2, 20; 27, 2, 25
ἀμήχανον, τό 26, 81
ἀμνημόνευτος 26, 67
ἀμόθεν (γέ ποθεν) 25, 63 (cj.)
ἀμύνειν 4 a, 26; 25, 141
ἀμφιλογεῖν 19, 7
ἀμφισβητήσιμος 12, 11
ἀμφότεροι... 25, 49, 81
ἀμφοτέρωθεν 27, 8
ἀναβάλλειν 26, 16
ἀνάγειν 5, 5; 11, 20; 24, 73
ἀναγκαῖος 4 a, 4
ἀναιρεῖν 25, 67; 26, 14
ἀναίρεσις 25, 65; 27, 17
ἀνακαλεῖν 5, 8
ἀναλλοίωτος 6, 10
ἀνάλογος 16, 6
ἀναμανθάνειν 26, 71
ἀναμιμνήσκειν 7, 8
ἀνάμνησις 14, 9

ἀναμφίλεκτος 26, 31; -ιλέκτως 7, 13
ἀνανεάζειν 27, 4
ἀνασκευάζειν 26, 100
ἀναστρέφειν 26, 69, 81 (v. l.); 28, 7
ἀνατρέπειν 25, 47; 26, 81 (v. l.)
ἀνατρέχειν 25, 3
ἀναχάζειν 27, 22
ἀναχεῖν 15, 10
ἀναχωρεῖν 1 a, 4
ἀνδραποδίζεσθαι 27, 38
ἀνεξαπάτητος 27, 14
ἀνήνυτος 8, 12
ἀνήρ 7, 6; 9, 3, 5; 23, 14; 24, 63, 71; 25, 37, 57; 27, 50
ἀνθρώπινος 14, 6, 17
ἄνθρωπος 2, 11; 14, 20; 17, 2, 5; 20, 8 (bis); 25, 151; 26, 102; 27, 51
ἀνοιγνύναι 26, 4, 14, 19, 38
ἀντιγράφειν 25, 116
ἀντιγραφή 27, 48
ἀντιλαμβάνειν 24, 67
ἀντιλέγειν 25, 28, 149; 26, 86
ἀντιλογία 26, 76; 27, 6
ἀντιλογικός 27, 9
ἀντιμετατιθέναι 24, 70
Ἀντίοχος 28, 11
Ἀντίπατρος 27, 43
Ἀντισθένης 24, 49
ἀντισοφιστεύειν 26, 72; 27, 61
ἀντιστρέφειν 27, 64
ἀντίτεχνος 25, 129; 26, 72; 27, 61
ἄνω 5, 23; 18, 5, 10
ἀξιόνικος 25, 129
ἀξιοπιστία 26, 85
ἄξιος 24, 18, 29; -ίως 25, 114
ἀξιοῦν 9, 6; 25, 37
ἀξίωμα 24, 74
ἀόριστος 3, 12; 4 a, 3 (bis); 8, 7
ἀπάγειν 27, 12
ἀπαλλάσσειν 4 a, 25
ἀπαξάπας 27, 17
ἅπας 26, 103
ἄπειρος (A) 25, 105; (B) 4 a, 2
ἀπερίοπτος 11, 19
ἀπέχειν 25, 120
ἀπιέναι 2, 10; 14, 4, 7; 18, 5
ἀπιστία 26, 85
ἀπιστούντως 26, 39
ἁπλοῦς 6, 10; 11, 13; -ῶς 25, 55

ἀποδεικνύναι 26, 60, 63
ἀπόδειξις 26, 61
ἀποδέχεσθαι 25, 53
ἀποδιδόναι 19, 12; 28, 2
ἀποδιδράσκειν 5, 10; 8, 6
ἀποκαλύπτειν 26, 92
ἀποκλείειν 26, 11, 15, 21, 36
ἀποκρούειν 25, 4
ἀποκτείνειν 23, 10
ἀπολαύειν 24, 26
ἀπολείπειν 14, 10
ἀποπλάζεσθαι 18, 7
ἀπορεῖν 26, 24, 79
ἀπορία 26, 7
ἀπορρηγνύναι 26, 43
ἀπόρρητος 27, 53
ἀποσβεννύναι 12, 19
ἀποστρέφειν 25, 124 (v. l.), 144
ἀποτρέπειν 25, 124 (v. l.)
ἀποφαίνεσθαι 25, 154; 27, 54
ἀποφέρειν 25, 130; 27, 6, 45
ἀποχραίνειν 19, 6
ἄπρακτος 27, 19
ἅπτεσθαι 11, 8, 20
ἄρα 3, 1, 3; 4 a, 18, 20
ἆρα 3, 8; 5, 18; 19, 3; 25, 154; 28, 1
ἀραρίσκειν 4 a, 28; 5, 25
ἀργός 12, 12
ἀριθμός 2, 21
ἀριστερός 5, 23
Ἀρίστιππος 24, 48; 26, 95
Ἀριστοτέλης 24, 66; 25, 103, 105, 107
ἀρχεῖν 16, 5; 25, 51
Ἀρκεσίλαος 25, 5, 14, 35, 74, 80, 101, 113, 115, 121, 129, 137, 142, 143, 147, 153; 26, 25, 28, 99; 27, 3, 14, 18
ἁρμονία 18, 8, 9
ἀρνητικός 27, 20
ἄρρητος 12, 9
ἀρρωστία 3, 10
ἄρτι 28, 1
ἀρτύνειν 25, 83
ἄρχειν 24, 37; 28, 11
ἄρχεσθαι 11, 11; 24, 13, 37; 25, 108; 26, 27, 33, 46, 72
ἀρχή 16, 5; 24, 65; 25, 56, 93, 94
ἀρωγή 25, 80
ἀσέβημα 24, 30
ἀσήμαντος 26, 57
ἀσθενής 25, 136
ἀσκέπτως 25, 50
ἀστασίαστος 24, 33

ἀσφαλῶς 23, 13; 24, 60
ἀσώματος 6, 14; 7, 2; τὸ ἀσώματον 4 a, 27, 31; 6, 3, 6
ἄτακτος 4 a, 5, 6
ἄτεχνος 26, 84; ἀτεχνῶς 2, 13
ἄτιμος 25, 118
ἄτρεπτος 8, 2
ἀττικίζειν 8, 14
αὖ 2, 5; 5, 11; 25, 46
αὖθις 25, 7, 47, 98, 126; 26, 15, 38
αὔξειν 4 a, 29; 26, 106; 28, 3
αὐστηρός 25, 13
αὐτάρκεια 26, 6
αὐτοάγαθον 16, 10, 14; 20, 11
αὐτοόν 17, 4
αὐτοποιεῖν 16, 11 (hapax?)
αὐτός ipse 2, 14; 4 a, 11; 5, 17 (bis); 6, 2, 13; 12, 11; 16, 3; 18, 8; 23, 15; 24, 25, 44, 57, 60, 74; 25, 31, 42, 66, 76, 104, 110, 112, 117, 133, 142; 26, 3, 4, 9, 19, 32, 37 (bis), 62, 65, 70, 86, 99; 27, 13, 23, 52; 28, 10
αὐτός (ὁ) idem 4 a, 18; 5, 15, 18, 19, 26; 6, 11; 8, 4; 11, 10; 13, 3; 14, 16, 18; 24, 9, 47, 56; 25, 36; 28, 6
αὐτοῦ... eius... 1 a, 6; 2, 19; 3, 4, 6, 10; 4 a, 3, 4, 18, 23, 24; 5, 22; 6, 5; 7, 13; 9, 8; 11, 16 (bis); 13, 5; 14, 11, 13; 16, 6, 7; 17, 6; 18, 4, 5, 7, 11; 19, 2, 10; 23, 5, 11, 16; 24, 19, 27, 29, 31, 38, 51, 54, 61, 65, 67; 25, 5, 8, 18, 22, 36, 53, 60, 67, 68, 76, 92, 93, 95, 98, 109, 116, 132, 133, 135, 141, 148; 26, 22, 29, 30, 45, 54, 59, 60, 61, 64, 66, 69, 70, 74, 90, 95, 96, 101; 27, 20, 43, 47, 62, 65, 69; 28, 6, 7
αὐτουργία 26, 6
ἀφαιρεῖν 14, 12; 25, 97
ἀφανής 27, 39, 69
ἀφανίζειν 27, 65
ἄφατος 2, 13
ἀφέλκειν 24, 47
ἀφιέναι 25, 137; 26, 23, 37, 48
ἀφιλότιμος 24, 15
ἀφιστάναι 27, 61
ἀφορμᾶν 25, 79

ἀφορμή 25, 94, 95
ἀφοσιοῦσθαι 12, 8
ἀφυής 25, 57, 59
ἄχρηστος 25, 152

βάθος 3, 11
βάλλειν 25, 91, 100, 103, 107
βαρύς 25, 102
βασιλεύς 12, 13
βάσις 25, 93
βέβαιος 5, 18; βεβαίως 27, 30
βία 27, 40
βιαίως 27, 22
βιβλίον 27, 48
βίος 12, 20; 15, 2
Βίων 25, 74
βιώσκεσθαι 12, 17
βλάπτειν 14, 8
βλέπειν 11, 19; 12, 16; 18, 10; 19, 12; 25, 52, 134
βοή 26, 85
βοήθεια 26, 80
βολή 2, 9
βούλεσθαι 24, 15, 62; 25, 112; 26, 1
βοῦς 20, 8 (bis)
βραδέως 24, 13 (cp.)
Βραχμᾶνες 1 a, 8
βραχύς 2, 8; 25, 152

γείτων 26, 82
γελᾶν 6, 6; 26, 44
γέλως 26, 44
γένεσις 7, 13; 16, 5, 7, 8
γενητός 3, 5
γενναῖος 25, 31
Γέτης 26, 50
γεωργός 13, 2
γῆ 3, 2
γίγνεσθαι 3, 6; 4 a, 29; 5, 6, 14, 19, 20; 6, 8; 9, 5; 11, 8, 9, 11, 20; 12, 6; 14, 7 (bis); 23, 11; 24, 21; 25, 5, 13, 17, 99; 26, 24, 93; 27, 43, 57; 28, 11
γιγνώσκειν 4 a, 5; 17, 3; 24, 56
γνώμη 24, 34, 64
γνώμων 11, 10
γνώριμος 24, 21; 25, 5; 26, 95; 27, 57
γνώρισμα 2, 4
γόης 27, 30
γοητεύειν 25, 41
γοῦν 4 a, 29; 7, 3; 9, 4; 25, 65; 26, 59, 68; 27, 30, 40, 43; 28, 12
γραμματεῖον 26, 11, 57

γράφειν 20, 4; 23, 4; 24, 60; 27, 44, 49
γρῦ 27, 47
γωνία 27, 48

Δακική 26, 51
δάκνειν 24, 17
Δάκος 26, 51
δακτύλιος 26, 12 (bis), 15, 16, 21, 38, 39, 41, 46
δεικνύναι 11, 11; 25, 150
δειματοῦν 25, 43
δεῖν 1 a, 3; 2, 7, 10, 19; 4 a, 18; 11, 7, 11; 12, 5; 25, 55, 132; 26, 10; 27, 9; τὸ δέον 25, 50
δεινολογεῖσθαι 26, 64, 84
δεινός 27, 28
δεινότης 25, 27
δεῖσθαι 4 a, 23; 26, 5
δεξιός 5, 23; 25, 37
δέος 25, 121
δέρκεσθαι 2, 9
δεύτερος 11, 2, 15; 15, 2, 3, 5, 7; 16, 10, 16; 19, 8, 11
δή 3, 1, 3; 4 a, 13, 22, 28; 5, 21; 7, 12; 8, 2; 11, 9; 19, 4 (bis); 20, 5; 24, 9, 10, 14, 40, 56, 58; 25, 3, 22, 63, 95, 101, 103; 26, 1, 13
δηλονότι 15, 3
δῆλος 24, 59, 60
δημιουργεῖν 12, 2, 3
δημιουργικός 12, 4, 13
δημιουργός 12, 7; 13, 4; 16, 4, 6, 8, 9, 11; 17, 3; 18, 6; 20, 3, 5, 10
Δημόκριτος 25, 63
δημοσιεύειν 27, 45
δημοτικός 24, 75
δήπου 8, 4; 25, 114
δήπουθεν 4 a, 5; 26, 87
δῆτα 6, 5; 28, 8
διάγειν 24, 58
διαδέχεσθαι 26, 96
διαδεικνύναι 25, 120
διαδοχή 24, 12
διάδοχος 24, 7; 27, 58
διαιρεῖν 11, 3, 11
διαιρετός 11, 14
διαίσθησις 28, 8
διαιτᾶν 25, 1
διακοσμεῖν 25, 27
διακούειν 24, 52
διακρούειν 18, 7
διαλέγεσθαι 4 a, 16
διαλεκτικός 25, 25
διανέμειν 18, 6

διάνοια 27, 41
διατείνειν 24, 9
διατιθέναι 1 a, 9
διατριβή 2, 14; 24, 33; 26, 75, 92, 97; 27, 46, 61; 28, 1; (tit.) 25, 73
διαφανής 26, 94
διαφερόντως 12, 6
διαφεύγειν 5, 10 (bis)
διαφορά 26, 103
διάφορος 24, 48
διδάσκαλος 25, 104
διδόναι 14, 3, 4, 11, 14, 15, 18; 27, 28
διελέγχειν 26, 45
διέλκειν 24, 69
διέξοδος 12, 15
διηγεῖσθαι 26, 1, 9
διιθύνειν 18, 3
διιστάναι 24, 13, 40; 25, 82, 99; 26, 102
δίκαιος 4 a, 31; δικαίως 26, 39
διό 14, 19
Διόδωρος 25, 15, 17, 24, 61
Διοκλῆς 25, 73
διολκή 24, 61
διόλου 11, 14
διομολογεῖσθαι 12, 11
διττός 16, 10
δόγμα 1 a, 7; 7, 5; 24, 9, 31, 61; 25, 77, 133; 26, 80
δοκεῖν 4 a, 10, 23, 27; 6, 14; 11, 6; 23, 10; 25, 3, 153, 154; 26, 30, 68, 81; 28, 3, 10
δόλος 27, 39
δόξα 8, 8; 26, 68
δοξαστός 8, 8
δοῦλος 26, 7 (bis), 17
δ' οὖν 24, 23; 25, 79, 99, 128; 27, 6, 44
δρᾶν 24, 17
δυάς 11, 16
δύναμις 5, 5
δύνασθαι 3, 9; 4 a, 26; 5, 16; 7, 7; 23, 13; 25, 136; 26, 14; 27, 49
δυνατός 9, 5, 9; 25, 92; -ῶς 27, 23 (cp.)
δύο 3, 2; 25, 100
δύσκριτος 25, 30; δυσκρίτως 25, 50
δυσμενής 24, 38
δύσνοια 24, 62
δυσχεραίνειν 23, 5

ἐάν 6, 6; 19, 6, 10; 24, 67; 25, 126
ἐᾶν 24, 68; 25, 42; 27, 33

ἑαυτοῦ... 5, 24; 8, 3; 11,10,
13 (bis), 18, 19; 12, 19;
16, 11; 19, 8; 24, 68, 70;
25, 49 (bis), 78, 104, 143;
26, 90, 10, 26, 34, 43, 71,
79, 80, 81; 27, 15, 23,
53; 28, 7
ἐγγύς 5, 5 (sup.)
ἐγκαλεῖν 26, 74
ἔγκλημα 26, 74
ἐγώ... 4 a, 10, 23, 26; 5, 9;
6, 2; 7, 3; 14, 19; 23, 10;
24, 16; 25, 2, 3, 79, 98,
114, 126; 26, 8, 31, 35,
40.— V. ἡμεῖς
ἐδωδή 23, 7
ἐθέλειν 5, 8; 7, 4; 24, 16;
25, 138
ἐθελούσιος 6, 11
ἔθνος 1 a, 5
εἰ caus. 15, 5; condit. 2, 7,
16; 3, 5; 4 a, 2, 3 (bis), 10,
15, 20, 22, 24; 5, 8, 16;
7, 5; 8, 2, 5; 12, 4, 7; 16,
2, 4; 19, 7; 23, 4, 15; 24,
10, 50; 25, 93, 113, 115,
128, 132, 142, 153; 26, 61,
80; 27, 9 ; interr. 25, 34,
35
εἰδέναι 17, 2; 24, 55; 25, 31,
32, 42, 46, 109, 117, 143
(cj.); 28, 8
εἰκάζειν 26, 8
εἰκῇ 24, 53
εἰκότως 20, 9 ; 24, 26
εἰκών 16, 7
εἶναι = ἐξεῖναι 3, 6; 7, 3;
25, 97 ; τὸ εἶναι 5, 13.
— V. ὄν, ὤν
εἴπερ 16, 8; 20, 10; 23, 9;
25, 22, 96
εἰρήνη 2, 14; 24, 31; 25, 115
εἰρωνεία 24, 73
εἰς 2, 9, 10; 3, 3; 5, 12, 14;
11, 15; 16, 15; 19, 13; 24,
33, 34; 25, 35, 94, 152;
26, 76, 96
εἰσιέναι 26, 57
εἰσπίπτειν 27, 11
εἴσω 26, 37.— V. ἔσω
εἶτα 23, 5; 25, 7, 15, 31; 26,
15, 16
εἴτε 26, 53; 27, 3 (bis)
εἰωθότως 23, 17; 24, 58
ἕκαστος 11, 5; 12, 16; 13, 6;
23, 17; 24, 52, 58
ἑκάτερος 26, 99; 27, 29
ἐκβαίνειν 25, 32

ἐκδέχεσθαι 24, 7; 26, 42; 27,
1; 28, 1
ἐκεῖ 26, 75
ἐκεῖθεν 13, 7; 24, 56; 25, 29;
26, 72
ἐκεῖθι 14, 6, 7 ; 27, 11
ἐκεῖνος 4 a, 25; 12, 9; 14,
13; 19, 6; 24, 13, 20; 25,
121, 130, 131; 26, 26, 55,
56, 65; 27, 14
ἐκεῖσε 24, 64; 25, 3
ἐκμανθάνειν 26, 53
ἐκμελετᾶν 2, 21
ἐκπλήττειν 25, 145; 28, 2
ἔκτοτε 26, 45
ἑκών 27, 25; 28, 10
ἔλασσον 5, 20
ἐλέγχειν 23, 17; 24, 37; 25,
76, 95, 117; 27, 62; 28, 9
ἔλεγχος 24, 38
ἐμαυτοῦ 26, 32, 36
ἐμβάλλειν 26, 46
ἐμμένειν 24, 12, 39; 25, 64
ἔμπαλιν 15, 4
ἐμπίνειν 26, 20
Ἔμπουσαι 25, 40
ἔμπροσθεν 4 a, 8
ἔναγχος 26, 68
ἐναίσιμος 24, 63
ἐναντίος 24, 24, 28; 25, 117;
28, 12; τοὐναντίον 25, 152
ἐνάργεια 28, 7
ἐναργής 26, 28
ἐνδέχεσθαι 6, 9
ἐνδιδόναι 27, 23
ἔνδον 26, 39, 41; 27, 67
ἔνδοξος 25, 106
ἐνεῖναι 2, 5; 25, 36; 27, 28
ἕνεκα 24, 9
ἔνθα 2, 11, 13
ἔνθεν 14, 7; 25, 63,79; 27,
28
ἐνθένδε 14, 6
ἐνιστάναι 5, 7, 8
ἐνοῦν 11, 16
ἐντεῦθεν 25, 29
ἐντυγχάνειν 2, 18
ἐξαπατᾶν 27, 15
ἐξάπτειν 14, 12, 14
ἐξαρνητικός 27, 8
ἐξεγείρειν 27, 10
ἐξεῖναι 2, 3; 26, 8
ἐξελαύνειν 9, 4
ἐξελέγχειν 26, 80
ἐξευλαβεῖσθσι 25, 76
ἐξηγεῖσθαι 9, 5
ἑξῆς 9, 2
ἕξις 14, 17

ἐξιστάναι 6, 11; 8, 3
ἐξίτηλος 28, 5
ἐοικέναι 5, 12; 12, 6; 24, 32,
35, 39
ἐπαγγέλλεσθαι 5, 11
ἐπάγειν 9, 7
ἐπαινεῖν 26, 6
ἐπακτρίς 2, 8
ἐπαλλάσσειν 3, 6
ἐπάν 11, 6; 25, 98
ἐπαναχεῖσθαι 27, 18
ἐπανατείνειν 27, 48
ἐπαναφέρειν 24, 64; 27, 4
ἐπαυρίσκεσθαι 12, 20
ἐπεί 23, 11; 24, 11; 25, 9,
52; 26, 52, 66, 85; 27, 24, 41
ἐπειδή 4 a, 16; 17, 2; 25, 103,
112; 26, 14, 18, 24
ἐπεῖναι 26, 61
ἔπειτα 2, 17; 11, 6; 16, 12;
26, 19, 33
ἐπεξιέναι 25, 75
ἐπέχειν 26, 103
ἐπιγράφειν 25, 73
ἐπιέναι 26, 40 (cj.); 27, 24
ἐπιζητεῖν 7, 4
ἐπίθετος 6, 14
ἐπιθυμητικός 11, 17
ἐπικαλεῖν 1 a, 5
Ἐπικούρειοι 24, 23, 27
Ἐπίκουρος 24, 24, 28, 33
ἐπικρύπτειν 24, 59
ἐπιλανθάνεσθαι 25, 82; 26, 62
ἐπιλύειν 9, 8
ἐπιμελεῖσθαι 11, 19
ἐπιπολάζειν 27, 68
ἐπίσημος 14, 5
ἐπισπᾶν 26, 30
ἐπίστασθαι 14, 9
ἐπιστήμη 14, 10, 14, 18
ἐπιστρέφειν 12, 16
ἐπιτηδεύειν 26, 99
ἐπιτιμᾶν 24, 46
ἐπιτίμησις 24, 42
ἐπιτυγχάνειν 27, 55
ἐπιχειρεῖν 11, 7
ἐπιχείρησις 26, 70, 100
ἐπορέγεσθαι 11, 21
ἔπος 25, 19, 151
ἐποχεῖσθαι 2, 15
ἐποχή 24,10; 25, 78 ; 26, 31,
101; 28, 6
ἐραστής 25, 58, 70
ἔργον 12, 12; 25, 152
ἔρεσθαι 7, 12
Ἐρετρικοί 24, 50
ἐρημία 2, 13
ἔρημος 2, 9

ἐριστικῶς 26, 105
ἐρωτικά, τά 25, 57
ἐσθίειν 26, 19
ἔσω 26, 13, 16, 46. — V. εἴσω
ἑταῖρος 27, 53
ἕτερος 2, 12; 6, 12; 7, 6; 14, 11; 16, 15; 17, 6; 24, 42 (bis), 44; 26, 49, 55; 27, 34, (bis); 28, 11
ἑτέρωθεν 12, 10
ἔτι 11, 21; 15, 6; 19, 7; 24, 39; 25, 58, 70; 26, 34, 44; 27, 58
εὖ 11, 6; 27, 24; 28, 9
Εὔανδρος 26, 96
εὐδαίμων 12, 20
εὐδοκιμεῖν 1 a, 6; 25, 134; 26, 3
εὐθημοσύνη 11, 6
εὐθύ 8, 6; 18, 4; 26, 53 (cj.)
εὐθύς 26, 53 (codd.)
Εὐθύφρων 23, 14
εὐμένεια 2, 15
εὐπρόσωπος 25, 51
εὑρίσκειν 16, 4; 25, 133; 26, 24; 27, 59
εὔχεσθαι 9, 5; 11, 12
ἐφέζεσθαι 18, 3
ἔφεσις 18, 12
ἐφίπτασθαι 2, 17
ἔχειν trans. 2, 9; 4 a, 13; 11, 17; 14, 12, 17; 23, 6; 24, 34; 25, 77, 93, 95, 101; 26, 86, 88; 27, 9; 28, 8; intr. 5, 16, 25; 11, 6; 20, 2; 25, 56; 26, 40, 42; « posse » 12, 6; 25, 43, 132 (bis), 137; 26, 31

Ζεύς 4 a, 23
ζῆν 12, 17, 20; 23, 12 (bis); 25, 139; 26, 92; 27, 58
Ζήνων 24, 66; 25, 5, 6, 80, 101(bis), 112, 125, 128; 26, 34
ζητεῖν 6, 6; 12, 4, 7
ζήτησις 25, 2; 27, 29
ζῷον 2, 12; 27, 21 (bis)
ᾗ 25, 3 (cj.), 92, 110
ᾗ interr. 4 a, 13; ἦ (που) 16, 9
ἡγεμονεῖν 12, 13
ἡγεμονικόν, τό 2, 15
Ἡγήσινος 27, 1 (cj.)
ἤδη 5, 10; 6, 4; 11, 6, 12; 24, 39; 27, 24; 28, 8
ἡδύς 6, 4 (cp.); 25, 52 (sup.); 26, 1, 8
ἦθος 2, 13; 11, 17, 21; 24, 8

ἥκειν 5, 12
ἡμεῖς... 2, 3; 5, 9; 11, 9; 12, 14, 16; 13, 7; 16, 12; 20, 6; 24, 64; 26, 92; ἡμῖν αὐτοῖς (= ἀλλήλοις) 4 a, 7, 16; 12, 11. — V. ἐγώ
ἡμέρα 27, 45
ἡρακλείτειος 25, 9
Ἡράκλειτος 25, 12, 13
ἠρεμεῖν 24, 31
ἤρεμον, τό 2, 15
ἡσυχία 25, 136
ἡττᾶν 25, 149; 26, 60
ἥττων 9, 3; ἧττον 4 a, 21; 25, 35

θάλαττα 18, 6, 9
θᾶττον 24, 13, 46
θαῦμα 27, 9
θαυμάζειν 15, 5
θαυμαστός 15, 6 (cp.); -ῶς 25, 45
θεά 26, 83
θεᾶσθαι 2, 21; 25, 51
θεῖος 2, 21; 14, 6; 17, 7 (cp.)
θέμις 5, 22
Θεοδώρειοι 25, 74
θεολογεῖν 23, 15
θεολογία 23, 5
θεός 9, 5; 11, 4, 10, 12, 14; 12, 3, 4, 12, 13, 17, 18, 18; 13, 3; 14, 18; 15, 2, 3; 16, 5, 6, 14; 18, 11; 24, 51, 67; 26, 82, 83
Θεόφραστος 25, 14, 56
θεραπεία 14, 4
θεραπεύειν 28, 2
θερμουργῶς 25, 60
θεσπέσιος 2, 13
θετικός 27, 20
θεωρεῖν 25, 129; 26, 58, 80
θεωρητικός 16, 12
θεωρία 18, 12
θήρ 27, 22
θηρᾶν 12, 10
θησαυρός 11, 9, 11
θνήσκειν 4 a, 17
θνητός 14, 5
θόρυβος 27, 12
θυμός 26, 19

Ἰαμβρῆς 9, 2
Ἰαννῆς 9, 2
ἰδέα 6, 10; 16, 2, 11; 18, 10; 20, 5, 8, 9, 11; 25, 108
ἴδιος 11, 21; 23, 16; ἰδίᾳ 20, 3; 24, 48 (bis), 49
ἱδρύειν 18, 8

ἵδρυσις 1 a, 7
ἰέναι 27, 23
ἰέναι 12, 14; 14, 20; 25, 1, 3, 53; 26, 13, 38, 39 (codd.), 54, 90
ἱερογραμματεύς 9, 2
ἰθύνειν 18, 9
ἵλεως 2, 15
ἵνα 4 a, 25; 25, 76; 26, 88; 28, 9
Ἰουδαῖοι 1 a, 8; 9, 3, 4
ἵππος 20, 9 (bis)
Ἰσοκράτης 25, 104
ἴσος 27, 33; -ως 24, 15, 20; 25, 115, 131; 26, 62
ἱστάναι 4 a, (bis), 28; 5, 25, 26; 8, 4; 15, 3; 26, 106
ἴσχειν 25, 15
ἰσχυρίζεσθαι 26, 30, 88
ἴτης 25, 18

καγχάζειν 26, 44
καθαιρεῖν 25, 130
καθηγητής 28, 13
καθῆσθαι 2, 7
καθορᾶν 2, 9; 25, 105
καινοτομεῖν 24, 30
καιρός 25, 98
καίτοι 24, 18; 27, 52
κακός 23, 10; 25, 46; -ῶς 23, 15; 25, 119 (cp.), 125; τὸ κακόν 27, 17 (bis), 37
καλεῖν 17, 4
καλλωπίζειν 16, 16; 27, 65
καλός 14, 9, 10; 16, 16; 25, 45, 54, 57; καλῶς 4 a, 2, 30; τὸ καλόν 16, 16
καπηλικῶς 27, 67 (cp.)
Καρνεάδης 26, 97; 27, 1, 18, 38, 41, 44, 51, 57, 58, 64
Καρχηδόνιοι 25, 145
καταγελᾶν 26, 22
καταγιγνώσκειν 24, 30
καταγλωττίζειν 25, 148; 26, 52
καταδοκεῖν 27, 51
καταθορυβεῖν 25, 43, 140
κατακυλίειν 26, 12
καταλαμβάνειν 26, 47; 27, 30, 59, 60; καταληπτός 27, 32
καταλείπειν 26, 23, 76; 27, 49
καταληπτικός 25, 97, 135; 27, 32
κατανοεῖν 26, 17
καταπιμπλάναι 27, 11
καταπλέκειν 25, 26
καταπλήττειν 25, 150
καταρτύειν 25, 64

κατασκευάζειν 25, 48
κατασκευή 26, 78
καταστωμύλλεσθαι 25, 28
κατατιθέναι 26, 11
καταφατικός 27, 8 (cj.; -φαντvel -φρονητικός codd.)
καταφρονητικός 27, 8 (codd.)
καταχαίρειν 25, 44
κατέχειν 4 a, 19, 22, 26
κατηγορεῖν 23, 6, 9 ; 25, 108
κάτω 5, 23; 12, 14; 18, 6; 27, 69
κενοδοξία 26, 45
κενός 26, 24; 27, 68
κεραννύναι 24, 74
κερδαίνειν 25, 142
κηδεύειν 12, 18
κήρινος 27, 36
Κηφισόδωρος 25, 102, 103, 111
κινδυνεύειν 6, 4
κινεῖν 4 a, 30; 5, 21, 22, 25; 15, 4; 27, 2
κίνησις 4 a, 30; 6, 9; 15, 7, 8
κλεῖθρον 26, 13, 17, 23
κλείς 26, 9, 14
Κλειτόμαχος 28, 3
κλέπτειν 26, 41; 27, 39
κλέπτης 26, 73
κλοπή 25, 44
Κνίδιος 25, 72
κοάλεμος 23, 15
κοῖλος 14, 5; 26, 11
κοινός 24, 34
κοινωνεῖν 12, 15
κομψός 25, 62; τὸ κομψόν 24, 73
κοσμίως 11, 7
κόσμος 15, 9; 16, 11, 16
κράζειν 26, 82
Κράντωρ 25, 15, 16, 58
κρατεῖν 26, 44
Κράτης 25, 8, 12, 14
κράτιστος 2, 19
Κράτυλος 6, 13
κρείττων 6, 9
κρίνειν 9, 3
κριτικόν, τό 18, 12
κριτής 25, 114
κυβερνήτης 18, 2
κυκᾶν 4 a, 25; 27, 53
κυκλικός 20, 3
κυνίζειν 25, 8
κυνικός 25, 14
Κυρηναῖος 26, 94
κύων 25, 119
κωμῳδικός 26, 50

λαβή 27, 28

λάβρος 27, 10
Λακύδης 26, 1, 2, 18, 23, 45, 67, 79, 93
λαλεῖν 26, 51
λαμβάνειν 2, 3, 6; 14, 3, 10, 15(bis), 19; 18, 11; 23, 9; 27, 48; ληπτός 26, 50
λανθάνειν 27, 16, 67
λέγειν 1 a, 3; 4 a, 2, 15; 5, 6, 14; 6, 4, 5 (bis); 7, 2, 3, 7, 8; 11, 6, 8; 12, 9; 17, 6, 7; 20, 4, 5, 7; 24, 15, 28, 53, 56, 57, 63; 25, 7, 18, 28, 36, 47, 69, 70, 72, 95, 115, 130, 136, 142, 145, 150; 26, 2, 34, 40, 59, 71, 85, 92, 101; 27, 16, 20, 29, 38, 41, 46; λεκτέος 26, 71
λεπτολογία 25, 25
λεπτολόγος 27, 7
λῃστής 27, 30, 39
λιπαρεῖν 2, 16
λογίζεσθαι 25, 8
λογισμός 25, 26
λόγος 1 a, 5; 4 a, 2; 5, 15; 7, 4; 8, 5; 11, 11; 12, 7(bis) 9, 10; 13, 2, 3; 24, 48; 25, 9, 27, 32, 36, 40, 43, 53, 81, 130; 26, 63, 75, 98, 101, 105; 27, 9, 45, 62
λυσιτελεῖν 26, 79
λύχνος 14, 12 (bis)

μαγεύειν 9, 3
Μάγοι 1 a, 8
μάθημα 2, 20, 21
μακρός 27, 4 (διὰ μακροῦ)
μάλα 26, 44; μάλιστα 4 a, 10; 13, 3; 25, 99; 27, 60; μᾶλλον 3, 10; 4 a, 19; 5, 25; 6, 4; 23, 12; 24, 16, 29, 43, 64; 25, 138, 154; 27, 22, 34(bis)
μανθάνειν 24, 23, 64; 26, 32
μανία 8, 7
μανικῶς 24, 68 (cp.)
μαρτυρία 1 a, 4
μάτην 26, 48
μάχεσθαι 25, 94, 111 (bis), 131
μάχη 25, 11, 101; 26, 86; 27, 4, 7
μαχητής 25, 13
μεγαλοφροσύνη 25, 120
Μεγαρικοί 24, 49
μέγας 2, 12; 5, 15; 7, 7; 24, 20; μέγα 7, 7
μεγεθύνειν 5, 19
μεθιέναι 25, 113; 26, 13

μέθοδος 2, 19
μειοῦν 5, 20
μέλαν, τό 25, 78
μέλειν 25, 142 (bis)
μελέτη 25, 41
μέλλειν 5, 11; 11, 4; 25, 99; 27, 22, 43
μέλος 24, 69
μένειν 3, 11; 4 a, 18, 20; 8, 3; 27, 13
μέντοι 4 a, 24; 11, 15; 12, 10; 17, 3; 24, 20, 46; 25, 112, 116, 127; 26, 39, 49; 27, 37
Μέντωρ 27, 57
μεσεύειν 24, 71
μέσος 18, 2; τὸ μέσον 5, 24; 24, 61; 26, 81
μεταβάλλειν 25, 47
μεταβολή 6, 9; 8, 6
μεταδιδόναι 14, 6
μεταθεῖν 5, 24
μετακυλινδεῖσθαι 25, 28
μετακύμιον 2, 9
μεταλαγχάνειν 13, 5; 19, 11
μεταξύ 3, 2
μετάρσιος 18, 5
μεταστρέφειν 12, 18; 25, 96
μετατιθέναι 24, 39, 70
μεταφυτεύειν 13, 6
μετέπειτα 24, 27, 41
μετέχειν 19, 2; 25, 9, 62; 26, 104
μετιέναι 12, 9; 14, 3
μετίσχειν 19, 2
μετουσία 16, 17; 19, 9; 20, 6, 10
μηδαμόθεν 24, 56
μηδείς 6, 9; 24, 28, 27; 25, 77, 152; 26, 28
μηδέπω 5, 14; 24, 37
μηκέτι 5, 11, 13; 26, 88
μῆκος 3, 12
μήν 5, 20 (cj.); 24, 16; 25, 120 (v. l.); 27, 57
μηνύειν 25, 98
μήπω 24, 10
μηχανή 2, 6; 25, 135
μικρολόγος 24, 44
μικρός. V. σμικρός
μίμημα 16, 8, 16
μιμητής 16, 7, 14
μιμνήσκειν 24, 29; 25, 6(bis) 98, 132; 27, 25
μῖξις 23, 7
Μνασέας 25, 65
μνήμη 26, 67
μνημονεύειν 7, 3; 26, 63

Μνήσαρχος 28, 13
μοιχός 27, 62
μόλις 26, 43
μονή 15, 9
μόνος 2, 8 (bis), 11 (bis); 4 a, 27; 5, 7; 8, 8; 16, 4; 17, 3; 19, 3, 5, 6 (bis); 20, 7; 26, 101; μόνον 4 a, 28; 25, 96
Μουσαῖος 9, 4, 7
μυρίοι 28, 13
Μωσῆς 8, 11

ναί 4 a, 15
ναῦς 2, 10; 18, 3, 9
νεανιεύεσθαι 2, 20
νεανικός 9, 8
νεκρός 4 a, 17
νεωτερίζειν 25, 126
νικᾶν 24, 54; 27, 41
νοεῖν 28, 7
νοητός 16, 2; τὸ νοητόν 7, 2; 11, 18; τὰ νοητά 15, 4, 5
νομίζειν 5, 13; 12, 3; 24, 59; 25, 109
νόμισμα 14, 5
νομοθέτης 13, 5
νοῦς 12, 14, 20; 16, 3; 17, 3, 6, 7; 18, 4; 20, 11; 22, 3; 24, 34
νῦν 6, 4; 24, 37, 66, 68(bis); 25, 2, 97, 132; 27, 49
νυνί 25, 8

Ξενοκράτης 24, 6, 7, 16; 25, 7
ξένος 14, 16; 28, 13

ὄγκος 24, 74
ὅδε 4 a, 15; 27, 21
ὁδός 6, 2; 18, 5; 25, 4
ὅθεν 8, 7; 25, 18 (cj.), 81; 26, 107
οἵ 26, 90
οἰακίζειν 18, 10
οἴαξ 18, 3
οἴεσθαι 2, 17; 5, 9 ; 7, 6; 24, 53; 25, 106, 142; 26, 10, 26, 56, 64, 67
οἰκία 26, 30, 77, 86
οἰκονομικός 26, 3
οἶκος 26, 13, 22
οἰκουρός 26, 89
οἷος 7, 7; 14, 6; 26, 50; οἷός τε 5, 12; 19, 9; οἷον 2, 7; 14, 11; 18, 8; 27, 10, 64; οἷα 25, 59
ὀκνεῖν 25, 75, 130
ὀλιγαρχικός 24, 40 (cp.)

ὅλος 16, 12 (v. l.); 24, 69, 70 ; 26, 33; τὰ ὅλα 4 a, 14; 15, 10; ὅλως 16, 12 (v. l.).
— V. διόλου
ὁμηρικός 25, 33
ὁμιλεῖν 2, 11; 25, 62
ὄμμα 18, 4, 11; 25, 55
ὁμοδοξία 24, 18
ὁμόθεν 25, 63 (codd.)
ὅμοιος 2, 4, 6; 25, 33; 27, 31, 32, 35
ὁμοίωσις 6, 13
ὁμολογεῖν 4 a, 8; 16, 3; 24, 25; 26, 35; 27, 54
ὁμολογία 12, 11; 28, 8
ὁμολογουμένως 1 a, 8
ὁμοῦ 5, 15; 25, 51
ὅμως 27, 51
ὅν, τό 2, 22; 3, 1, 8, 9; 4 a, 7, 9, 12; 5, 5, 6, 13, 17 (bis), 18, 24; 6, 7(bis),14; 7, 2, 12, 14; 8, 2; τὰ ὄντα 3, 3; τῷ ὄντι 2, 18. — V. ὤν
ὄναρ 27, 35 (bis)
ὄνειδος 25, 44
ὀνινάναι 14, 8, 10; 19, 4
ὄνομα 6, 3, 5, 7(bis),13; 16, 13; 25, 71, 134
ὀνομάζειν 25, 38
ὀξύ 2, 9; 19, 12
ὀξύρροπος 3, 11
ὄπη 24, 58
ὀπίσω 5, 22; 26, 16
ὀπόθεν 25, 29 (codd.)
ὅποι 26, 18
ὁπόσος 1 a, 8; 14, 3; 26, 7 (codd.)
ὁποσοσοῦν 26, 7 (cj.)
ὁπότερος 25, 34, 46
ὁποτέρωθεν 25, 29 (cj.)
ὅπως 24, 54, 71
ὁρᾶν 3, 6; 9, 8; 14, 11; 23, 12; 24, 23, 44, 75; 25, 104, 153; 26, 28, 38, 59
ὁρίζειν 5, 7
ὁρμᾶν 25, 63, 81
ὁρμητικόν, τό 18, 12
ὅρος 25, 96
ὅς dém. 26, 41; rel. 3, 4; 9, 7; 14, 8, 10, 12, 15; 15, 8 ; 16, 1 (cj.), 16; 17, 6; 19, 5, 9; 24, 34, 40; 25, 2, 12, 18 (codd.), 103, 109, 111 (bis), 116, 117, 118, 147, 149, 150; 26, 5, 7, 8, 36, 94, 96, 99, 105; 27, 13, 16, 19, 25, 42, 54, 68

ὅσος 5, 5; 7, 3; 24, 43; 25, 48; 26, 77, 83; 27, 2 (bis)
ὅσπερ 4 a, 7; 23, 16; 25, 97
ὄσπριον 27, 67
ὅστις 4 a, 6; 17, 4; 20, 6; 24, 29
ὁστισοῦν 27, 41
ὅτι 7, 5; 14, 17; 19, 12; 24, 17; 25, 8, 45, 117 (codd.); 28, 9
οὐδαμῇ 8, 3
οὐδαμῶς 8, 3; 24, 24, 70; 25, 37, 125
οὐδείς 2, 5, 6; 4 a, 29; 9, 3; 14, 16; 19, 2; 24, 24, 30; 25, 18, 31, 35, 42, 75, 130, 132, 141, 154 (bis); 26, 76, 90; 27, 41, 46; 28, 6; οὐδέν adv. 4 a, 15, 29; 25, 35, 75; 26, 90
οὐδέπω 5, 11
οὐδέτερος 27, 29
οὐκέτι 6, 2; 25, 138; 26, 46(bis)
οὔκουν 4 a, 11; 5, 12
οὖν 2, 3; 3, 3; 4 a, 13, 22; 5, 5, 8; 6, 2, 14; 7, 3; 11, 17; 12, 4, 16; 14, 5; 15, 4; 19, 5; 24, 39, 57, 71; 25, 6, 25, 38, 48, 52, 69, 79, 128, 151; 26, 17, 23, 34, 75, 98; 27, 3, 21, 35, 37, 66, 67
οὔποτε 27, 45
οὐρανός 12, 13; 18, 5, 10
οὐσία 2, 16; 6, 7; 14, 17; 16, 2, 5, 7, 9, 10, 15
οὗτος 1 a, 3; 2, 8; 3, 3; 4 a, 7, 13, 15, 20, 22, 27, 30; 5, 7, 14; 6, 5; 7, 2, 5; 8, 4, 7; 9, 6; 11, 19; 12, 6, 14; 19; 14, 9, 16; 15, 2, 6; 16, 2, 3, 6, 13, 14 ; 17, 5, 7; 18, 8; 19, 4, 6, 9 ; 20, 2; 23, 7; 24, 23, 25, 31, 44, 46, 50, 52, 56, 63, 73, 74; 25, 1, 47, 55, 59, 62, 79, 98, 115, 119, 128, 135, 155; 26, 3, 11, 17, 21, 26, 31, 41, 50, 69, 85, 91, 93 (bis), 95, 105; 27, 2, 6, 21; 28, 1
οὑτοσί 3, 1, 8, 9; 4 a, 7; 14, 5; 23, 9; 24, 10
οὕτω(ς) 2, 10, 21; 3, 8; 5, 14, 16; 11, 12; 12, 5; 17, 5 (bis); 18, 6; 19, 11; 20, 2, 9; 24, 66; 25, 63, 110 ; 26, 35, 56; 27, 50
ὀφείλειν 24, 23

ὄψις 27, 60

πάθη 4 a, 25; 26, 34
πάθημα 27, 67; 28, 7
πάθος 25, 152
παιγνιήμον, τό 24, 73
παιδιά 25, 128
παίζειν 26, 64, 66
παῖς 25, 56; 26, 49, 73, 87 (bis), 91
πάλαι 6, 5
παλαιστής 27, 28
παλίμβολος 25, 30
πάλιν 13, 2; 23, 10; 25, 5; 26, 14, 16
παλινάγρετος 3, 5; 25, 29
παλλακή 27, 58
πανουργεῖν 25, 62
παντάπασιν 17, 4
πάντῃ 8, 2; 24, 18
παντοδαπός 25, 18, 34
πάντως 8, 2
πάνυ 4 a, 5; 27, 40
παραγωγός 25, 19
παραιτεῖν 27, 60
παρακεῖσθαι 2, 4, 5
παρακεκινδυνευμένος 25, 30
παραλαμβάνειν 27, 31
παραλύειν 4 a, 24; 24, 11; 26, 54, 74
παραμένειν 14, 15
παραμυθεῖσθαι 7, 4
παρανόμημα 24, 29
παραπέτασμα 27, 66
παρασκευάζειν 27, 40
παρασκευή 25, 41
παρέχειν 23, 10; 24, 60; 26, 108; 27, 29
παρήγησις 27, 1 (codd.)
παριέναι 5, 9
παριστάναι 9, 6
πᾶς 4 a, 8, 10, 28; 12, 15; 13, 4; 24, 17, 18(bis), 53; 25, 65, 76, 135, 140; 26, 5, 35, 75, 81, 85, 95, 100, 104(bis); 27, 11, 40; τὸ πᾶν 2, 18; 26, 42; παντὸς (ἧττον) 4 a, 21; παντὸς (μᾶλλον) 3, 10; 4 a, 19
πάσχειν 11, 9; 24, 17, 47, 69; 27, 67
πατήρ 12, 3; 21, 1; 23, 7
πείθειν 25, 72, 79; 27, 16
πειρᾶσθαι 4 a, 16; 26, 32
πέλαγος 18, 2
πέμπειν 12, 15
Πενθεύς 24, 68
πενία 26, 6

περιγίγνεσθαι 27, 28
περιέπειν 11, 20
περιηγεῖσθαι 26, 33
περιιέναι 26, 63; 27, 14
περικρούειν 25, 147
περίοδος 26, 21
περίπατος 26, 18; 27, 46
περιυβρίζειν 25, 119
περιφέρειν 26, 10
περιωπή 12, 19
πηδάλιον 18, 3
πιθάνια, τά 25, 62 (hapax?)
πιθανός 25, 149; 26, 108; 27, 59; τὸ πιθανόν 25, 68; 27, 20, 29, 34
πιθανουργικός 25, 16
πίπτειν 25, 47; 26, 81
πιστεύειν 27, 60
πίστις 26, 84
Πιταναῖος 25, 153
πλάτος 3, 12
πλατύς 26, 44
Πλάτων 1 a, 4, 7; 6, 12; 7, 5, 8; 8, 8, 14; 14, 19; 17, 2; 19, 11; 20, 2; 23, 4, 9; 24, 6, 16, 19, 55; 25, 27, 106(bis), 108, 113, 116, 124, 125, 139, 141
Πλατωνικός 25, 15, 94
πλεῖν 18, 6
πλεῖστος 25, 114; (ἐπὶ) πλεῖστον 24, 27
πλείων 27, 37; πλεῖον (πλέον) 5, 20; 24, 43; (ἐπὶ) πλέον 26, 107
πλεοναχῶς 25, 48
πλῆθος 9, 6
πλήν 25, 50, 64, 71, 72, 110, 119
πλήρης 26, 23
πλήττειν 25, 118
πνεῖν 24, 54
ποθεν 25, 63
ποιεῖν 12, 5; 25, 117, 143; 26, 5, 21
ποικίλλειν 27, 7
ποικίλος 4 a, 15
πολεμεῖν 25, 107, 111, 112, 113
Πολέμων 24, 7; 25, 4, 7, 10, 82
πολιτεία 24, 33; (tit.) 20, 4
πολλαχῇ 24, 11
πολυθρύλητος 24, 10
πολυπραγμοσύνη 24, 45
πολύς 8, 7; 24, 31, 41 (bis); 25, 137; 26, 22, 94, 106, 108; 28, 8; οἱ πολλοί 26, 3, 106; πολύ 15, 6; 24, 46; 25, 119. — V. πλείων, πλεῖστος

πολυτιμητίζειν 24, 22
πομπεία 25, 140
πόρρω 2, 10
ποταμός 3, 11; 27, 10
ποτε 5, 6 (bis), 23, 24, 25; 11, 14; 24, 32; 25, 36, 126, 127, 153; 26, 29
που 16, 9; 18, 2; 25, 3; 26, 6; 27, 9
πρᾶγμα 6, 13; 16, 13; 24, 57; 25, 76; 26, 40, 88; 27, 26
πρᾶος 25, 57
πρεσβεύειν 4 a, 31
πρεσβύτερος 16, 3; 17, 7; 24, 63
πρίν 11, 8
προαιρεῖσθαι 23, 12; 26, 4
προαίρεσις 24, 14 (cj.)
προβάλλειν 25, 78
προδοκεῖν 25, 2; 27, 25
προϊέναι 26, 18; 28, 5
προκαθῆσθαι 26, 89
προκαταβάλλειν 13, 7
Προμηθεύς 14, 20
προσάγειν 18, 11
προσαναγκάζειν 6, 12
προσάπτειν 28, 13
προσβολή 26, 65
προσεθίζειν 25, 53
προσεῖναι 15, 7(bis); 19, 7; 27, 13
προσήκειν 24, 52, 69; 25, 119
προσκαλεῖν 11, 10
πρόσοδος 12, 6
προσομιλεῖν 23, 17; 26, 29
προσομνύναι 26, 65
προσονινάναι 14, 8
προσονομάζειν 25, 67
προσπολεμεῖν 27, 42
πρόσρησις 24, 26; 25, 64
προστυχῶς 24, 54
προσφέρειν 1 a, 6
προσχωρεῖν 25, 59
πρόσω 5, 22
πρόσωπον 25, 54
πρότερος 12, 5; 14, 12; 24, 41; -ον 11, 4; 24, 47; 26, 43
προτιθέναι 24, 65
πρωΐ 11, 8
πρῶτος 11, 4, 13; 12, 2, 4, 8, 12; 13, 3; 15, 2, 3, 4, 8; 16, 14, 15; 17, 3, 6; 19, 5, 9; 20, 7, 10, 11; 21, 2, 4; 22, 1; 24, 12, 40; 25, 133; τὰ πρῶτα 11, 8; 25, 44; πρῶτον 4 a, 15; 27, 15, 57
Πυθαγόρας 1 a, 5; 7, 7; 24, 19, 22, 71, 75
Πυθαγόρειος 24, 68

πυθαγορίζειν 24, 55
πῦρ 3, 2; 14, 13, 21
Πύρρων 25, 16, 17, 26, 62 (bis),65 (codd.)
πυρρώνειος subst. m. 25, 69, 71; pl. n. 25, 69;— ωνείως 25, 65 (cj.)
πω 5, 20; 24, 27; 25, 37 (v.l.); 26, 40
πῶς 3, 5; 7, 8; 19, 9; 26, 39
πως 25, 31, 150

ῥᾴδιος 2, 19; 4 a, 6; 25, 60
ῥεῖν 8, 5; 11,17; 27,10 (codd.)
ῥῆμα 24, 63
ῥηματίσκιον 25, 155
ῥήτωρ 25, 102
ῥοπή 27, 29
ῥοώδης 3, 11; 27, 10
ῥυθμός 24, 52

σέβεσθαι 24, 21
σείειν 25, 93
σεμνός 24, 75 (cp.); 25, 102; τό σεμνόν 24, 72
σημαίνειν 1 a, 3; 2, 3; 26, 12, 15, 21, 37, 58, 59, 61, 62
σηπία 25, 78
σκαριφητμός 24, 46
σκεπτικός, ὁ 25, 66 (bis); τό σκεπτικόν 25, 26
σκεῦος 26, 24
σκιαγραφία 25, 32
σκιδνάναι 4 a, 24
σκιομαχεῖν 25, 139
σκοπεῖσθαι 26, 57
σκοπή 2, 7
σμικρός 2, 12; 27, 19
σοφία 14, 19
σόφισμα 25, 43, 144; 26, 52
σοφιστής 25, 17, 75
σοφός 24, 25; 26, 66; 27, 31 (cp.); τό σοφόν 26, 17, 90
σπείρειν 13, 4
σπέρμα 13, 4
Σπεύσιππος 24, 6, 7
σποδός 11, 8
στασιάζειν 24, 36
στάσις 15, 8; 23, 6; 24, 61
Στίλπων 25, 8, 12, 13
στοιχεῖον 3, 1, 7
στόλος 12, 14
στόμα 25, 54
στοχάζεσθαι 26, 107
στρεβλοῦν 24, 12
στροφή 27, 7
στωϊκεύεσθαι 26, 87

στωϊκός adj. 24, 43 (cp.); 27, 52; subst. m. 25, 91, 122, 145; 26, 52, 71, 105, 108; 28, 3, 12; -ῶς 26, 73
στωμυλήθρα 26, 51
σύ... 14, 19; 26, 31. —V. ὑμεῖς
συγγίγνεσθαι 11, 14
συγκορυβαντιᾶν 27, 15
συγχωρεῖν 27, 27
συλλαβή 3, 7
συζῆν 24, 17 (codd.)
συλλήβδην 3, 3
συλλογίζεσθαι 16, 12
συλλογισμός 19, 11
συμβαίνειν 7, 6; 12, 17; 26, 26, 34; 27, 37
συμβάλλειν 25, 56
σύμβασις 19, 3
συμβουλεύεσθαι 5, 9
συμπαραλαμβάνειν 25, 11
σύμπας 12, 12; 13, 5
συμπολεμεῖν 25, 81
συμφέρειν 4 a, 9; 11, 15; 27, 7
συμφοιτᾶν 25, 10
συμφορά 9, 7
σύμφυτος 15, 8; 16, 10
συμφωνία 24, 31
συνανακολουθεῖν 24, 21
συνδεῖν 1 a, 4; 18, 8; 24, 57
συνδοκεῖν 24, 25
συνεῖναι 14, 15
συνεργάζεσθαι 27, 27
συνήθεια 28, 6
συνιέναι 11, 4
συνιστάναι 26, 97
συντάσσειν 12, 15
συντείνειν 18, 4
συντελεῖν 1 a, 7
συντελής 26, 78
συντυγχάνειν 19, 5
Συρακόσιος 25, 144
συσσύρειν 27, 12
σφεῖς... 25, 83; 26, 19; σφέας αὐτούς 25, 84
σφόδρα 27, 40
σφοδρῶς 27, 10 (codd.)
σφραγίς 26, 54, 58, 59, 61
σχεδόν 24, 8
σχῆμα 23, 14
σχηματίζειν 6, 3
σχηματισμός 23, 16
σχίζειν 11, 16
σχολάζειν 28, 12
σχολή 24, 7; 25, 127 (bis); 26, 95 ; σχολῇ (γε) 5, 16
σῴζειν 24, 17 (cj.)

Σωκράτης 23, 11, 16; 24, 47, 51, 55, 71, 74
σῶμα 2, 3, 12; 3, 8; 4 a, 11, 17, 25, 27; 8, 5; 12, 17
σωματικός 4 a, 28
Σωτήρ 4 a, 23
σωτηρία 15, 10

ταμεῖον 26, 4, 27, 33, 47, 89
ταμιεύειν 26, 9
τάξις 11, 5; 15, 9
τάσσειν 4 a, 5
ταύτῃ 19, 3
ταὐτότης 6, 11
τάχα 25, 138
ταχύ. — V. θᾶττον
τέκνον 23, 6
τελετή 1 a, 6
τελευτᾶν 24, 37; 25, 109; 26, 85
τέλος 25, 6
τέμνειν 25, 48, 49
τέσσαρες 3, 2; 16, 13 (bis)
τεχνικόν, τό 24, 43
τέως 26, 79
τῇδε 27, 11
τηνικαῦτα 27, 24
τιθέναι 20, 2; 23, 13; 24, 24, 51; 26, 77
Τίμαιος (tit.) 20, 4
Τίμων 25, 66
τιμωρία 23, 8
τίς 2, 21; 3, 1; 4 a, 14, 22; 7, 12; 8, 14; 25, 45, 46; 26, 34
τις 2, 6, 7, 8, 10, 11,12 (bis), 16; 3, 4; 4 a, 13, 27; 5, 8, 14, 16; 6, 6; 7, 6; 11, 6; 14, 20; 17, 5; 23, 15; 24, 10, 14, 15, 32, 38, 49, 69; 25, 19, 27, 31, 95, 96, 101, 153; 26, 1, 2, 6, 11, 29, 41, 61, 71, 75; 27, 9, 18, 21, 44, 47
τοιγαροῦν 25, 149; 27, 12
τοίνυν 24, 6; 25, 71
τοιόσδε 26, 36
τοιοῦτος 7, 3; 14, 14; 23, 8; 24, 11; 25, 37, 80; 26, 5
τολμᾶν 24, 31
τόλμημα 26, 53
τοπάζειν 17, 6
τοπικῶς 5, 21
τοσόνδε 7, 4
τοσοῦτος 6, 2; 25, 127
τότε 11, 6; 12, 17; 25, 151; 26, 54, 55; 27, 49, 51
τρεῖς 24, 50

τρέπειν 7, 14 (bis)
τρέχειν 25, 60
τρίτος 11, 15; 22, 3, 4; 26, 97
τρόπος 5, 13; 26, 2; 27, 27
τρυφᾶν 2, 17
Τρώς 25, 34
τυγχάνειν 4 a, 20; 19, 10; 25, 29, 58; 27, 24; 28, 9
τυποῦν 20, 8
τύχη 24, 54
τωθασμός 26, 75

ὑβριστής 26, 42
ὑβριστικός 25, 19
ὑγιής 26, 28
ὕδρα 25, 48
ὕδωρ 27, 68
ὕλη 3, 9, 11; 4 a, 3, 11; 11, 16, 18, 21; 14, 13; 18, 7, 9 (codd.)
ὑμεῖς 17, 6. — V. σύ
ὑμνεῖν 23, 8
ὑπάγειν 24, 72
ὑπαγορεύειν 7, 5; 25, 76
ὑπακούειν 25, 145
ὑπανιέναι 27, 22
ὑπάρχειν 3, 7; 12, 5; 24, 26, 40; 25, 106, 129, 151; 26, 7, 41
ὑπερβάλλειν 24, 45
ὑπερδικεῖν 25, 141
ὑπερεπιθυμεῖν 28, 9
ὑπερέχειν 27, 69
ὑπέρμεγας 27, 50
ὑπερφυῶς 26, 30
ὑπισχνεῖσθαι 26, 8
ὑπόγλισχος 26, 2
ὑποδέχεσθαι 26, 97
ὑποκλείειν 26, 4
ὑπολαμβάνειν 26, 65
ὑπομένειν 25, 70
ὑπονοεῖν 25, 110
ὑποσκελίζειν 25, 148
ὑποτείνειν 23, 4
ὑποτέμνειν 25, 148
ὑποτιθέναι 26, 55
ὕστερον 26, 13; 27, 49
ὑφιστάναι 27, 24
ὑφορᾶν 26, 90
ὑψίζυγος 18, 3

φαίνεσθαι 4 a, 31; 20, 6; 25, 77; 26, 106; 27, 39, 50
φάναι 4 a, 2, 11; 6, 3, 6, 12; 7, 12, 13; 8, 8; 14, 21; 15, 6, 8; 25, 21, 31; 26, 31, 40, 61, 62, 68, 102; 27, 47

φανερός 26, 35; εἰς τὸ φανερόν 23, 9; 24, 58; 25, 100; 27, 53
φανός 14, 20
φαντάζεσθαι 2, 17; 25, 33
φαντασία 25, 97, 135; 27, 21, 32, 35, 59
φάρμαξις 27, 14
φαρμάττειν 25, 41
φάσκειν 12, 5; 25, 73
φάσμα 25, 40
φαῦλος 6, 10; 27, 3
φέρειν 5, 5; 7, 8; 8, 6; 25, 4, 44
φεύγειν 28, 10
φθέγγεσθαι 27, 47
φθείρειν 5, 19; 6, 8
φθόνος 24, 62
φθορά 4 a, 26
φιλακόλουθος 24, 35
φιλάνθρωπον, τό 24, 72
Φιλόμηλος 25, 66
φιλονεικία 25, 61; 27, 52
φίλος 26, 69, 89
φιλοσοφεῖν 24, 51; 25, 75, 107, 114; 26, 25, 27, 48; 27, 64
φιλοσοφία 25, 126
φιλοτιμεῖσθαι 25, 10
φιλοφροσύνη 25, 55
Φίλων 28, 1, 10, 12
φλαῦρος 24, 15, 20 (cp.)
φληναφός 25, 27
φόβος 25, 74, 155
φοιτᾶν 25, 7; 26, 71
φορεῖν 4 a, 17; 18, 2
φόρταξ 26, 49
φράζειν 26, 32
φρονεῖν 19, 3; 28, 13
φροντίς 11, 11
φροῦδος 25, 3
φυλάττειν 27, 1
φύσις 3, 2; 4 a, 13, 17, 28; 25, 59
φυτεύειν 13, 2, 6
φῶς 14, 12

χαλᾶν 27, 18
χάρις 28, 2; Χάριτες 25, 147
χαρμονή 28, 2
χείρ 26, 37
χρή 4 a, 24; 5, 9; 7, 6; 11, 5; 12, 3; 24, 64; 25, 118; χρεών 12, 2; 27, 1
χρῆμα 14, 9, 14; χρήματα 13, 5; 14, 4; 27, 17
χρῆσθαι 25, 60, 135; 26, 7, 47, 98; 27, 66
χρηστός 27, 69

χρόνος 5, 7, 9; 26, 68; 28, 5
χωρίζειν 20, 3; 24, 65, 67

ψευδής 27, 36
ψεῦδος 25, 68; 27, 26, 31, 33
ψεῦμα 27, 65, 66
ψυχαγωγεῖν 27, 38
ψυχή 13, 4; 19, 7; 25, 47

ᾧδε 24, 57; 25, 56
ὤν, ὁ 13, 4. — V. ὄν
ᾠόν 27, 36, 37
ὡραῖος 25, 58
ὡς 4 a, 5; 5, 14; 8, 8; 19, 10; 20, 5; 24, 35, 68; 25, 31, 65 (codd.), 116, 140; 26, 13, 19, 30, 42; 27, 36, 59 (bis); 28, 5
ὡσαύτως 5, 26; 8, 4
ὥσπερ 13, 2; 17, 5; 20, 7; 23, 11; 24, 65; 25, 40, 67, 77; 27, 22, 27
ὥστε 4 a, 2; 26, 45, 67
ὠφελεῖν 26, 90

# The Prometheus Trust Catalogue

Platonic Texts and Translations Series

I Iamblichi Chalcidensis in Platonis Dialogos Commentariorum Fragmenta
John M Dillon   978-1-898910 45 9

II The Greek Commentaries on Plato's Phaedo (I – Olympiodorus)
L G Westerink   978-1-898910-46-6

III The Greek Commentaries on Plato's Phaedo (II – Damascius)
L G Westerink   978-1-898910-47-3

IV Damascius, Lectures on the Philebus
L G Westerink   978-1-898910-48-0

V The Anonymous Prolegomena to Platonic Philosophy
L G Westerink   978-1-898910-51-0

VI Proclus Commentary on the First Alcibiades
Text L G Westerink Trans. W O'Neill   978-1-898910-49-7

VII The Fragments of Numenius
R Petty   978-1-898910-52-7

The Thomas Taylor Series

1 Proclus' Elements of Theology
Proclus' Elements of Theology - 211 propositions which frame the metaphysics of the Late Athenian Academy. 978-1-898910-00-8

2 Select Works of Porphyry
Abstinence from Animal Food; Auxiliaries to the Perception of Intelligibles; Concerning Homer's Cave of the Nymphs; Taylor on the Wanderings of Ulysses. 978-1-898910-01-5

3 Collected Writings of Plotinus
Twenty-seven treatises being all the writings of Plotinus translated by Taylor. 978-1-898910-02-2

4 Writings on the Gods & the World
Sallust On the Gods & the World; Sentences of Demophilus; Ocellus on the Nature of the Universe; Taurus and Proclus on the Eternity of the World; Maternus on the Thema Mundi; The Emperor Julian's Orations to the Mother of Gods and to the Sovereign Sun; Synesius on Providence; Taylor's essays on the Mythology and the Theology of the Greeks. 978-1-898910-03-9

5 Hymns and Initiations
The Hymns of Orpheus together with all the published hymns translated or written by Taylor; Taylor's 1824 essay on Orpheus (together with the 1787 version). 978-1-898910-04-6

6 Dissertations of Maximus Tyrius
Forty-one treatises from the middle Platonist, and an essay from Taylor, The Triumph of the Wise Man over Fortune. 978-1-898910-05-3

7 Oracles and Mysteries
A Collection of Chaldean Oracles; Essays on the Eleusinian and Bacchic Mysteries; The History of the Restoration of the Platonic Theology; On the Immortality of the Soul. 978-1-898910-06-0

8 The Theology of Plato
The six books of Proclus on the Theology of Plato; to which is added a further book (by Taylor), replacing the original seventh book by Proclus, now lost. Extensive introduction and notes are also added. 978-1-898910-07-7

9 Works of Plato I
Taylor's General Introduction, Life of Plato, First Alcibiades (with much of Proclus' Commentary), Republic (with a section of Proclus' Commentary). 978-1-898910-08-4

10 Works of Plato II
Laws, Epinomis, Timæus (with notes from Proclus' Commentary), Critias. 978-1-898910-09-1

11 Works of Plato III
Parmenides (with a large part of Proclus' Commentary), Sophista, Phædrus (with notes from Hermias' Commentary), Greater Hippias, Banquet. 978-1-898910-10-7

12 Works of Plato IV
Theætetus, Politicus, Minos, Apology of Socrates, Crito, Phædo (with notes from the Commentaries of Damascius and Olympiodorus), Gorgias (with notes from the Commentary of Olympiodorus), Philebus (with notes from the Commentary of Olympiodorus), Second Alcibiades. 978-1-898910-11-4

13 Works of Plato V
Euthyphro, Meno, Protagoras, Theages, Laches, Lysis, Charmides, Lesser Hippias, Euthydemus, Hipparchus, Rivals, Menexenus, Clitopho, Io, Cratylus (together with virtually the whole of Proclus' Scholia), Epistles. An index to the extensive notes Taylor added to his five volumes of Plato. 978-1-898910-12-1

14 Apuleius' Golden Ass & Other Philosophical Writings
The Golden Ass (or Metamorphosis); On the Dæmon of Socrates; On the Philosophy of Plato. 978-1-898910-13-8

15 & 16 Proclus' Commentary on the Timæus of Plato
The Five Books of this Commentary in two volumes, with additional notes and short index. 978-1-898910-14-5 and 978-1-898910-15-2

17 Iamblichus on the Mysteries and Life of Pythagoras
Iamblichus On the Mysteries of the Egyptians, Chaldeans & Assyrians; Iamblichus' Life of Pythagoras; Fragments of the Ethical Writings of Pythagoreans; Political Fragments of Archytas, Charondas and other Pythagoreans. 978-1-898910-16-9

18 Essays and Fragments of Proclus
Providence, Fate and That Which is Within our Power; Ten Doubts concerning Providence; The Subsistence of Evil; The Life of Proclus; Fragments of Proclus' Writings. 978-1-898910-17-6

19 The Works of Aristotle I
The Physics, together with much of Simplicius' Commentary. A Glossary of Greek terms used by Aristotle. 978-1-898910-18-3

20 The Works of Aristotle II
The Organon: The Categories, On Interpretation, The Prior Analytics; The Posterior Analytics, The Topics, The Sophistical Elenchus; with extensive notes from the commentaries of Porphyry, Simplicius and Ammonius. 978-1-898910-19-0

21 The Works of Aristotle III
Great Ethics, Eudemian Ethics; Politics; Economics. 978-1-898910-20-6

22 The Works of Aristotle IV
Rhetorics; Nicomachean Ethics; Poetics. 978-1-898910-21-3

23 The Works of Aristotle V
The Metaphysics with notes from the Commentaries of Alexander Aphrodisiensis and Syrianus; Against the Dogmas of Xenophanes, Zeno and Gorgias; Mechanical Problems; On the World; On Virtues and Vices; On Audibles. 978-1-898910-22-0

24 The Works of Aristotle VI
On the Soul (with much of the Commentary of Simplicius); On Sense and Sensibles; On Memory and Reminiscence; On Sleep and Wakefulness; On Dreams; On Divination by Sleep; On the Common Motions of Animals; On the Generation of Animals; On Length and Shortness of Life; On Youth and Old Age, Life and Death; On Respiration. 978-1-898910-23-7

25 The Works of Aristotle VII
On the Heavens (with much of the Commentary of Simplicius); On Generation and Corruption; On Meteors (with much of the Commentary of Olympiodorus). 978-1-898910-24-4

26 The Works of Aristotle VIII
History of Animals, & the Treatise on Physiognomy. 978-1-898910-25-1

27 The Works of Aristotle IX
The Parts of Animals; The Progressive Motions of Animals, The Problems; On Indivisible Lines. 978-1-898910-26-8

28 The Philosophy of Aristotle
Taylor's four part dissertation on the philosophy of Aristotle which outlines his primary teachings, the harmony of Plato and Aristotle, and modern misunderstandings of Aristotle. 978-1-898910-27-5

29 Proclus' Commentary on Euclid
Proclus' Commentary on the First Book of Euclid's Elements; Taylor's four part Dissertation on the Platonic Doctrine of Ideas, on Demonstrative Syllogism, On the Nature of the Soul, and on the True End of Geometry. 978-1-898910-28-2

30 The Theoretical Arithmetic of the Pythagoreans
The Theoretic Arithmetic of the Pythagoreans, Medicina Mentis, Nullities & Diverging Series, The Elements of a New Arithmetic Notation, Elements of True Arithmetic of Infinities. 978-1-898910-29-9

31 & 32 Pausanias' Guide to Greece
Pausanias' Guide to Greece (in two volumes) with illustrations and extensive notes on mythology. 978-1-898910-30-5 & 978-1-898910-31-2

33 Against the Christians and Other Writings
The Arguments of Julian Against the Christians; Celsus, Porphyry and Julian Against the Christians; Writings of Thomas Taylor from his Collectanea, his Miscellanies in Prose and Verse, and his short works On Critics, An Answer to Dr Gillies, A Vindication of the Rights of Brutes, and his articles from the Classical Journal. Included is a Thomas Taylor bibliography. 978-1-898910-32-9

Students' Edition Paperbacks

The Sophist
Trans. Thomas Taylor. Includes extensive notes and introductory essays.

978-1-898910-93-0

The Symposium of Plato
Trans. Floyer Sydenham & Thomas Taylor. Includes Plotinus' *On Love* (En III, 5), and introductory essays.

978-1-898910-97-8

Know Thyself – The First Alcibiades & Commentary
Trans. Floyer Sydenham & Thomas Taylor. With introductory essays.

978-1-898910-96-1

Beyond the Shadows - The Metaphysics of the Platonic Tradition
Guy Wyndham-Jones and Tim Addey

978-1-898910-95-4

The Unfolding Wings - The Way of Perfection in the Platonic Tradition
Tim Addey

978-1-898910-94-7

Other titles available from the Prometheus Trust

Philosophy as a Rite of Rebirth – From Ancient Egypt to Neoplatonism

Algis Uždavinys

> 978-1-898910-35-0

The Philosophy of Proclus – the Final Phase of Ancient Thought

L J Rosán

> 978 1 898910-44-2

The Seven Myths of the Soul

Tim Addey

> 978-1-898910-37-4

Release Thyself – Three Philosophic Dialogues

Guy Wyndham-Jones

> 978-1-898910-56-5

An Index to Plato - A Subject Index using Stephanus pagination
> 978-1-898910-34-3

For further details please visit the Prometheus Trust website at:
www.prometheustrust.co.uk